A SHEARWATER BOOK

In the Thick of It
My Life in the Sierra Club

In the Thick of It
My Life in the Sierra Club

J. Michael McCloskey

To Diane

Mike McCloskey

◐ **ISLAND**PRESS / SHEARWATER BOOKS

Washington • Covelo • London

Library of Congress Cataloging-in-Publication data.
McCloskey, J. Michael (John Michael)
    In the thick of it : my life in the Sierra Club / J. Michael McCloskey.
      p. cm.
    Includes bibliographical references and index.
    ISBN 1-55963-979-2 (cloth : alk. paper)
    1. McCloskey, J. Michael (John Michael) 2. Environmentalists—United States—Biography. 3. Sierra Club. 4. Conservation of natural resources—United States. I. Title.
 GE56.M335M33 2005
 333.72'06'07—dc22

                                              2005014643

British Cataloguing-in-Publication data available.

For Maxine McCloskey

Contents

Introduction

In the 1950s, the conservation movement at the national level was described by one observer as "small, divided and frequently uncertain."[1] Two decades later, it was large, strong, and confident. And it had become an environmental movement, focusing on a panoply of issues such as pollution control as well as nature protection.

Of all the social movements that emerged in the latter half of the 20th century in the United States, the environmental movement is perhaps the most durable and well rooted, even though it still has much to accomplish. It has neither withered after its initial successes nor succumbed to personal rivalries. Together with the civil rights movement and the women's movement, it is viewed as having had the greatest impact of all of the social movements of that time.

The environmental movement has been instrumental in creating a significant body of public policy and has defended it vigilantly. In the scope and scale of its work, the movement has excelled. It has involved itself in an astonishing variety of issues, staying with them from inception through the intricacies of implementation.

The movement has also connected grassroot activists to sophisticated lobbying. Academics despaired of ever rousing the public to defend public goods that were broadly shared,[2] but the postwar social movements plunged ahead anyway. Through direct mail and other means, they collected core constituencies to build large organizations.

The environmental movement added more groups to the mix. It encouraged its activists to create separate groups to tackle specific issues, and the national organizations often encouraged development of local chapters. As new groups sprang up, more people became involved, and broad themes were sounded to connect local issues to national ones.

Although conditions may be different today, during the last part of the 20th century the environmental movement enjoyed a unique level of support among American institutions. Eight in ten Americans regarded themselves as environmentalists.[3] Half of them claimed to have contributed to environmental organizations. A third claimed to have been active in supporting environmental causes. Three-quarters said they had a high level of trust in national environmental organizations—more than twice as many as said they trusted large corporations, and many more than said they trusted political parties.[4]

Why did the environmental movement emerge and enjoy such success? Scholars cite various factors that set the stage. In the post–World War II period, sufficient affluence allowed many Americans to devote attention to issues other than the economy. And with the decline of loyalty to political parties (shown, for instance, by the rise of "independent" voters), people were eager to rally round other institutions. The discontent of youth in the 1960s played a part as well.

And the need was obviously urgent: Rivers were foaming and catching on fire; runaway oil wells were fouling the sea; forests were disappearing; open space was falling under subdivisions; highways were clogged and traffic was choking the air with smog. Faced with rising levels of pollution and open assaults on the natural environment, people were ready to do something.[5]

Established institutions also played a part in environmentalism's rise. Some of the older conservation groups were eager to meet the new environmental challenges, and they were led by individuals who embraced change. While they did not want to abandon their traditional issues, they wanted to move beyond them to fight pollution as well.

This memoir is the account of one such individual—me—and my relationship with one of those organizations, the Sierra Club. It describes the role I played in the evolution of the Sierra Club and the environmental movement.

Over its history, the Sierra Club has probably done more to shape the environmental laws and policies of the U.S. government than any other group. Other groups filled valuable niches (sometimes several of them), but in the 1970s and 1980s the Sierra Club had clout in Congress, in the voting booth, and in the courts. Other groups specialized in particular issues, but the Sierra Club specialized in making the issues it tackled politically relevant and in prodding the government to act.

The Sierra Club was a far different organization when I first began to work for it than it is today. In 1960, the Sierra Club was a California-oriented outdoor club, with an interest in conservation. Early in my career, for instance, I met an old woman who remembered hiking with "Mr. Muir"; she was referring to John Muir, who founded the Club in 1892. Between 1960 and 1970, however, the Sierra Club converted itself into a national environmental organization. By the mid-1970s it had chapters throughout the United States as well as in Canada and had opened offices abroad.

In 1960 the Sierra Club was primarily interested in the protection of nature. It focused on getting wilderness areas set aside in the national forests and getting national parks set up in suitable places elsewhere. But by the middle of the 1970s, it was also fighting pollution of all types through vehicles such as the Clean Water Act and the Clean Air Act; fostering programs to conserve energy, such as fuel-efficient cars; backing land use planning; and tackling environmental issues of every stripe, such as nuclear power and population growth. It had also become deeply involved in issues of international scope, such as mining in Antarctica.

The membership also mushroomed. In 1960, when I first became associated with it, the Club had only 16,000 members and a staff of 25. In 1999, when I retired, the Sierra Club had more than 700,000 members and a staff of more than 300.

The Sierra Club has various arrows in its quiver. It fields a major lobbying force at both the national and state levels. It endorses candidates for public office. It follows up its lobbying by going to court to litigate. It churns out an endless array of books, magazines, newsletters, audiovisual materials, and alerts. More recently, it has been able to field a force of organizers around various issues. And it provides a framework for absorbing volunteers into its work at the local, state, regional, and national levels.

At the local level, its units organize outings and events as well. Most of the more than 400 local groups run weekly outdoor excursions, and the national organization still runs longer outings. Some larger groups run short outings too, put on classes, and organize square dances. The largest group, in Los Angeles, may have as many as fifty different events on a given weekend.

While many fraternal clubs have fallen on hard times, the Sierra Club has not. It builds social capital because it has embraced a cause but continues to serve a social function. It is many things at the same time: an environmental organization, an outing organization, and a social organization. Some say it even has a touch of religion to it.

During the time when I was its executive director, the Sierra Club was "treated by the press as the quintessential expression of activist enviromentalism."[6] William Wyant, a journalist who wrote about the movement, termed the Club perhaps "the most effective of the conservation groups" of the 1970s.[7]

Most people who became leaders of the environmental movement had no background in public policy. If they had any particular training, it tended to be in natural resources. Only belatedly did they discover that they had to influence public policy. But my background was different: I earned degrees in both law and government, and served as an officer in the army. Because I thought I would find a career in politics and public life, I thought of myself as a politician in the making. I built the kind of résumé that often led to electoral success.

I tried to do all the things that would equip me to succeed in electoral politics. I led student political groups, canvassed on behalf of candidates, manned phone banks, stuffed envelopes, and tried to learn the art of politics from the ground up. I did research for a successful candidate for Congress. I worked on the campaign staff of a successful candidate for the U.S. Senate. I married a woman who had run the state office of a United States senator. I served as a precinct captain and on the county central committee of my local party. A year out of graduate school, I ran for the legislature myself. While I did not get elected, I ran creditably. I had the experience of campaigning—making speeches, shaking hands, and walking from door to door.

As a candidate, I found that I did not like having to address so many issues that did not really interest me, so I did not run again for public office. But I empathized with successful politicians. I knew their life was not easy, and I did not view them as skeptically as many do now. I knew that politicians had to weigh and balance competing concerns.

In my years with the Sierra Club, when I thought about how to talk to politicians, I tried to put myself in their place and frame the issues in a way that would allow them to say yes. I also tried to concentrate on making friends, not just enemies. I knew that our success depended on having good relations with important people. While I understood the ideology of the Sierra Club and shared it, I knew that ideological rigidity scared off many people. I tried to find reasons people could support us on the issue at hand. They did not have to sign on to our entire agenda.

I spent my entire career with the Sierra Club (although in my first few years, when I was on retainer, I represented a variety of regional conservation groups as well). After serving as a field organizer in the early 1960s, I moved on to become assistant to the president for a year. Then I became the Club's first conservation director, and after several more years I became the organization's executive director. I served in that capacity for as long as anyone has—seventeen years. And I finished out my career as the chairman.

I brought pragmatism and professionalism to my work for the Sierra Club. I always thought about how to move to the next step. As someone who trained to be a politician, it seemed second nature to me. A journalist and observer of the Club called me "the movement's most inveterate politician." And I always tried to find the most professional way to do our work. I took it seriously. I wanted us to always be thorough and prepared.

As this approach to influencing public policy took root in the Sierra Club, it also spread to other organizations. Many of the staff of the newer organizations, which arose after the first Earth Day in 1970, learned the business from our lobbyist, Lloyd Tupling, whom I had hired. Tupling had served for twelve years on Capitol Hill as a chief staffer for two U.S. senators. Collectively, Tupling and his counterparts in other organizations helped enact many of our nation's environmental laws.

In looking back over my four decades with the Sierra Club, I can see that I was fortunate to be at the right place at the right time with the right background. I began environmental work before it was popular, took advantage of opportunities, and was in a position of leadership as the environmental movement took off. I was on the ground floor in the thick of the struggles over the formation of America's environmental policies.

It was a magic moment in history.

1   *Growing Up in Oregon*

My earliest recollections are of California, but I was born in Oregon: in Eugene, in 1934, at the bottom of the Great Depression. My hometown stood at the head of the Willamette Valley, where the rivers from the mountains joined on the valley floor to flow lazily northward to Portland to meet the Columbia River.

Eugene then was a town of only 14,000 people, home to the University of Oregon and to a large lumbering business. The slow rains of mild winters nourished great stands of forests on the surrounding hills. Trees were being cut as fast as conditions permitted, but the federal forests farther from town had not been much touched. These old-growth stands of Douglas fir, hemlock, and cedar were among the greatest temperate rain forests that ever existed. More mass of wood was found in the average acre of these forests than in any other in the world.

Growing up at the edge of these magnificent forests, I took the lumber industry for granted, but I also took the old-growth forests as a given. Only slowly did I come to understand that the one spelled the end of the other. They could not coexist. As a child, I did not yet know the price of living in what was soon to become "the lumber capital of the world."

I exulted in the splendor of these forests in my youth. On family picnics in campgrounds at the edge of the McKenzie and Willamette rivers, I gloried in the ferns and deep festoons of moss hanging in the vine maples beneath the huge stems of the trees. As I grew up, I hiked the trails through the backcountry that roads, logging, and commerce had not yet reached. My sense of what was right in the environment was shaped by these experiences. To me, the unspoiled forests represented how things ought to be.

I was young and at large in Oregon's fir-clad mountains when its great forests were still largely intact. I could see the forests thinning on the nearby hills and knew that the families of my schoolmates worked in the mills. A procession of logging trucks trundled through town carrying immense logs, some of them so large that only one could be carried at a time. But I just assumed that logging would stop at the boundaries of the national forests—that I could count on these forests to remain forever.

I can trace my career to coming of age in this place, coupled with the shock of learning how wrong my assumptions had been. But my sense of place was also shaped by early experiences in California. In 1938, when I was four, my father took a leave of absence from teaching English at the University of Oregon to earn a Ph.D. at Stanford, and for two years we lived in Palo Alto. I remember still the flood of sunshine compared with Oregon's long, gray winters. And I remember sights of sophisticated life: San Francisco in the late 1930s, the World's Fair on Treasure Island, the foggy bay from the Berkeley Hills, and the old quadrangle at Stanford where my father had an office.

Most young people rebel when they reach adolescence, but I seem to have been most restive from the ages of four through six. In Palo Alto, I would disappear while exploring the town, making my parents frantic. Once the police found me along the El Camino Real, in search of a pony I had followed. When my parents locked me in their car after I misbehaved at a Fisherman's Wharf restaurant, I proudly sneaked out and sat defiantly on the bumper. When we returned to Eugene, I tried to run away after quarrels over trifles.

As a relatively small age cohort, my generation—"Depression babies"—was supposed to have been a quiet generation. But I didn't start out that way, nor did I seek retiring work over the course of my career. On the contrary, I often found myself deep in controversy and serving as a spokesperson for others. Yet I was usually characterized as unassuming just the same.

Parents and Family

My father, John C. McCloskey, was quite unassuming, though he gave lectures all his life and dealt with generations of students. He had the habits of a scholar and spent most evenings in our living room working on journal articles. He was the author of several textbooks on composition, but he tried to write novels too; none of them was ever published, which disappointed him immensely. He suffered from acute asthma, which, much to his lasting disappointment, led to his being rejected for military service in World War II.

In contrast, my mother, née Agnes M. Studer, was quite outgoing. She ran nursery schools and later taught in elementary schools. A natural leader, she was elected to run almost every group in which she was active. At various times, she headed the local branch of the League of Women Voters, the American Association of University Women, and her teachers association. She was vice chair of our county's Democratic Party for a while, and after World War II she organized a strike of housewives to protest the high cost of meat when wartime price controls were removed.

I was the eldest of three sons, the others six and thirteen years younger than I. The personality of my first brother, Jim, was most like that of my father, while my youngest brother, Dave, was most like my mother. I always felt that I was a blend of both my parents' temperaments, but not a fixed blend. As the firstborn, I found my own way and set the pace: my brothers were too young to have much influence on how I behaved.

My parents grew up in Iowa, where there was no wilderness to explore, and neither was an outdoor person. My father enjoyed playing tennis and, in later years, golf, which at least got him outdoors; but he did not hunt, fish, hike, or camp. Both of my parents were avid gardeners, however. Wherever we lived in Eugene, they planted large gardens full of flowers and, for quite a while, vegetables. Dad enjoyed dahlias, and both he and Mom loved roses and chrysanthemums. For a while, they were even officers in the local chrysanthemum society. I took some satisfaction in their gardening, but could always summon much more interest in wild flowers than in those grown in gardens. I suspect now that I was quietly rebelling.

Both my parents worked, and my father was employed throughout the Depression. When he could not get a job teaching summer school, he would work at the local cannery as a laborer. We lived modestly and frugally and almost never ate out. Butter was never bought because it was too expensive. In the summer, we ate vegetables and fruit that we grew in our garden. Meat was served on Sunday, with casseroles during the week.

During the Depression, I remember men coming to the door selling their wares or asking for food and to do odd jobs. When I visited the
homes of the poorest of my school friends, I saw families who subsisted
mainly on fried mush and what they could grow. They had their own
chicken coops, too. In the back of our house on Alder Street were the
remnants of a farm where chickens had been raised and cows grazed, but
my mother got our eggs from a friend at church who lived on a working farm.

After the age of six, I settled down to a happy childhood. I had good
friends, enjoyed playing outside with them, and thrived on school. I
seemed always to be busy and looking forward to new experiences. While
I did not excel at sports, I ran around the muddy playgrounds with the rest
of the boys. I can remember taking pitch from a favorite pine tree on the
playground to make gum. Life seemed full of adventure.

Environmental Hazards

In my family, growing up, we were aware of the more obvious forms of
local pollution, but not the more subtle hazards. I thought of Eugene at
the time as fairly clean—nothing like the industrial centers of the East.

We were all oblivious to dangers such as exposure to lead from gasoline fumes and the solder in the joints of our water pipes. We'd never
heard of secondhand smoke. Like thousands of other children, I liked to
see my toes wiggle in the X-ray machine in the shoe store, knowing
nothing of how unsafe these machines were. We weren't aware of the
excessive doses of dental X-rays used at the time, or of the dangers of
the mercury amalgam fillings in our mouths.

Parents kept warning us to stay away from the nearby Willamette
River, which was then grossly polluted from the untreated local sewage
that flowed into it. Refuse at the lumber mills was burned in so-called
wigwam burners, producing wood smoke that we now know was full of
carcinogens. And pulp mills were built later that sent sulfurous fumes
into the wind. The late summer skies were clotted with choking smoke
as farmers burned seed-grass fields following harvests to kill insects.

Pollution was not the biggest environmental problem that I then
understood. Bothering me most were the little red slivers from the bark
of the Douglas fir cordwood for our furnace, which would get painfully
lodged in my hands when I stacked the wood in our basement. I also
learned the hard way that the brush in the surrounding hills was filled

with poison oak, which severely blistered my skin when I touched it. We were warned about rattlesnakes in the hills, but I saw one only once. Somewhere out there were mountain lions as well, but the only ones I ever saw were dead ones brought in by a bounty hunter. And before the flood control reservoirs were built, the Willamette and its tributaries frequently pushed out onto their floodplains, rampaging across neighborhoods in their path.

Work

From an early age, work was part of my life. In my parochial school, children at about age nine were asked to sell Christmas stamps to neighbors after school. Since my nearest neighbors were sorority houses near the campus, I went to them. I was treated like a pet and taken from floor to floor, where the girls would cry out "man on second" and "man on third" and laugh. I didn't know why, but I sold lots of stamps. The following year I sold the *Saturday Evening Post* door to door to our other neighbors.

When I reached age eleven, I was expected to go into the fields with the other youngsters to pick string beans in the summertime. After the war, with labor still scarce, farmers relied on child labor. It was hot, backbreaking, stoop labor, and I was bad at it. I got a rash from the beanstalks, and my meager yield dropped quickly. By the third day I quit; I knew I was not suited to be a fieldworker.

The next year I got a job delivering newspapers to homes after school, and I stayed with that for five years, until the age of seventeen. We delivery boys rode around our routes on bicycles, tossing the rolled-up papers onto front porches.

Shortly after I began, the newspaper—the *Eugene Register-Guard*—asked us to deliver the papers to each door, forcing us to get off our bicycles repeatedly. I thought this unreasonable—unless we were paid a lot more. The work would take us twice as long, I argued. When management refused to pay more, I organized a wildcat strike by all of the delivery boys. After a three-hour standoff, management capitulated; no more was heard of "doorknob delivery." I was only twelve at the time.

On Sunday mornings, we had to get up at 4:30 a.m. to deliver the papers by 7:00 a.m. Afterward, some of us would gather at an all-night cafe to get cocoa and toast and wonder who the bleary-eyed characters sitting next to us were. Occasionally, I filled in on other jobs at the newspaper, handling the switchboard one summer for a while. I got to know many of the writers and editors, including one who became a federal judge.

The hardest job I ever had (that I stuck with) was stacking cans in a cannery where string beans and other vegetables were processed. My father had worked there and got me in. I did it one summer during high school and two more during college. My task was to stack restaurant-size, number 10 cans in the storage vaults in the basement, in endless rows, to a height of about six feet. This meant bending up and down for ten hours a day, six days a week—sometimes even on Sunday. Occasionally, when a defective can would explode, I would have to take the whole stack down to find the spoiled can, clean up the mess, and build the row all over again.

Once in a while, I would get a break and be transferred for the day to some other task. The hardest was unloading boxcars in the afternoon heat; at least the storage basement was cool. I spent a day with a fellow weighing huge casks filled with maraschino cherries that were curing in a putrid solution. These five-hundred-pound casks could easily get away from you and crush a bone.

The most enlightening respite was a day operating the labeling machine. We were given an assortment of cans with the same ingredients and were told to put labels on them—some for the cheaper kind of Blue Lake beans, some for the more expensive version. Thus I learned that you don't always get what you pay for.

The cannery job taught me what a sweatshop was. Supposedly no one cared, because this was just seasonal work using "temporaries." Some of us were high school and college boys, but others were itinerant laborers. While I knew I could survive hard manual labor at that age, I thought that sixty- to seventy-hour weeks of backbreaking labor were a bit much. In vain, I tried to get the labor union there, a Teamsters affiliate, to do something, but they chose to represent only the interests of the foremen, who were glad that we, rather than they, were doing the worst work. In the end, I wrote an article on the plant's deplorable conditions for the *Catholic Worker* newspaper.[1] That experience caused me to empathize with those whom labor unions are supposed to represent.

All through high school, I tried to get a job with the Forest Service on the crews that built and repaired trails. This kind of outdoor work appealed to me. When I was sixteen, the minimum age for this work was seventeen. When I was seventeen, it was eighteen. When I was eighteen, I decided I wanted to work as a seasonal ranger for the Park Service instead. But then I discovered that the pay was low and employees had to buy their own uniforms; I could earn more at the cannery, and needed to.

Alas, I never worked a day for a federal agency—except for a brief holiday stint in Boston for the Post Office. During a snowstorm, I kept doggedly delivering mail because I took seriously the motto that "the mail must go through," and I didn't want to appear to be a softie. Everyone else quit in that blizzard, but I didn't stop until my supervisor came out to get me and bring me in.

Play

The town of Eugene offered various entertainments to fascinate a child. The premier event was a pageant that was staged periodically at the county fairgrounds to celebrate the pioneers who had settled the country. Old Cal Young, who was born in a pioneer's cabin, led a parade of townspeople dressed in pioneer costumes. And on campus, every fall for Homecoming, the fraternity and sorority members put colorful displays on their lawns and lit a huge bonfire.

The campus at the time was a marvelous playground for kids. I watched WPA workers dig trenches for tunnels to hold steam pipes to heat the university. I dug fossils out of the shale of excavations for university buildings. I spied on ROTC students who were trying to disguise themselves with camouflage in the nearby woods as World War II began. My friends and I learned to climb along narrow ledges on the sides of university buildings and clamber up and over them.

I couldn't resist the lure of college football games played only blocks from where I lived. Lots of us boys who couldn't afford to pay found ways to sneak in. Because mounted sheriff patrols waited to intercept us as we scaled the fences, we developed strategies to outwit them. We would avoid the places where they were concentrated, and then we'd pour over the fences in great numbers and scatter. There were too many of us for them to run us all down, and we enjoyed many good games sitting near the fifty-yard line in the bleachers.

We also were drawn to the river's edge in the summertime. Though it was polluted and going there was forbidden, it was too much to resist. There were beaches, lagoons, and hobo jungles. To get there we had to cross the highway and the train tracks, dodge trucks that were working in a sand and gravel plant, and skirt the gas works, but it was worth it. A friend and I turned an old mixing box for concrete into a scow that we paddled through the lagoons. We waded into the current and played in the sand. On the way back—if trains were coming—we would flatten pennies by putting them on the train tracks.

I did worry about some hazards. As I rode my bike to school along the main avenues, I worried when overloaded log trucks would pass me. Would I ever be crushed by logs falling off these trucks? Probably there was a greater danger that the truck drivers might not see me.

Every summer my parents took our family to the beach just south of Waldport, on the central Oregon coast. Summer after summer, we played on Big Stump Beach, and I developed a love of strolling these wide beaches, which I still enjoy. One time, a friend of my father's took us out into Alsea Bay to go crabbing. I was carefully instructed in how to safely pick the crabs out of the nets as they were pulled aboard—"pick them up from the rear," I was told. By the end of that day, I thought I had it all figured out. But when I was helping my mother put our crabs into the pot at the cabin, I got careless, and one got my thumb between his big claws. I still have that scar.

One adventure during my youth did go a bit wrong, although it was not mine. When my younger brother Jim tried to climb up the cliffs of Judkins Point, a highway cut into columnar basalt, he got stuck, and the fire department had to rescue him. But one newspaperman always thought that it was I rather than my brother who had to be rescued. Over the years, he would keep dredging up this mistaken notion in his columns—to my continuing embarrassment.

Because I grew up in a land where it rained nine out of twelve months, everything looked wonderful when the sun shone in the summer. People in Oregon get somewhat crazed when the sun comes out (nowadays they call these periods "sun breaks"), and they come pouring from their houses. But I even liked being out in the Oregon rain, which mainly comes in the form of intermittent drizzles anyway. Nobody even used umbrellas then; that was regarded as giving in to the weather.

My parents took us on picnics in forest campgrounds along the highways that ran into the mountains. I wanted more, though—I wanted to go on hikes, to see more of what was behind the hills and woods around town and back of the highways. The way to do that was to join the Boy Scouts, so I did—as soon as I could, on my 12th birthday.

For a while the Boy Scouts seemed perfect; I liked their program, their structure, their uniforms, and the chance to earn merit badges. I especially enjoyed summer camp and its camaraderie at Camp Lucky Boy on Blue River, and later at Camp Melakwa in the high country near McKenzie Pass. I went for four straight years. We went on hikes into the areas beyond the end of roads—into what was in effect wilderness. It was entrancing to walk through the deep old forests of fir, hemlock, and cedar, along pure, wild mountain streams. And it was exciting to hike up to forest lookouts to see miles of unbroken forests—ridge after ridge unmarred.

I quickly yearned for better guidance, however. The Boy Scouts did not know much about the right kind of equipment. I didn't have real boots or a pack frame. And I began to see that not all of their leaders had that many outdoor skills. Gradually I learned where to get better equipment—mainly war-surplus mountain tents and down sleeping bags. I got myself boots with better support and a Trapper Nelson backpack. A buddy of mine and I started to upgrade our skills beyond what the Boy Scouts could offer.

But I had lots of good experiences with the Boy Scouts. They took me up my first real mountain with glaciers—the Middle Sister. I shinnied across rivers on logs, waded cold streams, and dodged trees falling in storms. I slept in old logs and on dark beaches, awakening to find the tide lapping at my toes. I tiptoed around thousands of tiny frogs at Frog Camp near McKenzie Pass. (The frogs subsequently disappeared, probably for environmental reasons; pesticides may have been the culprit.)

The Boy Scouts offered me challenges and I took to them, rising to become an Eagle Scout with a Silver Palm, their highest rank. Over time I became a junior assistant scout master and later an advisor to an Explorer Post. And I went to a national jamboree at Valley Forge, Pennsylvania, writing stories for our hometown newspaper about our boyish adventures along the way. I had no sense then that people would come to make fun of the Boy Scouts because of their straight-arrow earnestness.

My friend Gene Hebert and I did decide that we wanted to connect with outdoor people who knew more about what they were doing than many of the dads in scouting did. We were excited to hear of a local outdoor club called the Obsidians. We feared that they would have no interest in fourteen-year-old boys, so we were amazed to find ourselves admitted to membership in 1948. Through the Obsidians we learned about rock climbing, ice work, and good camping skills. It was the Obsidians that really got me into the backcountry and up most of the high peaks of Oregon's Cascades. As I grew older, I became a strong and speedy hiker.

On Mount Jefferson, I once barely escaped being knocked in the head by a falling rock while climbing up a chute. I flattened myself against the wall as a rock tumbled by, missing my head by a fraction of an inch. Helmets were not yet in use. I climbed this snow-clad peak twice because I fell in love with an amphitheater at its northern base—Jefferson Park—which is filled with scarlet paintbrush, ponds, and heather. It is the most beautiful place I have ever visited in Oregon's Cascades.

Eventually I became an Obsidian Chief, for having climbed the North, Middle, and South Sister mountains, but increasingly I wanted to understand what I was seeing rather than treating these ventures as a brand of athletics. My interest turned toward the natural scene and conservation. Later I became co-chairman of the conservation committee of the Obsidians.

While growing up, I also sampled other outdoor pursuits. Because I was curious, I tried to learn to fish. I never caught much, however, and found it boring to stand around the edge of rivers. I probably didn't know what I was doing. And I went out once with friends who were gun enthusiasts. I actually shot at a squirrel in a tree (missing it), but then wondered why I would want to kill it. Strangely enough, these same friends were afraid to go into wilderness without being armed, though I never found the slightest need to carry firearms there.

As a child in Eugene, I had little consciousness of race or ethnicity. The town had almost no blacks, Hispanics, or Native Americans. While my name was Irish, I had little sense of what that meant. On St. Patrick's Day, though, my father did send me to school sporting a humiliatingly large, floppy tie in kelly green with white polka dots. The butcher at the corner grocery used to kid me, saying, "Well, here is our little Swede" (I was towheaded), and then laugh. I didn't understand the gibe, though, so I wasn't offended.

The only overt sign of ethnicity around me was the Sons of Norway Lodge down the street, but no one ever saw anybody going there. Eugene had few first-generation immigrants so instead of remembering countries of origin, people in my town sought to remember the states from which they had come. Every summer, picnics were organized by groups such as the Iowa State Society or the Minnesota State Society.

Even though my parents came from Iowa, however, we never went to those picnics.

School

I had no experience with public schools until law school, though my parents taught in them. I went to parochial schools from the first grade through high school and spent my undergraduate years in a private college. I thrived in school from the first day, when my mother sent me off in knickers with my lunch box.

I was in no position to judge at that time, but I think I got a good education at St. Mary's and at St. Francis. The sisters of the Holy Names maintained strict discipline. Offending students got their knuckles rapped with a ruler. The discipline was in the mold of the parochial high school on the south side of Chicago where my father taught briefly in the 1920s. He told me how a prefect of discipline would roam the halls with a baseball bat. Once he was startled to hear a thump in the back of his class and turned to see a student lying prostrate—felled for stepping out of line in some indiscernible way.

My grades were always good, except for penmanship and typing; apparently I was lacking in some measure of eye-hand coordination. My parents encouraged me to study hard, but I also enjoyed learning. I liked writing papers; in high school I entered a national essay contest for parochial schools and won it, with my entry published in *Extension* magazine. It was a profile of the U.S. Attorney General at that time, J. Howard McGrath. Earlier I had won an essay contest sponsored by the local newspaper.

Upon entering high school, I was drawn into positions of student leadership. In my freshman year, in my innocence I was drafted to chair the prom committee—having never been to a prom and knowing nothing about them. I organized those who did know something, however, and it turned out successfully.

I was soon elected class president and then to the student council. In my junior year, I enrolled in a journalism class and then became editor of the school newspaper. I went to Boys' State and met other young student leaders and doers. About that time, I became ambitious and decided to run for student body president in my senior year.

Until then my campaigning had been sedate, but this time I printed up hundreds of handbills that showed up everywhere. (Some are probably still being found in odd places!) When the rules limited signs to only three throughout the whole school, my supporters, seeing no limitation on the size of the signs, painted a giant one that was hung on the front of the school. In a three-way contest against candidates from the popular crowd and the athletic circles, I ran as the candidate of the wallflowers—and won.

I can't remember now why I cared so much. But I suppose it was all training of sorts. It gave me a taste of politics—and a taste *for* politics.

2 *Politics, College Years, and the Army*

I first became aware of partisan politics during the 1940 presidential race. My parents were fervent New Deal Democrats and supported Franklin Roosevelt's bid for a third term. I remember arguing with the neighbor boy over the backyard fence about who should be president, Roosevelt or Wendell Willkie, having absorbed my parents' politics.

Four years later, my parents were again concerned that not enough was being done in our community to boost Roosevelt's chances, this time in his bid for a fourth term. They gathered Democrats in our living room to write a full-page advertisement to place in our local newspaper on his behalf.

In the decade following the war, my parents immersed themselves in local Democratic Party politics. They were in the vanguard of those who revived the party's fortunes in Oregon during that period. Returning veterans gathered at our home to lay plans. My folks went to endless party meetings and returned with dramatic tales of infighting. It seemed quite exciting.

By the early 1950s, my mother had become the vice chair of the Lane County Democratic Central Committee. That was about as high as a woman then could rise in organized party work in our county, which was the second most populous in the state. Statewide candidates sought her support, and she was deeply involved in the quixotic candidacy of Estes Kefauver in the 1952 Democratic presidential primary.

From the age of ten on, I became increasingly interested in national politics and attracted to the idea of promoting idealistic policies to

improve conditions. I listened avidly to a radio program featuring a liberal commentator and read speeches from the *Congressional Record* that
were sent to us by U.S. Senator Wayne Morse, who was soon to become
a Democrat and whom my parents knew from his days as a law professor in Eugene. I learned the party line on all of the programs being put
forth by the Truman administration, debating some of them in high
school.

I gradually came to notice that those who debated issues most skillfully tended to be lawyers. Then my parents backed a congressional candidate who was a Harvard-educated lawyer. At the age of twelve, I
decided that I wanted to be a lawyer too to get that training. Slowly the
idea took root that I would major in government in college and then
go to law school to prepare for a career in politics. I fastened onto that
career track at an early age without ever really looking into what lawyers
did to earn a living or what the everyday practice of law was like.

My parents seemed pleased with my ambitions, but it was clear that
they did not have the money to finance them. I would have to win schol-
arships and earn enough through summer and part-time jobs—which
I did.

I ended up applying to Harvard, Yale, Princeton, and Stanford, and
was accepted by all of them. Harvard offered me the largest scholarship,
so I went there. I also won a small scholarship from the Oregon AFL-
CIO, based on my knowledge of the history of organized labor, which
I had taken the trouble to learn. I had already begun cultivating my ties
to the labor movement.

When I arrived at Harvard in 1952, it was attempting to transform
itself from an exclusive Ivy League college for old wealth into a merit-
based institution that sought the best students from all over the nation.
I was admitted as part of the effort to change the composition of the student body, which was at that moment an odd mix of the old and the new
types, with all of us learning from one another.

In my freshman year, I won a Detur Prize for high grades. This prize
was awarded each year, under the terms of a 1637 grant, to "diligent
boys in the plantation colonies who show promise of being of future
service to their country." (Of course, it was a different country then.) I
hoped that was a good portent.

After my freshman year, I plunged into my major in American government. At Harvard, that major was not called political science because
Harvard did not believe in a statistical approach to the subject; instead,

the coursework emphasized relationships of power. I took courses in government from figures such as V. O. Key, Samuel Beer, and Samuel Huntington; in economics from John Kenneth Galbraith and John Dunlop; and in history from Oscar Handlin. I also took the only course given that touched upon natural resources—Arthur Maass's famous course on the dubious benefits of dam building.

When a family friend who was also a professor visited, he dubbed my friends and me "the young intellectuals," which struck me as an outlandish compliment. But perhaps, in retrospect, we *were* heading in that direction.

I kept grounded in other ways. I got a part-time job working in the dining halls as a dishwasher. The local help had little rapport with budding intellectuals, but I enjoyed the change of pace and the exercise.

Through the Philip Brooks House, I volunteered on Saturday mornings to work in local settlement houses. Usually I took boys aged eight to twelve on trips to see local sights. Sometimes this was even more of an adventure than I bargained for. When we went to see the USS *Constitution*, for instance, one of them threw a spike into its rotting sides. At the point where the spike struck, I was alarmed to see sawdust filtering out of a hole in the chipped paint. I almost panicked—would my kids sink the ship that the British couldn't?

Some of my time also went into politics at Harvard. I joined the Young Democrats rather than the Liberal Union because they seemed more practical in their orientation. I volunteered for Foster Furcolo's successful campaign for governor, as well as for other campaigns, where I learned how to do canvassing and phone banking. In my junior year, I was elected president of the Young Democrats. I even ran for the presidency of the Young Democratic Clubs of New England, but was beaten by a parliamentary maneuver as the rest of the clubs coalesced against "the candidate from the Boston area." I resolved to learn more about parliamentary procedure.

As president of the Young Democrats, I invited interesting figures to speak to the group. The most interesting of all was the former Boston mayor, Massachusetts governor, and ex-convict James Michael Curley. He had been convicted of taking a civil service exam for a constituent seeking a job at the Post Office. A tall, silver-haired figure with a rumbling voice, he relished telling Harvard types how he "shook down" bankers during the Depression to get money to feed the poor. He told the bankers they would be responsible for children starving—and he would make sure everyone knew it—if they would not extend further credit to the bankrupt city of Boston. He was then in the midst of his "last hurrah," a historic voice from an earlier era.

At the end of my junior year, I had a close call. I joined three other classmates driving home across the country in one of their cars. It was an old Ford station wagon—a "woodie"—and we drove around the clock. One night when I was driving near Mountain Home, Idaho, the car failed as I was heading up a long grade. When I tried to shift into a lower gear, the transmission froze and the brakes went out. The car came to a stop and started rolling backward. I barely got everyone awakened, and we bailed out as the car went over the edge into a ravine. We leaped blindly in the dark down a hundred-foot embankment. Just as we scrambled up the other side of the wash, the car came crashing below us. We escaped being crushed by a matter of seconds.

As we leaped down the embankment, all of us lost our wallets. Passing motorists called the sheriff, who took us into a nearby town, where we wired home for money to take a bus the rest of the way home. I know I should have learned something from this youthful escapade that went wrong, but I'm not sure I did. I've never had another auto accident, though.

In my senior year, 1956, I applied for a Rhodes Scholarship to Oxford. Harvard endorsed me for this scholarship, but I did not get the nod from the panel in my home state of Oregon, which had to concur. One of the panelists there later told my mother that they decided not to give it to me because they were not sure that I really wanted it. Apparently, in his letter of recommendation, my house master repeated something along this line that I had said to him in confidence.

But it was probably just as well. Had I gotten the scholarship, I might never have discovered what was to become my career. The opportunity for conservation fieldwork that presented itself in 1961 would not have been available two years later.

In June 1956 I graduated with high honors and prepared to enter the army. When I had begun college, the Korean War was still under way. Some in my high school had enlisted to serve in it, while others were drafted. To get a deferment, I signed up for the Reserve Officers Training Corps (ROTC) to be trained as an artillery officer in the U.S. Army. I correctly anticipated that the war would be over by the time I would have to serve on active duty.

Upon being commissioned as a second lieutenant, I looked forward to serving overseas. I thought Germany would be ideal. But as it turned out, I was the only person in my class assigned to Fort Sill, Oklahoma, the home training post of the artillery. In commencing my service there in December 1956, I thought I would drift through this service as I had ROTC. I needed a break from the challenges of college study. But my slack attitude got me into trouble. My first captain was a West Pointer who took me aside to give me a "dutch uncle" talk. I had a bad attitude, I was told, and needed to learn to "play the game rather than to fight the problem." I thought about what he had to say and decided that, as I was stuck there for two years, I might as well see whether I could master this game.

Artillery firing then relied on the use of slide rules, tables of data, surveying, and mathematics (matters now largely handled by computers and global positioning satellites). These were not subjects that came easily to me. But I became quite proficient in firing techniques and soon found myself commanding a firing battery of six self-propelled 155mm howitzers.

After a year, I was promoted to first lieutenant and became the acting C-3 of my battalion in charge of training. Usually a major handled that function, but all of the senior officers in my battalion, who were due to retire soon, spent most of their days closeted in their offices completing correspondence courses to prepare them for civilian careers. They effectively turned the running of the battalion over to me and the noncommissioned officers.

In the final evaluation of my performance, my superior gave me the highest possible efficiency ratings in all categories—straight "5s." I felt I had really learned how to "play the game." A few years later in the reserves, I was promoted to the final grade of captain.

While on active duty I did get an opportunity to become closely involved with the law. I was appointed to serve as counsel in Special Courts-Martial, which handle offenses punishable by up to six months of confinement. These lesser courts do not use trained lawyers as counsel.

In the beginning I was assigned the job of serving as counsel for the defense. These cases are tried before panels of fellow officers. I was slow to understand that the unspoken code was that the defense counsel was expected to not "try too hard."

I thought this was a chance to be like Perry Mason—so I did try hard. Surprisingly, I won every case I handled. After a while, the army got tired of seeing so many acquittals and moved me over to be the prosecutor. I found it easy to win all of those cases too.

With this legal experience under my belt, I was looking forward to law school.

Convinced that I was well suited to be a lawyer, I decided to return to my home state of Oregon, where I was accepted at the University of Oregon's law school.

I felt a bit bewildered returning to Eugene as just a student. I had been used to running a substantial operation, with men saluting and opening doors for me. I had written nationally published articles for the *Catholic Worker* newspaper and *Army Magazine*. Suddenly, I was no one again. What was worse, I was being hazed as a first-year law student, being shown how little I understood.

And I didn't like the way the law was being taught at the University of Oregon. The law school then was in transition. Many of its most respected faculty had left. The students were now supposed to learn the law largely through the case method—by analyzing court decisions. Some of the older professors continued to lecture, which I liked, while some of the newer ones were still struggling to learn to use the case method. The method seemed like looking for a needle in a haystack to me. I didn't yet know enough law to know what I was supposed to be looking for. And the school was using a lot of local attorneys, with little or no teaching experience, as adjunct faculty; these folks struggled even more to find their way in the classroom.

My undergraduate training in government also pointed me toward different kinds of questions than were pertinent in law school. I had trouble making the transition from political theory to legal logic. Law school was not at all what I had supposed it would be, and on top of that, I was being trained to practice business law, which held little appeal.

Perhaps as a consequence, for the first time in my schooling, I was not doing well. I was tempted a number of times to drop out. But I could never figure out a better type of graduate training to pursue.

I finally concluded that I wanted to be an advocate, but not just for anyone. I wanted to be an advocate for a cause I believed in. I wanted to shape the law, not just apply and interpret it. While becoming a politician was one way to do that, I could also work for a cause organization. The labor unions were one potential employer, but I was not sure of their future.

I asked myself which causes were relevant to the area where I lived. The answer was conservation. Oregon was then all about natural resources and the issues concerning their use and future. Richard L. Neuberger was elected senator in 1954 by championing conservation, and it was evident that conservation was a growing issue in the state. It was one I had long been interested in. A law degree might help me work for this cause, I concluded, but I didn't need to practice law. So I decided to stick it out in law school but not bother preparing for the bar exam.

Today the University of Oregon Law School is one of the nation's leaders in teaching environmental law. But at that time, the field of environmental law did not yet exist. I took all of the public law courses available, but no course on natural resource law was even offered then. Unguided, I prepared an extended note for the *Oregon Law Review* on the origins and meaning of the Forest Service's Multiple-Use Sustained-Yield Act of 1960, which was well received.[1] I argued that the Forest Service's basic law gave the agency the grounds to preserve the national forests as well as to log them. Oddly enough, the Forest Service took ten years to prepare an answer to my argument. In that article, I also predicted that citizen lawsuits would someday be brought under statutes like that. A decade later, I helped make that prediction come true by initiating pioneering legal cases as a leader of the Sierra Club.

Given my discontent over law school, I decided while still in school to pursue my other interests too, hoping that they might lead somewhere. As a member of Eugene's principal outdoor club since 1948, the Obsidians, I had followed emerging conservation issues in Oregon even while away at college and in the army. Now I joined their conservation committee and came under the tutelage of Karl D. Onthank, a dean at the university. Tall, spare, and balding, with an angular face, Onthank had been active in the field of conservation since the 1920s and knew everyone of consequence in the state. He was exactly the mentor I needed.

Onthank soon asked me to join him as co-chair of the conservation committee. Together we campaigned to stop the local municipal utility's reworked plans (their first had been rejected by the voters) for a set of dams on the upper McKenzie River (we lost). We also pursued efforts to preserve the natural setting and clarity of Waldo Lake, one of Oregon's larger lakes, near the Willamette Pass. The Forest Service wanted to push a new road into the area and make long-term commitments to logging. In response, we formed the Waldo Lake Committee to urge our case in the press. Unfortunately, these efforts were only partially successful.

The Obsidians were members of a larger entity known as the Federation of Western Outdoor Clubs. In 1959 Onthank persuaded me to join him and his wife, Ruth, as a delegate to the annual convention of the Federation. This was all new to me. There I met figures in the other clubs and from the national conservation movement. At a meeting on Hood Canal on Puget Sound, I met the heads of three major organizations: Olaus Murie of the Wilderness Society, Fred Packard of the National Parks Association, and David Brower of the Sierra Club. They were all figures of eminence and importance. It suddenly became clear to me that there were major organizations on the national scene that hired staff to lobby and organize around these issues.

I got to know Brower when serving with him on the Resolutions Committee at this convention. He was a tall, intense man with white hair who always attracted attention and was a bit of a legend. In the 1930s, he had made many first ascents. We saw eye to eye over the issues swirling about the Forest Service's new plans for massive logging, and the next summer he offered me a small job investigating plans for logging in the Minam Valley of the Wallowa Mountains of eastern Oregon. Justice William O. Douglas, who had spent time in that area, had privately appealed to Brower to stop this logging.

Working with photographer Phil Hyde, I hiked eighteen miles along the valley floor to develop the text of an appeal that Brower would put out. On that trip, Hyde and I soon parted company, as he was interested in seeing patterns in nature, while I was interested in seeing as much of the country as I could. Our appeal worked, and ultimately the Minam became part of the Eagle Cap Wilderness.

Through Onthank and Brower, I also learned that Douglas was urging the Sierra Club and the Federation to pool their resources to hire a full-time field organizer to resist this onslaught of logging. In the spring of 1961, these plans came together with a pledge of matching money from mattress manufacturer and noted skier Leo Gallagher, who was active in the Mountaineers Club of Seattle. Onthank told the two organizations that he knew just the man for the new job—namely me— and I was hired straight out of law school in the summer of that year. I wasn't even interviewed for the job, since the key people—Brower, Gallagher, and Onthank—already knew me.

All through law school I had also pursued my interests in party politics. Having learned how to do it at Harvard, I organized a club of Young Democrats at the University of Oregon. We signed up members at a table at the end of the registration line when school began in the fall. With four hundred members, we were the largest such club in the state, and I was elected president.

When John Kennedy came to the campus in the spring of 1960, as the president of the campus Young Democrats I was chosen to introduce him to a large audience in the student union. The next year I took his brother, Ted Kennedy, to the airport. On the way, the soon-to-be senator admitted that he had been at a loss as to how to answer a recent question about changes in the gold standard. He asked me for my opinion. I thought a moment, recalling what I could from my economics courses at Harvard, and gave him my advice. In the paper the next day, I saw that he had given that very answer to reporters in Portland when faced with the question again.

As the president of the largest Democratic club in the county, I was made a member of the Lane County Democratic Central Committee, and I was also elected as the Democratic committeeman for my voting precinct. In due course, Bob Straub, the leading state senator from the county (and later governor), appointed me as one of his alternates in case of incapacitation, under a law born of nuclear-age anxieties. Thus I became what was called an alternate state senator.

My involvement in the Young Democrats also brought me into contact with other such clubs around the state, because all were federated into an organization called the Young Democratic Clubs of Oregon. In the summer of 1956, while I was awaiting the call to active duty in the army, I did research to help elect a new Democratic congressman from eastern Oregon and volunteered my services in the reelection race of Senator Wayne Morse. In that capacity, I traveled around the state on his behalf organizing Students for Morse groups on college campuses.

In the late 1950s I became the executive secretary of the Young Democratic Clubs of Oregon. Within the politics of that organization, I became the champion of the downstate groups, which were vying against the groups from upstate, in the Portland area. My situation was now the reverse of what it had been in Boston, but I had learned my lessons from that earlier experience. I was now the master of parliamentary procedure.

One year out of law school, I ran for the state legislature in Lane County, of which Eugene was the largest city. In an at-large race, I was nominated as a Democrat and ran a creditable first-time race, with little money and employing mainly shoe leather. I lost by 2,500 votes out of 25,000 cast, but did well enough for my mentors to be encouraged about my prospects should I run again. I had the endorsement of the local AFL-CIO Central Labor Council, and in precincts in lumber country up the McKenzie River, I actually led the Democratic ticket. The timber workers in that area didn't seem to be offended by my conservation message.

I learned a lot in that one race. Typically, people who come out to hear candidates want to be entertained with banter and jokes, not to be burdened with lots of talk about issues. I also had to face the fact that most of the issues they were interested in were not issues I wanted to talk about. I didn't want to talk about cutting taxes or balancing budgets. I was interested primarily in conservation. And I learned that I had to raise more money if I wanted to compete.

Most of all, though, the experience convinced me that my interest in becoming a politician was misplaced (just as my desire to become a practicing attorney had been). I hadn't understood what being a politician was really like: it was a hard life and would become even more thankless in the years to come. But I had learned how politicians think and react, and had gained insights that would help me to become effective in influencing them.

3 *Field Organizer*

In August 1961, I embarked upon a very different career than the one I had long anticipated. Under the arrangement offered me, I became the first field organizer for the Sierra Club and the Federation of Western Outdoor Clubs. My mission was to help these organizations realize their goals for protecting nature, especially in wilderness areas and in national parks. My territory covered Oregon, Washington, Idaho, and western Montana. While other organizations had field representatives, the groups that hired me had no experience with such a position. I had to invent it.

And I had to invent it on very short rations. The retainer of $400 a month that I was paid was intended to both compensate me and cover my expenses. Accordingly, I learned to operate very economically. I continued to live with my parents. When traveling, I stayed in run-down hotels or campgrounds or with supporters, who also often fed me.

Around the Northwest

I traveled incessantly—both visiting supporters and scouting out areas that were threatened. I was probably on the road 60 percent of the time—day and night and on weekends in all seasons and weather—through winter storms and out to the ends of the logging roads. Once I slid off the road in my old Volkswagen into a snowbank near Yellowstone. On another occasion near Kalama, Washington, my car spun around twice after hitting a patch of flooded highway.

Though money was tight, I did open an office in Eugene in the dignified but fading Tiffany Building. If the office was small, the rent was cheap. I did my own typing and put out mailings from there. Local volunteers, particularly Bert Tepfer, helped plot Forest Service timber sales on maps I collected of every national forest in the Northwest.

When I began, conservationists in each locality felt embattled and outmatched. They struggled to understand the larger context of their battles. I invented systems to collect information about what was happening on conservation issues throughout this region. I subscribed to the *Lewiston (ID) Tribune*, the *Port Angeles (WA) Evening News*, and other regional newspapers that specialized in covering natural resource issues. Over time I built up a network of people such as Paul Bergman, living in the isolated community of Stehekin, Washington, who would send clippings, gossip, and cries for help to stop development schemes that appalled them. Gradually I gathered enough information to enable me to piece together patterns and see how the opposition was framing its arguments. In turn, I disseminated this information through a newsletter to my client clubs and through a constant stream of correspondence and phone calls.

I also developed a circuit of visits to cultivate contacts and to bring conservation news to our friends in various communities. These people were members of the clubs for which I worked as well as local activists who were coming to my attention. People in one community would then tell me of people I should meet in the next. Gradually I got to know more and more of them. They would give me news, and I would give them news. I would find out which tactics seemed to work and which didn't. I spread the news about promising approaches and helped local groups strategize about how to deal with agencies and developers.

Most of these activists felt abandoned. In the early 1960s they felt almost like heretics, particularly those in smaller communities. They welcomed me warmly, and I helped buck up their morale by bringing news of others like themselves facing the same struggles, showing them that they were not alone. I was almost like an itinerant preacher and was treated as a hero.

We met in homes and clubhouses. I often attended meetings of the conservation committees of the largest clubs in Portland, Seattle, and other cities. In Seattle, I was treated almost as an insider at the meetings of the Mountaineers, and I worked closely there with the officers of the North Cascades Conservation Council, which was also a client. Some of its key officers, such as Pat Goldsworthy, had begun in California with the Sierra Club, as had Polly and John Dyer. Polly had served as the president of the Federation (and was later to serve on the national board of the Sierra Club).

In Portland, the conservation committee of the Mazamas was split between the "old guard," who still supported the Forest Service, and the new critics of its logging policies, with each side trying to get its supporters to attend meetings in greater numbers. The outcome was often in doubt, though gradually our more critical side began to prevail.

I also attended meetings of the Pacific Northwest Chapter of the Sierra Club, which then covered the entire Northwest. (Separate chapters now exist in each state.) Fall meetings were held at the country place of a grande dame, Emily Haig, on the west side of Puget Sound, where we all looked forward to the ritual of prying fresh oysters out of the bay flats at low tide, then eating them on the spot.

In addition to organizing, I researched issues, drafted proposals to lay before the clubs and then agencies, and acted as a spokesman. At hearings, I would line up as many speakers as possible to support our position—trying to make sure they came from various areas and walks of life. I perfected a protocol about how to prepare for a hearing, which the Federation published in its newsletter.[1]

But I also offered expert testimony on technical aspects of the issues. And I cultivated key reporters to generate increasing coverage of our point of view. Sometimes I operated behind the scenes and sometimes out front. When I could get others to step forward, I stepped back. But when I couldn't, I was the spokesperson.

I also cultivated relationships with supportive members of Congress, senators especially. At that time, the senators from Oregon and Washington were all Democrats: Senators Wayne Morse and Maurine Neuberger from Oregon and Senators Henry Jackson and Warren Magnuson from Washington. I had good relations with all of them from my days in the Young Democrats, and I was particularly successful in getting Morse and Jackson involved in issues of Forest Service policy.

It was not entirely clear who my boss was. With regard to the Sierra Club, I looked to David Brower to play that role, but there was no single corresponding person in the Federation. I just tried to develop supportive and congenial relations with key players in as many of my client groups as I could.

Brower really did not want to try to direct my activity. He gave me very broad goals, such as "try to get a North Cascades National Park established and work with its supporters." He also told me stories about agencies and his experiences in working with them. At that time, he was pragmatic and measured in his outlook. For instance, he told me that while we would come to have differences with the Park Service, at least it was not in the business of logging, mining, or erecting dams. He shaped my view of the larger world of conservation and the Sierra Club, but he really left me on my own to figure out how to get things done. Perhaps this made sense given distances, the newness of the position, and that I was a contractor serving various clients.

Early in my career I was fortunate enough to meet Irving Brandt, Jr. A former newspaperman with the *St. Louis Star Times* and a Pulitzer Prize–winning biographer of James Madison, he had advised President Franklin Roosevelt during the New Deal. He had been a personal advisor to FDR on parks issues, and Roosevelt had relied on him as his eyes and ears during the battle for the Olympic National Park in the late 1930s. Brandt brought maps to the White House showing the boundaries he suggested the President support—based on his consultations and field inspection. Roosevelt pressed him to be sure that enough old growth was included in the park. He also asked why the river corridors on the west side (the Hoh, Queets, Quinault, and Bogachiel) were not longer and suggested they run to the sea. There ought to be a strip along the shore included too, Roosevelt added. He had a vision that none of his subordinate officials dared entertain. This story left me longing for that kind of leadership.

I also sought out other mentors, including Karl Onthank again. The Forest Service had been in a custodial stage of management until the early 1950s, he said. It was just suppressing fires and deferring the logging it had long desired to do until a market existed for its timber; in effect, it had been acting as a custodian rather than selling timber. With the advent of the Eisenhower administration in 1953, however, things began to change. Under its new chief, Richard McArdle, the Forest Service sought to remove heavily timbered areas from primitive areas (areas that had been roughly delineated in the 1920s, but were then having new boundaries set, under regulations for stricter protection that had been adopted in the late 1930s). It also enunciated the doctrine of multiple use (ostensibly balancing a variety of uses for the forests, but in reality making timbering dominant) and began to commit most old-growth forests to logging plans.

Onthank and his wife saw these changes firsthand as they struggled with the Forest Service in 1953–54 over its plans to dismember the western part of the Three Sisters Primitive Area in the central Oregon Cascades. In a few years, the Forest Service had changed its direction radically. The Forest Service had always hoped to sell a lot of trees for lumber, but market conditions had only now become favorable in Oregon and Washington. The private timber supply had declined sharply, and access roads could now be punched into the national forests. Few grasped the long-term implications of these changes.

One of the deans of forestry in the Northwest, Thornton Munger, told the outdoor clubs that they would have to get over their infatuation with big, old trees. The old growth was going to be converted into staggered stands of young growth. "We will have to learn to love little trees instead," he said. Indeed, Weyerhaeuser's magazine ads would show plots of little Christmas trees in glorified terms (always created by an artist, who could invent appealing scenes; realistic photographs were never used).

I learned of the "allowable cut effect." The Forest Service determined how much timber could be cut on a sustained-yield basis each year by making assumptions about the timbered area that would eventually be cut. Only a calculated portion of it would be sold and cut each year. By the late 1950s, plans had been made based on commitments of vast areas to eventual cutting. Whenever we would ask that an area be set aside for protection, the Forest Service would respond by pointing out that it would entail a reduction in how much timber could be cut generally each year in that forest, even when roads and logging were miles away from the particular place we sought to save. Reducing the cut would reduce the profits that timber companies would make and the amount of income that could be shared with local government, the argument went, and would affect jobs as well.

My constituency was outraged to learn that everything had already been decided. More than 90 percent of the timber in the national forests of the West that was economical to log (the so-called merchantable timber) had been committed to logging. The public was never asked whether this was what it wanted. No notice was given, nor were hearings held. Decisions were just made quietly in the inner councils of the Forest Service in the late 1950s.[2]

I was to learn later that this had been the plan from the outset—since the Forest Service's founder, Gifford Pinchot, had longed to make "forestry pay" and had promised to make the forests available for "use."

The Forest Service had been prevented from doing this for a half century because the lands were then inaccessible and too far from markets. I obtained copies of Forest Transportation System planning maps that showed projected road nets snaking through every corner of land. On the average, eight miles of roads would be built in every square mile of national forest land.

The Forest Service had given some thought to how to deal with the outdoor clubs and the conservationists. We were told that the "high country" was reserved for our use—in Oregon, generally the terrain above 5,000 feet of elevation. We were urged to focus our interests on the mountains and lakes in open, parklike country above the belt of heavy timber. On Forest Service planning maps, the high country was colored orange to show that it was oriented toward recreation as the dominant use, while the so-called low country was colored green to indicate that it was reserved for multiple use, which meant mainly timbering. The allowable cut was calculated based on the areas shown in green, usually in the low country, where the thick stands of old-growth Douglas fir, western hemlock, and red cedar were found. Cathedral-like stands filled with these trees clustered in the bottoms of valleys.

A few gurus whispered about the possibility of a grand trade-off. The high country would be managed as we wanted if we would agree to let the low country be logged as the timber industry wanted. Various professional foresters would mention this idea to me, but no one was in a position to act on it. And it certainly was not acceptable to us. Even the high country was not safe. In pursuing the issues involved with Waldo Lake in the Willamette National Forest, we found that the base for the allowable cut crept up onto the plateau of the high country.[3] Even open, parklike stands on the flanks of the high peaks (volcanoes such as Mount Hood) were subject to so-called sanitary logging—logging supposedly to remove "dead, dying, diseased, and damaged" trees.

But we also learned that foresters could make the case that almost any tree was diseased—and thus was vulnerable. The Forest Service was already marching through well-loved campgrounds in valley bottoms, taking out the oldest and largest trees under the assertion that they were diseased. Anytime in the next two centuries, they might die or fall over. Our protests over plans to build roads and to log around Waldo Lake spread to broader concerns about surreptitious logging in the high country. We learned that the orange areas shown on the maps were really not secure. Friends in the Forest Service leaked key documents to me. I brought this problem to the attention of Senators Morse and Jackson, who, in turn, pressed the Kennedy administration's secretary of agriculture, Orville Freeman, for a moratorium on logging in such areas.

He agreed, stopping development not only in the Waldo Lake area but in the North Cascades and the Minam Valley of northeastern Oregon. The secretary asked the Forest Service to be clearer about committing the high country to recreation. The upshot, in 1962, was a new statement from the Forest Service enunciating what it called the high mountain policy in the Pacific Northwest. In it, the agency pledged to keep logging to a minimum in this zone. Though the high mountain policy was not very strong, it marked the first time that the Forest Service had to respond in a significant way to pressures we orchestrated through a congressional delegation.[4]

In combating these Forest Service commitments to logging, we received aid from an unexpected quarter. I discovered that some members of the loggers' union (the International Woodworkers Association— CIO) in Oakridge, Oregon, were ready to act against their own ostensible economic interests and support our efforts to save the high country around Waldo Lake. I worked out of their union office to put out flyers on the plight of Waldo Lake.

That union had a long progressive tradition; in the 1930s it had supported preservation of large blocks of old-growth forest in Olympic National Park, and it later opposed shrinking the Three Sisters Primitive Area. It was frequently at odds with the millworkers, who were organized in an AFL union—the Lumber and Sawmill Workers Union (affiliated with the conservative Carpenters Union). Leaders of this latter union took their cues from the mill owners and fought every set-aside for conservation. Unlike the loggers, they had rarely seen the kinds of areas we were trying to save.

One fall day in the early 1960s, some of these loggers asked me to meet them in the woods at a special grove that they didn't want to log. It was a grove of giant western red cedar trees at the edge of the Willamette Swamp, at the headwaters of the North Fork of the Willamette River. It was reached via a poorly defined trail about two miles off the side of the access road. On arriving at the designated time in the middle of the afternoon, at first I saw no one. Then two men stepped from behind one of the huge trunks and said, "Dr. Livingston, I presume?" I replied, "Mr. Stanley, I presume." Then we laughed, introduced ourselves properly, and they showed me around.

We got along famously. They made it clear that some places, such as the grove in which we were standing, were just too fine to log. And I lost no time assuring them I would help them to save the grove. When we were done, I went back by myself because they had come a different way than I. But I hadn't realized how short the days were becoming. The light began to fail, and I had not brought a flashlight. After a while, I could barely see the trail. I was on the verge of losing my way when suddenly I saw a fire burning in the distance. I moved to it, with the light from the flames showing me the way. When I got there, no one was nearby, nor were there signs of any camp. The fire seemed safe enough in a ring of rocks, so I let it burn. The way along the remaining trail was much clearer, and I returned to my car without trouble.

That fortuitous fire kept me from spending a very cold night in the woods. I felt as if someone had been looking after me. But in the future, I always brought a flashlight.

Other Issues

About this same time (1962), the Friends of the Three Sisters Wilderness in Oregon sought my help to stop a proposal to quarry block pumice at Rock Mesa in the southern portion of that wilderness. While mining was inconsistent with the notion of wilderness, at that time the Mining Law of 1872 permitted claims to be filed within wilderness areas, since most had not been administratively "withdrawn" (that is, closed to mining and other projects). Operating a quarry there would entail building an access road into the wilderness, would deface a natural feature, and would put an industrial operation where it didn't belong.

After researching the claims that had been filed and reviewing the law (and visiting a pumice mine near Mono Craters in California run by the same company), I hit upon the idea of filing an administrative appeal of the Forest Service's decision to permit the mine operation to go forward. I found a provision in the Code of Federal Regulations that authorized such appeals. Apparently, until then the provisions had been used exclusively by commercial parties who were aggrieved. But nothing in the wording limited the use of the provision to commercial parties. Up until this time, those who objected to what was happening had simply written letters of protest. These could be filed away and forgotten. A formal administrative appeal had to be handled in a prescribed legal fashion, however, which often took years. And while the appeal was being processed, mining could not begin.

I developed an argument and filed what was probably the first administrative appeal of a Forest Service decision by conservationists.[5] At first the Forest Service tried to assert that we could not possibly use this provision, but after the issue was sufficiently publicized, they relented. The issue dragged on administratively for many years. Eventually, after this appeal was denied, Senator Mark Hatfield (who had succeeded Maurine Neuberger) and Congressman John Dellenbach (who represented the district) collaborated to pass legislation under which the federal government bought out the claims and permanently closed the area to mining.

This would prove to be the winning formula in many cases in the future. My appeal drew public attention to the issue and bought time until a political solution was possible. Eventually the Sierra Club's chapter in Oregon sent me a certificate recognizing the importance of my appeal.

From my days as an activist with the Obsidians, I had supported the proposal put forth by Oregon senator Richard Neuberger (and promoted by his wife, Maurine, who was elected to his seat following his death in 1960) for a national seashore in an area of huge sand dunes along the central Oregon coast. The National Park Service had identified this as a suitable area during its Pacific Coast Survey in the mid-1950s, and Neuberger immediately picked up its suggestion and introduced a bill. Most of the area, though, was then administered as part of the Siuslaw National Forest by the Forest Service, which resisted losing the area.

In my new work, I did what I could to build support in the early 1960s for a national seashore to be administered by the National Park Service. I organized witnesses for a field hearing and wrote a supportive article for the Club's magazine.[6] But the idea faced bitter resistance from local residents in the heart of the area around Florence, Oregon. They were allied with those who promoted use of the dunes by dune buggies (off-road vehicles designed for this purpose) and worked to stabilize the dunes through planting marram grass, or European beach grass. The chief contractor for these plantings, which were subsidized by the federal government, even threatened to sue me (on the grounds of "malicious business interference") for trying to end his work. I refused to be intimidated, and nothing came of his threat.

Oregon's senior senator, Wayne Morse, had decided to oppose the park idea, however. This should not have been unexpected, because in the late 1950s he had been quarreling over many matters with Senator Richard Neuberger (who, incidentally, had once had been his student in Oregon's law school). Also, some of Morse's friends from his days at the University of Oregon, such as our family friend Leavitt Wright, owned cabins near the area and worried that they might be condemned if a park were established.

Morse, who had always supported condemnation for public works, began to argue that in this instance it was not justified by the test of "necessity." He got into the curious position of arguing that while federal dams might be necessary, federal parks weren't. Later, to show his consistency, he even added a limitation on condemnation to the federal Wild and Scenic Rivers Act.

Despite Morse's opposition, we began to make headway. In preparing for the congressional hearings on the bill, the National Park Service developed detailed plans to show how it would manage the area. Wanting to avoid any surprises, I visited the agency's planners in San Francisco to see what they had in mind. I was aghast to find that they planned to pave a road along the beach south from the town of Florence (which the Forest Service did not favor). I told them this would be a mistake and urged them to drop it. But they were adamant; I finally told the regional director that we could not support Park Service management if it persisted in proposing to invade this area of wilderness beach.

But it did persist, and we withdrew our support. Thereafter, interest in turning the area over to the Park Service dwindled, and it never got it. In 1972 Senator Hatfield secured legislation establishing the area as a National Recreation Area under the Forest Service's management. But the objectionable road has never been built.

Primitive Area Reclassifications

In the early 1960s, the Forest Service was using its administrative powers to decide how much land it wanted to put into its new wilderness system. Areas in this system would have carefully considered boundaries and would be permanently managed as wilderness, without roads or logging. In contrast, the primitive areas, which had been set aside earlier under regulations of the 1920s, allowed some roads, had boundaries drawn with little study, and were only provisional in nature.

In response to pressures to better protect the primitive areas, the Forest Service had decided either to reclassify them as wilderness areas or to drop the provisional protection it had accorded them. The process grew out of regulations U-1 and U-2, promulgated in 1939. At this time, administrative protection was only accorded to wilderness areas, but that was better than nothing at all. We had to participate in this process to save acreage in the primitive areas and to extend it where possible.

During my days in the field in the Pacific Northwest, I dealt with reclassifications of four of these primitive areas—Mount Jefferson in the north-central portion of the Oregon Cascades, the Idaho Primitive Area and the Sawtooths in central Idaho, and the Cabinet Mountain Primitive Area in northwestern Montana. I also dealt with the aftermath of the reclassification of another—the Three Sisters Wilderness in the central Oregon Cascades.

This last case, beginning in the early 1950s, was the first of the post-war reclassifications. Conservationists vehemently objected to the Eisenhower administration's decision to lop off 53,000 acres from the west side of this former primitive area. Almost all of the deleted area, which had been added in 1938 at the behest of Bob Marshall, the originator of the wilderness system, was heavily timbered. The land added to the area in compensation lacked commercial timber. New wilderness areas set aside concurrently around Mount Washington and Diamond Peak also lacked such timber. This exchange of areas was supposed to look fair.

The Onthanks, sometimes with my assistance, raised objections for many years to subsequent decisions to log in this deleted area—calling for broader streamside corridors and a series of natural areas. A few of these were set aside. But instead of dying down, discontent over the loss of these 53,000 acres continued to grow. Subsequently, a campaign led by Dick Noyes, a University of Oregon professor and Sierra Club activist, focused on saving the southern portion of the area, which had not yet been logged—around French Pete Creek. After a twenty-five-year struggle, in 1978 Congress finally put 45,000 acres back into the Three Sisters Wilderness, including the west side of Waldo Lake, which I had labored to save in the late 1950s.

The first reclassification that I tackled on my own involved the Mount Jefferson Primitive Area east of Salem. This long, narrow area ran along the spine of the Cascades. Mount Jefferson anchored the area on the north, while a peak called Three Fingered Jack anchored it on the south; I had climbed both and knew the country around them. Popular Marion Lake abutted the boundary on the west.

I needed to examine the periphery of the primitive area carefully to see how suitable the old boundaries were. To my horror, I found that major logging roads had recently been built up to the edge of these boundaries in a number of places—even though large swaths of timber remained untouched back along the roads. I coined the phrase "leapfrog logging" to describe this tactic of trying to define future boundaries by preemptive road building and logging.[7] All too often, the Forest Service was confronting us with a fait accompli.

I drove every access road and hiked up to nearby viewpoints. By examining the terrain and developments (or absence of them), I was able to put together a proposal for new boundaries that would include as much unroaded contiguous acreage as possible. Subsequently, I conferred with my client clubs and refined my draft, gaining their backing for a final proposal, which I made public and submitted to the Forest Service. My proposal included detailed justifications for all of our proposed boundary changes, as well as arguments for why they would be advisable.[8] While the Forest Service ultimately decided to make few changes, it did include additional acreage on the west side, along Pamelia Creek, which I had recommended—acreage of lush old-growth forest.

In studying boundary changes at Mount Jefferson, I developed a technique that I applied in future cases. After I perfected it a bit more, I wrote it up for a Sierra Club manual on how to develop a proposal for a wilderness area. The technique involved sampling the core values of the area (via a backpacking trip, a horse pack trip, or an overflight); driving every road to the edge of the area; looking at every peripheral development; evaluating competing values and alternative uses of the resources found there; and then developing a concrete proposal and arguments for it. I would also consult with the hikers and climbers who were most knowledgeable about the area and would then line up support for the proposal among my constituents. People valued these areas for many reasons: to experience wild country, to see mountain scenery, to walk through old-growth forests, to hunt and fish in less crowded areas, and to simply get away from civilization.

The technique proved to be useful in evaluating the prospects for the giant Idaho Primitive Area. It embraced more than one million acres in the watershed of the Middle Fork of the Salmon River in north-central Idaho, with the Bighorn Crags along its eastern edge. This was sunny, open country with fields and forests of ponderosa pine. The area was riddled with mining claims and nonconforming roads penetrating well toward its center. Moreover, dozens of landing strips were scattered throughout the area. Owners of private holdings (called inholdings) had built lodges along the river, which was supposed to be wild, and packers had built permanent improvements, such as fences and corrals. In light of all of these blemishes, the Forest Service was thinking of declassifying the area as a lost cause.

My clients and I didn't think it was. I developed close relations with leaders in the influential Idaho Wildlife Federation—people such as Ernie Day (also a Sierra Club member)—to devise a strategy to salvage the area. To familiarize myself with the huge area, I surveyed it in a light plane, drove the peripheral roads, and went on a Sierra Club float trip down the river. I was assigned to the raft of the concessionaire's son. He was an expert boatman, but on the last day out, as we entered a place with the ominous name of Impassable Canyon, the rear of our raft got hung up on a submerged rock. The bow of the raft sank so low that water poured in, capsizing the raft and throwing all of us into the river.

Fortunately, I was wearing a life preserver, and I remembered trainers telling me to keep my head up to avoid being tumbled in the river (which would increase the risk of hitting one's head on a rock). I held my breath as I bobbed up and down in the ice-cold water and was carried through the canyon. The current was too strong to try to swim against it, but finally I hit slack water and dragged myself ashore. Shivering uncontrollably, I was on the verge of hypothermia. Fortunately, after one of the other boats came ashore, the crew built a fire and put dry clothes on me. It took hours, even in the heat of the day, for me to warm up.

Despite this inauspicious introduction to the area, I survived to put together a plan to salvage the idea of a continued wilderness area there. My plan, which the Idaho Wildlife Federation and other groups endorsed, foreshadowed approaches that later became common in dealing with nonconforming developments (that is, developments at odds with wilderness regulations). It featured narrow excluded strips along mining roads (so-called cherry-stem corridors); "cutouts" around inholdings (which might be acquired later), and phase-outs of the landing fields. The map I presented kept most of the area intact. The plan was designed to buy time until the political situation there would improve. In that respect, it was successful. Ultimately, many years later, the area was expanded vastly by Congress into the Frank Church–River of No Return Wilderness Area.

Not long after working on the Idaho Primitive Area, I also helped with the reclassification of the Sawtooth Primitive Area northwest of Sun Valley. While my investigations were limited, I put together a proposed boundary that was used at hearings, and I suggested areas that the agency later added on the southwest side. Eventually, a wilderness area of 216,000 acres was set aside. I was also drawn into the reclassification of the Cabinet Mountain Primitive Area, located in a range just south of Libby, Montana. I helped conservationists in Spokane put together a proposal for a hearing, which eventually resulted in a wilderness area of 94,272 acres being set aside, even though the area was burdened with an abundance of mining claims.[9]

During the early 1960s in the Pacific Northwest, the Forest Service was also deciding the future of what were termed Limited Areas, which were rougher versions of primitive areas. There were originally twenty of them, but they were quickly being disbanded. Five were declassified in 1960, with not one acre of them preserved in its natural state. Only a half dozen Limited Areas were left when I came on the scene. During my time, I decided to work on two of these in particular.

One was the Sky Lakes area in southern Oregon. This long, narrow strip, which runs south from Crater Lake National Park for twenty-five miles along the crest of the Cascades to Mount McLoughlin, was the least known of all of the Limited Areas. I feared that it might perish for lack of support.

The Sky Lakes area is composed of high forest land supporting lodgepole pine and Shasta red fir, punctuated by small lakes and occasional rocky outcrops. Chuck Collins, then the park director for Oregon's Douglas County, and I took a horse pack trip along the length of this serene, uncrowded area. The lateral boundaries of the area were already predetermined by access roads; there was not a lot of room for creativity. In any case, I was able to trigger sufficient interest to encourage the Forest Service to support designating the area as wilderness, and the Forest Service's final proposal closely resembled the plan that I developed. Congress eventually set aside a wilderness area of 116,300 acres.

The Alpine Lakes Limited Area, in the Cascades east of Seattle, between Snoqualmie Pass and Stevens Pass, required more study. I hiked into a number of high lake basins and vantage points. One of these hikes turned out poorly for me. Don Fager of Wenatchee and I decided to hike up a larch-covered ridge north of Icicle Creek near

Leavenworth on the east side of the Cascades. For reasons I can't explain, I foolishly decided to wear a new pair of rock-climbing boots. They provided no support whatsoever in coming 3,000 feet down off this high granite ridge. As my feet jammed repeatedly against the toes of the boots, my toenails took a terrible beating. I lost all of them for a while.

But I did get the data I needed to put together a proposal in 1963, which was endorsed by the Mountaineers, the Mazamas, the North Cascades Conservation Council (NCCC), and the Sierra Club. Although this landscape of lateral ridges and pockets of lakes at varied heights clearly was of the kind then regarded as suitable for wilderness, it was burdened by widespread checkerboard holdings of private land stemming from the original land grants to the Northern Pacific and the Great Northern railroads. Some of these lands later moved into other hands. It would have been all too easy for the Forest Service to give up on the idea of wilderness for this area.

To counter this risk, I drew boundaries that focused on what was public land, with only a limited amount of checkerboarded land included. My proposal embraced 275,000 acres of public land; if the private land were counted, its size grew to 334,000 acres. This was in contrast to the 256,000 acres in the original Limited Area. We hoped that this checkerboarded land could eventually be acquired by purchase or through exchanges. As it turned out, it took more than a dozen years to iron out these issues, but in 1976 Congress finally set aside a wilderness area of 305,400 acres, with an area around it to receive special management.

My successor as Northwest field representative, Brock Evans, has chided me for not thinking expansively enough about what could be accomplished at Alpine Lakes.[10] The final result was not that far from what I proposed, however, and it might be remembered that the art of the possible was quite different in 1963 than it was some years later. We were trying to salvage areas that were in trouble and to buy time. Moreover, at that time the Wilderness Act had not even been passed, and no one had yet developed the idea of designating "intended" or "escrow" wilderness—advance authorization by Congress to include a privately owned area in wilderness once it moved into federal hands. This concept eventually became a key feature of the Wilderness Act of 1976, which put the Alpine Lakes property into the wilderness system.

Colorado Organizer

In the fall of 1963 Dave Brower, the executive director of the Sierra Club, asked me to travel to Colorado to organize support for the Wilderness Act, the central focus of our movement at that time. The bill was designed to cure the problems that had emerged in the course of administrative reclassification of various primitive areas—decisions to remove protection for areas that had long enjoyed such protection. What had happened to the Three Sisters Primitive Area was a prime example, along with the fate of the Selway-Bitterroot Primitive Area on the Idaho-Montana border, where 400,000 acres were lost to logging. The bill was designed to prevent administrators from removing areas from protected status once such areas had been placed in a National Wilderness Preservation System. Only Congress would be able to remove them.

The bill faced an apparently immovable object—the obdurate chairman of the Interior Committee of the House of Representatives, Representative Wayne Aspinall, who represented the part of Colorado west of the crest of the continental divide. He responded sympathetically to opposition from constituents such as ranchers, miners, and irrigators (who wanted more dams and water) by refusing to let the bill out of his committee. My assignment was to organize enough support in his district to induce him to change his mind.

I was joined in this work by Bill Reavley of the National Wildlife Federation. He and I met in Grand Junction and decided to split the district between us; he took the northern half, and I took the southern half. I checked with people I knew in the Colorado Mountain Club in Denver, but unfortunately they couldn't tell me of any people to contact in western Colorado. Neither, it seemed, could anyone else. There was no Sierra Club organization in Colorado at that time, nor were there other statewide conservation groups to call upon for help. I was on my own.

After renting a car at the airport, I decided to drop by a sporting goods store in Grand Junction to learn what I could about the region. I asked a clerk at the store who around there might care about wilderness. The packers and guides did, he replied. They made their living by taking hunters into wilderness areas. When I asked how I would find them, he provided me with a list published by the Game Department. It had everything I needed: names, addresses, and phone numbers.

So I drove south on Highway 50 toward places such as Montrose, Ridgway, and Ouray, looking up each packer. I met packers in their corrals and kitchens and asked which wilderness they used and how. Then I told them that the future of these areas was not secure and that we were trying to get better protection for them. I let them know that their congressman needed to hear their views because he was standing in the way. Most of them were interested and eager to help. I would take down their words and send a telegram if they would tell me what they wanted to say. I had them sign what they dictated, and most of them even gave me seventy-five cents to send the wire. Then I went into the nearest town with a telegraph office and sent off their messages to Aspinall in Washington, D.C.

As the days passed, dozens of telegrams poured into Aspinall's office. He could almost plot the path of my travel by the source of these wires. He was hearing from real live constituents in their own words—people in western Colorado who wanted the Wilderness Act passed. He complained bitterly to the press about outside agitators being sent into his district, but before long a compromise was struck. He would get the provisions he sought, a study of public land law, and Congress would have to act affirmatively to put areas into the wilderness system. He then let the bill out of his committee, and it became law the following year. I am sure that the unexpected voices from his district played no small part in this success.

But I almost paid a very high price too. A bartender outside of Durango told me to contact the owner of the Turner Industrial Bank. The bank owner introduced me to his friends, who said they were willing to help. Then he told me of another contact he thought was excellent, near the Vallecitos Reservoir to the east, a venerable figure with a long white beard who took me around to a number of very helpful packers. As we were finishing, he thought of yet another fellow—a rancher who he thought did some packing. We greeted him in the lobby of the dance hall and bar he owned. As I made my pitch, he growled, "There was a shooting here last week, and there's just about to be another." My guide grabbed me by the arm, urging, "Let's get out of here!" I don't know whether my life was really in danger, but this was just about the only sour note in a very successful organizing trip.

During the following spring, I was deeply involved in a round of field hearings on the wilderness bill, held by Aspinall's committee. I spoke at, and helped organize witnesses to speak at, hearings in Denver; Olympia,

Washington; and elsewhere. A huge outpouring of support was evident, even though our opponents tried hard to turn out witnesses for their side. Our witnesses told stories, quoted poetry and history, and gave heartfelt testimonials about the importance of wilderness in their lives. To allow everyone to be heard, the hearings dragged on into the late evening hours.

Toward the end of this string of hearings in 1964, I got better acquainted with the longtime executive director of the Wilderness Society, Howard Zahniser, who went to every one of these hearings around the West. Zahnie, as he was called, had been the guiding force behind the long campaign for the Wilderness Act. He conceived of it, drafted it, found sponsors, lined up supporting organizations, and nursed the legislation through most of its critical stages. He was a beloved figure who was literally working himself to death.

I remember having a drink with him at his hotel following the last hearing in 1964. He said his doctor told him to have a drink or two at such times to relax, and he was in a genial mood. He knew that we were close to the end and were within reach of success. I reveled in his stories of how we had gotten that far. But I never saw him again. Within a few weeks, he was dead of a heart attack. He never lived to savor the moment when President Lyndon B. Johnson signed the bill on September 4, 1964. But I knew that he was confident that that moment would soon come.

In the aftermath of the intense work on behalf of the Wilderness Act, I decided to write a law review article on the subject. I had accumulated extensive files and had seen how people valued wilderness in so many different ways. Two years later this article, "The Wilderness Act of 1964: Its Background and Meaning," was published in the *Oregon Law Review*.[11] In it I combined legal analysis with a historical and intellectual account of the idea.

When I began my work in the Northwest, we faced a strategic dilemma. Our forces were pressing to have three new units added to the national park system in that region. Not only did we back a new national seashore along the Oregon Dunes, we also wanted to convert into a national park a portion of the central Oregon Cascades as well as the area in the Washington Cascades from Glacier Peak north. Not all of my clientele favored all of these parks, but the Sierra Club did. Moreover, I had also been retained by new groups organized to advance the cause of the Oregon Cascades park (the Oregon Cascades Conservation Council) and the park in the North Cascades (the NCCC).

We simply did not have the resources, however, to mount credible campaigns on behalf of all of these proposals simultaneously. We had to assign priorities to our work. The NCCC in Washington state, under Pat Goldsworthy, was much more solidly established than the similar group in Oregon. And the Sierra Club viewed the North Cascades park as its priority. Only a few of my clients were deeply devoted to the Oregon Dunes proposal, and thus it seemed clear that the North Cascades was to get priority over the Oregon Cascades.

But Dave Brower had trouble reconciling himself to this choice. He certainly was enthusiastic about the North Cascades, but he also cared about the Oregon Cascades and could not forget the work of a young man by the name of David Simons who came from my home area in Oregon. Oddly enough, I never knew him. Simons had written beguiling pleas for both of these new national park candidates in the Cascades; in the late 1950s Brower had published his articles on each area in the Club's monthly magazine, the *Sierra Club Bulletin*. About the time I returned from the army, Simons entered the army and before long died from a rare form of hepatitis.

I finally persuaded Brower that the needs of the Oregon Cascades would not be forgotten. For the areas that Simons proposed be put in the park, we would try to achieve protection through other means, such as designation as wilderness areas. This would have to be tackled on a piecemeal basis, but it would not entail a change in the administering agency—which was preferable, since it was never easy to get Congress to agree to take public land from the Forest Service and to transfer it to the National Park Service.

To some extent, we succeeded over the years in acting on this plan. In the end, we also found a way to get the attention that we wanted for the Oregon Dunes without transferring jurisdiction. But with the North Cascades, there was no question that our aim was to take land away from the Forest Service and give it to the Park Service instead.

North Cascades

The area between the Canadian border on the north and Glacier Peak on the south was spectacular country, with glaciers, needle peaks, finger lakes, and deep, forested valleys. While it did have two classic snow-clad volcanoes—Mount Baker and Glacier Peak—most of the mountains were alpine, with serrated crests and twisting terrain. At that time, there were no highways across the area (the North Cross-state Highway was built later), and much of the region was wilderness and little known. Of all the Cascade volcanoes, Glacier Peak was the least accessible. Climbing it entailed a long but beautiful hike through the thick forests of the Suiattle Valley.

Disillusionment with the Forest Service over its management of this area was slow in coming, but by the late 1950s key leaders in our wilderness movement in the Seattle area were demanding change. In the 1930s, Forest Service administrators themselves had recognized the park quality of the area. But by the 1950s, their successors were planning logging roads instead. The 1960 reclassification of the Glacier Peak Limited Area as a wilderness area was the turning point. Wilderness was assigned to the high peaks and radiating ridgelines, but many of the forested valleys on the west, such as the Suiattle, were excluded. Our folks decried this pattern of "wilderness on the rocks."

Not everyone in the inner councils of the NCCC was eager to embrace the Park Service as the alternative for preserving the land, but hope of influencing the Forest Service was dying. Pleas and petitions were routinely ignored. We remembered Brower's reminder that while the Park Service would give us problems, at least it wasn't in the business of promoting logging.

There were a few exceptions. When the Bureau of Outdoor Recreation was established in 1963, a former superintendent of Olympic National Park, Fred Overly, became its regional director in Seattle. Early in his tenure, I paid a courtesy call to get acquainted. When he learned who I represented, he started berating me. "Your people got me fired as superintendent of Olympic National Park," he fumed. Overly was one of the few foresters to enter the Park Service, and apparently he didn't like to see sound timber rot. In the 1950s, he had arranged for commercial loggers to take not only downed timber out of the park but some standing timber too—all as part of a so-called salvage sale. This led to a huge outcry over his betraying park principles.

Most of those who resisted the Park Service were concerned that it would build too many roads. Those problems had been surmounted in Olympic National Park and at Kings Canyon National Park in California, however. The pace of Forest Service road building and logging finally brought the doubters, such as NCCC board member William Halliday, around.

For the North Cascades, the question was: What kind of national park did we want? I generally advised my clients to come up with specific proposals; legislators could not really assess what you had in mind until you got specific. I was taught in my government courses in college that to be an effective lobbyist you needed to know exactly what you wanted, who could give it to you, and how they were influenced and made decisions. This was the thinking behind the technique that I had developed for studying wilderness reclassifications.

After I persuaded leaders in the NCCC and the Mountaineers that this was so, they then turned to me to figure out how to develop such a proposal. While I did sample this area and drove the surrounding roads, the region was too vast for me to know enough to draw the boundaries. Instead, I picked the brains of the climbers, backpackers, and mountain photographers who had gotten to know various parts of the area quite well over the years. People such as John Warth of Seattle and Chuck Hessey of Yakima were invaluable in giving me this kind of information.

I asked each person where the most valuable areas were that should be saved in a park and got people to sketch out their ideas on maps for the various sectors. I pressed them too to give me the reasoning behind their ideas. Gradually I pieced together all of the information, and boundaries emerged from their collective judgments.

Then I searched out every piece of information I could find about competing values. I went to state agencies to learn about mining and minerals and water resources; I got detailed maps from the Forest Service showing types of forests, including prime timber stands; and I got transportation maps showing projected road extensions. I wanted to know what arguments would be made against including a given area in the park and how well founded they were. After I evaluated these competing values, I put together what I felt was a defensible proposal for a new national park of 1.3 million acres. It also involved a complementary National Recreation Area around Lake Chelan on the east, which was no longer entirely natural, since its lake level had been raised by a small dam and a small community was located at its head.

I called this a "Prospectus for a North Cascades National Park." My report ran to 130 pages and was endorsed by my client organizations.[12] Published in 1963, it was distributed to federal agencies, the media, and political leaders. Senator Henry Jackson of Washington state responded with interest and induced the administration of President John Kennedy to set up a process to study the idea. The study group, composed of a team of officials from federal natural resource agencies, held administrative hearings, and I helped turn out our supporters to attend them.

Many in the Kennedy administration tended to see conservation issues in the West through the prism of the past. Except for Interior Secretary Stewart Udall, they tended to view them in terms of developing natural resources instead of protecting nature. They wanted to cultivate our emerging popular forces, but did not know how to talk to us and didn't quite understand why so many controversies were emerging. This was particularly true of the leaders of the Agriculture Department under Orville Freeman.

Eventually this team—by the narrowest of margins—did recommend establishment of a new national park in the North Cascades region, but a much smaller one that embraced only the northern portions of the area. I was tempted to denounce it as shortsighted and a disappointment, but Dave Brower cautioned me not to. He wanted to nurture the park idea, feeling that we could build on it later and encourage its expansion. The important thing was to gain credence for the idea of a national park there. "Let's get on a train that is going somewhere; once we are under way, we can figure out how to get it to go farther," he quoted Richard Neuberger as having said. This was sound advice, and I learned from it.

The most immediate obstacles to progress in establishing this new national park were the two congressmen who represented the areas involved. Both were Republicans who adamantly opposed the idea. So I took a leave of absence in the fall of 1962 to work in the campaigns of their opponents—Lloyd Meeds on the west side of the Cascades and Tom Foley on the east side—both of whom were open to the park idea. I worked particularly hard on behalf of Meeds and remember spending one day in the fall with Senator Jackson, both of us working the streets of Everett on Meeds's behalf. To my delight, both Meeds and Foley won. While Foley was more reserved than Meeds about the park idea, he was a former aide to Jackson and was apt to follow his lead.

The North Cascades campaign continued for a number of years after I left the Northwest, and my successors, especially Brock Evans, worked energetically for the park that we backed. Finally, in 1968, a North Cascades National Park was established, along with flanking National Recreation Areas (NRAs)—a Ross Lake NRA on the north and a Lake Chelan NRA on the east. All told, 684,200 acres were transferred to the National Park Service.

This was short of the 1.3 million acres that we wanted. In the ensuing years, however, battling by our folks continued to expand the boundaries of the Glacier Peak Wilderness and brought protection to other nearby areas. Eventually, Evans told me, every single acre that was included in my 1963 prospectus got statutory protection under one designation or another.

In advancing such an ambitious plan for the North Cascades in 1963, I was no longer merely trying to salvage damaged goods, as had been the case with so many of the primitive areas. I was able to put forth what seemed an ideal plan and to mobilize our forces around it. It took the efforts of many people over many years, but it was finally realized. This experience convinced me that there was a time and place for visionary proposals, but they had to be well founded. In putting forth this plan, I was also privately delighted that for once I had been the visionary while Dave Brower had been the cautious one (though he also had been right; we did build on the original disappointing plan).

I had accomplished things, but I was also wrongly blamed for things I did not do. In his 1977 book on Hells Canyon, William Ashworth claims that I discouraged efforts early on to save Hells Canyon, an immense canyon on the Oregon-Idaho border that had outstanding natural values and needed some protective designation. At one point it had been threatened with high dams.[13]

Ashworth refers in his book to the chilly reception that I gave to one Floyd Harvey from the area, who was looking for help. Allegedly I told him in my Seattle office in 1965 that the cause was lost and that he was wasting his time. But I never had an office in Seattle, and by that time I was no longer in the Northwest. Ashworth is undoubtedly talking about my successor, Rodger Pegues, who had taken over then and was in Seattle.

I served as the first field organizer for the Sierra Club (and the Federation of Western Outdoor Clubs) until the end of 1964—for three and a half years. This was the most satisfying job I ever had with the Sierra Club. I explored marvelous country, worked with warm and supportive people, and was given lots of latitude to do my job. And I felt that I was charting new paths and was making a contribution to conservation.[14]

Midway through this period—near the end of 1962—I was offered a job with the Oregon legislature. It paid better, and I was tempted. When I told Dave Brower about it, he countered by giving me a raise and taking me on as a regular salaried employee. So I decided to keep going, and I never looked back. When I took this job, I thought that I might do it for a while and have some fun, then look for a "real" job. But it turned out to be my life's work.

At the end of 1964, I was offered a job in San Francisco as assistant to the president of the Sierra Club. The pay was much better, long-term career prospects seemed brighter, and I would take part in the Club's new campaign for a Redwood National Park. So I accepted the offer.

As I wound up my service in the Northwest, my friends thought I would be miscast in San Francisco. A lawyer on the conservation committee of the Mountaineers, Jesse Epstein, for example, thought I was a "field man" through and through; he felt I would never adapt to office work. They expected me to be miserable.

My client clubs were sorry to see me go. When I visited them in Yakima, I was greeted with a huge "goodbye" banner on the airport terminal. In an editorial, *Salem Oregon Statesman* editor and former governor Charles Sprague observed that "[McCloskey] has battled so long and hard for wilderness protection in the Northwest states that he will leave a chunk of his heart here," while Bob Frazier of the *Eugene Register-Guard* spoke of the debt that "our grandchildren will owe . . . to people like Mike McCloskey who have put aside the personal comforts of today in favor of the long-range good of the continent and its people."

I basked in these good wishes and thanks, but I really didn't feel that I had given up anything. I had been given an opportunity—the chance to be part of history.

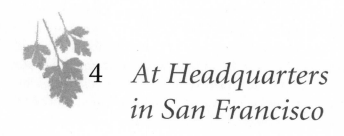

4   At Headquarters in San Francisco

In January 1965, I packed my few belongings in my Volkswagen and drove to San Francisco to assume my new position as assistant to the president of the Sierra Club. A lamp was jammed in the backseat on top of clothes, papers, and my portable typewriter. After a few days, I rented an apartment in North Beach, at the corner of Stockton and Bay, from which I could easily walk to work.

My new office was located in the Sierra Club's headquarters, on the tenth floor of the Mills Tower building at 220 Bush Street in the financial district. The offices of the Club had been in the Mills Building since 1903 and had expanded into the adjoining Mills Tower building after it was built in the 1920s. When the Club's offices were remodeled after World War II, cracks from the 1906 earthquake were found in the thick brick walls. Indeed, Richard Leonard, a longtime Club leader with law offices in the building, was fond of explaining that the Mills Building had developed a tilt out over Bush Street as a result of the 1906 quake (spacers in bolts holding it together permitted it to shift a bit).

The Sierra Club in 1965 had about 45,000 members, most of them on the two coasts. I was joining a staff of thirty-five, almost all of them in San Francisco. Most were then involved in processing membership applications, accounting, serving the outings program, or putting out publications. Other than the executive director, hardly any of them did conservation work on a full-time basis.

I was put in an office far from the center of things. I soon discovered why. My role was to assist the Sierra Club's volunteer president in taking on a growing load of conservation work. The club's executive director, Dave Brower, had become infatuated with producing elaborate pictorial books—what some derisively called coffee-table books, which he called exhibit-format books. He was spending more and more of his time in the East on these projects, rather than doing conservation work. Yet the tempo of conservation challenges was rising as the 1960s progressed, demanding a response from the Club. Since Brower was not there often enough to deal with most of them, by default they were falling into the lap of Club presidents.

My job was to help the president of the national Club, Will Siri, cope with this onslaught. While Siri, by training a physicist and by avocation a mountaineer, was a forceful and decisive person, he wanted me to share his load and was anxious to draw upon my expertise. I took over the burden of wide-ranging correspondence, initiating inquiries, urging action, and passing along information to Club leaders. At that time, government officials actually responded to my letters.

Though assigned to serve the president of the Club, technically I worked for Brower, who had already become a national figure. He was hired as the Club's first executive director in 1952 and had been in this position for more than a dozen years. Before that, he had served on the board of directors and as the volunteer editor of the Club magazine. Prior to that, he had been an editor at the University of California Press and had once worked in public relations for The Yosemite Park and Curry Company.

Brower was not happy that presidents of the Club were assuming functions that he felt were rightfully his. At this time he was not getting along well with some members of his board, however—those he viewed as the "old guard." He feared that Club presidents were out to seize power from him and set themselves up as rivals, and he was afraid that I would simply make them more formidable rivals. I quickly ascertained that there were indeed those who hoped to use me as a pawn against the executive director. I didn't want to get built up to be a counterweight to Brower or be forced into an antagonistic role.

I made a point of sharing information with Brower and consulting with him when he was in town. Brower, in turn, was receptive and cultivated me. Before long, I concluded that I could get along with the various parties. I suggested to Siri that what the Club really needed was a conservation director—someone who could give the program direction with Brower away so much and coordinate the growing body of conservation business coming to the Club. The conservation director, I suggested, would work under the executive director but with the aim of helping all of the people who would act on the Club's behalf in this field. That would include club presidents, who changed regularly; the executive director; and other leaders of the Club who were heading up projects. In this way, the work would get done, but without setting up rivalries.

Both Brower and Siri liked the approach, and so did the board of directors, which quickly approved it. Soon thereafter, they offered me the very job I had proposed, and I took it happily. As conservation director, I felt I could grow with the organization.

That was in the fall of 1965. The past twelve months had been momentous ones for me in other respects too. In September of the prior year, when I was in Washington, D.C., as the Wilderness Act was being signed, my father had died of an asthma attack. After playing a game of golf that was too strenuous for his hard-pressed lungs, he drove himself to the hospital to breathe his last breath. Then in December of that year, just weeks before I moved to San Francisco, my brother Jim was killed tragically in a traffic accident while driving home for Christmas from Seattle, where he was working on his doctorate in genetics. His car skidded on black ice into traffic in the opposing lane.

But that year was filled with great joy as well. During the years when I was active in Democratic Party politics in Oregon, I had met Maxine Johnson, a very attractive woman from Portland who worked with Senator Richard Neuberger's office and then with his widow and successor, Maurine. I first noticed her at a state party convention, when she served as secretary at the head table for a committee before which I spoke. At a later reception, we met and felt an affinity. I subsequently learned that she was married and had four children, however.

A few months later, when I visited the Portland office of Maurine Neuberger, Vera Springer, who ran that office, mentioned that Maxine was now widowed. After Vera contrived to get us together, we dated a bit in 1964. At the time, Maxine represented Senator Maurine Neuberger as her alternate at the Democratic National Convention, serving on the platform committee. I saw her off on the train. In August, together with her children, we visited the Wallowa Mountains in northeastern Oregon, listening to the Republican convention on the car radio at night to see what they were up to. I took the whole family on a horseback ride into the Eagle Cap Wilderness.

Maxine and I shared many interests and had similar viewpoints. We enjoyed each other's company and felt a bond growing between us. I invited her to visit me in San Francisco in the spring of 1965. A few months later, on June 17, 1965, we were married in Eugene. I was so innocent about wedding ceremonies that I did not even know I was supposed to "kiss the bride." But I made up for that later.

With my marriage, I instantly became the stepfather of four children—three girls and one boy (Claire, Laura, James, and Rosemary)—ranging then in ages from fifteen to eight. I suddenly had a full-fledged family. Almost at once I was learning about the rites of passage for teenagers. But I liked the children, and they seemed to accept me.

I suggested to Maxine that we take a boat trip through the Grand Canyon for our honeymoon. The Club was then engaged in a great effort to keep dams out of the canyon, and I wanted to see the area first-hand. One of the Club's board members and the travel editor of *Sunset* magazine, Martin Litton, was then running trips through the canyon on McKenzie River dories, wide rowboats with high prows on both ends.

Maxine and I joined Martin's boating party at Lees Ferry, near Page, Arizona. We pushed off to enjoy a fabulous experience and laughed as Martin regaled us with stories about the capricious "river gods," whose plans for unsuspecting humans were impossible to foresee.

Thereupon the gods apparently decided to teach us not to be too self-satisfied. At the first major rapid—House Rock Rapids—our boat capsized, and we were cast into the foaming water. In the upset, I hit my head and came up underneath the overturned boat. Stunned, it took me a moment to realize where I was as I looked bleary-eyed into the half light under the boat. Then I dove under the boat to surface along its side, only to see my new bride disappear into a cauldron of foaming water. I had a horrible feeling—what had I done?

Fortunately, our life preservers provided buoyancy, and the other boats in our party were soon able to pick up Maxine as well as the rest of us. Besides our composure, the only thing lost was my glasses. Being nearsighted, I squinted my way through the rest of the trip, concentrating on things that were close at hand, like my wife, the crew, and the river spray. We got into the relaxing rhythms of life on the river. We slept in caverns and under ledges, and shook scorpions out of our boots each morning. To document the scenery that was merely a blur to me, I took lots of photographs. Later, when I examined the slides from the trip, I saw how magnificent it had all been. My wife, who saw more than I did, reveled in the experience.

As it turned out, Maxine had spent some time in the Bay Area in the late 1940s and knew some of the key figures in the Sierra Club before I did. She had been to the house of Stewart Dole, a lawyer from the Dole pineapple family who chaired the Club's bylaw committee, and was a friend of Jim Harkins, a Club outings leader. She had also met Richard Leonard, a former Club president and climber, and his wife, Doris.

After our honeymoon, Maxine spent the rest of the summer hunting for a house for us, while her mother tended the children in Portland. She finally found a Monterey colonial that we liked in Piedmont, in the East Bay hills. It was to be our home for the next twenty-one years. It had a bit of a view of the bay and was graced with the cooling effects of the summer fog without being enveloped by the mists.

Maxine helped me in my work in many ways. When I married her, she was about to begin a doctoral program in history at the University of Oregon, having already earned a master's degree from Reed College. Our marriage sidetracked those plans, but she did go on to teach American history and government at various community colleges in the Bay Area. She was an ideal person with whom to talk over my work. She understood what I was facing. Not only was she a source of emotional support, she was the source of many of my ideas.

Early on she assumed the role of executive secretary for two successive Club-sponsored wilderness conferences, in 1967 and 1969. Afterward, she edited the conference proceedings that the Club published, and a few years later she became the editor of the newsletter for the Federation of Western Outdoor Clubs.

Following the wilderness conferences, Maxine developed her own distinct interests. She became the president of Project Jonah, which was among the first groups trying to save whales, and in 1978 she organized the Whale Center, located in Oakland, which she ran for a decade. Not only did the center have a storefront office, a staff of eight, and a membership of 3,000, but it also ran whale-watching trips and lobbied the U.S. government on whale-protection policy. Maxine also served on the U.S. delegation to the annual meetings of the International Whaling Commission eight times, under both Democratic and Republican

presidents. She played an important role in shifting the popular emphasis from catching whales to watching them.

Maxine subsequently became the chair of a California state advisory
committee on nongame wildlife. Here she laid the groundwork for the
idea of "watchable wildlife," which extended the thinking behind whale
watching to other species on land. Public value would be derived from
enjoying the sight of wildlife in its habitat rather than killing it. That
work led eventually to service for nine years on the board of directors of
Defenders of Wildlife.

Her interests in whales continued and grew into a concern for their
extended habitat. She developed the idea of wilderness reserves on the
high seas, presenting her ideas to the International Union for the
Conservation of Nature (IUCN) and later at a World Wilderness
Congress. That led to appointment to the parks commission of the
IUCN, where she headed up a project promoting the idea of establishing marine protected areas on the high seas.

San Francisco Days

When Maxine and I arrived in San Francisco in the mid-1960s, the
habits and style of a more traditional society were still in place, but the
rebellious youth of the period were about to make their mark. Men still
wore suits and ties to work in offices downtown, with black shoes (no
"brown in town"). Some women still wore hats and gloves. The financial district, not surprisingly, was a bastion of such conservatism. The
West Coast stock exchange was at the back of our building, and numerous banks that no longer exist were nearby: the Crocker-Anglo Bank,
the Bank of California, and the Hibernia Bank. The Bank of America
(which of course lives on) still had descendants of the founder on its
board, from the time when it was called the Bank of Italy. Some fine old
establishments, such as the City of Paris department store, Sloane's fur-
niture store, Newbegin's bookstore, Blums' confectioner, and the Old
Poodle Dog restaurant, were still fashionable.

The *San Francisco Chronicle* was the newspaper everyone read. It
emphasized the entertaining aspects of living in the city, with a clutch of
eccentric columnists. The star was Herb Caen, who practiced a humor-
ous version of "three-dot journalism" and from time to time mentioned
the Sierra Club. At lunch with him one day, I discovered he couldn't help
being funny even in casual conversation; I felt like taking notes.

Dave Brower used to take the senior staff to lunch at In the Alley, a quaint cafe a block from the office on Belden Place. Service was mainly on an outdoor patio hidden from general view under umbrellas. Sierra Club posters covered the walls. We ate hangtown fries, shrimp Louis, and frittatas along with the special sourdough bread made for San Francisco restaurants. Brower always had martinis with his lunch, but I passed on that pleasure.

I also got into the habit of having weekly lunches with Ed Wayburn, who was president of the Club during much of the 1960s, and that continued for about twenty years. Brower refused such invitations, viewing them as "summons" to pay court to club officers, but I always found them rewarding. When I would arrive, Dr. Wayburn was usually on the phone to some government official about a conservation problem. We often ate on the terrace of his building's rooftop restaurant, which at 490 Post Street afforded a glorious view of Nob Hill. Over lunch, I learned what he had been told and shared what I knew. I also got lots of good exercise, because Dr. Wayburn didn't believe in using elevators. He bounded up the stairs two steps at a time, with me struggling to keep up.

When Club officers met to discuss our business over dinner, they tended to go to old-line fish and chop houses where there was room for a party of six to eight. The closest was Sam's Grill on Bush Street, where we ate in enclosed booths. We also had dinner meetings in paneled private rooms upstairs at Jack's on Sacramento Street. I particularly remember one long evening at Jack's when Will Siri was intensely lobbying a state official who smoked an endless succession of cigars. I was about to choke to death by the end. Occasionally we would be invited by business leaders, such as utility executives, to meet in august private clubs such as the Bohemian Club on Taylor Street and the Pacific Union Club, a somber brownstone at the top of Nob Hill.

Throughout the sixties, the Club's board of directors usually met in the banquet rooms of major hotels in downtown San Francisco. The favorite was the ornate Empire Room of the Sir Francis Drake Hotel near Union Square. The Club's annual banquet in early May was usually held in the larger rooms in grand hotels such as the Palace, the St. Francis, or the Claremont in Berkeley.

When I first started to attend board meetings in San Francisco in the early sixties, Brower was still on cordial terms with board members. I will never forget being taken by him one Saturday night to the home of Ansel Adams, who then lived in a pretty Queen Anne–style home in

San Francisco. (He later moved to Carmel.) With board members gathered round, Brower and Adams sat together at his piano playing a duet in the friendliest fashion. Adams had once studied to be a concert pianist, and Brower played light music with an accomplished hand. This harmony wasn't to last, alas, and not for much longer did I see Brower socializing with board members.

Ed Wayburn and his wife, Peggy, did entertain a great deal, however, at their spacious home in the Seacliff neighborhood near the ocean. They hosted a huge party every year at Christmastime and frequently invited selected friends attending board meetings to their home afterward. I could see that these opportunities to socialize deepened bonds between Club leaders. As the Club grew, those playing formal roles no longer could draw upon earlier bonds that they had developed on outings. We needed to provide new opportunities for them to get to know one another on a friendly basis. In due course, Maxine and I would hold such parties too.

Soon after we arrived in San Francisco, the age of rock and roll and the counterculture arrived too. The genteel styles of the past were being displaced by the tastes and demands of a huge new boomer generation. Having been born before World War II, I was not a member of this generation and did not define myself in terms of rebellion against established norms. But a new mood was taking hold: the Summer of Love was under way in Haight-Ashbury, posters for rock concerts were everywhere, the battle in Berkeley over People's Park had begun, and *Ramparts* magazine was cutting a wide swath with its exposés. At some point, it seemed, any speaker worth his or her salt made a harangue on the steps of Sproul Hall at the University of California at Berkeley, and I was no exception.

I couldn't help wondering how all of this change would affect the Sierra Club. And indeed, in just a few years these currents would change the Club into a far different organization.

In 1967, Maxine decided that she wanted a different kind of poster for the wilderness conference she was organizing, one that would connect more with youth. Through a series of referrals, we were directed to Stanley Mouse, a leading artist for the psychedelic posters of the time. Thus we found ourselves at an abandoned wooden fire station in the Fillmore district. After making our way through the first-floor gloom and litter and up the steps to his loft, we found the unassuming artist with a huge mop of hair ready to hear our proposal. Though rock concert posters were his forte, he accepted our job for a reasonable fee.

His creation featured a reproduction of the famous image depicting a sad Indian on horseback, raising his hands toward heaven ("Appeal to the Great Spirit"), surrounded by a wreath of foliage. Rendered in striking green and gold, it was a great success and gave the conference a new cachet. It was later featured in *Life* magazine and even appeared in the movie *Bullitt*. Whenever copies of the poster were tacked on Berkeley campus bulletin boards, they were torn down by collectors almost immediately (they are now worth thousands of dollars). Only many years later did we learn that the decorative foliage on the poster was composed of marijuana leaves; we were too square to know what they looked like.

Becoming Conservation Director

When I began my work as conservation director in 1966, my office was moved to adjoin that of the executive director. There was a private back door into his office. Clearly, I had moved from "outer darkness" into the inner sanctum. I would pop into Brower's office whenever I could to brief him on what was going on and to learn about information that had come to him directly. And I had a secretary for the first time.

From time to time, Brower would send me on a special mission. Once he sent me to testify before the San Francisco Board of Supervisors in their ornately paneled chambers on a purely local matter. I was also sent out to solicit donations from major givers. I remember being turned down by Stephen Bechtel of Bechtel Engineering, who had supported book projects in the past, because he resented Brower's criticism of nuclear power plants. I had been told that Bill Hewlett, who was making money in computers and was a onetime Club climber, had also turned on Brower for similar reasons. It seemed that Brower was causing some donors to become alienated from the Club. But I tried hard to be responsive and to work well with him. For the most part, he let me define the job, and our relationship was one of mutual respect and restraint.

My job involved keeping in touch with as many of our leaders as possible and staying abreast of conservation issues. I counseled Club leaders about tactics and tried to promote a coordinated approach. I worked with Will Siri, Ray Sherwin, and Ed Wayburn on the issues that they were pursuing: Mineral King (blocking a ski resort planned by Walt Disney), Minaret Summit (keeping the Sierra free of a new highway across it), and establishment of a Redwood National Park. Brower himself was heading up the campaign to keep dams out of the Grand

Canyon, and I coordinated volunteers who were providing critiques of the economics of the dams proposed in the canyon. Interestingly, many of them were associated with the RAND Corporation, a Defense Department think tank near Los Angeles.[1]

I also tried to stay in touch with the Club's growing cadre of field staff. Brower had hired some of them on his own, without seeking permission from the board. These included Jeff Ingram in the Southwest and Gary Soucie in the East. I interviewed and chose my own successors as Northwest field representative: first Rod Pegues, and then Brock Evans in 1967. Both were attorneys.

And I was in close touch with our lobbyist in the nation's capital. Bill Zimmerman, who had filled this post since 1962, died in 1967. I persuaded Brower to hire Lloyd Tupling to replace him; Tupling had been the administrative assistant for Senator Richard Neuberger and later for Senator Maurine Neuberger. Before long we also hired someone to lobby the state legislature in Sacramento, John Zierold. In theory, all of these field staff reported to me, and decisions on how to position the Club on issues were supposed to be cleared through me. Tupling, Evans, and Zierold were responsive to my direction, but Ingram and Soucie acted as though they reported directly to Brower, though Soucie did send me copies of his reports to Brower.

I was also in charge of organizing the conservation agenda for meetings of the board of directors. I collected information on all proposals for new policy; advised the Club president on whether they were ripe for action; and helped put the proposals in the form desired by the board, which included an analysis of the pros and cons. Before long, I too was proposing new policy to keep the Club abreast of trends.

In 1966 I persuaded the board of directors to adopt a policy on urban environmental amenities, which I thought should include not only aesthetics but matters of planning and clean air as well. I felt the Club should recognize these as within its purview, since most of us lived in urban areas. Some scholars now think this was one of the first signs that a newer, broader movement was about to emerge: the environmental movement.

Over time, I also developed a network of contacts among Club activists who would call and write me to tell of their concerns and hopes. George Marshall (brother of Bob Marshall and Club president in 1967) wrote me long letters, as did board member Fred Eissler from Santa Barbara. My communicants also included leaders of the regional conservation committees that began to blossom around the country. When in 1966 I had recommended to Siri that a conservation department be established, I had also recommended setting up regional boards (or conservation committees) to coordinate volunteer conservation work as the Club developed chapters around the country. This suggestion had been adopted too. These regional conservation committees were patterned on an existing one that the Club had in southern California. Their formation transferred some of the burden of coordination into the hands of experienced activists around the country.

Many activists pressed me for help on their favorite issues. At first I was tempted to respond, as I had as a field organizer in the Northwest, but I soon realized that with my other responsibilities I could not play that role anymore. I could not immerse myself in every issue in California or elsewhere. While I could provide advice, I could not play a hands-on role. As the Club hired more staff in the field, either they had to assume that first-line role, or volunteer leaders would have to.

These cries for help also compelled the Club to set clear priorities. In 1965, after passage of the Wilderness Act, the board of directors had decided to assign priority to three campaigns: establishment of a Redwood National Park, establishment of a North Cascades National Park, and keeping the Grand Canyon free of dams. Activists in the Santa Barbara community, such as Nevis Fortney, wanted the Club to give priority to establishment of a new national park around islands in the Santa Barbara channel, but there was no broad constituency for this. The one board member from that area, Fred Eissler, was more interested in establishing a marine sanctuary in the Santa Barbara channel and blocking oil drilling and nuclear plants along the coast. I helped him frame legislation that was introduced in 1966 by Senator Clair Engle, a Democrat from California, and later was included as Title III of the Ocean Dumping Act of 1972. It provided the basis for America's growing system of marine sanctuaries.

I learned some things the hard way. On my frequent trips to Washington, D.C., for instance, I soon learned to be careful of who might overhear my conversations. One night in the lounge of the Mayflower Hotel, I was giving information to an agent of Drew Pearson and Jack Anderson for use in their popular newspaper column. I rambled on about the costs and side effects of the proposed Central Arizona Project, which diverted water from the Colorado River to Arizona cities such as Tucson and would then depend on water power generated by dams proposed for the Grand Canyon. After my eyes had adjusted to the dim light, I realized to my consternation that seated next to us in the lounge was one of Arizona's senators, who certainly took a contrary point of view. Fortunately, he hadn't seemed to take any notice of us. Just the same, we found an excuse to move.

Ironically, not long after that, I agreed to share a taxi one blustery day with a group of men who turned out to be lobbyists for the Central Arizona Project. They took no note of me, but I listened intently as they discussed all of their lobbying plans, which I then quickly passed on to our own lobbyists.

In the late 1960s, the Sierra Club redefined its priorities to include rounding out the national park system and the wilderness system. At Dr. Wayburn's behest, protecting lands of national interest in Alaska was also made a priority. He had just returned from his first trip there brimming with enthusiasm (which George Marshall viewed with bemusement, since his brother Bob had written of the area's importance in the 1930s, after his extended wilderness explorations).

In an indirect way, I also contributed to the effort that led to expanded protection for wilderness on the Kern Plateau in the southern Sierra. Local Sierra Club leaders were so discouraged with the Forest Service's indifference to wilderness values in the area that they were ready to embrace the idea of National Park Service management instead. They asked me to draft legislation to add the area to Sequoia National Park, just as the Kings Canyon area had once been added to that park.

The bill I drafted was introduced in Congress by Representative Phillip Burton from San Francisco. While the bill was never enacted, fear of losing the area may have made the Forest Service more willing to entertain wilderness designation. Ultimately, much of this area was incorporated into the Golden Trout Wilderness, an area of 306,000 acres, in 1978. The rest was ultimately made part of the Giant Sequoia National Monument at the end of the Clinton administration. In both cases, board members Joe Fontaine (who ultimately became Club president) and Martin Litton provided much of the leadership.

Through the second half of the 1960s, the Sierra Club also began to be drawn into using the courts as a forum for pursuing its concerns. By the end of 1967, the Club, through its local chapters, was a plaintiff in cases affecting Storm King Mountain in New York, Hells Canyon in Oregon and Idaho, the Grand Canyon in Arizona, and San Francisco

Bay in California. In the following year, the Club became involved in cases dealing with logging in southeast Alaska and the Mineral King issue. The latter entailed efforts to add the Mineral King enclave, at the headwaters of the East Fork of the Kaweah River, to Sequoia National Park. Because that effort never received any priority from the Club (although it eventually succeeded), I had us turn to litigation instead to challenge development proposed there.

At the end of 1967, I proposed that the Club set up a Sierra Club Legal Defense Fund to coordinate this growing body of litigation. It took time (and frustration with the increasing tempo of the work) for this idea to be digested, but finally in 1971 the Fund was established as a separate operating entity. Within a few years it became the leading litigating group in the environmental field. Litigation gave us another weapon that put agencies on the defensive as well as putting us in the news. It often gave us a way of buying time as projects were blocked.

I also helped handle press relations and plan media initiatives. In the winter of 1965, Brower and Wayburn felt that the Club needed to dramatize our case to the country in both the redwood and the Grand Canyon campaigns. We decided to run a series of full-page advertisements in selected newspapers, principally the *New York Times* and the *San Francisco Chronicle*, the former to reach a national audience and the latter to reach our core local audience. (Another factor was that people in those two markets responded well to coupons asking for contributions to defray the ads' costs.)

Brower was not sure whether he needed to hire an agency to produce the ads. After all, he had been a public relations man himself, was a good writer, and had a strong sense of design. For our first ad, on the Redwood National Park, he decided to retain an agency to write and design one ad, while he would write and design another—both with the same message. They would be put out in a "split run": half of the subscribers would get one version, while the rest would get the other. By counting the coupons returned, Brower would assess which was more successful.

By a modest margin, the ad agency's version did better. So we hired Freeman, Mander and Gossage to produce the rest of the series. They had previously distinguished themselves by designing a clever series of ads for Irish Distillers. All through the following spring Brower and I, and occasionally Wayburn, would troop over to the agency's stylish offices in Jackson Square to plan these ads. The Club ran them quite regularly over the next two years, and they aroused so much political attention that the IRS revoked the Club's tax deductibility after six months (a development I discuss further in chapter 10). Thus we succeeded in getting attention that we didn't exactly seek!

I usually outlined the basic material, while Brower would decide who would be the target (for example, the president, the secretary of the Interior, or the chairman of the House Interior Committee). Mander would write the copy, while Freeman's staff handled design work. Gossage, Brower, Mander, and I would brainstorm to come up with the catchiest headline. After a while, we were writing ideas all over the walls of their office. Brower came up with a Sistine Chapel headline, while I helped concoct the headline "Legislation by Chainsaw." The former asked whether we should dam the Sistine Chapel so that tourists could get closer to its ceiling, while the latter asked whether the loggers should be allowed to preempt Congress's job of defining the boundaries of the projected Redwood National Park with their chainsaws. Both were designed to trigger a public outcry over what was going on. This may have been the most successful series of advocacy ads ever run. They triggered an avalanche of protests to Congress, an upsurge of good publicity, and an influx of donations. The ads succeeded in breaking the back of the opposition too. It was great fun, and I think the agency knew the ads were making history.

Implementation of the Wilderness Act

By the spring of 1966, the Forest Service was generating a huge number of proposals to implement the 1964 Wilderness Act. Hearings were being held in many places across the West on its proposals to redraw the boundaries of primitive areas. In the form that the Wilderness Act finally took, areas could be put into the National Wilderness Preservation System, or taken out of it, only by an act of Congress. So we had to decide what we thought of the Forest Service's proposals, get witnesses to the hearings, and organize a decent turnout of our supporters. The reclassification process was entirely a political one.

The Club had already been sending teams of volunteers from California out to evaluate the wilderness potential of various remote areas in the West. These so-called Exploration and Reconnaissance (E & R) teams went to states where the Club had no chapters at the time, such as Wyoming and Montana. But the teams were slow to write up their findings and were protective of their role. I tried to focus them on areas coming up earliest on the review schedule and to speed up their evaluations. I recruited new activists to report back on proposals already before us. And I wrote up the techniques that I had pioneered in the Northwest in a handbook on evaluating wilderness proposals.

Coordinating our response to the drumfire of hearings that we faced was a consuming task. There were dozens of them. I managed the process of finding people to take charge and determine our position. Then I put out appeals for support and strove to turn out a crowd for each hearing—often in rural areas. For the most part, we pressed for larger wilderness areas and questioned deletions. But the Club also faced new issues in this work to implement the Wilderness Act, all of which required analysis, discussion, and strategizing.

With the Forest Service we faced issues over solitude, buffers, and "purity." The Forest Service wanted to limit the amount of acreage deemed suitable for wilderness. Toward that end, it decided not to propose areas for wilderness that were exposed to the "sights and sounds" of civilization. These places would not afford opportunities for solitude, which the agency asserted was a necessary ingredient of wilderness. In many primitive areas along narrow mountain ranges in the intermountain West, however, there were few spots where one could not see barns and highways in settled valleys. This criterion, which was not clearly required by the act, would eliminate many existing primitive areas.

This position was also inconsistent with the Forest Service's long refusal to set aside buffer areas outside the boundaries of wilderness areas. It logged and built roads right up to their borders. The Forest Service had insisted that any needed buffers would be inside the borders of a wilderness area. But such buffers inside wilderness boundaries would necessarily, in varying degrees, be exposed to the sights and sounds of civilization that were found along their edges and thus could not afford the same level of solitude as their interior.

Finally, the Forest Service announced that it did not want any areas in the system that had been compromised by human impacts, but wanted only so-called pure areas. This argument for "purity" also had the effect of minimizing the amount of land that could qualify for inclusion in the system. In its controlling language, the Wilderness Act called for areas that "generally appeared to have been primarily affected by the forces of nature." We thought that this provision allowed for some blemishes, which could be erased over time: small stub roads, stumps, and even small catch dams.

I dealt with this issue in a personal way during the reclassification of the Desolation Valley Wilderness Area west of Lake Tahoe. That area was riddled with small rock-faced dams, four to five feet high, put there by utilities to increase water storage. These were relatively inconspicuous, although there was one twenty-foot-high dam on the northern side of the wilderness.

Notwithstanding these dams, we decided that the area did generally *appear* to have been primarily affected by the forces of nature. Through my fieldwork with Luis and Laverne Ireland and Francis Wolcott, the Club was able to get additional acreage included along Lyons Creek on the southwest. And Congress accepted our argument regarding purity there. The issue was not put to rest, though, until the Eastern Wilderness Act was passed in 1975. Through that act, Congress made it clear that it would put recovered areas into the system.

The National Park Service, which was supposed to look for zones of wilderness within the boundaries of its holdings, also thought of ways to say no. The Park Service had never been enthusiastic about being included under the act in the first place. It didn't like having its discretion circumscribed. It wanted to be able to build roads and lodges wherever it wanted. Thus it proposed to leave lots of room along existing roads and around existing lodges to add more of them in the future. Its early proposals provided for substantial setbacks from these features for the boundaries of wilderness zones proposed within the parks. These intervening areas were labeled "thresholds" for wilderness. In effect, the Park Service was putting its buffers outside of its wilderness.

This issue first arose in connection with a proposal for Lassen Volcanic National Park in northern California. Club officers were crystal clear that they opposed these thresholds and sent me to scout out the area and prepare our testimony. At a theoretical level, I was less sure of the wisdom of trying to do master planning in reverse via wilderness zoning. But I studied the area on the ground, and then the agency's proposal, and became convinced that the agency had overreached. Its proposal was driven not by any real need for more roads or lodges but just by a policy of routinely making setbacks. With a good conscience, I delivered our testimony. In response, Congress finally made some adjustments.

While agencies exerted themselves to finish the reviews of their holdings under a schedule mandated by the Wilderness Act, it was up to the wilderness groups to persuade Congress to act once these reviews landed on its doorstep. Otherwise, they would sit there like lumps of clay. Traditionally, Congress deals with broad legislation that establishes a framework for agency action. It likes to leave the detailed work to agencies and does not like to have to address a huge flow of implementing legislation. But it now faced just that under the affirmative action provision of the Wilderness Act.

Questions of strategy faced us in persuading Congress to come to grips with all of these reclassifications. Seeing such a large number of areas to be sent through the process (involving three, and later four, agencies), I felt that it was important to get a fast start. It would be to our advantage to show Congress that it would not be a painful process to put areas into the new wilderness system. This would encourage them to move forward with processing the hundreds of proposals that would be coming to them from agencies.[2]

Stewart Brandborg, Howard Zahniser's successor in the Wilderness Society, had a different idea, however. He wanted the Forest Service to understand that Congress would not blindly rubber-stamp its proposals. So in 1967–68, Brandborg made a major issue of the reclassification of the San Rafael Primitive Area, in the mountains back of Santa Barbara. The local chapter of the Sierra Club had pushed the Forest Service into embracing a proposal to substantially expand the area—from nearly 75,000 acres to nearly 143,000 acres. But Brandborg seized on an issue involving 2,200 acres along its northern edge, which the Forest Service wanted as a fuel break. Brandborg embroiled both the House and Senate in a bitter fight to include this area—ultimately to no avail. Many key members of Congress were left with a sour taste in their mouths. I told Brandborg I thought he had made a strategic mistake.

We also faced a question about which agency's proposals we should push in Congress. For better or worse, the Sierra Club and the Wilderness Society decided to give priority to wilderness proposals coming from the Forest Service. Commercial pressures on the Forest Service were so strong that we needed to assure protection of their areas without delay. We felt that the land in units of the national park system and the system of national wildlife refuges were in far less danger.

While I agreed in general with this prioritization, I was never comfortable with leaving the proposals of the Park Service and the Fish and Wildlife Service in limbo for long periods of time, which was what often happened. Unless we pushed these proposals in Congress, they would

get little attention. I feared that they would lose legitimacy and momentum if neglected for scores of years. The pressures that developed later
to drill in the Arctic National Wildlife Refuge showed that such areas
were vulnerable too.

The quickening tempo of the work to implement the Wilderness Act
gave us a taste of what was to come. It had taught us that we needed to
generate the political energy to shape better proposals and to get
Congress to respond. Without our organizing, we had learned, little
would happen.

5 Campaigning for a Redwood National Park

Even before I moved to the Sierra Club's San Francisco offices in January 1965, I knew I would be splitting my time between in-house duties under Dave Brower's direction and the campaign to establish a new national park in the coastal redwoods of northern California, one of the Club's top priorities after the Wilderness Act became law. This project was to be a preoccupation for the next four years.

The campaign was managed by Ed Wayburn, who made the decisions, secured needed backing from the Club's board of directors, and was our principal spokesman. Ed had just served three years as president of the Club and before then had served as chairman of the Club's conservation committee, so he was in an excellent position to take the lead.

My role was to assist Ed. I acted as tactical advisor, furnished technical support, and, much as I had in the Pacific Northwest, did field organizing. In time, I also became the Club's principal lobbyist in Congress for the park, as well as a frequent spokesman for it.

The Club's redwoods campaign, perhaps more so than any other, illustrates everything it takes to get a measure through Congress. Customarily, Congress develops an appetite for action on an issue only when it feels enough pressure from constituents. Then it usually looks to the interest groups that embody the hopes of those constituents to do much of the work. Accordingly, it fell to us to bear this burden in the redwoods campaign, meaning that we had to master the full legislative process. In this case I did much of the work, which made it an invaluable learning experience for what was to follow.

I prepared for this campaign by visiting every significant redwood grove in northern California. I wanted to learn to recognize differences among the stands—the bottom stands, specimen trees, and slope stands—and all the varied situations in which they grew. I wanted to be able to comment knowledgeably about what had already been done and to make a persuasive case for what we proposed to do.

Dave Brower had become involved in this issue in 1963 when he arranged Club publication of a large-format book on the plight of the redwoods, *The Last Redwoods*, with text by Francois Leydet and photographs by Ansel Adams. He also helped oversee my work and develop full-page newspaper ads, but most of his attention was focused on the Club's Grand Canyon campaign.

So, for the most part, it was Ed and I who put together the Club's campaign for a Redwood National Park. Of course, many others played important roles. Martin Litton, who was then travel editor of *Sunset* magazine and who sat on the Club's board of directors, spurred us on, brought news of the latest outrages, and acted as roving reporter. With a light plane at his command, he frequently flew over the area. Gradually we formed a cadre of supporters in Humboldt County, where the best trees were.

Interest in the redwoods had been building throughout the 1960s. Only about 10 percent of the original stands of coastal redwoods (*Sequoia sempervirens*) still survived as that decade began. And only about 2.5 percent had been protected in state parks.[1] The only stands the federal government had protected were in tiny Muir Woods National Monument near San Francisco.

Most of the 150,000 acres of unprotected virgin redwood stands were being rapidly logged. Moreover, the highway department in California was trying to push freeways north along Highway 101 into the redwood region. It had already routed a freeway through the edge of Humboldt Redwoods State Park, south of Eureka, and was looking at routes that would slice through groves located in two more state parks farther north. Hundreds of prime trees would be lost—ones that were supposed to be inviolate.

Humboldt Redwoods State Park, then protecting only stands on flats, had also suffered from bad flooding along Bull Creek because its watershed had not been acquired; logging in it had unleashed debris that damaged the magnificent stands on Bull Creek Flat. Additional floods of record size in 1964 and 1965 had heightened concern over the need to protect the unacquired slopes above the parklands.

The pace at which the virgin stands of redwoods were vanishing was beginning to become evident to the public. It had been standard practice for companies logging their own stands to leave strips of uncut forest along highways in order to shield the public from scenes of devastation. But beginning in the mid-1960s, most of the lumber companies ended even this practice. Cutting down to the roadside left drivers aghast.

These concerns, and the Club's publication of *The Last Redwoods* in 1963, engendered new interest in the future of the coastal redwoods. The National Park Service decided to study the stands again to see if anything remained that would merit protection as a national park. At the Club's biennial wilderness conference in 1961, Ed and Peggy Wayburn had prompted Interior Secretary Stewart Udall to look into this possibility. The Park Service had conducted previous studies, but only many years before, in 1920 and in 1935. Congress had never responded to those studies; had it done so, most observers agreed, the best stands could have been protected, particularly along the lower Klamath River.

The National Park Service put study teams into the field in 1963–64, working under a grant from the National Geographic Society. The teams found the tallest known trees in the world along Redwood Creek in northern Humboldt County, on lumber company lands. The tallest redwood stood 367 feet, although it is now shorter because of later storm damage. News of this discovery, published by the National Geographic Society, caused a sensation. In 1964, the Park Service issued a report on three alternative designs for a new national park in Redwood Creek and asked for public comment, which—on balance—was supportive of the idea. The Park Service was expected to release a final set of recommendations the following year.

Serving on the Park Service Study Team was a career landscape architect by the name of Paul Fritz. Outgoing and ebullient, Fritz made friends easily and used his time in the redwoods to identify people who could be helpful to the cause of a park. He cultivated Ed Wayburn and kept him informed of what the field team was finding and was planning to recommend.

I had known Fritz from the time he had served at parks in the Pacific Northwest, and I trusted him. Fritz convinced Wayburn that the park should be located along Redwood Creek, where the new discoveries had been made and the largest unprotected stands of virgin redwoods were. Based on this expert opinion, Wayburn committed the Sierra Club to support a new national park in this location, and we got to work.

The campaign for a Redwood National Park proved to be daunting. In some ways, it challenged the Sierra Club far more than the battle for the Wilderness Act, on which the Wilderness Society had carried more of the burden. The obstacles we faced in this battle were greater and more concentrated, and we were on our own. We had to learn to master more tools and arts of persuasion in shaping public policy. In some ways, this battle was a precursor of the campaigns that would challenge the Club in the decade to follow.

And unlike the simultaneous campaign it was waging to defeat dams in the Grand Canyon, in this campaign the Sierra Club had to persuade Congress to act, rather than keep it from acting. We had the affirmative burden of surmounting the twenty-two steps of the congressional process to transform our vision into law. It was the more difficult task, and we faced opposition from timber companies every step of the way.

In December 1964, before I had begun in San Francisco, I flew to Eureka, California, to get started. I drove north to Orick, at the mouth of Redwood Creek, to meet Jean Hagood, a local supporter who owned a motel there. Then I drove out the Bald Hills Road to take a good look at the slopes of virgin redwoods along Redwood Creek—seeing for the first time the vistas of unbroken forests stretching southeasterly along this narrow valley. Only a clearcut along the first part of the road marred the scene. But visibility was limited because of winter mists. Nor was it possible to see the Tall Tree Grove, which was then closed to public entry. But I could see that there was much here to save.

A visit to nearby Prairie Creek Redwoods State Park reminded me how beautiful the coastal redwood trees were, with their thick red bark and flat evergreen needles. Thriving mainly in the foggy zone along the coasts of northern California, they grow taller than any other species of tree. While they are not the species that lives the longest, some nonetheless live for more than 2,000 years. In contrast to the redwoods of the Sierra (*Sequoia giganteadendron*), these trees are known for their height rather than for their girth or age.

On returning to Eureka, I began looking up the thirty-five people Paul Fritz thought sympathetic, and over the next few months I got to know many of them. I wanted to set up a local group that would publicly support establishment of the park. While most were sympathetic, not all were willing to be publicly identified as supporters or to stand up to a local power structure that was hostile to the park idea. But a core group was willing to form an organization called Citizens for a Redwood National Park.

Ed Wayburn also cultivated these local leaders. One of them, Ray Peart, a member of the county board of supervisors, also wrote sympathetically for the local newspaper. In the final analysis, the existence of this group may have helped to keep the local Republican congressman, Don Clausen, from becoming an intransigent opponent of the park (although the large number of Democrats in the southern portion of his district who favored the park was probably a more critical factor).

Over time, more supporters emerged in the area, especially in the nearby town of Arcata, where faculty and students at Humboldt State College tended to support the initiative. Rudolf Becking, a forestry professor there, was generally helpful, though he kept his own counsel. David Van de Mark was indefatigable in finding ways to get into privately owned Redwood Creek to take photographs documenting stands of special significance. More and more students and other young enthusiasts began to infiltrate the lands of the lumber companies, to see what was at stake and to run the eight miles of lower Redwood Creek in rafts and canoes. While we did not officially countenance trespassing, those who got onto those lands brought us photographs that convinced us we were on the right track.

Some time after becoming a frequent visitor to the region, I finally squeezed onto a sanctioned trip into the Tall Tree Grove, where I could actually see the trees that had started it all. With these trees crowded onto a small flat, it was hard to appreciate their exceptional height. In among them, one was more conscious of huge trunks and burls than soaring shafts. Because of their size, it was difficult to see them as a whole; one saw either sections of their bases or scenes of the forest. Afterward I canoed with others down the stream to Orick, treasuring the views along eight miles of virgin forest.

I studied every piece of evidence about these stands that I could lay my hands on. I believed we needed to know exactly what we wanted the government to do and why. Once again, I quizzed those who were most knowledgeable. We obtained type maps of the timber stands from the county assessor and whatever we could from Paul Fritz, who began to feel constrained in how much he could tell us. We began to map out our own proposal, reflecting what we thought Fritz and the Park Service field team really hoped would be recommended by the Interior Department. As this work became more technical, the Club hired its own professional forestry consultant: Gordon Robinson, the former chief forester for the Southern Pacific Land Company.

As 1965 dragged on, the Interior Department failed to issue its expected final report on the park. The Johnson administration had promised that the report would be forthcoming at the beginning of 1965, so something was holding it up. Our informants in Congress told us that they would not take up the matter until the administration made clear what it wanted.

Interior Secretary Udall would not tell us where the report was or what was causing the delay. While he generally exhorted conservationists to think big and be bold, he seemed immobilized on this issue. We did everything we could to persuade him of the importance of moving fast, before much was lost to logging, and we made the case for the wonders of Redwood Creek as the place for the park.

Only later did we learn how little influence Udall had with President Johnson. As a leftover from President Kennedy's administration, Udall may have felt insecure in his relationship with his successor. He tried to cultivate President Johnson by assisting Lady Bird with her program to promote protection of "natural beauty," but he was constantly outflanked by Laurance Rockefeller and his aides, who were presidential advisors and were close to the Save-the-Redwoods League.

Gradually we came to understand the reason for the delay: the Save-the-Redwoods League was not on board. Since 1918 this organization had been the leader in efforts to save coastal redwoods and to have them protected in parkland. It was a fund-raising group, with only nominal members. While it had once championed the goal of establishing a national park in the redwoods, its longtime leader and co-founder, Newton Drury, had given up on the idea. Since the best stands, which once existed along the lower Klamath River, no longer existed to form the core of a national park, Drury had concluded that the time for such a park had passed.

Instead, he and his associates had focused on raising funds to buy small stands of bottomland redwoods for the system of state parks. After the floods at Bull Creek Flat, the League became convinced that it needed to acquire more upper slope areas too. To succeed in doing this, Drury felt that the League needed to maintain cordial relationships with the lumber companies owning these lands, since they had to be persuaded to sell. He felt that the Sierra Club was engendering hostility and alarm among the companies and would ruin the League's chances of buying more stands.

Under Drury, the Save-the-Redwoods League had decided that it should try to replicate its lesson from Bull Creek Flat at Jedediah Smith

Redwoods State Park to the north. The League sought to acquire the entire upper watershed of Mill Creek, which drained northward into the Stout Grove and other areas in the northernmost of the major redwood state parks near Crescent City. These lands were owned by the Miller-Rellim Company. Drury decided to capture the momentum for a national park in the redwoods to further his project of acquiring the rest of Mill Creek. If the Park Service bought the Miller-Rellim lands, he would not have to.[2]

Ever since the 1920s, Drury had had a close relationship with the Rockefeller family, which had provided the money to buy the forests in Humboldt Redwoods State Park. He now prevailed upon Laurance Rockefeller to persuade the Johnson administration to locate its proposed park at Mill Creek rather than at Redwood Creek. Rockefeller had developed a close relationship with LBJ through staffing the President's Committee on Natural Beauty, and as it turned out, Rockefeller had more clout with LBJ than Udall did.

Drury was a formidable opponent. Not only was he a founder of the League along with his brother, but he was also a former director of both the National Park Service and the state park agency. He had the kind of expertise and connections in the East that impressed Lyndon Johnson (who lacked them).

Moreover, Drury resented having the Sierra Club poach on what he perceived to be his turf. Nor did he take kindly to having Ed Wayburn assert greater knowledge and expertise on the matter of redwoods, although I managed to maintain good relations with the League's field director, John DeWitt, who had also been active in the Club. Moreover, as relations cooled between Wayburn and Dick Leonard (a longtime Club leader and former president), Leonard became more involved with the affairs of the League. I believe he encouraged Drury to take issue with the Club.

Because of the split between the Sierra Club and the Save-the-Redwoods League, other conservation organizations tended to shy away from the Redwood National Park issue. They didn't want to get involved in an intramural fight between old-line organizations in California. At the national level, the only significant support the Club received was from the Wilderness Society and the Garden Club of America, in which Mrs. Thomas Waller was an influential voice (ironically, her family had once owned some of the stands in Redwood Creek). And we also received support from the United Auto Workers in

Detroit, whose recreation director was on our side. But most of the conservation organizations left it to us in California to "duke it out." So
we had to do it pretty much on our own.

California's various governors did not support the park either. When
Edmund "Pat" Brown was governor in 1965 and 1966, he actually
opposed establishing a national park at Redwood Creek. And when
Ronald Reagan campaigned for governor, he dismissed the redwoods
with the blithe comment, "If you've seen one redwood, you've seen
them all" (though historians now argue about whether those were his
precise words).

When he took office in 1967, however, Reagan appointed Norman
"Ike" Livermore as the administrator of the California Resources
Agency. Livermore had been not only a lumber company executive but
also a high-country packer who had served on the Sierra Club's board
of directors and initiated its series of wilderness conferences. He worked
skillfully to keep the state government under Reagan from drifting into
hard-line opposition to the idea of a national park. His action was crucial to our eventual success.

Our campaign was infinitely more difficult because the lands
involved were privately owned, not public. Unlike other park campaigns
in the West, ours was not trying to shift the management of public lands
from one agency to another. Instead, we needed to get the federal government to acquire private lands from three lumber companies that
owned them: Arcata Redwood Company, the Georgia-Pacific Lumber
Company, and the Simpson Timber Company. We were not at odds
with the Miller-Rellim Company since we did not seek a park on their
lands at Mill Creek, though the League did. Meanwhile, all these companies fiercely opposed the park and conducted skillful campaigns
against it.

Not only did we face political opposition from these companies, but
we also faced three other problems that arose out of their ownership.
First, we could not gain ready access to these lands to show people what
we were talking about; the permission once extended to the Park Service
had now been denied to everyone else. Second, the lumber companies
began to accelerate the process of logging these lands, including the
construction of damaging access roads. In effect, we were dealing with
a "wasting asset" whose value for park purposes was being destroyed
while we talked. Much of the rehabilitation subsequently undertaken by
the Park Service addressed damage done during this campaign. And

third, the cost of acquiring these lands for park purposes was proving to be inordinately high.

The Bureau of the Budget (now known as the Office of Management and Budget) also had a chokehold on our progress. It would allocate only $60 million to acquire lands for this park—wherever it was located. In addition, the administration would support a park in only one location, not two—presumably to control costs. The park we wanted in Redwood Creek, it was them thought, might require twice that amount—as much as $120 million. In the summer of 1965, when Interior Secretary Udall tried to get the Bureau of the Budget to clear a park proposal of 93,000 acres in Redwood Creek, it turned him down.

Udall's Interior Department was caught in a cross fire. If it tried to fashion a compromise between the Save-the-Redwoods League and the Sierra Club, it would run afoul of the Bureau of the Budget's stricture against trying to stretch the park over two locations, and it would be hard to stay within the $60 million limit. (Eventually, the administration simply embraced the cheaper proposal of the League and endorsed a park at Mill Creek of only 43,000 acres. Thus it turned its back on all of the research of the National Park Service's own team in the field, an astounding repudiation of its own agency's work.)

In California we were thus facing two formidable opponents—not just the lumber companies, but the Save-the-Redwoods League as well. Furthermore, in backing the Park Service's field team, we enjoyed little support from other groups, and the Park Service itself had been silenced. The Johnson administration lacked conviction, and the state dragged its feet. The local congressman was not supportive, nor were most local media. The resource was continuing to disappear before our eyes as it was logged, and the costs of acquiring the land were incredibly high.

But our case caught the fancy of the public nonetheless. People were intrigued by the idea of unknown trees of stupendous height. The behavior of both the Johnson administration and the lumber companies seemed reprehensible. And every day brought news of some further outrage, some key stand laid low. These were the openings we needed.

The administration tried to build the case for its choice of Mill Creek by bringing in a firm of consulting foresters (Hammond, Jensen, and Wallen) to assess the quality of the stands. We argued that they ought to also assess the quality of the Redwood Creek stands, which they finally did, finding that there were ten times more trees of superior size in Redwood Creek and four times more virgin stands. The Park Service's field team knew what they were talking about: far more value could be obtained in Redwood Creek for the money available.

In the fall of 1965, we decided that we could wait no longer. We would have to put forth a bill ourselves. Having worked with Ed Wayburn to define the optimal boundaries, I drafted a bill that would have set up a national park of 90,000 acres along the lower miles of Redwood Creek, including 34,000 acres of virgin redwoods. I shopped it around in Congress to find sponsors.

Our lead sponsor in the House of Representatives was Jeffrey Cohelan of the East Bay, my own congressman. Not only was he a Californian, but he was somebody we could work closely with. I spent many hours in his office, drafting not only the bill (which the Legislative Counsel perfected) but also many of his remarks about it for the floor of the House. I also helped find forty co-sponsors in the House, both Democrats and Republicans.

In the Senate, I persuaded Lee Metcalf, a Democrat from Montana, to be the lead sponsor and found sixteen co-sponsors. Though Metcalf was not from California, he was from a Western state with a lumber industry and was in the majority party of that time. Neither of California's senators was yet ready to get involved, given the split between the Sierra Club and the Save-the-Redwoods League.

When Cohelan introduced his bill on October 25, we backed it up with a well-orchestrated public relations campaign. The Club organized a press conference and provided television stations throughout the state with film clips of the site. In the ensuing days, we made widespread mailings to the media and cultivated those who might write on the issue. Among the California press, the *San Francisco Chronicle* covered the issue thoroughly, as did the *Sacramento Bee*. National newspapers, such as the *New York Times*, were also eager to write about it.

Over time, the Club produced books, films, slide shows, pamphlets, fact sheets, posters, campaign buttons, and other items to promote its Redwood Creek park proposal. I wrote articles for the *Saturday Review*, the *Sierra Club Bulletin*, and other nationally distributed periodicals.[3] We worked with KING-TV of Seattle to produce a documentary on the issue, which won an Academy Award. We took writers and influential people to see the area and fostered as much media coverage as we could. With this treatment and a generally receptive public, it quickly became a national issue.

Still, the Johnson administration did not act. So in December 1965, the Sierra Club decided to undertake a campaign of paid advertisements in newspapers across the country, as mentioned in the previous chapter. Over the following six months, the Club ran ads on both the redwood issue and the Grand Canyon campaign, but we began with an ad on the redwood issue.

The headline in that first ad read: "Mr. President: There is one great forest of redwoods left on earth, but the one you are trying to save isn't it. Meanwhile, they are cutting down both of them." The ad called for letters to the president and to members of the House and Senate Interior Committees. It also asked for donations to defray the costs of the ad. Initially we ran it in the *New York Times*, the leading San Francisco newspaper, and papers in Denver and Salt Lake City.

The response was overwhelming. The donations we received more than paid for the ads, and other newspapers begged us to run them in their papers. The ads became a news event in their own right. And wires and letters poured into Washington, D.C. In the following eighteen months, we ran more ads. We commented on the irony that this nation could afford to send a man to the moon but thought it couldn't afford to save the best redwoods left on this earth. With the headline "Legislation by Chainsaw," we rubbed the face of Congress in the fact that it had let the lumber companies usurp its job of deciding the boundaries of the Redwood National Park.

The initial series of ads continued through June 1966, when the IRS revoked the Club's tax deductibility, ostensibly because our lobbying efforts were too brazen. But that action only brought us more attention and sympathy as an underdog that the government was trying to silence, and we became even more active.

Ours may have been the most successful issue-ad campaign ever undertaken by an advocacy organization. People remember many of the ads to this day. The success they enjoyed, though, may have been the product of many ingredients. Certainly the ads were novel and fresh, well-written, dramatic, and witty. But they were also successful because they were aimed at one person (the president) who had to make the right decision. The need for action was clearly urgent too, and the values at stake were being undermined by forces who were clearly villains. These ingredients would not always be in place in the future when we hoped to enjoy this same level of success with new ads.

The year of 1966 did not bring presidential action for us, though. The Johnson administration spent most of the year trying to rally support for its Mill Creek proposal, with little to show for it. In June the Senate Interior Committee did hold two days of hearings in the field at Crescent City, close to Mill Creek, however. No local support whatsoever was evident for the administration's proposal. Of those who spoke in favor of a national park at all, three-quarters supported the Redwood Creek site. At a subsequent Interior Committee hearing in August in the Capitol, witnesses again overwhelmingly preferred the Redwood Creek site, with little opposition evident there to the idea of establishing a park. I encouraged supporters to turn out at both hearings, and Ed Wayburn and I both testified at the Washington, D.C., hearing, with Wayburn laying out the basic case while I amplified and handled rebuttal.

Congress then indicated that it might give the president the power he asked for to condemn logging rights for one year to stop the ongoing destruction. To stave off this prospect, the companies agreed to limit their logging in the area for a year—until September 1967. This suspension created something of a deadline, which put pressure on Congress to act.

Senator Thomas Kuchel was a pivotal figure. A moderate Republican, he was not only the senior senator from California but also the ranking minority member of the Senate Interior Committee. In August 1967 he decided to abandon the Johnson administration's Mill Creek proposal, which he had sponsored as a courtesy. Seeing that its proposal lacked any popular support, Kuchel decided the administration's plan was not viable. He was now interested in fashioning a compromise, and the Club indicated that it was flexible as to the size of the park and the inclusion of other units, as long as the key areas in Redwood Creek were part of the plan.

While Kuchel was not beholden to conservative forces, he was mindful of his relations with other Republicans in California. It would have been far more difficult for him to exert leadership on this issue had he faced adamant opposition from Governor Reagan's administration and from the Republican member of Congress from that district, Don Clausen. But neither dug himself into such a position.

I worked closely to fashion a compromise with E. Lewis Reid on Kuchel's staff and with the staff of the committee chairman, Senator Henry Jackson, a Democrat from Washington state, whom I knew well from my days in the Northwest. Sterling Munro of Jackson's staff actually gave me a desk in their offices from which to work. Shuttling back and forth between the offices, I helped them fashion a compromise that they could both support and that we could get behind. They wanted a compromise that included some of the best features of both areas and that would bridge the differences between the Save-the-Redwoods League and the Sierra Club. They were not too concerned over opposition from the lumber companies, which they took for granted.

While I was working out of Jackson's offices one day, I ran into Laurance Rockefeller, waiting in the anteroom to see the senator. I am sure he was there to make a last plea on behalf of the Save-the-Redwoods League. His face dropped as he saw me coming out of Jackson's offices. I am sure he knew this meant that things were not going his way.

The key to working out a compromise was finding a way to pay for a larger, two-unit park. That key was found in a proposal that Ike Livermore had crafted on behalf of the Reagan administration in California. Whereas the Johnson administration had tried to induce the state to transfer various redwood state parks to the federal government by offering various federal properties to California in return (for example, the Bureau of Land Management's King Range and two national monuments, Muir Woods and Devils Postpile), Livermore made it clear that the state was more interested in getting beach lands in federal military reservations transferred to it instead. And he wanted a Forest Service area just north of the Klamath River, known as the Redwood Purchase Unit (initially bought for a Redwood National Forest that never materialized), to be traded to the lumber companies for their land. Over time, the Forest Service planned to log most of the old-growth redwood there, which was thought to be worth $40 million. With that value factored in, there might be enough wherewithal to acquire lands in both Redwood Creek and Mill Creek.

Thus, a plan was fashioned that put three-quarters of the acquisition value in Redwood Creek and one-fourth in Mill Creek. The bill reported out of the Senate Interior Committee, and subsequently passed by the Senate, would have created a national park of 64,000 acres costing an estimated $100 million (of which the Purchase Unit would have provide $40 million). It would have extended protection to 13,000 acres of virgin redwood. The bill included a declaration of "instant taking" by the federal government, which was carried over into the measure that ultimately became law. Thereby the federal government would acquire the parkland by eminent domain at the moment the bill was signed and became law.

The Forest Service was outraged over the plan to trade away its lands, however, and that suddenly became the focus of concern when the bill was debated on the Senate floor. Some were concerned about the precedent of selling off national forest land to finance new parks, though this plan involved land that had never become a national forest. I lobbied every Senate office to gather support for the bill. In a showdown vote, an amendment to drop the Purchase Unit was defeated, with fifty-one senators opposed to the amendment and only thirty favoring it. On the final vote that followed, only six senators voted against passage of the bill to create the park.

While the Senate had acted before the moratorium on logging expired that fall, the House had not. Despite the imminence of congressional action, Georgia-Pacific resumed logging soon after the yearlong moratorium expired—at a site within the boundaries of the measure to create the park passed by the Senate. The Sierra Club exposed this action at a press conference. Georgia-Pacific and the Club then responded to each other in a series of ads in various newspapers. In December 1967, Georgia-Pacific commenced logging in the newly discovered Emerald Mile—a gallery of magnificent trees flanking Redwood Creek upstream from the Tall Tree Grove. As 1968 began, the other two companies with holdings in the drainage of Redwood Creek resumed logging too. The gauntlet had been thrown down.

By the spring of 1968, the House Interior Committee was compelled by public opinion to act. It could no longer drag its feet in deference to the lumber companies, which had the ear of the committee's chairman, Wayne Aspinall. At hearings in April and May, most of those who testified in favor of a park supported the bill passed by the Senate. While the Johnson administration now indicated that it could support the Senate bill, the Agriculture Department, which oversaw the Forest Service, was vehemently opposed, and each of the lumber companies now tried to arrange separate terms under which it would cooperate.

In late June when Aspinall unveiled his own park proposal, however, we were stunned. His plan consisted of no more than the 25,000 acres along nine miles of Redwood Creek that the lumber companies had now agreed to sell. Even these could not be acquired until the state of California had donated two nearby state parks. No use was made of the lands in the Purchase Unit, nor was there authority for an "instant taking." Mill Creek was not included. Aspinall, who had said that the lumber companies would not like his bill, now justified it by claiming that he wanted to take a bill to the floor that could pass easily, so as to speed the process of getting to conference with the Senate.

Outraged, I worked feverishly to line up votes to overturn this proposal. I found champions on the subcommittee who were willing to offer amendments to add key areas that were in the Senate bill, such as Lost Man Creek, Little Lost Man Creek, and the Skunk Cabbage Creek area. In some cases, members of the subcommittee could not be present to vote but gave me their proxies. I put those proxies in the hands of the ranking Republican, John Saylor, who was very sympathetic, as well as the next ranking Democrat, Morris Udall, with whom we were now working well. But at the subcommittee meeting, our amendments lost on a vote of seven in favor, with ten opposed. The proxies I had provided were not voted, nor did Saylor and Udall support us. It seemed that the ranking Democrat and Republican were not willing to go that far to challenge the chairman's leadership.

Everyone sensed that the situation was precarious. I slipped a note to Representative William Fitts Ryan of New York suggesting a follow-up amendment, which he offered, to add a block of land to beef up the corridor along the mainstem of Redwood Creek, as well as to add the Emerald Mile to the proposal. In the confusion, however, I wasn't able to clarify where the added land would be. He thought it was all supposed to be above the Emerald Mile. At that point, Aspinall, who was worried about losing control of the process, indicated that he would accept Ryan's amendment. It was accepted then on a voice vote. With that amendment, Aspinall's plan looked like a snake with a kite tied to its tail. The shape had no logic, but we had won a small moral victory. Of course, if all of the proxies I had rounded up had been voted, we would have won a real victory.

Aspinall's bill would have extended protection to only 5,360 acres of virgin redwoods, at an estimated cost of $56 million. He was able to get his bill through the full committee only by assuring members that they would have ample opportunity on the floor to amend and improve it. I went to work with a number of offices to draft one-minute speeches to be delivered on the floor of the House. I was helped by Doug Scott, later the Club's conservation director but then an intern at the Wilderness Society, who sat in the visitors gallery drafting such speeches, which we quickly sent to members to deliver on the floor. In lobbying for this bill, I visited the office of every member of the House.

When Aspinall took his bill to the floor, he did it under a suspension of the rules, which precludes amendments. He claimed to be using that procedure so the bill could get to conference sooner. Morris Udall assured me that the problems with the House version would all be corrected in the conference committee, on which he would serve. I organized members who were ready to confront Aspinall over his procedure, and when they threatened to deny Aspinall the two-thirds vote he needed to prevail on the floor under that rule, he pledged "to try to find in conference the answers by which the acreage can be increased to a reasonable and logical amount." Thereupon, the House passed the bill by a vote of 388–15.

The final bill that emerged from the Senate-House conference did substantially resemble the Senate bill. It provided authority to acquire 58,000 acres of land at an estimated cost of $92 million, saving 11,000 acres of virgin redwoods. Udall and Aspinall had been true to their word. More than four times more private land was to be acquired in the southern unit along Redwood Creek than in the northern unit around Mill Creek. Only a small band of land was to be acquired along the southern edge of Jedediah Smith Redwoods State Park. Skunk Cabbage Creek was dropped from the plan, however, while the Emerald Mile was added, thanks to Representative Ryan's amendment. The Purchase Unit was to be used to reduce costs, and the measure included the Senate's "declaration of instant taking." The conference committee recommendations were then easily passed by both houses and sent to the president for signature.

At the signing ceremony on October 2, 1968, I watched President Lyndon Johnson sign S. 2515, the act to establish a Redwood National Park. When he lifted his pen from the page, I realized that, at that moment, all 28,101 acres of private land in the park had moved into federal ownership. This may have constituted the most aggressive use ever made of a legislative taking. I also rejoiced because at the same ceremony, the president signed a bill to establish the North Cascades National Park, on which I had done so much early work. The national system of Wild and Scenic Rivers (making them off-limits to dams) was also created at that signing ceremony, as was a system of national trails. I brought home one of the pens the president used in signing these measures, as well as a photograph of me shaking his hand.[4]

Oddly enough, though, I was not invited to the original ceremony to dedicate the Redwood National Park. Later the Nixon administration had its own dedication ceremony, at which Republicans and the Save-the-Redwoods League personnel were featured, not surprisingly.

A few days after the president signed the redwoods bill, I traveled to the park to celebrate with local supporters. As we gloried in the trees along Lost Man Creek that had been saved, we were accosted by the chief forester for Arcata Redwood Company, Gene Hofsted, who roared up in his jeep to accuse us of trespassing—ordering us off their land. We had the pleasure of replying, "This land is now part of the Redwood National Park. It is you who don't belong here anymore."

Based on the original proposal of the Johnson administration, the national park was designed around three state redwoods parks there (Prairie Creek, Del Norte Coast, and Jedediah Smith). It was assumed that they would be conveyed to the National Park Service, but this never happened; there was really never any constituency for it. Ed Wayburn and I tried to encourage transfer, but rangers in the state parks were opposed to losing this land. The transfer almost took place during the time when Jerry Brown was governor of California and Jimmy Carter was president. But at the last moment, our friend Bill Whelan from San Francisco, then director of the National Park Service, raised objections to some of the details. To this day, two systems of parks exist side by side there.

The act passed in 1968 represented the best that could be accomplished at that time. But the boundaries of the corridor along Redwood Creek were unsatisfactory. That corridor was exposed to erosion, landslides, and floods. As logging accelerated in the lands above and outside the park, a major concentration of rock, mud, and debris began to move down the course of Redwood Creek, endangering the Emerald Mile and the Tall Tree Grove.

We all knew that the boundaries were unsatisfactory, but we also knew that we could not go back to Congress right away with any expectation of success. During the Nixon administration, we got the U.S. Geological Survey to study the unstable geological conditions there. The Club filed a series of lawsuits arguing that the secretary of the Interior had a high duty to care for national park land and seeking to compel him to deal with threats to the park from erosion and debris.

By the mid-1970s, the Club had launched a second campaign to achieve its original boundaries, this time focusing on the need to acquire and rehabilitate the slopes above the corridor to protect its integrity. We had to demonstrate the scope and severity of the damage that was occurring.

In 1978 Congress did intervene, with Representative Phil Burton of San Francisco leading the way. The park was expanded to include all of the lands that we had put in the original Cohelan bill—though with far fewer trees than existed in 1965—plus other lands to the north. It included a park protection zone for cutover areas that needed to be rehabilitated by plantings, removing logging roads, and restoring stream courses. This zone included areas that no longer had resources of park caliber but that were needed to protect parklands, an idea for which I developed the conceptual basis. The National Park Service has been hard at work restoring ecological health to this area. It may constitute the largest rehabilitation effort undertaken in the United States, with tens of thousands of acres already restored.

As a result of these two acts of Congress, 20,000 acres of virgin redwoods were given protection. This was a major milestone in the history of protecting coastal redwoods. Newton Drury of the Save-the-Redwoods League was not impressed, however. He reacted sourly to this achievement, focusing only on how we had alienated the lumber companies and made it difficult for the Save-the-Redwoods League to buy redwood forests for the various state parks. In truth, there were few left to buy.

Under the legislative taking, the former owners of the lands taken for the park were directed to file claims for compensation in the U.S. Court of Claims. Litigation dragged on for many years. The companies made outrageous claims, but had little evidence of transactions involving sales on a scale large enough to indicate the value of the lands taken. They had evidence only of sales of small parcels, which often cost more and were unrepresentative. Ultimately, though, the claimants were able to use this unrepresentative evidence to push the payments to them to $1.6 billion, including interest. This process made the redwood park the most expensive national park ever acquired.

I had thought the lands in the Cohelan bill could be acquired for $120 million, but this estimate was based on the taxes the companies were paying on their lands. I never envisioned a process that would allow claims to be pumped up so high. I am proud, though, that even when faced with higher costs than expected, this country did not back away from its desire to create a great park in this special area.

In its second act, Congress agreed to pay additional sums to the affected locality. Representative Burton established a generous package of payments to displaced timber workers. The locality never seemed willing to help itself, however, by properly promoting the tourist potential of the Redwood National Park. To this day, the local chambers of commerce virtually ignore the park, promoting tourism to the overall redwood region instead. Die-hard opponents of the park complain that the tourism boom we promised never materialized. But they have only themselves to blame because they have never done anything to make it happen.

The National Park Service is also to blame, however. It started off on the wrong foot by putting the headquarters in an illogical place— Crescent City, in deference to Drury, despite the fact that federal holdings near there are minimal. Little land was acquired in pursuit of Drury's national park. Then, when the Park Service finally built a visitor center at Orick, it did little to interpret the redwoods as the prime feature of the park. Instead, the agency treated the facility as a nature center to interpret common flora and fauna of the coastal region, and was slow to develop trails into the best groves.

The Park Service's work in rehabilitating the abused areas of the park has been first rate, however. It has put many miles of roads "to bed," nursed many tributary streams back to health, and planted new forests that will green the hillsides again. In time, this park will heal and its promise will be realized.

As for the Sierra Club, the contentious and complicated campaign for the redwoods prepared us well for the challenges that would soon face us.

6   *The Brower Affair*

As the 1960s progressed, the Sierra Club's reputation and membership grew. But even as its impact was growing, internal dissonance was developing. Many new members were attracted by the dashing style of its executive director, David Brower, and identified that style with the Sierra Club. But some members of the Club's board of directors were becoming increasingly upset by his behavior.

Brower had made a name for himself both as a climber and as a conservationist. During World War II, he fought in the Tenth Mountain Division and taught climbing and skiing. With other returning veterans, he became one of the Young Turks intent on changing the once staid organization into a vigorous advocate of conservation. In 1952 that group took control of the board and hired the forty-year-old Brower to be the Club's first executive director.

Brower threw himself into the job and took the lead in the successful battle to keep dams out of tributaries of the Colorado River in Dinosaur National Monument in western Colorado. He helped put together the national coalition that waged an imaginative campaign to save the area in the mid-1950s. After carefully examining the government's calculations on evaporation rates, he identified errors that undermined the case for the dams. Realizing that water in that basin was in short supply, Brower showed that less water would be lost to evaporation by building a higher Glen Canyon Dam than by building the various dams proposed in the Dinosaur National Monument. Brower thereby acquiesced in building the Glen Canyon Dam downstream as the price of keeping dams out of the Dinosaur Monument upstream.

The board of directors was delighted with his performance in this campaign. Brower worked with others, paid attention to detail, and found a way to win by compromising. He also looked to board members such as Ansel Adams for suggestions. In the late 1950s Adams pushed Brower to strengthen the Club's stand in opposing resort development in Yosemite National Park. Brower was also drawn by transplanted Club members in Seattle to get involved with the future of the North Cascades.

Late in the 1950s, Brower became particularly critical of the Forest Service and its decision to start logging its holdings in a big way. Plans were put into effect to commit most old-growth timber to systematic, year-by-year liquidation—to convert a "stagnant forest," which was supposed to be decaying, into a dynamic one. Brower's sense of alarm rose over the scale of logging planned, and his criticism grew in intensity and bite. Club members in Oregon had told him of threats to Forest Service wilderness there, and I had brought similar stories to his attention when we used to meet at conventions of the Federation of Western Outdoor Clubs.

Brower himself had protested so-called sanitary logging sales at Deadman Summit on the east side of the Sierra. Sanitary logging allowed commercially valuable timber to be removed from recreation areas under the pretense that only "dead, diseased, dying, and down trees" would be taken out to leave a healthier forest. In 1959, Brower reprinted an article in the *Sierra Club Bulletin* that accused a Forest Service officer in that area of accepting a bribe.

The Club's board of directors was uncomfortable with such disparagement of public officials and adopted a policy that forbade the staff from impugning the integrity of any public official. Brower interpreted the policy as a kind of "gag order" that would prevent him from criticizing officials in a forthright fashion. The order itself did not really prevent forthright criticism on the merits, only ad hominem attacks, but Brower felt hobbled. And in their oral histories, both Ansel Adams and Richard Leonard make it clear that at this time they wanted to continue to have amicable relations with agencies such as the Forest Service. They resented Brower's turn toward confrontation.

Over the next few years, Brower's relations with the Club's board of directors deteriorated. Earlier, Brower had been able to get his way by threatening to resign if the board did not go along with his plans, but by the early 1960s this tactic no longer worked. In 1962, during his first presidency, Ed Wayburn cautioned Brower against offering his resignation anymore—lest it be accepted.

Brower responded in several ways. He found a new voice in having the Club publish books by others that were designed to express his vision. Even if *he* were censored, he felt that no one in the Club would want to censor the words of outside authors. And this was a line of work that he knew and understood from his days at the University of California Press. After helping Ansel Adams put on a photographic exhibit in 1960 at the Club's Le Conte Lodge in Yosemite Valley, he turned it into a stunning pictorial book—the first of a series of exhibit-format books. These books attracted critical acclaim and a wide audience, but they were expensive to produce and began to lose money.

Ansel Adams was enthusiastic about finding a wider audience for his work, but his support for the books program waned once Brower featured new talent, such as Eliot Porter. Porter's photographic work in color (in contrast to Adams's in black and white) was seen as the new wave. Brower, somewhat tactlessly, proclaimed that Porter was now the Club's "most valuable asset." Adams felt rejected and became increasingly critical of the way that Brower was running the book publishing program and the Club.

Brower tried to shore up his position with the board by recruiting well-known national figures to stand as candidates for election to the board. Their reputations would help them get elected, even though they had not been active in the organization. Brower hoped these new board members, in turn, would support him.

Various talented figures gradually joined the board as a result of Brower's recruitment efforts. A board of longtime outings leaders and conservationists suddenly had to absorb figures of wide experience and expertise such as Supreme Court Justice William O. Douglas, who hailed from Yakima, Washington, and had traveled the globe; Eliot Porter, a physician who became a noted landscape photographer; Luna Leopold, the chief hydrologist for the U.S. Geological Survey and brother of Aldo Leopold; novelist and English professor Wallace Stegner; Paul Brooks of Houghton Mifflin, who edited Rachel Carson's work; and John Oakes, who came to edit the editorial page of the *New York Times*. Unfortunately, few of these luminaries had much interest in or time for the intramural business of the organization, and it was also far from clear that they did much to increase the Club's visibility.

Some of these new board members did support Brower for a while, but others did not. Douglas quickly resigned, deciding that board membership was not a good use of his time, and Brooks and Stegner eventually abandoned Brower. But thanks to this recruiting strategem, Brower did barely manage to maintain a supportive majority on the board through most of the 1960s.

As Brower and the board struggled over various issues, three factions emerged. Brower's supporters were basically willing to give him a free hand and judge him by the Club's overall success, while a second faction had become disenchanted with him. Among this faction were old-guard types who wanted the Club to be primarily an outings organization, as it once had been, with conservation as a sideline. Others in this faction, such as Ansel Adams and Richard Leonard, had themselves been Young Turks who had favored turning the Club into primarily a conservation organization, but who now thought Brower was running away with the group and needed to be brought under control. And finally, in a third faction were people such as Ed Wayburn, Will Siri, George Marshall, and Phil Berry, who liked Brower's brand of conservation and the Club's evolution but agreed that he needed to be controlled.

Brower tended to think of those who were trying to rein him in as just being old-guard types. Some were, but many were not. Most of those who were disenchanted also wanted the Club, first and foremost, to be a conservation organization, and an aggressive one. But they wanted the elected board and officers to be in control.

Oral histories of Brower's critics,[1] however, reveal just how much a few board members really did want to go back to the old days, to the way the Club was prior to 1952, when outings were paramount. Ansel Adams had once urged a more aggressive approach, for instance, but by the 1960s he had come to identify with Francis Farquhar, an influential former president, who felt the organization "should be an elite club with a definite purpose [and should] stay with Sierra Nevada," for which it was named. Then honorary president of the Club, Farquhar had never agreed with the Club's 1952 decisions to grow and become a major force for conservation. And throughout the early 1960s, board members such as attorney and outings leader Bestor Robinson urged a more conciliatory approach in working with agencies. Richard Leonard, who had

been part of the Club's 1952 decisions to expand its numbers and purpose, now also came to see things more as Robinson did.

Fundamental questions did underlie the struggle. On one hand, the
board faced the question of what kind of organization the Sierra Club
should be: an outings organization with conservation interests or a conservation organization with an outings program. On the other hand was
the question of whether the Sierra Club was really a membership-
oriented organization or merely one that reflected the vision and the
personality of its executive director. And if the Sierra Club was primarily a conservation organization, what style should it have: one that was
assertive and hard hitting or one that was measured and kept a low profile? If it should be assertive and hard hitting, could it still do its homework, be accurate, and avoid impugning motives? And in any event,
could the Club behave this way and be well managed too?

As conservation director, I was pleased to see the Club convert itself
from an outdoor club into a conservation organization, and I wanted it
to be assertive and hard hitting. I saw no point in impugning motives,
however (and actually, Brower seldom did that); I believed that we
should do our homework (Brower used to urge that too) and that we
ought to be accurate (Brower was less careful about this). I also thought
the organization could be better managed and tried to do that within my
sphere, but Brower believed that inspiring people—and moving as fast
as he could—was the way to manage.

As the Club grappled with these issues, confusion abounded over
who held the executive powers of the organization. Was the executive
director the de facto chief executive officer (CEO), or did the volunteer
president fill this role? When Ed Wayburn first served as president
(1961–64), he tended to defer to the executive director as if the latter
held the power. Serving as president again in 1967–69, when tensions
with Brower came to a head, Wayburn acted as if the president held the
executive power.

The bylaws did not seem to resolve the question. They said the
president should "exercise general supervision over the affairs of the
club," but what did that mean when specific questions were at issue?
Indeed, it was not until the late 1970s that the board finally resolved
this question by making the executive director, me at the time, the
CEO.

In the 1960s, however, Brower felt that he already had inherent
executive powers as executive director and had the right to lead the

organization where he felt it needed to go. He felt compelled by the needs of the moment to pull the organization along—willing or not. In fact, he often failed to ask for permission, fearing that he might not get it.

As the 1960s wore on, Club presidents increasingly felt that Brower was going too far and needed to seek approval in advance for his major decisions. Brower opened field offices without permission and rushed forward with commitments to publish books before gaining the assent of the Publications Committee. Full-page advertisements appeared in major newspapers without the Club president even being consulted. And Brower never accepted limitations on his spending authority, finding ways to confuse the accounting department about how much he spent.

In many ways, Brower was growing faster in his grasp of the field than was his board. He traveled widely, meeting many prominent people concerned about a growing set of issues. He was seeing environmental problems in a wider perspective than were many on the board, and he wanted the Sierra Club to be in the forefront of meeting these challenges. He felt a sense of urgency to act and resented having to bring along a board that was not ready. He took chances and plunged ahead, ignoring restraints that the board tried to impose upon him. In his own oral history, Brower admits that "I led them on a merry chase. I felt that I had to—that there were a lot of things that had to be done, and if I took the risk, I would rather do it than not."

Brower also underwent a personality change. In his first decade as executive director, he had been much more pragmatic and attentive to detail. He had been willing to compromise. Early in my career, he cautioned me against wearing a hat that was too jaunty. When I wanted to denounce a weak plan for a North Cascades National Park put forth by the Kennedy administration, as discussed in chapter 3, he urged restraint, quoting our frequent ally Senator Richard Neuberger: "Let's get on a train that's going somewhere; we can get it to go farther later." He told me stories of how many national parks had begun on a small scale and gradually been expanded, thus making the case for incrementalism. He resented the belief of many rank-and-file activists that national parks were generally overdeveloped. Influenced perhaps by his time working for a concessionaire, The Yosemite Valley and Curry Company, he did not then think Yosemite Valley was being degraded by too much development. In fact, Ansel Adams had to push him in the late 1950s to do more to resist development in the valley. Adams wanted to roll back the level of development there and tried to resign from the board of directors in 1957 to force the Club to take a stronger stand.

Brower had decided not to fight the Glen Canyon Dam in order to assure the defeat of the dams proposed in Dinosaur National Monument. As he became concerned about too many rivers being dammed, he thought nuclear power might provide an alternate source of power for the West. Later he embraced a coal-fired power plant near the Grand Canyon, the Navajo plant, as an alternative to dams there. And he also went along with the Hooker Dam on the Gila River, as the price of getting a Central Arizona Project bill enacted that did not include dams in the Grand Canyon.

In time, he came to regret all of these compromises. We can only speculate about whether the victories at the time could have been won without them, but Brower saw that they did not turn out well in the end. His bitter experiences moved him to regard compromise with suspicion. Increasingly, he tended to take a harder line. But in doing so, Brower was becoming strident, Adams and Leonard felt; they called him "a shin kicker." Brower thus fell out with these onetime climbing associates of his. Increasingly preoccupied with the big picture and becoming apocalyptic in his outlook, Brower spent more time in New York working on books and making friends there, and less and less time at the headquarters in San Francisco managing the organization.

Things began to go wrong. The monthly magazine, the *Sierra Club Bulletin*, rarely came out on time. Annuals were not produced; the Club's handbook was not revised. Expensive pictorial books were often late in getting to stores for the crucial Christmas sales season. For a while, books were published without contracts being drawn up. And the Club's budget was strained as it poured more and more capital into publishing books and paying for heavy promotional efforts. Some charged that Brower had diverted money from the permanent fund, which was supposed to be "safely and securely invested," into capitalizing the books. As an investment, the books were neither safe nor secure, they averred.

And the Publications Committee, which was charged with overseeing the books program, felt that Brower evaded the controls it had established. He would commit major sums to book projects before gaining authorization. Once so much money had been committed, the committee had no option but to approve the books. The committee became increasingly alienated as it was confronted with one fait accompli after another.

Club membership was growing rapidly, however, almost doubling between 1966 and 1969, and the conservation campaigns, which I was managing as conservation director, were going well. I took up as much slack as I was allowed to and tried to keep the machinery running, but I had no role with regard to the lagging publications. I tried to interpret the board's desires to Brower and Brower's to the board and its officers. I walked a delicate line in trying to be loyal to Brower but also to serve the officers, in whom ultimate authority resided.

Over time, I came to be the one person toward the top whom everyone trusted. As the level of contention grew, I tried to stay out of the line of fire, and most were happy to spare me. In fact, I think that most of the board members wanted me to survive the strife. But it was like walking through a minefield. Club presidents turned to me, as their "staff," for advice in coping with Brower, but I was mindful that in fact I worked for Brower.

Brower trusted me with information that he did not want disclosed to Club officers, and I kept his trust, even though I felt he should have been sharing the information. I kept my own counsel, while both sides suspected that I sided with them. As much as I could, I focused on the conservation job to be done rather than on internal politics. I just waited for the agony to end.

Things came to a head in the years 1967 and 1968.[2] At board meeting after board meeting, Brower clashed with a growing number of board members and officers over various issues. Ed Wayburn was brought back as president, under the assumption that he was the only person who could handle Brower. Wayburn turned to me for guidance on parliamentary procedure and sought my advice on how to keep these contentious meetings from breaking down.

For a while, Wayburn thought he could keep relations with Brower from collapsing. Wayburn was firm, fair, and patient. He was confident that he could sort through the difficulties and keep things on an even keel. He began to think of himself as the key person in the organization. The meetings over which Wayburn presided, which were open to the public as always, were held in downtown San Francisco hotels in front of large audiences, who watched wide-eyed at the exchange of harsh charges. Bad feelings, which had been contained in private sessions of the board, now spilled into public wrangling, culminating in a May 1967 board meeting at which three board members presented an indictment of the executive director. Followers of each side in the audience would wildly applaud meeting speakers who gave voice to their views.

The board and Brower quarreled over finances too. Brower questioned figures compiled by controllers and resented the board's decision to make the controller directly accountable to it. Brower thought too much overhead was being assigned to the books program, making it look bad; his critics charged that he manipulated figures to make the books program look good.

After losing the Club's tax deductibility in 1966 owing to newspaper ads on issues before Congress (which the IRS found too blatant an attempt to influence legislation), Brower sought to have the newly organized Sierra Club Foundation—a sister organization that had been chartered in the mid-1950s and kept in readiness in case the IRS cracked down on the Club—underwrite capitalization of the book publishing program. It refused to do so, provoking Brower into refusing, in turn, to raise any money for the Foundation. Brower then came to believe that the Club's attorney, Gary Torre, was not fighting hard enough to regain the Club's tax deductibility. He told the IRS that Torre no longer represented the Club. President Ed Wayburn, in turn, countermanded that order.

Brower also disagreed with the board's decision to support siting a nuclear power plant at Diablo Canyon on the central California coast. This idea arose out of negotiations by Will Siri, when he was president, to keep such a plant out of the Nipomo Dunes, which were slated to be a state park. Brower's supporters on the board convinced him that the new site was unacceptable, and Brower began to criticize it.[3] When the issue was put before Club members for a vote in the spring of 1967, Brower put out an edition of the *Sierra Club Bulletin* without a statement supporting the board's position. (Siri, though, it should be said, did miss the deadline for submitting it.) This behavior outraged Brower's critics.

Even without the statement, Club members voted to support the board's position, and they did so again a year later on a similar ballot measure. Brower came to feel that the utility proposing the Diablo Canyon plant (Pacific Gas and Electric) was out to get him. I stayed out of this intramural fight, feeling that the board had to back up the commitments its president had made, though I regretted the loss of the alternate site.

In 1967, when Will Siri was still president, he and the Club treasurer, Charles Huestis (both climbers who had become friends on an Everest expedition), put forth a plan to send Brower to New York to run the publications program, with someone else—unspecified—to take over running things in San Francisco. Brower rejected that idea. Siri and Huestis asserted that the Club effectively had a negative net worth and that the finances were in desperate shape.

In May 1967, three board members—Richard Leonard, Ansel Adams, and Richard Sill—proposed that Brower be fired. Brower was charged with insubordination (violating orders of officers and acting against policy); neglect of his duties (being away from the office too much and failing to move business forward); and imperiling the finances of the Club by pushing it toward insolvency. Adams proposed that I be appointed as acting executive director instead. Former presidents of the Club also signed a joint letter critical of Brower.

But Brower learned in advance of this effort to oust him and leaked the story to a friendly columnist in San Francisco, who publicized it. This brought out Brower's supporters, causing the effort to fail. His critics also provided too little in the way of particulars to support their charges. At that meeting Wayburn was brought back as president, and I helped him put out a press release affirming the board's continuing confidence in Brower. But the issue did not go away, and the same points were argued again at meetings in the fall of 1967 and throughout 1968.

There were other sources of discontent, too. Some felt that Brower was trying to develop a cult of personality around himself and change the organization from being member-controlled to one that he dominated, by tactics such as pushing his friends to run for the board. Brower replied that he could not become a "nonperson." He felt that new members were pouring in because they were attracted by what he was doing.

His critics also claimed that Brower was extravagant in his personal spending. He had taken an apartment in New York City—at Club expense. Elsewhere, he stayed at first-class hotels and treated staff and visitors to expensive luncheons. Some thought he "double-dipped" in drawing up book contracts under which he was paid a fee for editing services—while he was already being paid for his full-time efforts on behalf of the Club. Brower was slow, too, in accounting for his reimbursable expenses and evasive in justifying his use of discretionary funds, which some sought to cut off.

In addition, Brower was compulsive about using certain techniques to publicize conservation aims, regardless of whether a better way might exist under the particular circumstances and regardless of who needed to be persuaded. He tended to run full-page newspaper ads in the *New York Times* and the *San Francisco Chronicle*, even though their readers might have had little influence on the members of Congress who needed to be convinced. He printed brochures for campaigns with little thought as to how they would be distributed; sometimes they sat in warehouses. And Brower thought that every campaign would benefit from having a book written about it. In this regard, means often became ends in his mind. Later even Brower admitted that he had become "addicted to books."

Brower also came to have an antagonistic relationship with the Sierra Club Council, an assembly of leaders from chapters around the country. While it lacked independent authority, it was influential and advised the board, largely on organizational questions. Brower sought to abolish the Council as a needless layer of bureaucracy that was trying to act like a second board of directors. The Council, in turn, sought to get rid of Brower—though Brower did retain a body of support in the Atlantic Chapter, which was centered in New York City, where he cultivated friends during his frequent stays. In general, the Council stood for more grassroots control of the Club and felt that Brower was centralizing control in himself.

During Wayburn's second stint as president (1967–69), he ordered Brower to clear with him all copy that would be printed in the *Sierra Club Bulletin*. Wayburn also insisted on approving each newspaper ad and its text. Brower felt these restrictions were unworkable and demeaning. He revived a onetime books newsletter to get around these restrictions so that he could publicize a new set of books on the Galapagos Islands, but his critics charged that he did so improperly.

Brower also wanted to launch the Club into the international arena. He used a special donation (which could be spent only in the United Kingdom) to open an office, hire staff, and charter a new branch there. Officers were even chosen. Board members felt they had never authorized this and were aghast. I was intrigued and amazed.

Brower also wanted to launch a new series of international books. At a special meeting in December 1968, the board told him he could not. But in mid-January 1969, Brower went ahead anyway, announcing a forthcoming series of a hundred new titles in newspaper ads that ran under the banner of "Earth National Park." Brower did even not try to get Wayburn's permission.

I knew in advance what Brower was planning to do. When Wayburn began to hear rumors, he quizzed me about them, but I felt I could not betray my boss. Wayburn knew something surprising was about to happen, though, and when the ads came out, he saw that his authority had been directly challenged. He thereupon suspended Brower's authority to spend Club funds. Ansel Adams felt that Brower "just went berserk" and that something had to be done. I felt that Brower was deliberately pushing things to a head to force a decision over whether he was in control or not. Wayburn, who agreed substantively with much that Brower was doing, had tried to salvage Brower's talents, but finally gave up. Brower wanted either to be given a free hand or to leave.

At a meeting of the board a few weeks later, in February 1969, Wayburn's actions were upheld. Brower then took a leave of absence to head a slate of candidates for election to the board of directors. He would try to build a board that would stand firmly behind him. I was given the title of chief of staff, with the powers to act as executive director. At this juncture, however, I was simply filling in for the absent Brower, who might return if his forces were to win in the coming election.

Both sides quickly organized themselves into competing slates of candidates for the board election in the spring of 1969. Brower's slate styled itself as the ABC slate (which variously stood for either "Aggressive Brower-Style Conservationists" or "Active, Bold, Constructive"). Its opponents, headed by Ansel Adams, called themselves the CMC slate ("Concerned Members for Conservation").

The board of directors rescinded previous campaign regulations, such as limits on spending. Flyers were put out, mass mailings were sent, and recriminations flew about the amounts being spent in the campaign. The issues were put squarely before the members for them to decide, and the press avidly covered the contest.

There were five candidates on each slate, and they campaigned at chapter meetings all over the country. Each slate put its case in stark terms that lingered in members' minds for many years and left confused expectations. Wallace Stegner supported the CMC slate, asserting that "in his grab for absolute power [Brower] . . . will wreck the Sierra Club";

he "had been bitten by the worm of power." The ABC slate charged that its opponents wanted the Club "to revert to its days as a society of 'companions of the trail'" and pledged themselves to an uncompromising program for "the total environment," implying that the other side was less committed to that goal. In reality, the survival of the Club was not in jeopardy, nor was it about to retreat from the field of activism. Both sides, however, felt that ultimate issues were at stake and acted as if Armageddon was at hand.

When the votes were counted in mid-April, the CMC slate had won decisively, with all of its candidates receiving more votes than Brower. Longtime members voted overwhelmingly against Brower, but even new members did so by a large margin. The winners interpreted their victory as a vote for membership control, not as a vote to back away from conservation. Others were not so sure.

Facing a new board now arrayed against him by a 10–5 margin, Brower submitted his resignation at the May 3, 1969, meeting, after seventeen years as executive director. If he had not resigned, he would have been fired.

When Brower left, I wrote him a letter expressing my admiration for his vision and saying that I had tried to be loyal to him and to all of those for whom I worked. I later learned that he appreciated receiving it. When he was elected to the board of directors some years later as a petition candidate (and under very different circumstances), he was quite supportive of me. We always remained on friendly terms.

In retrospect, Brower's very success in building a larger, more aggressive organization had undermined his ability to run it as a reflection of his own personality. During his term as executive director, the Club grew from 7,000 to nearly 70,000 members. There were now too many centers of power with people who wanted to be consulted, and popular culture was moving toward more collegial styles of management. Brower was no longer suited for the kind of organization that the Club had become. Moreover, it was no longer appropriate in a member-oriented organization to cater to the growing needs of his ego. He had ceased to be a good fit.

The staff had been polarized by the conflict. The board had told us to stay out of Club politics, but most of those who worked with Brower in the *Bulletin* and book departments supported him, as did two field representatives who were close to him, Gary Soucie in the East and Jeff

Ingram in the Southwest. I stayed out of the battle, as did our field representative in the Northwest, Brock Evans, and our Washington, D.C., lobbyist, Lloyd Tupling, both of whom I had hired. Staffs of the accounting, membership, and outings programs also stayed on the sidelines. Soon after Brower resigned, those who had supported Brower either left voluntarily or were let go.

I stayed out of the battle for a number of reasons. First, we had been told to by the board. And I did not believe that there was much danger of the Club retreating to the old days as an outings-only organization. There were those who wanted to, but they were in a shrinking minority. The centrist board members, with whom I worked most closely—such as Ed Wayburn, Will Siri, Phil Berry, and George Marshall—certainly did not want to retreat. Through the 1960s, the board had expressed little opposition to the hard-hitting approach we were taking on conservation. And our growing membership did not want to go backward. Council delegates may have been concerned about grassroots control, but they were not speaking out against our stands on the redwoods or the Grand Canyon. And the popular mood was certainly not heading in that direction: public opinion surveys showed rising support for the stands we were taking.

Moreover, I was too steeped in legal realities to believe that it made sense to challenge the authority of a board of directors. While I often agreed with Brower's aims in conservation, I did not agree that it made sense to defy the authority of the board. Instead, I thought one should try to cultivate its support and earn its trust. I would soon learn that was not easy.

Ultimately, it may actually have been fortunate that there were issues over Brower's behavior. He became the lightning rod for longtime members' anxieties over change. With the Club changing so rapidly in response to changing times, it is likely that some catharsis would have occurred anyway. As it happened, the issues became personalized, and pent-up pressures found release in debate over them. But the transformation of the organization was never in jeopardy.

By 1969, the Sierra Club had firmly shifted from being an outings organization (with an interest in conservation) into a conservation organization (with an outings program), and it was on the eve of becoming an environmental organization. It had also transformed itself through the 1960s into a national organization with international interests, instead of an organization focused on the state of California. Whereas once volunteers ran everything, the organization's volunteer leadership was now struggling to define its relationship and share leadership with a substantial complement of staff. The Sierra Club was quickly becoming one of the most complicated and far reaching of all environmental organizations.

7 *Taking Over as Enviromentalism Takes Off*

My role would evolve and change as a new wave of interest in our cause emerged, with productive results, over the next few years. While Brower was now out, the political infighting that had arisen around him continued. Every elected office in the Club was contested when the new board of fifteen directors convened in May 1969. But the faction allied with Brower could not muster more than six votes for any position. Quite surprisingly, Ed Wayburn decided that he wanted to run for president again, but Phil Berry defeated him on an 8–6 vote. Even though Wayburn had run on the anti-Brower CMC ticket, he lost; the new anti-Brower faction preferred a fresh face. Wayburn was made vice president instead, with Ray Sherwin elected as secretary. Chuck Huestis was made treasurer, and Dick Sill was chosen as the fifth officer on the executive committee.[1]

My tenure as acting executive director expired at this meeting. The new board was clearly happy to rely on me to hold things together for a while, but they were not sure they wanted me to be the new executive director. The Brower faction was in favor of it, but the reigning CMC faction was undecided. The upshot was that I held three titles for a time. They called me chief of staff to suggest that my role was limited to managing the staff, not the organization. But I was also given the title of acting executive director so that someone would have the needed authority to carry on business. And I still held the title of conservation director.

It was not even clear that the members of the CMC faction still wanted there to be an executive director. It was seen as the position that

Brower had shaped, and they were distrustful of the power reposed in it. Oddly enough, I was seen both as someone who was not "Brower-like enough" (that is, not sharply outspoken) and as someone who needed to be kept from becoming too powerful. The newly empowered CMC faction was intent on taking back control of "their Club" from the staff; they wanted me to be merely a mechanic to keep things going along the lines they indicated.

The Brower Aftermath

As the new Club president, Phil Berry approached the office much in the manner of his predecessor, Ed Wayburn. He acted as if he were the CEO and the Club's chief spokesman. Berry had grown up on Club outings and was a self-assured young trial attorney doing defense work in his father's firm in Oakland. But Berry's strong assertion of control did not cause me to retreat into the wings. Through managing the Club's conservation programs, I was on top of the flow of information and was in a position to speak out. By this time, I was not about to acquiesce in the notion that I was a lesser figure.

Management of the Club's affairs was in a kind of receivership at that time, however. Members of the new executive committee felt that they had to meet every two weeks to get on top of the Club's internal affairs. Payment of every substantial bill now had to be approved by them. Vacant positions could be filled only by their authorization, and they insisted on interviewing finalists for all positions of consequence. This intense focus on internal management was happening at the very time that a new wave of interest in the environment was bursting forth in the larger world, and I was trying to keep abreast of that too.

Under my three job titles, I struggled to keep the ship afloat. Brower had run annual deficits through most of the 1960s, and by the end of the 1969 fiscal year, the Club's net worth was less than half of what it had been just three years earlier. We no longer had enough cash coming in to pay our bills on time.

Many on the staff had departed when Brower did. At least that kept payroll costs down. But there was no one to put out the *Sierra Club Bulletin* each month. The book publishing staff had left too, as had the personal assistants to the executive director. Fortunately, the membership, accounting, and outings staffs were still in place, as were most of the conservation staff. Before long, though, the two field representatives closest to Brower—Jeff Ingram and Gary Soucie—left too. I was authorized to hire an assistant to help me direct the conservation program, and I took on Jonathan Ela, who later became our first field organizer in the Midwest.

I had to make quick hiring decisions to rebuild the depleted staff. I didn't have the luxury of long searches. Julie Cannon, whom I hired to put out a weekly newsletter on conservation, had to fill in to get the magazine out. To manage the books program, which was moved to New York and charged with putting out about a half dozen books a year, I hired John Mitchell, a journalist then covering the environmental beat for *Newsweek*, whom I had gotten to know in the campaign for the Redwood National Park.

Many observers in the media expected that the Sierra Club would collapse without Brower. They had come to identify the Club so closely with him that they could not imagine the organization "making it" in his absence.

What ultimately saved us was the incredible growth in the Club's membership. When I took over as acting executive director in February 1969, the Club had 79,000 members. By the end of 1971, we had 131,000. Our membership soared by 23 percent in 1969, by nearly 30 percent in 1970, and by 23 percent again in 1971. Even though revenues from book publishing collapsed for a while, revenues from membership more than doubled in these years, which kept us afloat.

The Club's membership had been increasing throughout the 1960s, but it grew even more after Brower left. It is hard to know exactly why growth in the past had occurred. At that time, the Sierra Club did not have an organized program to solicit members. Most new members came in "over the transom"—that is, interested people wrote to us asking to join. Only a small share were solicited by existing members.

But there is no doubt that this new surge in our membership was caused in large measure by the explosion in media coverage of all things environmental in the months leading up to the first Earth Day, on April 22, 1970. This exploding coverage created a new market for environmentalism, and in this market, the Sierra Club was already a well-established brand. I did everything possible to keep our "brand name" before the public; we wanted to have a high profile and be mentioned in the press. We wanted to make news.

Because Dave Brower had become such a divisive figure in the Club, I decided to change the imagery that had become associated with him.

I switched our advertising agency to the firm of Pritikin and Gibbons.[2] Instead of using scenes from Brower's books on our letterhead, I reinstated use of our traditional seals, though reinterpreted in a more contemporary vein; I even replaced Brower's favorite type styles. I hired new designers to restyle all of our printed materials. Instead of quoting Brower in our membership brochure, I selected a quote from Wallace Stegner about wilderness and the "geography of hope."

To fill the void caused by Brower's departure, I decided that we should venerate our founder, John Muir, instead. At the bottom of our letterhead I put a quote from him that hinted at an ecological perspective: "When we try to pick out anything by itself, we find it hitched to everything else in the Universe." We began to celebrate Muir's birthday each year and put photos of him on our walls. The officers welcomed these changes.

I worked with Berry and the executive committee to shift the Club's program away from books and toward conservation. We started a weekly newsletter on conservation for our leaders around the country (the *National News Report*, or NNR). We connected our various offices by teletype machines to facilitate instant printed communication. We restyled the magazine, putting it on a regular schedule, providing more background in stories, and introducing color on a regular basis. We started a public-service advertising program to obtain free space in millions of issues of commercial magazines. In the books program, we changed the emphasis from coffee-table books to books that would be of use to activists, starting a new line of topical "battle books."

Before long, I was no longer referred to as the chief of staff. And by the end of my first year in the job, I was no longer the "acting" executive director. I had been made the executive director. And it was just in time—because the Club was on the verge of being completely transformed.

Soon after the new board took over in 1969, it acted to quell doubts about its resolve. Acting unanimously, it proclaimed: "The Sierra Club will pursue conservation objectives without pause, with full determination, and with all of the resources at its command." Berry and I were united in our determination that the Sierra Club was not going to retreat or shy away from controversy. We were going to seize the opportunity and meet rising public expectations.

We enmeshed ourselves in a whirlwind of activity whose breadth and pace was unlike anything before. In the first six weeks after I took over that May, the Club testified nineteen times before various committees of Congress on pending bills. We held press conferences, issued frequent statements to the press, and made speeches. Again and again, our members were urged to write to their legislators.

The Club's Atlantic Chapter in New York invited me to its annual banquet to be introduced. Justice William O. Douglas of the Supreme Court was the guest speaker. I sat in the front row expecting a word of encouragement. After all, my first work for the Sierra Club, writing a brochure on the threatened Minam River valley of eastern Oregon, had been at his behest. He had helped conceive the idea of a field organizer in the Northwest, and I was the first to hold that job. I had known him on the Sierra Club's board, and I had met with him once at the Double K dude ranch west of Yakima, Washington. Instead I listened to him warn the Sierra Club against "going soft" without Brower—knowing that I was now in charge and sitting in front of him. I felt let down, even insulted. His forebodings may have had more to do with the policies he anticipated from the Nixon administration, however, which had been in office only a few months.

When Richard Nixon was elected, some old hands in the conservation movement were filled with pessimism as they anticipated attacks on conservation. Stewart Brandborg of the Wilderness Society counseled us all to "circle the wagons" and hunker down defensively. He felt that the progress we had been making in the 1960s was about to end.

Nixon's term certainly began inauspiciously. In late January, oil spewed from a broken drilling rig in the Santa Barbara channel, an area we had warned about earlier. Oil and other waste so polluted the Cuyahoga River in Ohio that it caught fire in June. Pipes were being stockpiled in Alaska to build a new oil line from the Prudhoe Bay petroleum discoveries, with little concern for the dangers posed by permafrost. And Alaska's cheerleader for the new oil fields, Governor Walter Hickel, was to be Nixon's new interior secretary.

But this was not what the public wanted to hear and see. Scenes of oil boiling up in the Santa Barbara channel alarmed them. When another blowout of an oil well occurred off Louisiana's coast, Berry and I went out in a helicopter to see it firsthand and voice our concerns. When Chevron's tankers ran aground in San Francisco Bay, we organized a picket line in front of the company's offices, which were right across the street from ours; I simply pointed out the window to show our picketers where to march.

Fearing that foxes were being enlisted to guard the henhouse, we organized a massive campaign against Hickel's appointment as secretary of the interior. A detective we hired discovered that Hickel had oil holdings himself, giving him a direct conflict of interest, which columnist Drew Pearson quickly publicized. The confirmation fight in the Senate Interior Committee became so bruising that Hickel changed his stance and pledged to protect the environment. He changed so much that he lasted less than two years in the Nixon administration. In any case, the process of working over a nominee in this fashion became known as "Hickelizing."

As the year progressed, we waged a spirited campaign against the National Timber Supply Bill, which I describe later in this chapter. We were also among the few groups to lend strong support to the enactment of the pathbreaking National Environmental Policy Act (NEPA), which committed the federal government to giving serious attention to the environment as a matter of policy. Even though I gave the lead testimony for the supporting groups before the Senate Interior Committee, I must confess that even I did not foresee the importance of its requirement that agencies document the impact of their proposals on the environment and inform the public of their findings. In future years, however, the Sierra Club would make repeated use of that provision in court.

In 1969 I also persuaded the Sierra Club to sue Walt Disney Productions and the Forest Service to stop them from developing a massive winter resort in the Sierra Nevada in what was then a wildlife refuge. In one of the first environmental lawsuits instigated as part of a coordinated campaign, we won a preliminary injunction against the project in July of that year. The case, filed by San Francisco attorney Lee Selna,[3] eventually reached the Supreme Court and liberalized the rules of standing, which determine who can bring suits. In a dissent, Justice Douglas also suggested that suits could be filed on behalf of non-humans. In pursuit of this idea, the Club subsequently sued successfully on behalf of the palila, an endangered bird in Hawaii, in a case that established the precedent that habitat destruction was a kind of taking under the Endangered Species Act.[4]

Other lawsuits were filed on behalf of the Club that year, in Colorado, Maryland, and New York,[5] and plans were laid for more—especially in Alaska. Over time, most met with success. For the first time, federal courts were willing to question what agencies were proposing. They no longer seemed to be stymied by the "presumption of administrative regularity"—the presumption that agencies were operating properly and lawfully.

In the late 1960s, the California legislature also began to be receptive to our message. The Club's lobbyist in Sacramento, John Zierold, was very skillful and had good access to key legislators. The Club began to make breakthroughs in Sacramento before it did in Washington, D.C., and I occasionally went there to testify.

In 1969 negotiations were deadlocked between California and Nevada over how to set up an interstate compact to better protect the Lake Tahoe Basin. This was a key issue for the Club at the time. California wanted mechanisms in place that would allow it to be stricter than Nevada, and Zierold told me he was concerned that negotiations might collapse. In response, I suggested that California set up a commission of its own within the larger bi-state compact. Zierold put the suggestion forward and to my surprise, it was the idea that broke the impasse, and it was adopted for a number of years.

Earth Day, 1970

The first Earth Day, in the spring of 1970, further galvanized the public mood. It was designed to send a message to the Nixon administration and others that the public now demanded a more enlightened approach to environmental affairs. With the encouragement of Senator Gaylord Nelson of Wisconsin, graduate student Denis Hayes took the lead in coordinating the organizing effort, which included activities at campuses and in city centers all over the country. Campus organizers in particular planned demonstrations and teach-ins like those that had been held in the 1960s around other causes.

The Sierra Club wasn't sure it had much expertise when it came to mass demonstrations, and we did not particularly identify with the counterculture that was heavily involved in Earth Day organizing. We believed more in mastering the arts of political persuasion than in demonstrating to show our discontent.

We had a suspicion, nonetheless, that this event might be important, so we gave our local chapters leeway to participate and produced materials that would appeal to the Earth Day audience. We hastily stitched together a new book of hard-hitting essays, *Ecotactics*, for which I wrote the foreword.[6] It sold more than 400,000 copies. Some of our activists on college campuses, such as Doug Scott, then a graduate student at the University of Michigan, became leaders in Earth Day organizing.

A sense of rising expectations infused our work through the latter part of 1969. We felt that a strong tide was suddenly beginning to flow in our direction. January 1970 broke with a drumbeat of activities under way. While April 22 was to be Earth Day itself, events were planned every week through May. In February I attended a huge event in a field house at Ann Arbor, Michigan, where thousands of students applauded wildly for the most provocative speaker. Walter Reuther, the head of the United Auto Workers union, was actually booed because he sounded so tame.

Across the country, student demonstrators competed to devise stunts to attract attention. Cars were buried, polluters were trashed, and pro-environment banners were hung high from buildings. Crowds marched down Fifth Avenue in New York and gathered on the Mall in Washington, D.C.

I remember addressing a crowd of 3,000 as the keynoter at the University of Minnesota on Earth Day itself. I tried to get the students to think about how to make a difference over the long run, urging them to make a lifelong commitment to environmental work. While I was well received, I felt they might have liked a "fire breather" even more. When I participated in teach-ins, many students acted as if the Sierra Club could wave a magic wand to make all the bad things go away. They seemed to think achieving a healthy environment was simply a matter of having the will and taking a stand rather than entailing difficult and sustained effort over many years.

In mid-May, I gave my last Earth Day speech of that year at Tulane University. Suddenly, it was all over. The turnout there was sparse. Hostilities in Vietnam had intensified, the United States had invaded Cambodia, and students at Kent State University had been shot and killed by National Guardsmen. In light of these arresting events, students' attention turned back to the war.

But Earth Day proved to be more than simply a series of student demonstrations. Its effect was not fleeting. Somehow, almost miraculously, Earth Day catalyzed the formation of a new movement—the environmental movement. Suddenly our concerns expanded across the entire spectrum of issues affecting the environment. Whereas we once had been solely focused on conserving nature, now we were also concerned with pollution, public health, population growth, land use, energy, transportation policy, and almost any other issue touching even remotely upon the environment. Almost overnight, our agenda grew a hundredfold.[7] The new environmental movement differed from the old conservation movement in its breadth, confidence, and holistic nature. It seemed more open to new ideas, evolved more quickly, and addressed human concerns more directly.

Not only did a new consensus emerge about the movement's agenda, a new philosophy and approach emerged almost overnight too. In short order, networks spread that enunciated a new basis for thinking about our habitat on this planet. While much of the thinking was sound, sometimes it stooped to trivia. I remember how amazed I was by the number of people who suddenly claimed to have all the answers. While I was struggling to keep up, others had just learned new norms and told me so in no uncertain terms. Recycling was important, and suddenly everybody was doing it. First we couldn't use colored paper napkins anymore; then that had been superseded and we couldn't use paper napkins at all—only cloth ones were acceptable.

And, finally, public opinion shifted with Earth Day. The huge amount of publicity that the media gave to Earth Day increased public support for environmental protection to a new level. Now a majority of the public felt that the pollution around them was serious and should get attention from the government. One observer declared: "A miracle of public opinion has been the unprecedented speed and urgency with which ecological issues have burst into American consciousness. Alarm about the environment sprang from nowhere to major proportions in a few short years."[8] While public opinion would fluctuate over the ensuing years, thereafter environmental protection always enjoyed majority support. We were now on the popular side of the issue.

To some extent, the new environmental movement became so dominant that it eclipsed the older conservation movement and the splits within it. The distinctions once so important, between the Pinchot and Muir wings (that is, the utilitarian and nonutilitarian wings), no longer seemed very important, though they didn't go away. Divisions emerged along new lines, however.

It soon became evident that the new ecology centers had a different analysis of the problem than did the Sierra Club. Indeed, our whole idea of how to work effectively was completely different. Some in the movement, particularly on college campuses, were not interested in using public policy to effect change. They regarded such approaches as "power strategies." Instead, they wanted to change the "inner person" and persuade people to choose simpler lifestyles and to consume less. Their mantra was "reduce, reuse, and recycle." While we felt society would benefit from such steps, we did not consider them sufficient. The powerful who were polluting needed to be confronted with the power of government, not just with hit-or-miss voluntary action.

Most of the youthful protesters disappeared from public view in time. But a few continued to use direct-action techniques on issues related to nuclear testing and nuclear power. They organized in groups like the Clamshell Alliance, which used civil disobedience and other forms of protest to oppose a proposed nuclear plant at Seabrook, New Hampshire. The protesters typically addressed less tractable issues and operated through loose networks under consensus decision making. Most of us working on public policy, though, had little contact with them.

While David Brower had promised when he left the Sierra Club that he would not set up a "splinter group" that would compete with the Club, in the fall of 1969 he did just that. The group was called Friends of the Earth, and a few of the Club's former employees joined its staff. While many of its positions were similar to those of the Sierra Club, it tried to champion avant-garde issues as well, such as genetic engineering. Friends of the Earth enjoyed modest success in the United States and opened some offices abroad, but in due course Brower had a falling-out with it too.

Many other new groups came into existence in the wake of Earth Day. Most notable was the Natural Resources Defense Council, with which the Club has subsequently been closely aligned on many issues.

New Directions

In the face of changing times and new competition, Phil Berry and I both decided that the Sierra Club should position itself as a strong player. We would take on all of the new issues, use all of the latest tools, and attract as much support as we could. We would work actively to flesh out our organization throughout the country. We would assume a high profile and take risks. In this new time, we would seek to become the best-known and most productive environmental group working on public policy.

Not all of the old-line conservation organizations reacted in this fashion. In fact, at first, none of the others did. Over time, the National Wildlife Federation and the National Audubon Society cloaked themselves in the mantle of environmentalism, but neither did it with the relish and commitment that we did; conservation issues remained their focus. Some groups, such as the Izaak Walton League, never embraced the new issues and thus never grew. Though many of the new groups came to assume important roles in the environmental movement, the Sierra Club, more than any other, became synonymous with aggressive, pragmatic environmentalism.

In retrospect, it seems amazing that both Berry and I thought rising to the challenge in this way was the thing to do. If we had reacted differently, the Sierra Club might have stumbled and not gone forward. Indeed, there were those in the old-guard CMC faction who hoped that Brower's ouster meant that the Club would return to its earlier days as an outings-focused organization. They chose Berry as the new face for their hopes. But he, as well as his successor Ray Sherwin, had no interest in this quest. Indeed, Berry, Sherwin, and I all wanted to show that those ambitions would not be realized. Berry, in particular, wanted to disprove Brower's charge that the Club would go backward without him. If Berry had not brought the board of directors along, I could not have done it alone. That we agreed on where to go was fortunate for the cause and, indeed, society.

The new winds unleashed by Earth Day brought both opportunities and perils. Various firms wanted to associate their products with the newly popular cause and with the Sierra Club. The Club did license its name to a series of decorative plates that celebrated endangered species, a very lucrative deal that helped the Club's bottom line at a critical time.

Another firm wanted the Club to do a weekly radio program on "ecology" (not on the science, but on environmental issues). They would sponsor the program and air their commercials at breaks. At first this sounded appealing, particularly since the sponsor's product was a cleansing product. But then we began to wonder whether the factory in upstate New York where the product was manufactured was also clean, and we discovered that the state had cited it for water pollution violations. The company said it was willing to sign an agreement with the state to quickly get into compliance, which was encouraging. Then someone asked about the pollution that might be produced in obtaining the raw materials for this factory. The whole project raised questions about how far we could reasonably pursue our scruples.

Ultimately, we decided to proceed, but the day before I was set to sign the contract for the radio program, the Food and Drug Administration announced that it was citing the company for selling a product that the agency thought posed a risk of cancer to newborn babies. Thereupon, the firm withdrew the product from the market (later to reformulate it). Needless to say, I didn't sign the contract. Our association would have been a public relations disaster. The experience opened our eyes to the many pitfalls hidden in commercial proposals of this sort, and the Club's officers became increasingly gun-shy with respect to them.

With the public demanding action, Congress also now began to embrace the environmental agenda. And not only did Congress begin to change with the times, so also did the administration of President Richard Nixon. Nixon feared that he would have to face Senator Edmund Muskie of Maine as his opponent in the 1972 election. Like Senator Jackson, Muskie was a champion of the environmental cause. For some years he had been trying, as the chairman of the Commerce Committee, to pass strong legislation to curb air and water pollution.

So that Muskie would not be the only candidate to benefit from identifying with this cause, Nixon decided to send a special message on the environment to Congress in February 1970. By the end of the year, he had set up the Environmental Protection Agency by executive order. He salted his administration with a number of Republicans who had real environmental credentials, such as Russell Train, the chairman of his Council on Environmental Quality, a man I had known from his years at the Conservation Foundation.[9]

The first sign that things were changing in Congress occurred in the House of Representatives in February 1970. Since late in the fall, it had become clear that the timber industry was soon going to make a major push to gain approval for its National Timber Supply Bill, legislation designed to facilitate ramping up timber sales in the national forests by earmarking their proceeds to support expansion of the timber sales program. We thought the existing program was already destroying too many roadless areas and were fearful that more areas would be lost to an enlarged program. In December 1969 I had written an article in *The New Republic* criticizing the legislation.[10] We cobbled together a coalition of eight groups to fight the bill, including the Wilderness Society, the National Audubon Society, Friends of the Earth, and Trout Unlimited. I put Brock Evans from our Northwest office in charge of our campaign; the coalition quickly accepted him as its leader, and all of the groups sent staff to the Hill to work on the campaign.

We enlisted the doughty Representative John Dingell, Democrat of Michigan, to head up our forces in Congress. He provided space for us to set up an operations room in the Rayburn House Office Building. Teams lobbied every member of the House, reporting back on the inclination of each. Assignments were handed out to increase pressure in districts where it was needed. One hundred and fifty thousand letters and wires from concerned constituents poured into Congress within a few weeks.

When its proponents tried to bring the bill to the floor early in February, they had to withdraw it for lack of support. Finally, on February 23, they tried again, but their move was rejected by an overwhelming vote of 228 to 150. The bill was not even sent back to committee, because neither the Interior Committee chair nor the Agriculture Committee chair would support it. Despite pressure from the National Forest Products Association and the National Association of Home Builders, the Nixon administration withheld its support too. We began the new environmental era with a resounding victory.

The method by which we lobbied on the National Timber Supply Bill was typical of much of our efforts. We identified which members of Congress were committed to us, opposed to us, leaning our way, leaning against us, or undecided. We focused on moving those leaning our way into the committed column; moving the undecideds into leaning our way; and moving those leaning against us into the undecided column. These were the swing votes, and we concentrated on asking Club members in their districts to write to their representatives in Congress. Often our ranks there were thin, and our few members there heard from us often.

Following this fight, I thought we needed to divert the attention of the timber industry away from the national forests. So I had our forester, Gordon Robinson, work with Senator Lee Metcalf, a Democrat from Montana, to develop a bill that would impose a regulatory framework on private, industrial forest lands. I wanted to draw off some of the industry's energy into opposing this legislation, which they would bitterly resist.

In 1971 Metcalf introduced a bill that would have allowed logging only under state supervision and under plans drawn by professional foresters. This bill was basically a replay of one introduced in 1920 by Senator Arthur Capper of Kansas and championed by Forest Service founder Gifford Pinchot. While the bill did not go anywhere, field hearings were held on it, drawing industry opposition. I sent Robinson to testify at one in the South. This was our first effort to change the politics affecting national forest issues, with the industry at least on notice that they were no longer going to have a free hand in controlling the agenda on forest issues.

A few months after our clash over the Timber Supply Act, the Sierra Club was in the midst of another campaign in Congress, but on a very different issue. Since 1967 the Club had opposed development of civilian aircraft that would produce sonic booms audible at the surface of the earth. By 1970 Congress was being urged to provide federal subsidies for Boeing's development of a civilian supersonic aircraft, the SST, for the Department of Transportation.

Laurence I. Moss, an engineer and MIT graduate who then held a position at the National Academy of Engineering and was on the Club's board, had served as a White House fellow in 1968, at which time he was assigned to the Department of Transportation. In that role, he made contacts with important members of Congress. He also came to have a very negative view of the proposed SST.

In the spring of 1970, Moss took the lead in getting staff from the offices of a number of the members of Congress who opposed the SST (such as Senators William Proxmire and Clifford Case, and Representatives Henry Reuss and Sidney Yates) to meet with staff of the Club and Friends of the Earth in Washington, D.C. They decided to form the Coalition Against the SST, which soon included fourteen organizations. This was a new type of coalition in that it included not only environmental groups but other groups as well, such as the Consumer Federation of America and the Federation of American Scientists. Arthur Godfrey served as its honorary chairman.

Shortly before Earth Day, the coalition announced to the world that it intended to kill funding for the SST. It called the SST a technology out of control, one that would "bombard millions with ear-splitting shock waves, cause unprecedented airport noise, cause heavy discharge of pollutants, and could cause possible climate changes."

I helped Lloyd Tupling, who then ran our Washington, D.C., office (and represented us in the coalition), distribute the coalition's press release to the national media. Neither the *New York Times* nor the *Washington Post* considered our effort to be the least bit newsworthy, though. The SST looked unstoppable. But within fourteen months, it was dead. The media itself had not yet learned how quickly things were changing.

In mid-May, Senator Proxmire held a hearing to showcase revelations by a former White House expert, Richard Garwin, who had evaluated the

SST. Revealing the contents of his report, which had been suppressed, he concluded that the technology to make the SST "economically and environmentally acceptable . . . did not yet exist." The biggest problem was the excessive noise its engines would make before takeoff. After the publicity the coalition gave to Garwin's testimony, the House was able to muster only the slimmest majority to continue funding for the project.

To cast further light on the shaky underpinnings of the project, the coalition hit upon the idea of asking a panel of fifteen prestigious economists, representing a full spectrum of views, for their thoughts on the proposal to subsidize the SST. All but one opposed it. Other opposition was mobilized, including the association representing the operators of airports across the country. The media finally began to cover the issue seriously, and Congress began to hear from constituents.

When in December the issue finally was brought before the Senate in a lame-duck session, funding for the SST went down to defeat by a margin of 52 to 41, notwithstanding the best efforts of Senators Henry Jackson and Warren Magnuson. These senators favored the project because Boeing, which would have built it, was headquartered in their state of Washington. Despite efforts in the ensuing months to keep it going, the project sputtered to an end.

The campaign against the SST gave the new environmental movement confidence that it could win not only on traditional issues but on the new "environmental" ones as well. The subject matter might be different and took time to master; new networks of expert advisors would need to be cultivated. But the mechanics of many of the ensuing environmental campaigns were the same.

The 91st Congress acted affirmatively to support the environmental agenda again and again. Among its conservation measures, it authorized three new national seashores or lakeshores, Gulf Islands (Mississippi), Sleeping Bear Dunes (Michigan), and Apostle Islands (Wisconsin); one new national park, Voyageurs, in Minnesota; and one new national monument, Florissant, in Colorado. Local Club activists had sought them all and persuaded their congressional delegations to push for them. They took me to see each of these treasures. I also took part in meetings at which Senator Jackson handed out assignments to environmental leaders to line up various senators' support for increasing the Land and Water Conservation Fund to $300 million.

Congress also added a number of units to the National Wilderness Preservation System: Ventana Wilderness and Desolation Wilderness in California, and Mount Baldy in Arizona (all Forest Service units), as well as wilderness within twenty-three units of the system of national wildlife refuges.

By the end of the year, buoyed by the popular euphoria over environmental action, Muskie had succeeded in having Congress enact the strongest federal law ever passed to clean up the nation's air: the Clean Air Act of 1970. After having been stalled in prior Congresses, it was now passed with virtually no opposition. It required automakers to cut their emissions by 90 percent in five years, it obliged those who would build new sources of industrial pollution to use the best available control technology, it directed EPA to establish national standards for ambient air quality to protect health and property (none had been established by the states under the ineffectual 1967 Clean Air Act), and it directed the states to develop plans to implement the goals of the act. While arguments over it would continue for years, the Clean Air Act of 1970 set the benchmark for what should happen across the land to protect our air. The Sierra Club, though not yet active on clean air issues, would join the cause in future years.

Arguments continued in 1970 over the construction of a pipeline to transport oil in Alaska across the North Slope. The U.S. Geological Survey pointed to the dangers of melting permafrost if a line full of hot oil were to be buried along the proposed route. Two injunctions barred the pipeline's way—one resulting from a case brought by the Wilderness Society, using the provision of the new National Environmental Policy Act calling for an environmental impact statement (EIS). No EIS had been prepared for the pipeline as such, nor were there answers yet about how to deal with the permafrost issue. The Sierra Club was not a party to that suit, though it had been preparing one of its own before the Wilderness Society, which did not have local chapter leaders to confer with, beat us to the courthouse door.

I decided that I needed to see the area firsthand to best understand the issues. In July 1970, my wife and I flew to Alaska and to the North Slope. The Bureau of Land Management (BLM) flew us around in a light plane, landing at various sites where preparations for construction were under way. Notwithstanding the absence of final permits, huge stacks of the four-foot-wide pipe were already stockpiled along the route. The pipe had been brought in over a winter snow road, which was already deteriorating in the summer sun. Fleets of heavy earth-moving equipment were lined up ready to go. The oil companies were acting as if this were going to be another Oklahoma land rush. They wanted to push ahead without delay—in the absence of environmental planning.

On the trip, we experienced the magnificence of Alaska's scenery and space, and I had no trouble agreeing with the Club's commitment to making protection of this place a top priority.

We also had the pleasure of visiting Alaska's native peoples. When our plane landed at Anaktuvuk Pass in the Brooks Range, the children of the Inuit village there flocked around it and took Maxine happily by the hand to escort her into their village. We were treated like rare visitors from another world who had descended into theirs. An elder even told me that as a boy he had met the explorer Roald Amundsen when he had come through the area. We were shown new frame houses, built by the Bureau of Indian Affairs, which stood exposed to the wind and weather, and then were taken into more-sensible traditional houses, which were built into the ground to keep the villagers warm. We could see how their lives were already changing and knew they would change even more with the advent of oil development. We wondered whether anyone had asked them what they wanted.

The Sierra Club began to file more lawsuits in 1970 on a variety of issues. One contested long-term timber sales in southeast Alaska. Another helped in an effort to prevent a freeway from being built through Overton Park in Memphis, Tennessee. A third concerned DDT: as an outgrowth of a petition to the secretary of agriculture to cancel the registration of DDT for use on crops, the Club joined in a lawsuit in which a federal judge ordered the secretary to respond. (In the future, the Club would be part of further legal efforts to end the use of DDT.)

Part of the compromise permitting the Wilderness Act to go forward in the House of Representatives in 1963–64 was an agreement to conduct an in-depth study of the public land laws. Finally, in late June 1970, that report was released by the Public Land Law Review Commission. This commission had been at work since 1964 and was charged with helping to guide Congress in determining the future of public lands, particularly those under the purview of the BLM. Interior Committee Chairman Wayne Aspinall of Colorado was the political architect of this commission, and its work bore his imprint.

While the commission's massive report did call for retaining the bulk of these lands in federal ownership, it also called for replacing the concept of multiple use with the concept of "dominant use"—that is, frankly setting aside many areas for grazing, mining, or timbering as their principal use. Environmental concerns would get short shrift by law. There was much to trouble us otherwise in this report. I remember studying it and typing my notes in the back of a rented Volkswagen van as my wife drove us and our daughter Rosemary to a conference on that topic in Wyoming. Both Phil Berry and I wrote articles on the report for the *Sierra Club Bulletin*.[11] Over the next half dozen years, the future of BLM lands became a major concern of the Club.

The "Earth Day years" of 1969 and 1970 turned out quite differently than some expected. The Sierra Club did not fall apart despite David Brower's departure; in fact, it thrived. I did not turn into a caretaker but became a full-fledged executive director. Our cause did not go into decline but mushroomed and transformed itself into a new movement. And the government responded with alacrity, setting up new institutions and programs. This turnabout was simply breathtaking. And there was much more to come.

8　*More Contentious Times*

Once the spate of Earth Day 1970 events had run their course, media coverage of environmental issues dropped sharply. While some newspapers had hired environmental reporters, many treated the issue as a passing fad. As coverage diminished, "the environment" fell from the position it held briefly as the most pressing issue in public opinion polls, though it continued to draw strong levels of support.

The business community had been caught off guard by the blitz of coverage that gave credence to the need for environmental protection. Thus it had failed to organize any credible opposition in Congress to withstand the environmental onslaught in 1970. But as the media blitz abated, corporations regrouped to lay plans to resist regulations or at least shift them to be more in their favor. They hired public relations firms to advise them and to develop fresh lines of argument.

By 1971 the new lineup on the environmental side had also firmed up. New groups had joined the ranks: the Environmental Defense Fund (initially fighting pesticides), Friends of the Earth (Brower's new group), Environmental Action (reflecting Earth Day concerns), and the Natural Resources Defense Council (based in New York and closely allied with the Sierra Club). The Sierra Club Legal Defense Fund came into being that year too, and the National Wildlife Federation soon developed a legal arm as well. In Oregon and some other states, environmental councils were formed to lobby for strong new state laws on recycling, energy conservation, land use planning, and the like.

In 1971 the business community launched its public relations counter-attack. The environmental movement was attacked for ostensibly promot-ing a "no growth" agenda that, it charged, would stunt the economy and dry up jobs. Campaigns were launched to target labor unions and minori-ties, warning them that we were a threat to their employment and their well-being. Particular efforts were made to develop cooperative programs with trade unions in the construction industry. In California, former gov-ernor Pat Brown was enlisted to head up an antagonistic group called the California Environmental Trade Alliance, which comprised figures drawn both from these unions and from major businesses. Similar front groups were formed in many other Western states.

In the late 1960s and early 1970s, environmentalists were faced with a barrage of proposals for mega-developments. An unbelievable num-ber of energy facilities were being proposed: nuclear power plants would hopscotch up and down the coasts, supertanker ports would follow, thousands of miles of new pipelines would be laid, and a huge number of new coal-fired power plants would swarm across the arid West. There seemed to be no process for vetting them—for determining which were needed, where they should go, and how best to protect the environment in the whole process. In the absence of any safeguards, environmental-ists generally just pushed back and said no. In many cases, they were able to defeat ill-conceived projects. With government unwilling to regulate and plan, they often became de facto regulators.

In response, the energy industry openly predicted a backlash from the public. It issued dire warnings of shortages, brownouts, and black-outs. Engineers and other specialists in their employ belittled us as being technically "beyond our depth" and ill equipped to debate matters of policy with them.

Not all of the politicians who swung our way in 1970 were really convinced of the depth of the environmental problems the nation faced. Many wanted to believe that environmentalism was a flash in the pan; they were anxious to get back to doing business the old way. Some also did not see us as a serious contender in the political arena that would put up money for elections the way labor and business did.

An embattled President Nixon was among those who wanted to walk away from any commitment to environmentalism. Once Earth Day was over, Nixon tried to have it both ways. He tried to increase logging in the national forests by more than one billion board feet and endorsed the findings of panels he appointed that called for increasing logging by another six billion board feet. (We eventually blocked both.) When I persuaded the President's Council on Environmental Quality, through council member Bob Cahn, to seek a moratorium on logging in roadless areas in 1971, Nixon acceded to the timber industry's entreaties and refused to issue such an order.

Nixon did approve a number of new environmental measures in 1972, including measures creating four new national recreation areas (Gateway East and Gateway West, Cumberland Island National Seashore, and Glen Canyon NRA), the Marine Mammal Protection Act, the Ocean Dumping Act, and the somewhat flawed Federal Insecticide, Fungicide, and Rodenticide Act.

But he vetoed the sweeping and critical new bill that Congress passed to clean up water pollution, the Clean Water Act of 1972. That landmark act set a goal of zero discharges of effluents by 1983, and it aimed to make the waters throughout the nation clean enough to fish and swim in. Congress enacted it over Nixon's veto. He also vetoed a measure that would have established an environmental data bank to centralize the collection of key information that could undergird further action. Nixon no longer felt politically obliged to go along with each new congressional effort to improve the environment. At that point, he was probably more concerned with reinforcing the business community's loyalty to his administration.

The environmental movement met this heavy new opposition, from both business and the Nixon administration, head on. None of us had expected to get our way without opposition for long, and experienced groups like the Sierra Club were used to these shifting tides. I was still getting used to opposition from within the Club, however. Though we appeared unified to the world at large, internally factions were still contending, and I was about to be challenged personally.

In May 1971, Phil Berry's tenure as president of the Sierra Club was at an end. Traditionally one did not serve for more than two years in this position. (Officers were actually elected for terms of only one year at a time, but a president was usually elected for a second year without any contest.)

Berry's successor was Judge Raymond Sherwin of Vallejo, who had been serving as secretary. He had limited experience in the Club, having worked mainly to oppose the Minaret Summit Road across the Sierra. He was a striking figure, with a florid face and a shock of white hair. Closely allied with Berry on the fifteen-member board, he was part

of the voting bloc that the CMC coalition had brought to power following Brower's ouster. This group came to be called the East Bay bloc
because many of its most prominent members came from the communities on the east side of San Francisco Bay. The bloc included not only
Berry and Sherwin but also August Frugé, head of the University of
California Press; Will Siri, a physics professor at Berkeley; and Richard
Leonard, a longtime Club leader and attorney. Maynard Munger, an
Orinda Realtor, voted with the bloc at the outset but soon parted company. Ansel Adams and Charles Huestis were also members of the bloc,
though they did not live in the East Bay.

Despite the bloc's support, Sherwin's succession was not an easy one.
Once again, the election was highly contentious. In the advance skirmishing, Sherwin was opposed for the presidency by Laurence I. Moss, often
called Larry (not to be confused with Larry E. Moss, who later served
on the staff). Because Richard Sill from Reno voted for himself, each of
the leading contenders could muster only seven of the fifteen votes. This
deadlock continued through many ballots. Eventually, it was broken in
favor of Sherwin when Martin Litton finally abandoned Moss over his
failure to support a forthcoming ballot measure in California. Because
emotions ran high, the exchanges were heated and feelings bruised.

Thereafter, for several years, the East Bay bloc quarreled with others on the board—and with me. The biggest quarrel occurred shortly
after the election of new officers in May 1971. Because Phil Berry had
enjoyed his time in the limelight, he decided he would like to continue
in a comparable role. He felt that he had done well—and he had. A reorganization committee that he appointed, headed by Will Siri, recommended that he be made the permanent, paid president of the Sierra
Club (Sherwin held an unpaid leadership post and would probably have
been given a different title had this proposal been adopted). For all
intents and purposes, that would have made Berry the head of the staff.
He would have been the highest-paid person in the hierarchy. Having
just been given the job of executive director, I was not personally happy
about the prospect of either being displaced as the leading salaried person or living indefinitely with Berry's heavy-handed style.

Moreover, this would have marked a distinct change in the basic
structure of the Sierra Club leadership, with long-term implications. No
one in the extended leadership of the Club—in the Council or the
chapters—had been consulted about it. Finally, it seemed strange for
the CMC faction, which had just rebelled against Brower's "cult of per-

sonality," to be now trying to similarly enshrine Phil Berry. That faction had also taken great umbrage at Brower's wanting to cross the line from serving as staff to serving at the same time as a member of the board. If that were inappropriate, why wouldn't it be equally inappropriate for a member of the board to serve simultaneously as paid staff?

Ed Wayburn strongly opposed the permanent-president idea, believing it was important to continue to have rotating, elected presidents. He had served longer in this position than anyone else in modern times. He did not think the outcome of the proposal was foreordained; he urged me to resist and not to acquiesce to playing "second fiddle."

My assistant, Jonathan Ela, had become friendly with a newly elected board member from Menlo Park, Claire Dedrick (who would subsequently become California's resources secretary under Governor Jerry Brown). He told her of my unhappiness. She agreed that the proposal for a permanent, paid president was a bad idea and spread the word among the chapters that they should demand to be consulted on the matter.

As a result of the protests, action on the reorganization report was not taken at the regular board meeting on May 6 but instead was deferred until June 26–27, when a special meeting of the board was to be held. But at the May 6 board meeting, I gave an executive director's report that sounded more like a farewell report. It sounded, just as I intended, as if I might resign if the reorganization report were accepted. I reviewed the highlights of my ten years with the Club and thanked the many who had made so much possible. I was given a sustained ovation at the end.

When Ray Sherwin opened the special June board meeting, he announced that he had received "a mountain of mail" on the topic of reorganization. He then called upon Kent Gill, head of the Sierra Club Council, for his report. The Council was strongly opposed to the changes proposed and wanted the presidency to continue to be a volunteer position, with the addition of a paid person to provide support to the president. It further recommended that a single, responsible officer should head the staff, with clearly defined duties, and that an administrative services officer and an associate conservation director should be added to the staff.

At this point, even Siri dropped his insistence on the reorganization plan because so much opposition was manifest, saying that the proposal to turn the executive director's job into a chief operating officer "is not acceptable." Wayburn, who supported the Council report, warned against creating an assistant to the president who might compete with the executive director. President Sherwin, who wanted the presidential assistant to be a senior person, revealed in his oral history that what he had really wanted was for the executive director to serve as an assistant to the president and as a coordinator of volunteer affairs.

The board then heard from a procession of speakers from chapters around the country. Beginning with the Bay Chapter, they all opposed the reorganization plan and supported the Council report. Not one speaker from the floor supported the original proposal. The board concluded by adopting a motion put forth by Wayburn and Dedrick that encapsulated the Council report—specifying that "the volunteer presidency is retained" and "the staff will be led by the executive director." The board also decided to authorize the president to hire his own assistant, at a lesser level, who would not be part of the regular staff.

Phil Berry felt this rejection intensely, others have told me, and our relations were strained for a number of years as a result of the struggle. Eventually, many years later, we came to be on good terms again.

During the showdown, I did not know whether I would survive or want to stay, and I began to take soundings about other employment options. There were certainly openings at the EPA, and a number of the Club's activists who had worked at the RAND Corporation and then had gone to work for the EPA would have welcomed me. But as it turned out, I stayed because I felt that my tenure would become more secure as time went on.

Through the summer of 1971 the officers quarreled over priorities in hiring; the East Bay bloc felt priority should be given to hiring the administrator and the president's assistant, while others wanted conservation staff to be a priority.

Because of these disagreements, the board refused to ratify actions taken along this line by the executive committee. And when it came time for the board to adopt a new budget for the fiscal year beginning October 1, the board chose different priorities entirely—with more money for conservation instead of internal positions.

In reality, there was little money for any new positions. Throughout the summer and fall of 1971, cash flow became a problem. Membership growth had slowed, probably reflecting declining media coverage. Because of problems with a computer conversion, publishing-program invoices were slow in being sent out. Incoming bills were piling up, our billings to others were slow to be paid, and the Club had borrowed to its authorized limit.

An austerity plan was implemented, including deferring raises in salaries. With the softening in membership growth, I projected a net membership increase of only 10 percent in 1972, instead of the 28 percent that had been forecast based on the pattern of prior years. The board decided to cut the adopted budget by more than a half million dollars based on the budget cuts I had suggested.

When the final figures came in, 1971 still turned out to be a fiscal disaster. The Club ran a record deficit of almost $470,000 and was plunged into negative net worth. All of the fiscal progress of the past two years had been erased.

As it turned out, membership growth in 1972 was even less than I projected—only 3.4 percent. The revised budget for 1972 was still too optimistic. At a special board meeting in February, another $333,000 was cut from the budget. Over objections from the East Bay bloc, the campus organizing program they favored was terminated, as well as the research program. Field offices in New York City and in the Southeast were eliminated, and expenses for the legal program were also cut.

This budget-cutting session focused especially on the book publishing program, which was seen as a drain on the Club's capital. Not only was its budget reduced, but an acrimonious debate ensued, which I attempted to defuse, about whether its finances could ever be set straight, whether it should be moved to the Club headquarters in San Francisco, whether the Publications Committee had misled the board about its prospects, and whether I was attempting to seize control of it. My competence as a manager even became an issue, though many years later the board member who questioned it apologized.

At this meeting, the board also authorized the establishment of a Budget Committee for the first time, which was an improvement. Previously, staff and I had simply been asked to collate budget requests from all cost centers and present them in a packaged form to the board. Now they would go first to the Budget Committee, which would check the technical assumptions underlying the figures.

But the board still didn't trust staff enough to task them with the job of wrestling the budget into shape. Board members believed that those who shaped the budget shaped the organization, and they wanted to retain that control. Through most of the 1970s, the board insisted on putting itself through the agony of doing the "hands-on" job itself as a committee of the whole. The process became more and more unworkable.

Cash flow continued to be tight through the rest of the fiscal year. With an unexpected bequest of $100,000, however, the Club did finish the year of 1972 in the black. By the fall of that year, book sales had also improved, as had cash flow. Nonetheless, caution was the watchword, with a no-growth budget adopted for 1973. By the following spring, bank loans had been paid off, and the Club's net worth had finally become positive once again.

In the course of 1972, President Sherwin developed a strategy for clipping my wings. He resented the high-profile role that staff had assumed in conservation (by doing daily lobbying and speaking to the press, for instance), so he conceived of a way to develop a counterforce. He wanted to appoint a series of volunteer committees that would develop expertise on important issues to rival that of the staff, after which he would put them in charge of running the various campaigns. Sherwin told me bluntly, "I am going to cut your nuts off." I was flabbergasted at such talk. I didn't realize how bitter he had become over his own feelings of impotence.

Not only did Sherwin have no use for me, but he also harbored negative feelings about Brock Evans and Carl Pope, then our staff air pollution specialist. Evans turned out to be one of the most durable and respected figures in the environmental movement, working for Audubon and eventually heading the Endangered Species Coalition, while Pope eventually became one of the Club's most respected executive directors.

Sherwin and Berry came to believe that I feared having strong figures around me. In most everybody else's eyes, however, Evans and Pope looked like strong people, as did Doug Scott, whom I had hired and who in due course became associate executive director. Fran Gendlin, who came to edit the *Sierra Club Bulletin* under me, was also certainly a strong figure. In fact, the Club has drawn for many years now on the talents of the strong and capable people whom I hired.

In the early 1970s, Sherwin began to pursue his strategy, appointing committees dealing with issues such as energy and wildlife. I had mixed feelings about these committees. Often they were composed of people who knew the issues well but did not have much sense of how to lobby or deal with political crosscurrents. On the other hand, they did turn out to be very helpful in framing policy proposals to lay before the board. They were never put in charge of campaigns, even though Sherwin sought to do so, and it was ticklish to find a way to integrate them into the lobbying process. Eventually, some years later, we developed a workable solution: "campaign steering committees" composed of both veteran volunteer leaders and staff, whose task was to guide lobbyists and publicists.

Despite Sherwin's dire talk, the seed he planted by creating these committees proved to be productive. Those that addressed issues (on which staff were not working) actually handled a degree of implementation. By the mid-1990s, when efforts were undertaken to reduce the number of these committees, which had proliferated to nearly one hundred, I actually became something of a champion of them. Many had become quite productive and experienced, and I was sorry to see them sent packing.

At the end of the normal presidential tenure of two years, Sherwin did not go easily. He actually tried to run for a third term. In the preliminary skirmishing, he was again locked in a tie for many ballots with Larry Moss, with Richard Sill once again holding out by voting for himself. But eventually Moss prevailed and became the new president. Sherwin was reduced to serving as the fifth officer on the executive committee; all the other members of the East Bay bloc were removed from the committee. Kent Gill, who had now been elected to the board, became vice president, with June Viavant as secretary and Paul Swatek as treasurer. At last there were officers with whom I could work comfortably.

Larry Moss immediately indicated that he wanted to work closely with me and would not need the kind of assistant that Sherwin had demanded. Instead, Moss's wife, Ann, typed his letters, for which she was compensated by the Club.

The new executive committee did intend to make changes, though. It decided to assert greater control over the still controversial book publishing program. With some issues, such as nuclear power, the text of new books had gone beyond Club policy; this had led to concern among officers. The Publications Committee's authority to approve new titles was revoked and was assumed by the executive committee. Moreover, when a new chair was selected for the Publications Committee, the staff director of the book program in New York interpreted the move as a vote of no confidence and resigned, allowing the program to be moved to San Francisco, where I was able to integrate it more into the Club's conservation program. I hired a career professional in publishing to run it.

The new executive committee also decided that it was no longer appropriate for it to control all hiring. It wanted to be involved in hiring only at the managerial level, although that was still a lot of work. Sherwin began to be a chronic critic. He objected to the growing size of the staff. He thought too much money was being spent on the Northwest office. He proposed major cuts in spending in the Washington, D.C., lobbying office. He warned against infringements on the permanent fund; when the Club borrowed money from a bank, it had long been our practice, including during Sherwin's presidency, to use the permanent fund as collateral.

Meanwhile, a number of the other board members began to object to the seriousness of the matters being decided by the executive committee. This new faction was not just the old East Bay bloc. The "outer ten" were restive over the power being wielded by the "inner five" and wanted them to content themselves with handling routine matters. Thereafter, the committee mainly focused on ratifying decisions to become involved in lawsuits and on approving use of the Club's name under trademark law.

But the East Bay bloc had one final opportunity to "settle the score" with its opponents. Concern over the safety of nuclear power had been growing among chapters of the Club. The Utah chapter wanted the board to adopt a policy against nuclear power. Larry Moss, a nuclear engineer, supported nuclear power; Paul Swatek sided with him, as did former president Will Siri, a nuclear physicist. They were confident that all of its problems (that is, operating safety, the risk of proliferation, and the disposal of radioactive waste) could be solved technically.

Phil Berry and August Frugé suddenly embraced the anti–nuclear power position and pushed for a resolution opposing it. The new and old leadership split dramatically over this issue. But ultimately, Moss and Swatek were unable to resist the grassroots demand that the Club stand up and be counted among the opponents of nuclear power. Against their opposition and on a split vote, the board voted in 1974 to oppose nuclear power until its various problems could be resolved. I did not insert myself into this contretemps, although I was happy enough to see the Club adopt this stance (and subsequently defended it in public many times).[1] But I was not happy to see the Club's new officers put in an embarrassing position.

Later in the 1970s, efforts were made to heal the wounds left from the days when the East Bay bloc was in power. Berry was given the

Club's highest award, the John Muir Award, in 1978. To my surprise, I was given the very same award the following year. Both of us then felt better appreciated. Berry stayed on the board for many years, serving briefly again as president in the centennial year of 1992. At that time, he asked me to make one of the commemorative speeches. Sherwin left the board in 1975, and eventually an award for service to the Club in the international arena was named after him.

As the Sierra Club struggled with its internal management issues, events were not letting up in the world at large. The time of our greatest opportunity to shape America's environmental policy was at hand.

9 *The Glory Years*

Between 1972 and 1984, more than a hundred environmental measures were passed in which the Sierra Club played a leading role. The period of 1972–77 was particularly productive. These were the years when so many of America's basic laws and programs to protect the environment were set in place.

Public opinion was still supportive of environmental causes, even though business had begun to fight back. Because of the opposition, bills did not slide through Congress the way that NEPA and the Clean Air Act had in 1970, but the contests were winnable. Despite spirited resistance, Congress passed measure after measure. Legislative accomplishments that otherwise would have taken years took a matter of months.

When I would come home each night, Maxine would ask, "What did you save today?" Surprisingly often, I had something to tell her. The successes I told her about, of course, were the successes of the Sierra Club and the environmental movement, not my personal achievements. But I was leading the Club and framing the grand strategy. These were the glory years of the environmental movement. We had the sense that sooner or later, everything would get dealt with by Congress.

A number of broad strategies guided our work.

We believed that voluntary action by those who chose to change their lifestyles was not enough to effect sufficient environmental change. We didn't agree with Pogo's slogan, "We have met the enemy, and he is us," though we recognized that wasteful lifestyles needed to change. We felt that the power of the business community needed to be confronted by the power of the federal government because business was shaping the consumer society, polluting in major ways, resisting environmental reform, and trying to bend the political system to its ends. A patchwork of personal responses would not be enough.

Unlike those demonstrating against the war in Vietnam, we did not feel excluded from or disenfranchised by the normal political process. We felt encouraged by the success of many of our past efforts. We did not see the federal government as the enemy, though we did struggle over the direction the "ship of state" should take, and we had to work hard to get it to head in our direction. But to us, the federal government was a constructive force that could be used to counter the forces of environmental destruction.

The national scope of so many problems required solutions at the national level, we felt. Some kinds of air pollution, for example, were carried long distances over state boundaries. Large corporations made decisions at the national level. Many water pollution problems could not be solved locally. Thus we had a perspective quite different from the bioregionalists, who were promoting localism, the idea that problems are best solved at the lowest possible level. While that may be true in an ideal world, the forces that we confronted were operating on a broader stage. Only at the national, and sometimes even the international, level could we muster the forces necessary to contend with large corporations and the problems facing us. We had no alternative but to meet them on that stage. We could not retreat unilaterally to the local stage.

As we injected ourselves into the politics of the nation, we decided that simply bearing witness—or standing for the "right things"—was not enough. We wanted to make things better; we wanted to be effective. Thus the Sierra Club stood for a kind of ambitious, tough-minded pragmatism.

We also wanted to be newsworthy. Dave Brower had argued that we would have to seek free coverage for our cause because we could not afford to buy that coverage, though we did run paid ads on occasion. Strong advocacy and activism made the Club newsworthy, we recognized. And as we garnered free publicity, citizens would learn of the issues and take sides. During my tenure as executive director, we took this policy a step further and interjected ourselves into the debates on the principal issues of the day, such as energy. As we garnered added publicity as a participant, we became a player of more consequence. The establishment had to deal with us. At every level, from local to national, we had something to say and got in the news.

We also believed in setting forth ambitious goals that we hoped
would inspire our followers to act. But these goals needed to be within
the bounds of political plausibility, achievable over time if not at the outset. In due course, we would thus change the definition of political reality. I walked a fine line between Brower's followers, who denigrated
those who wanted to be "reasonable," and those like Doug Scott, later
associate executive director, who were excessively pragmatic. For
instance, Scott did not think the timber industry in Oregon could be
overcome, just when it was in fact about to crumble. I always believed in
taking on hard cases—but not impossible ones.

Moreover, in lobbying Congress, there was a world of difference
between affirmative and negative cases. It was easy to take a strong stand
and never waver when you were merely trying to defeat a project (though,
of course, not all such cases are winnable). Many of Brower's celebrated
campaigns involved negative cases, such as keeping dams out of the Grand
Canyon. But affirmative cases—trying to get a national park established,
for example, or, even more challenging, a new pollution control program—
were immeasurably tougher. In standing against something, you had to prevail only once in the legislative process; in affirmative cases, you had to prevail every step of the way. For example, you had to secure a hearing on your
desired bill, get it reported out of committee for action, get it through the
House Rules Committee, and get it adopted on the floor. All told, you had
to prevail twenty-one times in a row. In this process, it is expected that there
will be compromises; you almost always get "half a cup."

But we took the long view and came back again and again for more.
Over time, we believed, if we were persistent, we could approach the
ideal. The wilderness system and the National Park System, after all,
were built in this fashion, brick by brick. Often it was a test of staying
power. We were in it for the long run.

Many in the organization, such as Phil Berry, were nervous about
compromise. But it was Congress that was making the compromises, not
us. Compromise was the way the system worked when you were trying
to pass legislation. And it was a shock to realize that a campaign, which
you had controlled for so long, was no longer in your hands. The price
of success in having Congress pick up your ideas was that they dealt with
them as they wished.

During the Arab oil embargo of 1973–74, the business community tried
to convince members of Congress that public interest in environmental

programs had collapsed. It argued that the public had learned its lesson and was no longer infatuated with environmentalism, and that this "environmental nonsense" was over at last.

But the public didn't see it that way. When members of Congress went home at Christmastime in 1973, they found their constituents blaming the gasoline shortages on the oil companies, not on environmentalists. The public didn't buy business's argument that the Clean Air Act needed to be weakened. By June 1974, almost none of the oil companies' demands had been met.

In quick succession in 1974–75, Congress passed three measures to promote good energy policies: a fuel-economy requirement for new cars, energy efficiency labels for new appliances, and a strategic oil storage program, which would reduce pressure for new oil drilling.[1] A surcharge on large cars with poor mileage was added a few years later, as well as funding to promote solar power. At times, congressional committees actually used a "Sierra Club" committee print (a draft of legislation prepared by committee staff to help members as they considered options) as the standard against which their bills would be judged.

The auto industry dragged its feet in complying with the Clean Air Act of 1970, as did the power industry. When the auto industry provoked a crisis in 1976–77, Congress was forced to wrestle again with the Clean Air Act. Two lobbyists from the Natural Resources Defense Council (NRDC) transferred to the Sierra Club payroll to handle the crisis.[2] (NRDC's tax status as a 501(c)(3) organization limited its ability to work on legislation, whereas the Sierra Club, as a 501(c)(4), had no such restrictions.) Congress ended up emphasizing compliance. The Club was given funding for its work on this issue by a manufacturer of catalytic converters, who wanted automakers to have to install its product, which was fully compatible with our aims.

During this time, the Sierra Club also joined other groups in filing a successful lawsuit against DDT, which resulted in the EPA administrator being ordered to eliminate its use for most purposes. In another pathbreaking decision, the EPA was commanded to protect all air of good quality in the nation, especially the air over wilderness areas and national parks, in an order "preventing significant deterioration" (PSD). Congress passed the Ports and Waterways Safety Act in the aftermath of oil spills in San Francisco Bay. It tightened safety regulations to lessen the chances of another such mishap.

Spurred by the efforts of the Sierra Club and other lobbyists in 1976, Congress finally imposed environmental constraints on oil industry development of the Outer Continental Shelf and also passed the Toxic Substances Control Act, which, in theory, if not later in practice, regulated the safety of new products on store shelves. And the Club joined other groups in lobbying successfully to regulate strip mining for coal on private lands.

On public land issues Chuck Clusen, the Club's assistant conservation director, led the way. He organized sufficient support to enact the California Coastal Act in 1972, which prevented overdevelopment near the shoreline, and he turned back the effort to give federal wildlife refuges to the states. I sent him to Washington, D.C., to lobby against the worst impulses of the Public Land Law Review Commission and to get the laws off the books for the BLM, which allowed public lands to be disposed of. In 1976 this culminated in a good organic act (that is, a framework statute) for that public land agency. Fortunately, the leaders of the Sagebrush Rebellion, which opposed the idea of federally owned public land in the West, didn't wake up until this debate was over. I wrote several articles for the *Sierra Club Bulletin* on what was at stake.

In 1974 Congress decided to let restored wilderness in the East be added to the National Wilderness Preservation System (sometimes known as the Eastern Wilderness Areas Act). Club leaders worked hard for the areas in their states, such as Alabama, North Carolina, and New Hampshire.

Jim Moorman, while he was at the helm of the Sierra Club Legal Defense Fund, took the lead in lobbying for a new organic act, or framework statute, for the national forests. The National Forest Management Act of 1976 (NFMA) stemmed from a successful lawsuit brought by the Fund to stop logging of the Monongahela National Forest in West Virginia. Trees slated for logging in clear-cuts were not being marked as required. The lawsuit, which was designed to provoke a crisis and put the issue before Congress, was brought in cooperation with the Izaak Walton League.

Following the court judgment, Moorman drafted a sweeping reform bill that was then introduced by Senator Jennings Randolph of West Virginia. Though the measure that finally passed was a compromise, it contained some valuable provisions, such as a requirement that natural diversity be maintained in the conversion of virgin forests to managed ones. The NFMA was the culmination of years of controversy in which we blocked the timber industry's bills[3] and they blocked ours. Finally a denouement was achieved.

Many controversies over valuable places were also settled in this period. The Grand Canyon National Park was enlarged. Mining was kept out of the Lake Mead National Recreation Area, and dams were kept out of the Delaware Water Gap in Pennsylvania. The Oregon Dunes were placed in a National Recreation Area. The St. Croix River in Minnesota, the Chattahoochee River in Georgia, and the Big South Fork of the Cumberland River in Tennessee were protected from dams and bankside development. So were the Big Thicket in Texas and the Big Cypress in Florida, both of which were made preserves under the National Park Service. The Congaree Swamp in South Carolina was made a national monument. On the Idaho-Oregon border, Hells Canyon was protected as a National Recreation Area, as was Glen Canyon in Utah.

The Club did not play a significant role in the lobbying for the Clean Water Act of 1977, the Resource Conservation and Recovery Act of 1976, or the Safe Drinking Water Act, though we agreed that they were important. Nor did the Club then involve itself in many wildlife issues, though the bills we did push saved a lot of habitat. We were ready to help with the Endangered Species Act in 1973, but the measure was not then controversial, nor did we help with the Marine Mammal Protection Act of 1972, though I had drafted its third title. There were limits to what the Club could handle, and we knew that other groups were championing these causes.

While most of the work on behalf of the Club's campaigns was handled by our staff, I was personally involved in a number of issues: national forest matters, transfer of the Mineral King enclave to the Park Service, hearings on Interior Department secretaries, Alaska, and energy and land use planning.

In 1971 I went to talk to the President's Council on Environmental Quality, with Stewart Brandborg of the Wilderness Society, to propose a moratorium on logging in de facto wilderness areas (the term "roadless areas" was not yet in use). The Forest Service refused to protect them, but it did agree to study the areas to determine their future. This involved establishing where such areas were and how large they were. In 1972 the agency completed its first study, the RARE I (Roadless Area Review and Evaluation) survey. It was grossly deficient and left out approximately 8 to 9 million acres. In talking to a reporter for the *Denver Post*, I got carried away; he goaded me into threatening to sue the Forest Service over the shortcomings of the study.

Once I promised to sue the Forest Service, I had to make good on the threat. After conferring with the Sierra Club Legal Defense Fund about who should handle the suit, we asked Bruce Terris, a Washington, D.C., attorney in private practice, to be our counsel. He brought an action in federal district court in San Francisco against the secretary of agriculture, under whose jurisdiction the Forest Service operates, for failure to comply with the National Environmental Policy Act (NEPA). I sat at the table for the counsel for the plaintiff, and much to our surprise, he won—we won. In one of the early rulings under the new law, the court held that under NEPA, every timber sale in a roadless area had to be accompanied by an environmental impact statement—an evaluation of all foreseeable impacts on the environment, along with a range of alternatives that would avoid or mitigate those impacts. After that, the rate of attrition of roadless areas was far less.

Mineral King

One issue with which I was associated for a long time involved the fate of the Mineral King area,[4] a 15,000-acre tract of land located at the headwaters of the East Fork of the Kaweah River in the southern Sierra of California. Because of its suspected mineral values, it had been left out of Sequoia National Park and remained part of the national forest when the park was expanded in the 1920s (though Congress had designated it as a game refuge). The park surrounded this thumb of land on three sides. The Club wanted Mineral King to be included in the park, so that neither mining nor major resort development could occur there. I was involved with this campaign from its conception in 1965 through 1978. Many others played important roles at various times, but as the Club's conservation and executive director, I guided the campaign through all those years.[5]

When the campaign began, everybody was against us. Even our own board of directors was split. John Muir had drawn lines for an ideal Sequoia National Park in 1911, with this area in the park. All of Muir's areas but Mineral King were eventually added to the park by Congress. In 1946, seeking (successfully) to deflect pressures to build a ski resort in the San Gorgonio Wilderness, the Club deviated from the Muir vision and announced that Mineral King would be a suitable area for a modest skiing development. But when the Forest Service awarded a contract to the Disney Corporation in 1965, it was for a giant "Disneyland" in this alpine area, not the modest development the Club had envisaged. By a narrow margin (some directors felt bound by past decisions), the board opposed this scale of development.

The Disney Corporation had lined up most of the political power structure on its side. The congressional delegation from California supported it. So did President Lyndon Johnson, Governor Pat Brown, the legislature, county supervisors, and the state highway commission. Even the National Park Service and some conservation groups went along, as did editorial writers in Los Angeles and San Francisco.

We started alone. We bought time in the late 1960s by filing a lawsuit, which eventually went to the Supreme Court, stalling the project while we built support. The case alleged that the Disney development was inconsistent with the area's status as a game refuge and that the development exceeded legal limits. National articles were written on the struggle, a film was produced, bumper stickers were printed, and patches for jackets were made. Publicity committees were organized. Sit-ins were held at the site, and demonstrations were staged at meetings of Disney's board of directors. Thousands of letters were written to members of Congress.

By 1978, we had turned the situation around entirely and had stopped the Disney project dead in its tracks. The Forest Service was spending its time preparing an environmental impact statement (which we had asked for in the lawsuit, which we had refiled). After Interior Secretary Stewart Udall had dragged his feet in the late 1960s and later court action curtailed work, the administration of President Jimmy Carter, elected in 1976, was supportive of our position. The National Park Service was now working with us. At the state level, the administration of Jerry Brown was supportive too, as was the legislature. The proposed access highway had never been built; the state didn't want to provide the money for it, and the Park Service wouldn't provide the rights-of-way. Now the editorial writers supported our side.

I drafted a bill to add the Mineral King area to the park, which Representative Phillip Burton of San Francisco introduced. Eventually a supportive congressman, John Krebs, was elected from the district in which Mineral King was located, and he introduced the bill too, as did Senator Alan Cranston of California. These bills were finally enacted.

The Disney interests didn't even get a provision in the park bill "buying out" their investment in planning the resort. About the only interest that was not supportive of the park idea was the U.S. Ski Association, which sought fruitlessly to keep the potential for its sport alive at that site.

The campaign for Mineral King illustrated several characteristics of successful environmental action. It showed the value of persistence and the power of idealism—of fighting for what you believe in, regardless of the odds. And it showed the importance of a historical perspective. Bit by bit, John Muir's vision was realized, and Mineral King was eventually added at last to Sequoia National Park.

Confirming Secretaries

During the administrations of Presidents Richard Nixon and Gerald Ford in the 1970s, we found ourselves time and again opposing the confirmation of various interior secretary nominees with terrible environmental records. I testified against a number of them. In one case, we also prepared a series of questions for a friendly senator to ask the secretary-designate. Each one built on what we supposed would be wormed out of the nominee with the preceding question. I took the senator who had agreed to ask these questions out for cocktails on the eve of the hearing. After we had a few drinks, I briefed him on the line of questioning. Apparently he had had too many drinks, however, and I turned out to have been too clever by half.

The following day he did ask the right questions—but of the wrong person. Instead of asking them of the person nominated as secretary, he waited until I testified and mistakenly asked them all of me. With each question, I squirmed and explained that the answers would be better sought from the nominee. But he persisted. Apparently all he remembered was that these questions had some connection to me. It was a complete fiasco.

After a while we learned our lesson and ceased trying to "Hickelize" each nominee (working over a nominee in such a bruising fashion that he comes over to our side). Given the nature of its work, we thought the Interior Department ought to be run by people who were clearly in our camp. But ordinary politicians kept being appointed, largely from the West to our disappointment. Our campaign did drive former Wyoming governor Stanley Hathaway from the post after just four months in office, though. The pressure was just too much.

During the Nixon administration, our campaign against interior nominee Rogers Morton seriously alienated him. Ed Wayburn, however, found
an inventive way to overcome this breach. Morton was charged with making decisions by a deadline to set aside areas in Alaska while Congress delib-
erated. When Morton found himself recuperating in Stanford Medical
Center from a cancer operation, Wayburn, a doctor attached to that hospital, would visit and chat about Alaska. Eventually, Morton did the right
thing. He and I met later and remained on good terms.

Alaska

That was just one small part of our greatest campaign in the 1970s,
which was led by Ed Wayburn: to establish new national parks, wildlife
refuges, and wild rivers in Alaska. The state and the natives had been
given huge amounts of land there, and the oil companies had been given
tracts for their development. We thought the American people as a
whole should be given their share too. The chance came in 1971, under
an Alaska Native Claims Settlement Act provision that required the secretary of the interior to set aside lands temporarily to afford Congress
time to act. I was on the scene to lobby for this provision with Stewart
Brandborg of the Wilderness Society. Rogers Morton finally acted on
the matter (after his bedside chats with Wayburn), setting aside almost
80 million acres for this purpose in late 1973.

I thought I might be called before Congress to testify on allocating
Alaskan lands to various uses, so I decided I had better go see the areas
involved. In the summer of 1974, Maxine and I toured this region to visit
as many of the areas as we could, in a light floatplane flown by the son
of the president of Wien Airlines. We flew into McCarthy to see the
Wrangell Mountains, with the village's old Kennicott mine in the background. We flew into the Lake Clark area to the west to see its limpid
waters. We saw the places where the Katmai National Monument, to
the south, needed expansion. We visited Afognak Island, the most west-
erly forested island, which the Forest Service wanted to log. And we flew
out along the Aleutian Peninsula to the Aniakchak Crater, which the
Park Service felt should become a national monument, even landing on
the lake in its crater.

When the issue finally came before Congress, Senator Ted Stevens
of Alaska quizzed me intently when I testified before the Interior
Committee. Had I even been to these areas about which I was testifying

so glibly, he wanted to know. Had I been to the Wrangells? Yes sir, I replied. Had I been to Lake Clark? Yes sir, I answered again. He persisted. Had I been to Katmai National Monument? Yes, I had been, I said. Well, he asked, had I ever been to the Aniakchak Crater? Again, I answered yes. Finally, he gave up.

Fortunately, he gave up in time. There were still important areas I had not seen, such as the Kobuk Sand Dunes, the Noatak River, and the Gates of the Arctic region, which bad weather prevented me from visiting.

In my testimony I tried, of course, to put the case for action in Alaska in the best light. I began by reminding Congress that "there have been few moments in the history of our country when the fate of so much land had to be decided. There have been few moments when decisions of such magnitude had to be decided in such a short time. . . . And there have been few moments when land of such quality was at stake. . . . This is the one great opportunity in history to do something right for once. . . . Now the Congress is at another crossroads: will it act so that there are no regrets tomorrow—so that history will not look with dismay?"

With the knowledge that I had acquired through my trips, I was able to begin drafting the bill that was eventually introduced to set aside these areas. When the coalition first met in Washington, D.C., I worked with Jack Hession, our expert in Alaska, to get a draft under way. It evolved a great deal as it was shaped by Congress, but some of my language survived—particularly in what were called "subsistence provisions," which allowed native peoples to take wildlife for their own use within various federal reservations. When Congress was through, it had set aside all of the areas that had been studied, in a package that exceeded 110 million acres. The American people got their share at last.

Hanging on to these areas was another matter. In the ensuing years, the Sierra Club fought off efforts to allow hunting in some areas administered by the National Park Service and to shrink the boundaries of others. In the Arctic National Wildlife Refuge, the Club beat back efforts to allow oil drilling. Most of this area, on the Arctic Ocean next to Canada, was designated a wilderness and thus was off-limits to oil drilling. A zone in the refuge along the Arctic Coast was kept out of wilderness, however, because Congress couldn't agree on its future.

I felt strongly that oil drilling was not compatible with the land's purposes as a refuge. This was a prime breeding ground for caribou and polar bear. In the 1980s, however, the Reagan administration pushed hard to get Congress to grant permission for drilling to begin.

Some environmentalists, feeling that it was inevitable, sought a deal that would limit the damage. In sessions of the Group of Ten—composed of the heads of the ten largest environmental groups, who met periodically to coordinate strategy—I led the faction that opposed this, and we ultimately convinced our colleagues. Stalwart resistance was not only the right policy, it was a good tactic. No one was ready to make a deal with us. Mitigation to limit the damage was likely to be offered only if the resistance was firm. Firm resistance kept oil development at bay for many years, though the threats to the area are now greater than ever.

Land Use Planning and Energy Projects

While the Sierra Club was well known for its concern with public lands, it was also concerned with private land. In the early 1970s, we had supported legislation to encourage states to undertake comprehensive land use planning. This legislation passed the Senate but never made it to the floor of the House. To garner support from conservatives when he was facing impeachment, Nixon switched from supporting to opposing the bill, and in the spring of 1975 it went down to defeat in the House Interior Committee by a vote of 19 to 23. Some farm interests kindled opposition with the argument that planning could cause their land to be "taken" without compensation.

But the Sierra Club itself had concerns over the direction that the legislation was taking. To overcome opposition, the Senate put provisions in the bill to reserve "areas of critical industrial concern." This provision was supposed to counterbalance a provision requiring states to identify "areas of critical environmental concern." I became concerned that more provisions along this line would appear. Such a bill in unfriendly hands could do more harm than good, I felt.[6]

Plans for construction of a huge number of energy supply facilities were then before regulatory agencies. I began to fear that such legislation requiring land use planning under federal guidelines might facilitate the process of approving them. Industry executives were already complaining about the obstacles in their way and arguing for "one-stop licensing." They claimed that in some states, there were as many as thirty-four hurdles that they had to clear. In the nuclear field, they were calling for federal preemption of state land use processes. Was this bill a step toward doing this in other areas as well?

Moreover, we were already calling for the reverse notion in some cases. In the case of the Coastal Zone Management Act, we were calling for federal plans (such as to allow oil drilling) to be consistent with state plans (such as to protect coastal areas). Thus, we were beginning to champion a greater role for the states. The two sides were beginning to switch positions in the course of the debate over this bill.

Because of these concerns, we never pushed thereafter for the land use planning bill. I made the decision to accept the negative stance of the House Interior Committee. Ironically, at an earlier time when the bill was regarded as likely to pass, a provision requiring the BLM to identify "areas of critical environmental concern" had been put in its organic act, which did pass in 1976. This was the only enduring result of the land use planning bill.

While I believed in the importance of land use planning for environmental purposes, it was not clear whom we could trust to do it. I felt the need for a clear strategy in dealing with the onslaught of proposals for power plants. We needed to be able to figure out where to concentrate our fire. It was impossible to fight everything, and it was poor public relations to appear to be opposed to every possibility.

Club activists implicitly didn't want to approve any of the power plant proposals, but in effect, we had developed a strategy of letting some plants be developed, in areas we cared about less. The Club decided which proposals would get bogged down and blocked by its actions and which wouldn't. For all intents and purpose, the Club became the licensing authority. Those who were congenitally opposed to public planning never recognized that groups such as the Club were doing the planning instead. Through our lawsuits, we were making the decisions about which power plants would get built and which would not.

Environmental groups never found a forum where they could argue in a straightforward fashion about whether more nuclear plants should be authorized. Instead, they attacked nuclear power collaterally by trying to end the Price-Anderson Act, which limited liability in the event of accidents—without success. They were successful in killing the Clinch River breeder reactor and the idea of an interim storage facility for nuclear waste, but those successes didn't get at the basic problem. The Atomic Energy Commission (AEC) and its successor, the Nuclear Regulatory Commission (NRC), were filled with proponents of nuclear power. They would never turn down any utility that asked for a license to build a nuclear plant, nor would they revoke a nuclear plant's license—no matter how many safety issues emerged.

This lack of neutrality constituted one of democracy's real failures. These commissions were not a fair tribunal, and it seemed we could never win there. This fact helps explain why so many environmentalists resorted to demonstrating on this issue, though not the Club. The huge demonstrations at the site of the proposed nuclear power plant at Seabrook, New Hampshire, embodied this frustration. On this issue only, American environmentalists were more like their European counterparts, who felt that demonstrating was their only recourse. The system wasn't working in this case.

But in a way, it was. Despite the closed minds at the regulatory agency, the real-world problems of nuclear power kept emerging, and the Sierra Club found ways to work within the system. In the early 1970s, for example, the Club's chapter in Kansas found that the AEC proposed to dispose of nuclear waste by burying it in the salt formations near Lyons, Kansas. The repositories for these wastes, which could be radioactive for as many as 250,000 years, needed to be dry to be effective, and the AEC asserted that they were. But in working closely with the state geologist in Kansas, our activists found that the salt beds the AEC chose were not dry at all. The formations were riddled with holes that early-20th-century miners had bored into them, and surface waters had poured down these holes. In great embarrassment, the AEC was forced to abandon this particular site.

As more and more safety problems with nuclear power came to light, the Sierra Club and other groups intervened in a series of licensing contests. While the licenses were never turned down, the AEC/NRC was forced to ratchet up its safety standards and require a stream of upgrades. These raised the costs of construction and operation. Many plants were also shut down frequently for repairs. Over time, the utilities learned that nuclear fission was an expensive and difficult way to boil water to produce steam so as to generate power.

After the Sierra Club went on record against nuclear power (we actually stood for a moratorium on construction until problems were resolved), I found myself invited to address a conference of nuclear engineers to explain our position. In 1974, in a major speech to the American Nuclear Society in Portland, Oregon, I reviewed at length the industry's safety problems. I thought I had stated the case against nuclear power well, but I found myself mocked. The audience was incredulous. Yet within a few years, the utilities themselves turned to other sources for power, and their infatuation with nuclear power came to an end.

During the early 1970s, I served on the Ford Foundation's Energy Policy Project, a high-level panel composed of both environmentalists and business representatives who sought to chart the nation's energy future. I found myself pitted against the president of a major oil company. He was used to dominating boards, but I was not about to let him do it in this case. When it became evident that the project staff would produce a pro-conservation report, the oil man threatened to have his own staff write a counterreport in the guise of an extended dissent. I then moved to limit dissents to a defined and reasonable length to block this attempt at intimidation. My motion carried, which made him furious. He never was able to get the project to print his huge counterreport. In a magazine interview he called me a nut, while I called him a bully. He threatened to sue me for libel, but never followed through. If he had, it would only have proved my point.

The Energy Policy Project eventually issued a far-reaching call for energy conservation and use of alternative fuels. Its report served as the basis for the Carter administration's energy policy in the late 1970s. Through service on various boards such as this one, I came to feel that a "bridging fuel" was needed, an energy source that could be used until conservation had reached sufficient levels and alternative fuels were plentiful. We had already ruled out nuclear power and any more hydroelectric projects; I thought we needed to suggest a bridging fuel in order to have some credibility with the press and policy makers. I wondered whether coal might even be that fuel if its various problems, such as air pollution and mining-related issues, could be reduced.

The Club's Energy Committee could never agree on a bridging fuel, however. Members saw problems with every possibility and could not agree on most of the scenarios forecasting which fuel supplies would be available in the future. Only in 2001 did the Club finally acknowledge the need for planning on the supply side—though it had no problems with planning to reduce demand, which was clearly important as well. Over the years the Club encouraged a wide variety of programs designed to reduce demand, such as those that improved building standards to reduce heat loss.

Eventually natural gas gained favor as the bridging fuel, but few felt at the time that the supplies of it were adequate. Almost everyone was wrong about its future, including me, although I changed my views after the 1970s. In the 1980s, I came to embrace natural gas as the least troubling source of readily available energy. By now, however, we understand that it also generates some greenhouse gases, though far less than coal or oil.

Since I realized at the time that natural gas had fewer environmental drawbacks than coal, I did not want us to be perceived as standing in its way, notwithstanding the Club's Energy Committee. We were trying to get the votes of many people in the center of the political spectrum in Congress.

Importing natural gas in liquefied form was one way to overcome the domestic shortage of it. In the early 1970s, officials of the Columbia Natural Gas Company approached us to seek resolution of a problem they were having in gaining approval to build a liquefied natural gas plant at Calvert Cliffs, on the western shore of Chesapeake Bay in Maryland. A few years before, the Club had been a participant in a successful lawsuit that had made it more difficult to build a nuclear power plant at the Calvert Cliffs site because the environmental impacts had not been considered from the outset. Officials of the gas company, fearing potential Club opposition to their own plans, came to San Francisco to talk with us. Local Maryland conservationists—including members of the Sierra Club—opposed the plant because they didn't want the facility to be visible from hiking trails in the nearby state park.

After poring over maps and discussing the proposal, it occurred to me that a compromise was possible. What if the liquefied natural gas, to be imported from Libya, were unloaded at an inconspicuous single mooring facility far offshore and brought ashore in a buried pipeline? While the mooring facility might be visible, it would not be conspicuous, and the buried line would be invisible. The company "bought" the idea, local conservationists thought the compromise was acceptable, and the project went forward as we proposed. It has operated there ever since, with few problems.

The foundations of federal law to protect the environment were laid during the 1970s: the National Environmental Policy Act, the Clean Air and Water Acts, the Toxic Substances Control Act, and various energy conservation laws, as well as the Endangered Species Act and basic laws to reform the management of the national forests and other lands in the public domain.

The most important work was done during the period between 1972 and 1977, and the Sierra Club was in the thick of most of the battles, as I have described. The pace of action during this period set our heads spinning. It was exhilarating and taxing. Some said the Sierra Club was a "horse that couldn't be ridden." But I rode it, and a huge amount was accomplished. There never was a time like it.

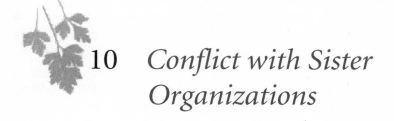

10   *Conflict with Sister Organizations*

Beginning in the 1950s, the Sierra Club spun off a number of allied organizations to handle operations that required special treatment under the U.S. tax laws. The federal agencies that regulate not-for-profit organizations can determine whether they thrive or wither. The agencies regulate whether such organizations can have access to tax deductions for those who contribute to them, whether they can benefit from advantageous postal rates, and, in general, whether they can operate optimally. The Sierra Club learned the hard way that it had to pay close attention to its relations with these agencies.

The Sierra Club's board of directors had anticipated that the organization might get into trouble with the Internal Revenue Service (IRS) for lobbying too much, so in the 1950s it set up a group called Trustees for Conservation to be the "lightning rod" organization that would do most of the lobbying. The Sierra Club Foundation, mentioned briefly in chapter 6, was established separately under section 501(c)(3) of the tax code. It was to be the tax-deductible arm of the organization, as well as being tax-exempt; donors would be able to deduct gifts to the Foundation as charitable contributions on their income tax returns. To avoid placing its tax status in any jeopardy, the Foundation would do no lobbying at all. By creating these two sister organizations, board members thought they were giving the Club the flexibility to address every situation.

Things did not work out as they planned. It proved hard to raise money for Trustees for Conservation because donors' gifts were not tax-deductible. An additional problem, pointed out by William Losh, a public relations expert hired to run Trustees, was that no one was familiar with the group. Without an established reputation and following, and with little money at its disposal, Trustees could not do very much.

Because Trustees was able to do so little, the Sierra Club itself was gradually forced to take up the slack, despite its status then as a tax-deductible organization, 501(c)(3). (Some years later, in 1973, Trustees was dissolved.) IRS regulations severely limited how much lobbying any tax-deductible organization could do. But the Club, with its directors concurring, decided that it had to do more and more overt lobbying, regardless of the risk to its tax status.

Notwithstanding the decision to take a calculated risk, it was a shock when the Sierra Club actually lost its tax deductibility. While the Club had been running full-page newspaper ads for almost six months prior, it was only in late June 1966 that it got into trouble. Its advertisement to protect the Grand Canyon had outraged Congressman Morris Udall, Democrat of Arizona, who later was to be so friendly and helpful, but who was then championing the Central Arizona Project—a project to divert Colorado River water into southern Arizona. Two dams proposed on the Colorado River, which we opposed, would have provided power and profits to pump the water southward.

When Udall saw the Club's ad in the *Washington Post* at breakfast one morning, he called his friend Joseph Barr, who was then undersecretary of the Treasury, to complain bitterly. Barr immediately called the commissioner of the IRS to order him to act. In less than twenty-four hours the decision was made, and that day a notice revoking the Club's tax deductibility was hand-carried by IRS agents to our offices. Rarely—even in times of war—had the federal government acted with so much dispatch.

The IRS claimed that the Sierra Club had been too brazen in its lobbying. While the agency could tolerate a certain amount of lobbying (one previous ruling held that as much as 5 percent of an organization's budget could be devoted to the activity), it could not tolerate an unremitting fusillade of propaganda designed to influence legislation. If the Club had been willing to be less effective, it might have stayed out of trouble, some suggested. Businesses, of course, suffered from no similar constraints. While they didn't enjoy tax deductibility with respect to donations, businesses could deduct lobbying expenses as business expenses, and there were no limitations on how "brazen" their messages could be.

The Club decided to file an administrative appeal of the decision with the IRS. Gary Torre, of the San Francisco law firm that was handling the Club's other legal matters, led the effort. We were surprised to discover that the IRS had an unusual interpretation of the law. Ostensibly, we had violated the language of the tax code granting deductibility to an organization "no substantial part of whose activity is involved in carrying propaganda or otherwise influencing legislation."

We thought they were alleging that we spent too much, relatively, on lobbying, but this did not turn out to be the IRS's argument. Instead, the agency argued that the Club's legislative work by itself was too substantial and too obvious to be acceptable. Regardless of whether the Club's lobbying activity was less than 5 percent of its efforts (or budget), it was too much. This was a novel interpretation of the words of the statute. It was as if the words "no substantial part" were not even in the statute.

The fallout from this situation was interesting. Brower was not blamed by the Club's board of directors because they had accepted the risk all along. Though the Club lost the administrative appeal in the fall of 1968, Torre himself began a long run as an officer of the Sierra Club Foundation. And the Club garnered a great deal of sympathetic publicity as a victim of persecution.

After the Club lost its administrative appeal, it decided not to contest the decision. By then it had become even more active legislatively, and it planned to become more active still. So the Club settled for tax status as a civic league, under section 501(c)(4) of the tax code; this entitled it to an exemption from taxes but not to deductibility. If donors wished deductibility, we could route their donations through the Sierra Club Foundation, since its work did not involve lobbying. Although running a tandem (c)(3)/(c)(4) operation was not easy, it was possible. It was the best we could do, it seemed.

In June 1970, the other shoe dropped. Thinking the issues were parallel, the Postal Service decided to revoke the Sierra Club's access to the preferred, nonprofit rates for third-class mail. Under its regulations, only organizations that were either educational or philanthropic were entitled to the preferred rates, and it held that we were neither. In its eyes, the Sierra Club was a "conservation" organization rather than an educational organization.

It mattered not that we had been a conservation organization all along and that education was one of our means, not an end. We filed lawsuits to contest this decision, but to no avail. Now that we were deprived of these special postal rates, it was no longer economically feasible to use direct mail to seek new members. Membership development via the mail was simply too expensive. In the mid-1970s, then, while other conservation groups were able to build their memberships via the mail, the Sierra Club, to its detriment, could not. The Audubon Society, for example, which had been about the same size as the Club in the 1960s, grew rapidly, while the Sierra Club did not.

Some glimmer of relief came in 1976, however, when Congress passed the Conable Act (ironically promoted by the CEO of the Audubon Society), which permitted charities to devote a larger percentage of their time to lobbying within established limits. The Sierra Club did not benefit directly; it chose to remain a (c)(4) organization so it would not be subject to any limits. But passage of the act did plant a seed in the minds of Postal Service officials. They could see that Congress did not think it out of line to be both a charity and a group that lobbied.

The Sierra Club decided it was now time to seek to regain access to those preferred mailing rates. A lawyer at the firm of Arnold and Porter, Richard Hubbard, agreed to take our case on a pro bono basis, and by the late 1970s he had persuaded the Postal Service that it had been wrong in revoking our third-class rates. The Club then started to use the mails again in a big way to find new members. Next it sought rebates for the extra amounts it had had to pay the Postal Service for regular operations over the years, which it obtained in 1981.

In the mid-1970s the Sierra Club decided that it should also register as a lobbying organization with the House of Representatives. For many years, we had thought that registration was not required because the Club's funds were raised for general purposes, not specifically for lobbying.[1] The Club now decided that it should register, though, because many thought it was supposed to and it did not want any appearance of impropriety. But registering and reporting fully—as the Club decided to do—did have a downside. It boosted the Club into the ranks of the big-time lobbying organizations, because many on the other side fudged their figures and presented unduly small numbers. In press reports, the Sierra Club soon appeared to be one of the nation's largest lobbies. Ultimately, the Club came to register twenty-seven different people as lobbyists, though many of them were field representatives who came to Washington, D.C., to lobby only on occasion.

For a while the Sierra Club had its regulatory problems in hand. When it was audited in 1974–75, the IRS found no problems. But the

IRS did detect problems in the mid-1980s. It found that the Club had been too active in managing its relationship with a credit card company. In the early 1980s, the Sierra Club had pioneered in developing an affinity credit card, a special card with the Club's name on it that was marketed to members. Whenever members used the card, the Club received a small payment from the company. The arrangement proved very lucrative for the Club.

But in looking at returns for the years 1984–86, the IRS claimed that the Club owed back taxes. The Club was not passive enough, the IRS argued; it regarded the Club as a partner in the credit card business. The Club challenged this assessment in the U.S. Tax Court, and for fifteen years it sought vindication, arguing that it was merely being paid royalties and was not running a business. I was called upon to testify about stale matters involving people who were dead and facts that seemed even deader. On two different occasions, the U.S. Tax Court ruled in the Club's favor. Finally, the IRS agreed that the Club had not been too active. The Club benefited at last by being able to use the funds it had set aside in case it lost that suit.

In many of these encounters, the Club felt that it was being singled out to serve as an example. Its offense was that it had been too outspoken and, in the process, effective. While the issues were often cloaked in technical terms, what was at stake was the ability of organizations such as the Sierra Club to speak out and play their role as vigorous advocates. It became clear too that the financial viability of the Club turned on questions of a technical nature, such as those raised in these cases, and that our ability to compete in the public debate depended on staying healthy financially.

Despite these tax issues, the Sierra Club's structure continued to expand during the 1970s. By 1980 the Sierra Club family had grown to include a number of organizations, principally the Sierra Club Foundation, the Sierra Club Political Action Committee, and the Sierra Club Legal Defense Fund. During the late 1960s especially, the idea of decentralization was popular. As the Club's functions grew in number, it was regarded as progressive to "spin off" separate organizations to handle them. While the seeds for these organizations were planted by Club leaders, several of the groups did not want to be seen as offspring. They jealously guarded their turf and were fiercely independent. And they certainly did not think they should defer to me. I spent a lot of time coping with their idiosyncrasies.

Sierra Club Foundation

The Sierra Club Foundation's first years, following its founding in 1966, reflected the strained relations that characterized David Brower's tenure as the Club's executive director. The Foundation's initial board of directors was composed of former Sierra Club presidents, who regarded Brower with disdain—almost as a wayward child. They regarded the Club, too, as being in the hands of undependable people.

In their eyes, I was a junior figure entitled to little respect. When I meekly approached the Foundation to ask for grants to the Club, I felt as though I was having to sing for my supper. The board thought nothing of giving the Foundation's money (raised largely in the name of the Sierra Club) to other groups. This attitude persisted into the days when I was executive director.

Throughout the 1970s, the Sierra Club tried to take on too much and its budget was often strained. The attitude of the Foundation, including its first executive director, Nick Clinch, was that the Club was reckless with money. The Foundation allied itself with the conservative faction in Club politics, which warned us smugly "not to spend the money before it was raised." This might have made sense if the Club had had a comfortable endowment to fall back on. It didn't, however. All of the money in its budget for each year had to be raised.

At the same time that the Foundation was passing on homilies about fiscal conservatism, its president of the early 1970s, Ed Wayburn, was telling the Club's board of directors that additional projects could be tackled with "soft money" (i.e., tax-deductible contributions) and that the Club merely had to ask for it. He acted as if such money were easy to raise and pressed for more funding in particular for his favorite programs in Alaska.

From 1973 through the rest of the decade, the two organizations fussed about money and who was the top dog. The Club thought the Foundation was raising too little money and that its overhead was too high. The Foundation thought the Club was a bottomless pit of demands.

Around 1974, the Club looked into the possibility of setting up a separate fund, which it would control, that could receive tax-deductible funds directly. The Club would show that it could do without the Foundation. The Club's attorney, Clark Maser, thought this could be done legally, but the Foundation bitterly resisted it. Foundation board

members Wayburn and Siri, who were not attorneys, argued that setting up a new fund was neither legally possible nor necessary. Siri felt
very protective of Clinch as a fellow mountain climber. Ted Snyder, an
attorney who was then Club treasurer, argued for the new fund. He saw
it as a hedge against uncertainty: Who knew what the Foundation's attitude would be in the future? I gave Snyder lots of ammunition.

Frictions also developed over how bequests were to be handled and
over the administration of funds. Denny Wilcher, a staff member I had
inherited from Brower, raised funds (both tax-deductible and not) for
both organizations but was on the payroll of the Club. Originally a book
salesman, he had drifted into fund-raising as a sideline but proved to
be quite effective at it. He got along poorly with the Foundation staff,
however; he endlessly found fault with them, and they felt he was picking on them. Wilcher contended that the Foundation staff raised only
about 20 percent of the funds they had available to grant; the rest were
funds the Club had generated and routed to the Foundation.

Talks were held over a number of years to find ways to improve relations. The participants agreed that the organizations should have a common attorney so they would receive the same—rather than conflicting—
advice. This system did not last for long, however. Finally, in the summer
of 1978 they agreed to set up a Joint Fund Raising Center, but this expe-
dient solved little. So further negotiations were held, with Ted Snyder,
then Club president, and Denny Shaffer, then Club treasurer, leading the
way in negotiating for the Club. I advised both of them and participated
in the negotiations. Phil Berry tried to deflect the negotiations onto a different path, but his efforts yielded little result.

Relations with the Foundation finally began to improve when three
things occurred. First, the Sierra Club actually got the IRS to authorize it to set up a controlled account for tax-deductible funds (the "Sierra
Club Fund"), with the executive committee of the Club's board serving as its trustees. The Club then had an alternative way to handle the
tax-deductible funds it raised, allowing it to call the bluff of the
Foundation. Second, Wilcher left the Club's employment, removing an
irritant to the Foundation. And last, the Club began to get professional
advice on more effective fund-raising from a national consultant. The
Foundation then perceived that the Club was intent on building a professional fund-raising operation of its own and saw no point in competing with that. The Foundation became much more cooperative and
agreed to let the Club raise tax-deductible funds on its behalf.

Sierra Club Political Action Committee

In a theoretical sense, the Sierra Club always knew that the electoral process determined who would sit in Congress and whom it would have to lobby. But the tax laws prevented the Club from doing anything to shape that process—or so we thought. Moreover, we knew that about one-third of the Club's members were Republicans. We feared initially that endorsing candidates would be intensely controversial and would tear the organization apart.

Pressures began to push us toward getting involved, however. As early as 1971, the Sierra Club Council (composed of chapter leaders) had urged Club activists to get involved with outside political action groups. I also began to hear different views of what the law allowed from various lawyers. Some claimed that we could be active in electoral campaigns in limited ways. On looking into it further, we found that we could at least set up a "committee on political education" if funds were raised separately for this purpose.

So in 1976 the Club set up the Sierra Club Committee on Political Education, or SCCOPE, to educate its members on the records and positions of candidates for public office. We quickly learned that federal law permitted us to help some candidates more than others. We could rent our mailing lists to candidates that we preferred, for example. Our board, though, was treading carefully and voted not to let the candidates in the Democratic presidential primary rent our lists. Even in the general election, the act of printing profiles of both presidential candidates in the *Sierra Club Bulletin*—indicating their environmental records—proved to be contentious, though the board finally approved it.

But when I was lobbying Congress in 1980, then Senator John Culver, a Democrat from Iowa with an excellent voting record, gave me a Dutch uncle talk. We were always asking people like him to do things for us, he complained, but he perceived that we did not want to do things for him. He wanted our help in securing his reelection. He insisted that "this has to be a two-way street." He claimed that we would not have many friends left in Congress if we did not stir ourselves to make sure that they came back. (His concerns proved to be well founded personally, because he did not win reelection.)

I took his message back to the Club's board of directors. It was true—we were losing our friends in Congress. We had to do something more: lobbying could only do so much. As it turned out, one of the upsides of

having status as a "civic league" under the tax laws was that such entities were now allowed to have political action committees (PACs).
Accordingly, in 1980 the Sierra Club decided to organize such a committee, though with safeguards in place against unrestrained partisanship;
for example, both the national and local chapters had to agree to endorse
a candidate, and both approvals had to be by a two-thirds margin.

In that first year, the board decided to free me to give my personal
endorsement to President Jimmy Carter, who had a strong environmental record. Carter had phoned me personally to ask for support in his bid
for reelection. Should he be reelected, he promised to let me interview
any future candidate for secretary of the interior (Cecil Andrus, the
incumbent, was not willing to serve another term) before he made his
final decision on whom to appoint. In October 1980, I traveled to the
Rose Garden to stand with other CEOs of environmental groups to
endorse Carter. I also raised some money for him from our staff.

In its first foray into electoral action that year, the board endorsed
only candidates running for the California legislature. Since there was
no adverse reaction, in 1982 the Sierra Club PAC began to endorse candidates for Congress. I put Carl Pope, who was then splitting his time
between the Club and the California League of Conservation Voters, in
charge of the Club's PAC, and he handled the post skillfully. In 1984,
the Club proceeded with the final step: it endorsed a candidate for president. While our candidate, Walter Mondale, failed to get elected, about
74 percent of the 190 candidates that the Club endorsed for election to
Congress were successful. The Club raised more than $250,000 for its
electoral work that year. It had now become a major player among the
PACs in the environmental field.

In contrast to the work of raising deductible funds, this electoral
work went smoothly. It may have been because this operation was never
spun off into a separate organization. No competitive behavior ever
emerged with regards to it. But it certainly did with regard to the way
we handled litigation.

Sierra Club Legal Defense Fund

The Sierra Club Legal Defense Fund was organized in 1971. The Mineral
King litigation had cost us so much that we realized we could have our
own lawyers for the amount of money that we were paying to others. Phil
Berry, who did the spadework to set up the Fund, was supposed to have

its leaders sign a license for use of the Club's name. He never got around to it, however, which eventually became the source of many problems.

The Fund came to manage ongoing cases as well as bring new lawsuits. While it was understood from the outset that it could bring cases on behalf of other clients, for a long time the Sierra Club was its principal client. Decisions to file lawsuits on behalf of the Club were made by a three-member Litigation Review Committee. As executive director, I was one member of this committee; the Club president was another; and Phil Berry was the third. Through this group, I joined in authorizing hundreds of suits.

At the outset, Dick Sill, a very independent member of the Club's board of directors, raised questions about liability. He wondered whether opponents might sue the Sierra Club and win costly judgments against us. Board member Berry, the Fund's chief protector, assured the rest of the board that there was nothing to worry about. But there was. Over the years, the Sierra Club was sued often—for "malicious business interference." Whenever the Club stopped a timber sale or a subdivision, it was vulnerable to such a suit. These were dubbed "SLAPP suits" by onetime Club board member and law professor George Pring—Strategic Lawsuits Against Public Participation.

At one time, the Club had more than $100 million in claims pending against it in suits of this sort. To win such cases, "malice" had to be proved—which it never was, so the Club was fortunately able to beat back all such challenges. But it was intimidating, particularly for an organization without deep pockets. The NAACP Legal Defense Fund in Mississippi was almost wiped out by one such successful suit. And the Sierra Club always defended all of its agents whenever they became entangled in such suits. Nonetheless, the Club persisted and kept bringing cases.

Over the years, the Fund won about three-quarters of the cases that it brought. On the average, the Fund would have between one hundred and two hundred cases pending at any one time—almost all of them against government agencies. No organization brought more recorded state and federal cases of landmark significance in the environmental field than the Sierra Club Legal Defense Fund.

For the first few years, my relations with the Fund were good. In part, this was because Denny Wilcher worked for it as well as for the Sierra Club, and he was a peacemaker of sorts, smoothing relations between the two groups—despite his more antagonistic reputation with the Foundation. But it was also because Jim Moorman, its first executive director, and I liked each other and worked together well.

Moorman did not stay long, however. And where he was straightforward, his long-term successor, Rick (Frederick) Sutherland, was brash and cocksure. For some reason he had taken a dislike to the Sierra Club, which was clear from our first meeting before he even took the job. He also regarded the Club (his client) as his competitor. He wanted the Fund to be run as a separate organization that could go its own way— and even "show up" the Club. He proceeded to build up the Fund's membership and, contrary to the Fund's agreement with the Club, hired his own Washington, D.C., lobbyist, resulting in considerable confusion among lawmakers when our views differed.

Under IRS regulations, a client entity such as the Sierra Club could not pay a public-interest law firm for its services. Donors had to provide the funding to pay for the firm's work. But the Sierra Club could urge its donors to give to the Fund, and the Club agreed at the outset to do that. The Fund, in turn, got into the habit of telling the Club how much it should raise each year for the Fund's services. In 1972, this sum was only $140,000. But by the next year, it had risen to $158,000. By 1976, it was $200,000. And it went up steadily thereafter.

Sutherland and I clashed repeatedly over this sum. While it was not a bill, he treated it as one. Instead of negotiating with me, he merely told me how much the Club owed the Fund and complained that we were not raising enough money for him. Under our accounting, over time we more than met our obligations to the Fund, considering the excess sums we raised in some years as offsetting shortfalls in others. But throughout the process, Sutherland showed his disdain for our organization while lauding the value of his group's services.

During the 1970s while Denny Wilcher was on the scene, he urged that we not press the Fund very hard on the questions that divided us. Wilcher's approach in this instance was very different than his behavior regarding the Sierra Club Foundation. I began to wonder where his loyalties lay, since he worked part-time for the Fund.

I also began to wonder how valuable the services of the Fund actually were. Our relations with most of the Fund's attorneys remained good, but by the end of the 1970s I realized that it had been a long time since I had been shown a roster of cases and their status. All I saw was a report on the highlights of selected cases, and I could only guess about the rest.

Moreover, Sutherland refused to write a contract to clarify these questions and further refused to agree to a licensing arrangement for the use of the Club's name. As the Club pressed hard for these, he dodged our requests.

Before things came to a head, Rick Sutherland was killed in a tragic auto mishap in which he fell out of a moving vehicle. Although his passing changed the tone of things it did not really change their substance. Eventually the Club came to a parting of the ways with the Fund. It had come to have too strong a desire to run its own show, and it no longer wanted to be thought of as a legal adjunct of the Sierra Club. In the mid-1990s, it relinquished the Sierra Club name and went its separate way as an organization called Earthjustice. Today the Sierra Club has its own legal arm within its structure.

Over my time the Sierra Club changed its mind about the value of spinning off organizations to undertake specialized functions. While the Club no longer had to worry about the management details of the organizations it spun off, it had to worry about a host of conflicts: over operations, money, and control, as I have described. I came to feel that it was simply not worth doing, and many board members agreed.

11 *Finding Our Way Internationally*

As the 1970s began, it became increasingly clear that environmental problems were not limited to the United States. All developed nations were suffering from variations of the same problems—pollution, congestion, and degraded habitat. Developing countries typically suffered from environmental problems too, sometimes of a different sort. International commons were about to be assaulted by mining on the bed of the high seas and in Antarctica. And almost everywhere, native forests were in trouble.

The Sierra Club was ambivalent about what it should do in the international arena.[1] The scope of the problems was evident, but it was not certain that the Club could stretch its resources even further. It was just now growing into a national role; how could it extend even further, into an international one? Moreover, would we be welcomed, and were there ways we could be effective, as Americans?

Dave Brower had announced to the world in the 1960s that the Sierra Club planned to publish a series of books with an international focus, and he had set up an operation in the United Kingdom. The Club had already published books on the Galapagos and on Aldabra Island in the Indian Ocean, then threatened by a military base. After leaving the Club in 1969, Brower had been busy setting up chapters of his new group, Friends of the Earth, around the world.

Many expected that the Club would do likewise. In 1970, the Club's board authorized groups abroad to use the Club's name as long as their purposes conformed to those of the U.S.-based Sierra Club and as long as their members controlled their operations. The Club's bylaws were amended to provide a basis for worldwide operations, and groups sprung up among Americans in the Panama Canal Zone (which was then still in American hands) and in American Samoa.

The board was not sure that steps should be taken to promote chapters abroad and referred the question to the Council for study. In the meantime, members in Canada acted on their own. They organized chapters in British Columbia and Ontario before Club lawyers succeeded in reserving the name. The Club in the United States thus was confronted with a fait accompli.

The Sierra Club's board of directors in the United States struggled to catch up with events. It authorized the formation of a sanctioned Club chapter in western Canada, which incorporated the Sierra Club of British Columbia, and initiated negotiations with the new Canadian chapters, which varied widely in temperament. At an all-Canada Sierra Club meeting in Calgary that I attended in the mid-1970s, members from eastern and western Canada could hardly get along. The Ontario chapter was composed of relatively conservative young professionals, while the British Columbia chapter was dominated by liberals who felt everyone needed to pursue a more ecologically sound lifestyle. I had to run a kind of shuttle diplomacy to interpret each to the other. Moreover, many in the British Columbia chapter were Americans who had emigrated to Canada to avoid service in the Vietnam War, and they still had a chip on their shoulder toward the establishment. Some of them went on to found Greenpeace.

As an aside, I should point out that people opposed to the Vietnam War made strenuous efforts to get the Sierra Club in the United States to declare itself against the war. I felt then that the Club should stick to issues that had an environmental basis, although later I would agree that the Club could take on social issues that were connected in some way to the environment. But there were those who wanted the Club to adopt the whole liberal agenda regardless of its relevance to the environment, just as if it were a political party. I felt that the Club would be more effective and have more credibility if it stuck to its environmental agenda, even though I personally shared much of the liberal viewpoint. The Club did end up opposing the use in Vietnam of Agent Orange, a defoliant containing dioxin as a contaminant, which was indisputably an environmental issue.

When the Club sanctioned the chapters in Canada after the fact, I anticipated that this might be the start of a move toward having chapters abroad. At the beginning of 1973, a process was set up for reviewing applications from foreign chapters. The U.S. Club would simply charter affiliates, who would run and finance their own operations, as our chapters in Canada were doing and as Friends of the Earth was doing.

Earlier, in the spring of 1972, on a trip to Mexico City to speak to a National Wildlife Federation convention being held there, I sought out local Club members to get acquainted with them. We met at the hotel over a long breakfast. About a half dozen influential people came, and I learned about the growing environmental sentiment in Mexico at the time. They were all native-born members who had somehow found out about and then joined the Club. I also sounded them out about their interest in forming a Sierra Club chapter in Mexico. While it was too soon to push the issue, there seemed to be interest in developing a closer relationship; in time there might be interest in forming a chapter.

In June 1972 the United Nations held the first of a series of global meetings on the environment in Stockholm, and I attended as part of a Sierra Club delegation. We were eager to encourage the United Nations' interest in the environment, and it was from this meeting that the United Nations Environmental Programme was developed. I met with Sierra Club members there just as I had in Mexico City. Overall, there were by this time more than 3,000 Club members in various countries abroad.

Following the conference, my wife and I traveled to the United Kingdom to meet Club members there. One enthusiast, John Pontin, actually put on a conference in Buxton, in the Midlands, sponsored by the Sierra Club of the United Kingdom. A huge banner was put up on the auditorium with the Club's name on it. More than two hundred people attended, and I spoke to an enthusiastic audience. Later I spoke to another session at the University of London, where about half of the attendees were Americans working abroad and the other half were Britons.

I suppose I was using the organizing skills that I had honed in the United States to organize abroad. Members welcomed contact and, where their numbers were great enough, they wanted to organize. Some members in the United States worried about the image of the "Ugly American" and feared that we would be viewed as carpetbaggers, but I felt that the potential was there to recruit and organize effectively abroad.

Alas, that potential was not to be realized. In 1972 an engaging young international lawyer by the name of Nicholas Robinson, who had grown up in Palo Alto but now lived in New York City, convinced the board that the Club should establish a staff-run program on a regular basis to deal with international issues. But he strongly opposed having foreign affiliates. He thought that only homegrown groups could be effective and that the Club's name and approach would not work abroad. He was willing to make an exception only for Canada.

I disagreed with his conclusion. I saw that other groups, such as Friends of the Earth, Greenpeace, and the World Wildlife Fund, were having success in organizing abroad and felt that we could too. I was especially reluctant to close down the Sierra Club operation in the United Kingdom, where there was a critical mass of members who wanted to be active. I did not feel it was right to tell them that they could not operate in an organized fashion. But I had no choice.

At the end of 1974, Robinson prevailed on the board to adopt a new set of guidelines for the Club's international program, which stated that the Club would not establish units outside the United States, its territories, and Canada. Thereafter, the Club never wavered from this policy, even though over time we heard from people in almost three dozen countries—places as diverse as Australia, Colombia, and Thailand—asking us to organize "Sierra Clubs" there or proposing that various people be given that authority.

I always felt that there was a distinction between proselytizing and telling existing members of the Club that they could not organize where they wanted to. To a certain extent, I could also understand the reluctance to charter Sierra Clubs in places with very different cultures, but I did not understand why we needed to say no to members in England and Australia. Apparently the board was worried about lawsuits, liability for bad debts, and never-ending appeals for financial help. But other organizations found ways to deal with those issues.

The international program that Robinson established was focused on the United Nations in New York City. Our staff there operated under the theory that delegations from small countries, who usually lacked government instructions on environmental questions before them, could be lobbied. Patricia Rambach (later Scharlin) was hired to lobby the United Nations and to organize the program. Robinson told the board that the program could be funded almost entirely by grants from foundations and friendly corporations.

Robinson had a penchant, it would seem, for focusing his attention on bodies that were cumbersome and difficult to deal with. He dragged the Club into trying to influence not only the United Nations but the Soviet Union and the International Union for the Conservation of Nature and Natural Resources (IUCN).

Although Rambach enjoyed some success in building a program, the effort seemed very separate from the rest of the Sierra Club. Rambach recruited representatives in European capitals where U.N. agencies were located, such as Rome, Paris, and London. She put on annual conferences at Talloires, France, on environmental issues. In due course, special projects were developed to influence negotiation of the Law of the Sea Treaty, to influence negotiation of a protocol to the Antarctic Treaty, and to promote forest protection in Venezuela. Special reports were commissioned, and observers were sent to an endless series of conferences. But few Club members knew what was going on or seemed to care.

Board members reflected this sense of estrangement, resenting the $20,000 to $30,000 each year, which they paid to support the program despite having been promised that it would be self-supporting. They also began to question the line taken by the international program's publications. When its reports on questions of ABC (atomic, bacteriological, and chemical) warfare voiced stands that went beyond the Club's positions, the board decided that in the future, its permission would be required before such reports could be published. Some board members asserted that the program was "out of control."

After giving Robinson permission to put on a conference in New York City, the International Earthcare Conference, with the understanding that it would be self-supporting, the board was unhappy when the conference in fact ran a large deficit. Robinson's subsequent plea for an even larger subsidy for the international program fell on deaf ears. Board members began to be restive, too, over some of the corporations that were supporting the program, such as Exxon, and over Robinson's proposal in the mid-1970s to contract with a tour company to run the program's own excursions in East Africa.

Robinson was so exasperated by the frosty reception he received from the board on such occasions that he decided to run for the board himself as a petition candidate, and he succeeded. During his years on the board, from 1977 to 1983, overt complaining about the program ceased, but the underlying restiveness persisted. Most board members did not have the sense that the international program was integrated into the Club's structure; it seemed almost like a separate organization that contracted to do work for the Club.

In 1985, after Robinson left the board, I led an effort to redefine the focus of the international program. With the Club's large base of members in the United States, it made more sense to focus on the policies of the U.S. government abroad than on the policies of the United Nations. In this period, during the Cold War, the United Nations had become largely impotent. But steps taken in Congress could influence our own government's foreign policy, and our members could influence their representatives in Congress. As a result of my recommendation, the board decided to move the program to Washington, D.C., and to make these changes.

Robinson's ideas were not without merit, but he achieved too much influence too soon. At first, board members were dazzled by his apparent mastery of this field, but subsequently they came to have doubts. Initially they thought they were getting a free ride with the program, but as they learned about the real costs, they finally chose to have the program they wanted rather than one he wanted.

The Sierra Club's involvement with the International Union for the Conservation of Nature and Natural Resources preceded Nick Robinson, but he encouraged us to become more involved with it during his club years. The IUCN, founded in Europe a few years after World War II and headquartered in Switzerland, is an unusual amalgam of representatives of governmental agencies from about seventy-five countries and representatives of environmental groups (nongovernmental organizations, or NGOs). It has a strong scientific cast, which is designed to reduce political tensions, though NGOs and governments constantly tug in different directions. It provides the only forum where NGOs can work together and lay plans at the global level. It traditionally operates through various commissions in which volunteers, aided by staff, do most of the work. The IUCN does valuable things in developing programs to protect endangered species, in setting standards for national parks and other protected areas, and in helping developing countries to draft environmental codes.

From the outset, the Sierra Club has been active in the IUCN. Longtime board member Richard Leonard and his wife, Doris, represented the Club at the IUCN in the early years. My predecessor, Dave Brower, was involved for a while. I first got involved at the 1972 United

Nations meeting in Stockholm, when Nick Robinson and I met with the IUCN's director general and his aides. When we urged them to embrace a more activist role on the world scene, we got only a bemused response.

Thereafter, I urged our staff member in New York, Pat Scharlin, to become active in the American Committee for International Conservation (ACIC), the U.S. group that was organized to provide liaison with the IUCN. In due course Scharlin became an officer of the ACIC, and I attended some of their meetings when I was in Washington, D.C.

One of the staff members of the President's Council on Environmental Quality, Lee Talbot, a friend who had been very active in the U.S. delegation at the Stockholm conference, had long been active in ACIC as well. Scharlin and Talbot worked together to lead an American delegation to a momentous IUCN convention in Zaire in 1976 that demanded change in the organization. They got it—in fact, something like a revolution occurred at the conference, and the IUCN henceforth was supposed to welcome participation by its members and take more aggressive stands.

When in a few years Talbot became director general of the IUCN, I was offered a volunteer position as a vice chair of its Commission on Environmental Policy, Law, and Administration (CEPLA). The commission had long been led by a strong-minded German, Wolfgang Burhenne, and his wife. He was used to running it as he wanted, and he raised most of its budget. Talbot thought it should be more open and collaborative.

At my first CEPLA meeting, in Geneva in 1977, I expected that Burhenne would treat me as a colleague and welcome input on what the commission should do. I pressed for an annual review of the commission's work plan by the executive committee, of which I was now a member. But Burhenne was not ready to welcome new ideas at all, and I was treated as an outsider. As my ideas were brushed aside, I became incensed and expressed my displeasure in strong terms. This meeting so alienated me that thereafter I began to play the role of a gadfly at IUCN meetings.

Talbot didn't last long as director general. Thereafter, the IUCN's secretariat acted as if the "revolution" in Zaire had never taken place. Another uprising by the membership took place later, at a General Assembly in Buenos Aires in 1994, but the secretariat again behaved as if nothing had happened.

At numerous General Assemblies of the IUCN, which were held every three years, I took pains to organize NGOs to bring pressure on the secretariat to be more receptive to NGOs and often chaired the NGO caucus. Frequently I collaborated with NGOs from Australia, such as the Australian Conservation Foundation in the early years and the Wilderness Society later.

At a General Assembly in Madrid, despite considerable hostility, I successfully championed the admission of Greenpeace as a member. I became a master of the rules of procedure and frequently quarreled with official rulings. I kept the assembly from reducing the votes to which American NGOs were entitled. At the meeting in Perth, Australia, the Sierra Club led the way in preventing the IUCN from abandoning its traditional focus on protecting nature. The secretariat wanted to placate Third World opinion by switching the IUCN's focus to "sustainable development," but I felt that the IUCN should not back away from nature protection and should not be at all embarrassed about that position. I rallied NGOs to resist acquiescing in this latest fad, which would have had the IUCN become something quite different. The secretariat viewed me as a "conservative force"—wedded to the past.

At assemblies such as the one in Buenos Aires, I championed the cause of small NGOs who wanted the legitimization that grew out of getting the IUCN to endorse their stands on homegrown issues. They would come to me for advice, and if they had to leave early, they would give me their voting cards. When it came time to vote on resolutions, most of the NGOs began to look to me for cues on how to vote. At the Montreal assembly, for example, I ended up with a sheaf of voting cards from NGOs who left early. I stayed to the bitter end.

Frequently, NGOs were trying to get a park established over the opposition of their own government, which often was beholden to developers, or to stop a dam or water project. These groups felt their stand would be validated by getting an international imprimatur, and they could use it at home to strengthen their hand. The secretariat of the IUCN, on the other hand, felt that such resolutions were a waste of time, since the umbrella organization didn't plan to do anything to implement them. The IUCN administration never understood the NGO viewpoint. But again and again, we prevailed on the floor. Most governments abstained rather than resist NGOs in a direct way. But while the secretariat's view was often overruled on the floor, they did everything they could afterward to undermine the stands taken there.

When I first started attending these conferences, those of us from the Sierra Club often took the lead in championing the cause of nature. This sometimes estranged us from the delegates of Third World countries, who didn't yet fear overdevelopment or see the urgency in protecting nature. By the end of my time with the Club, however, attitudes had changed completely. Now we could sit back and watch the delegates from the Third World take the lead—even on protecting nature. They would exert the leadership, and we would then rise to support them.

Efforts were made to bring me into the mainstream at the IUCN. The organization's establishment figures put me on the Resolutions Committee a number of times. I even ran unsuccessfully for the governing council. But I always felt that I was at odds with the ruling clique. I simply did not see things the way they did.

The only time I was able to make a truly lasting impact was when I was appointed to a drafting committee in 1978 to work on a Charter for Nature. It was to be the equivalent for nature of the United Nations' Universal Declaration of Human Rights. Quite remarkably, the president of Zaire had asked the United Nations to draft such a document at the IUCN General Assembly that took place in his country. The task was eventually referred to the IUCN's Commission on Environmental Policy, Law, and Administration, of which both Nick Robinson and I were members, and a task force was established with both of us on it. Neither Nick nor I cared for the weak, colorless draft prepared by the secretariat, and we worked together to prepare an alternative. I prepared the initial draft, and Robinson polished it. Surprisingly, our draft was adopted for discussion purposes by the task force. After further honing by that group, it was eventually adopted and sent to the United Nations. The United Nations, in turn, referred our draft to the United Nations Environmental Programme, which initiated its own lengthy review process. But ultimately, the draft it produced went to the United Nations. Some of my original language even survived. Finally, the United Nations adopted the Charter for Nature almost unanimously. The only negative vote was cast by the United States, then under the rule of the Reagan administration.

I also had some impact as a member of the IUCN's Commission on National Parks and Protected Areas. Ed Wayburn, who also served on the parks commission, and I teamed up to try to get the commission to recognize wilderness as a category in its nomenclature for types of protected areas. Some delegates from South America resisted strongly, feeling that wilderness was not something they wanted in their countries; they argued that it was culturally alien to them. I was never sure why they were so bothered by this notion. We argued that it was a simple reality that many countries had wilderness areas, and that fact deserved to be recognized. I wrote an article for the *Journal of Forestry* pointing out that eleven countries then had versions of wilderness protected by law. Ultimately we prevailed. Ironically, I discovered later that the 1940 Convention on Nature Protection and Wild Life Preservation in the Western Hemisphere, which most South American countries had signed, explicitly sanctioned setting aside wilderness reserves—using that very term.

I was one of a very few to have attended most of the World Parks Congresses sponsored by the IUCN's parks commission at ten-year intervals. I was too inexperienced to get into the first one, held in Seattle in 1962, and merely languished at the gates. But I did attend the next one, at Wyoming's Grand Teton National Park in 1972—albeit without my luggage, thanks to the airline. At that conference, Nick Clinch, who had been to Antarctica as an explorer and climber and was then with the Sierra Club Foundation, put forth a dramatic idea—protecting Antarctica as a world park. Although the delegates did not take up his vision, this may well have marked the beginning of the efforts to keep that continent free of development.

By 1982, I was an invited speaker and arrived with luggage intact. At that conference, held in Bali, Ed Wayburn and I teamed up again to lodge a protest over the conference slogan, "Parks for Sustainable Development." We did not object to making development more sustainable, but we thought that parks did not find their justification in development, whether sustainable or not. Our complaints made little difference, but at least everyone knew the conference attendees were split on this question.

We did make headway in getting the parks commission to adopt a new program to recognize parks around the world that were endangered, just as is done for World Heritage Sites. (That endangered parks idea was later abandoned, however, because of opposition from too many governments.) Ever since 1913, when the Club had suffered the setback of seeing a dam authorized at Hetch Hetchy in Yosemite National Park, the Club had tried to spread the notion that national parks should be viewed as inviolable, and I tried to keep up that tradition. I rallied NGOs to insist that protected areas be off-limits to extractive development such as mining, drilling, or logging. This stance was embodied in something called the New Delhi principles, which were endorsed once again by the conference, though we caused a plan to weaken them to be rejected. I also spoke at the Fourth World Parks Congress in Caracas, Venezuela, in 1992.

The work of the IUCN was too important to be ignored, and it did have an impact. Yet it was a very frustrating organization to deal with, I found time and again. Its efforts to bring NGOs and governments into the same forum were probably preordained to be difficult. Yet Robinson thrived in this environment. While he seemed to agree that we needed to push the organization, he got along with its leaders in ways that I never could. Yet I rallied NGOs in ways that he never did.

Aside from his IUCN work, Nick Robinson also developed a deep interest in the Soviet Union and its environmental policies. He felt the Sierra Club should have a fraternal relationship with the largest and oldest conservation group in that country, the All-Russia Society for the Conservation of Nature. The U.S. State Department had negotiated a protocol with the Soviet Union for exchanges of citizens, and our exchanges with the All-Russia Society were conducted under its provisions. The All-Russia Society was another sprawling, unwieldy group—in this case, one that operated under the Soviet government's auspices. While its work was bona fide (though tame), it counted among its members workers in tractor factories and schoolchildren who were told to donate a few kopecks. Through this process, it had accumulated an immense putative following.

In 1979 I was the leader of our first delegation to the Soviet Union. Although I vowed in advance that I would not get coerced into swilling vodka in toasts, I found myself doing just that at the opening dinner. As the toasts went on forever, recounting legends and wondrous events, I soon learned the art of pretending to drink, as others became increasingly intoxicated. Sometimes I hid my glass behind other things or emptied the contents into flowerpots. But I sipped enough to know that the vodka we were served was very smooth and not bad tasting at all.

Because of these protracted drinking rounds, lunch was served very late—sometimes not till 5 p.m.—by which time we were famished. After these meals, everyone was taken back to their hotels to sober up. We learned to carry breakfast rolls with us during the day to stave off hunger and to gorge on rolls as soon as we arrived at the dinner table to soak up the vodka.

One of our hosts was an affable manager of a nearby wildlife refuge. He had traveled to the United States before, to tend the Soviet exhibit at the world's fair in Spokane, Washington, in 1974. He had enjoyed the experience immensely, he said, and one night at our hotel he was telling us all about it—until the phone rang. He was summoned away and never showed up again to guide us. Apparently there were listening devices in the walls, and he was overheard saying something he should not have. And, closer to home, the lining of my wife's suitcase was slit open. Someone came to the room while we were out to search for contraband. Of course, nothing was there.

We searched in vain to discover what we had in common with the All-Russia Society. They engaged in mild forms of conservation education, while we operated in an open society to lobby our government. While we talked bravely about various possibilities, they never made much sense. I guess we were simply promoting "people-to-people diplomacy." We were helping to reduce tensions in the Cold War. At extended intervals, this exchange went on for many years.

Many other engagements took me to Europe in the 1970s. On one occasion, during the Carter administration, I made a series of speeches in Western Europe under the auspices of the U.S. Information Agency. After making presentations in Spain and Germany, I traveled to Rome for my last one. While I was there, a local environmental group asked me to attend its press conference the next day in downtown Rome. They were announcing their opposition to nuclear power and wanted me to sit at the head table.

This made my USIA handlers very nervous. Since they were paying my travel expenses, I was under their immediate control. They reluctantly consented, on the condition that they could read the press release first. The local group agreed, but told the handlers they would have to wait, as the press release was being finished at the last moment. As I sat comfortably at the head table, my handlers sat in the audience reading the press release, which had been rushed into the room right as the conference began. I expected them to try to yank me from the head table at any moment as the main speaker droned on in Italian, which I didn't understand. Thankfully, that didn't happen.

The Sierra Club was caught in crosscurrents on the Japanese whaling controversy. In the spring of 1974, it endorsed a boycott of Japanese goods because of that country's continued whaling. The Stockholm conference had called for a moratorium on whaling. Later the Club endorsed the specific boycott of yellowfin tuna sponsored by Project Jonah, an anti-whaling group in which my wife was active. I heard a lot about the problem from her, but the Club also heard about the Japanese side of the issue because its Outings Committee was operating "foreign outings" in Japan. Tony Look, who ran the trips, feared that the boycott would be interpreted as "Japan bashing" and thought it should be called off. In time, the Club's International Committee came to feel similarly. Some board members vehemently opposed the boycott, while the Club's Wildlife Committee felt it should continue. Eventually, however, the Club did withdraw from it.

On one trip to Japan, my wife took pains to visit various Japanese whaling stations to see how substantial they were. Representations had been made that whaling was an important part of Japan's economy and traditional way of life. (This was before Japan tried to justify its whaling purely in terms of scientific research.) She found the stations in southern Japan to be small operations, but we were told that there was a big one on the northern island of Hokkaido.

Once in Hokkaido, we found ourselves in the hands of a local conservation group nearby that was almost too hospitable. We had trouble disengaging ourselves from them to see the whaling station—while there was still daylight for us to take photographs. The station was in the city of Abashiri, a fishing and resort city on the northeast corner of the island. When we finally got there, we found only two signs of the whaling enterprise. One was a locker for tools by the side of a small slipway, the other a small garage where the meat was prepared. Somehow our new friends must have been put under pressure to keep us from seeing what an insubstantial operation this really was. The claim that whaling was economically important there seemed hollow indeed. But the Sierra Club had already made its decision to withdraw from the boycott.

As the 1970s progressed I was feeling more confident personally about operating abroad, but the Club was struggling to find a role for itself that would make sense to activists who currently operated exclusively at the domestic level. There were too few in the Club's leadership who had experience at both levels. As a consequence, mutual understanding was in short supply.

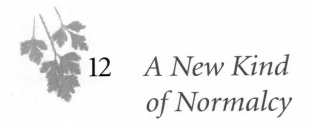

12 A New Kind of Normalcy

During the late 1970s, public opinion surveys showed that protection of the environment had become something almost everybody sought and supported. Some called environmentalism a "valence value"—the only question was how much weight to place on it. Those in vocal opposition had shrunk to a tiny minority. Environmental protection was now a normal, accepted value.

President Jimmy Carter's election in 1976 seemed to embody this change. While his predecessors gave lip service to environmental values, Carter came into office really meaning it. We found that whenever we could talk directly to him, we got somewhere. It was his aides who often tried to keep him from going too far in our direction.

Carter was like no president we had ever seen. Perhaps Teddy Roosevelt and FDR were as enthusiastic, but those in the last couple of decades definitely were not. Kennedy and Johnson were old-style Democrats who had pushed public development. Nixon appointed some good people but vacillated, and in the end he turned against environmentalism. Ford wanted to be seen as a friend of the national parks, but he was a conventional, business-oriented president. Carter, though, was firmly in our camp. On one occasion, he even invited me to go canoeing with him.

His vice president, Walter Mondale, seemed less enthusiastic. He had known serious opposition to environmentalism in northern Minnesota, where mining was entrenched, and he would soon see it in the West too.

Early in his administration, Carter tried to cancel scores of proposed dams in that region. Although it was correct in theory, I never thought this move was well considered politically because it was too abrupt and alienated too many important congressional allies in the West. In any case, it caused an uproar that Mondale was put in charge of trying to quell. He traveled throughout the West after the fact, listening and trying to mend fences. Mondale's chief aide, Bert Carp, worked to moderate Carter's tendencies to favor our interests. We finally met personally with Mondale, but heard only reassuring platitudes rather than anything that responded to our concerns.

Carter put more than forty figures from the environmental movement into his administration. Jim Moorman, of our own Sierra Club Legal Defense Fund, moved into the Justice Department to head the Division of Lands and Natural Resources. Rupert Cutler, whom I had first met at the Wilderness Society (and who did his doctoral dissertation on our Mineral King case), became an assistant secretary of agriculture and oversaw the Forest Service. Charlie Warren from California's legislature (who was recommended by our lobbyist there, John Zierold) became the chair of the President's Council on Environmental Quality. The Natural Resources Defense Council lost so many staffers to the administration that it became a shadow of its former self for a while, and a number of staff from our organization moved into the Interior Department at mid levels.

Some of these appointees acquitted themselves quite well, but strangely enough, many became cautious bureaucrats. On the whole, they seemed to do no better than average. Many felt they had to live down their past and avoid the implication of bias in our direction. They didn't seem to recognize their former friends.

Soon after Carter's election, in late 1976, he invited the CEOs of the major environmental organizations to visit him in Georgia to consult. We were directed to meet him at the home of his mother ("Miss Lillian") near Plains, Georgia. Not wanting to be late, some of us arrived early. In fact, we even got to the house ahead of the Secret Service. As we were passing time, we inspected the vegetation around the foundation. Some of Carter's newly appointed staff probably thought we were the Secret Service looking for bombs. Fortunately, we did not find any.

That meeting with the president started a practice that continued well into his administration. Environmental organizations in the Group of Ten were the principal ones invited to these meetings.[1] Carter wanted to meet every six months to find out what we were thinking. At these meetings, each member of our group would offer comments on our top concerns. We always met in advance to agree on what to address and what would be said, by whom, and in what order. Each person spoke for a minute or two, and Carter, always well informed, would interject from time to time. The exchange of views was very useful; it meant we could understand each other without intermediaries, could secure commitments, and learn what issues might move in the administration. Unfortunately, this practice tapered off as Carter became too busy, and it was not continued by his successors at all.

After our meeting at Miss Lillian's home, some of us flew back to Washington, D.C., with members of the cabinet on Air Force One. I sat with Charles Schultze of the Brookings Institution, who was soon to become chairman of the Council of Economic Advisors. We discussed energy policy, and he seemed receptive to our views.

Carter knew that we were quite concerned about who would be secretary of the interior. I worked with Larry Rockefeller of NRDC (the son of Lawrence Rockefeller, Sr., and definitely a person of a new age) to develop a series of questions to put to the candidates. Leaders of environmental groups then met to discuss the various candidates; Brock Evans represented us in that process. At one of their private meetings, Evans mentioned some negative information that had been forwarded by conservationists in Idaho concerning their governor, Cecil Andrus, who wanted to head the Interior Department. Evans did not want to put too much weight on it, however. He had dealt with Andrus directly during the years he spent running the Sierra Club's Northwest office and was already familiar with Andrus's pluses and minuses.

But the negative information leaked out. Evans's name was associated with criticism of Andrus and opposition to his appointment, and the Sierra Club's name was associated with Evans. Although Andrus got the job, he remained furious over the criticism. Ever after, our relations with him were prickly. Others in the Interior Department were accessible to us, but Andrus was not.

My name was put forward to head the Bureau of Outdoor Recreation in the Interior Department, but I declined the offer. I was more interested in the National Park Service, but that was not offered; after what had happened, Andrus was not about to offer such a major post to a leader of the Sierra Club. The Bureau of Outdoor Recreation, on the other hand, was a small agency that had been carved out of the Park

Service, and I was never sure I really approved of that. Oddly enough, James Watt was chief of the Bureau of Outdoor Recreation during the Nixon administration. Clearly, I failed to recognize what a stepping-stone this post could be.

Our problematic relations with Andrus were compounded when he later sought control over the Forest Service. Efforts were made during the Carter administration to revive the idea of creating a Department of Natural Resources, first floated in the 1930s by Harold Ickes, FDR's interior secretary. Various agencies would have been added to the Interior Department under this plan, including the Forest Service. Before he became governor of Idaho, Andrus had been a logger, and he refused to extend assurances to us that the Forest Service's emphasis on logging would be reduced if the agency were transferred to the Interior Department. In fact, the timber industry itself felt that logging might be increased if the merger went through because of Andrus's background. As a result, we withheld our support for the idea, and it died for lack of support.

Campaigns

Despite our tepid relations with Andrus, we worked closely with many of his people on planning for the protection of lands and waters in Alaska. Ultimately, Congress and the president took the key steps that protected millions of acres there, but the groundwork was laid by planners in the National Park Service and other agencies.

All the same, Congress delayed taking action by the statutory deadline to set aside new parks and refuges in Alaska because of implacable opposition from the Alaska delegation in Congress. It was Carter who broke the impasse, using his executive powers to preserve 80 million acres as national monuments in Alaska. This step was so offensive to the Alaska delegation that they urged Congress to reverse the president's action, but their pleas were in vain. Carter's action took immense courage and was a landmark achievement.

During the Carter years, the Sierra Club was in the thick of many battles. In 1977, for instance, we worked to extend the Clean Air Act with amendments requiring, among other things, that EPA set national air-quality standards by strict deadlines. In 1980 we waged a particularly intense campaign to enact legislation authorizing the Superfund program, which provided funds to clean up sites where hazardous wastes had been dumped.

Wilderness protection also made major progress during the Carter years—not only in Alaska, but in portions of the lower 48 states as well. Doug Scott, then in our Northwest office, put together the Endangered American Wilderness Act, which was enacted in 1978. It protected 1.3 million acres of wilderness in areas that lacked any designation and stood in the greatest peril. No bills of this sort had been enacted before; Congress had acted only on legislation embodying agency recommendations.

Wilderness protection was also garnered for the Golden Trout Wilderness in California, in 1978; the French Pete Creek Wilderness in Oregon, on which I had once worked, in 1978; and the huge River-of-No-Return Wilderness in Idaho, in 1980. When Congress finished with it, the area protected, 2.2 million acres, was three times larger than I had once thought possible. The basic law for the Boundary Waters Canoe Area in Minnesota was strengthened in 1978, and acreage was added to it as well as to other areas. Two million acres of land within national parks were designated as wilderness, where roads and lodges could not be built. In 1978, a total of 4.5 million acres were added to the Wilderness System. And in 1980, four million more acres of wilderness were established in various states outside of Alaska.

Moreover, a better inventory was done of de facto wilderness in the national forests. Assistant Secretary of Agriculture Rupert Cutler ordered a new study (RARE II) to remedy the defects of the study done earlier in the decade, which had left out many areas. The new study found that there were 62 million acres of Forest Service lands that were roadless, undeveloped, and unprotected, for example, whereas the earlier study had found only 56 million acres of this type.

While the Carter administration did recommend that more of this inventory actually gain protection as wilderness in the future (15 million acres, in comparison to the 12 million acres recommended as an outgrowth of the first Nixon inventory), our attention now turned to how much the administration proposed to release to be logged: 36 million acres. Because Carter believed that increased logging on public lands would help combat inflation, environmentalists were doubly anxious. In light of the Clinton administration's proposal, many years later, that as many as 58 million acres be kept roadless, this proposal seems particularly ill considered. In any case, it sounded the first down note in our relations with Carter.

In the furor over inflation during the Carter years, the timber industry managed to get the Council on Wage and Price Stability to back an increase in logging on public lands; this would reduce housing costs, the industry argued, because it would increase the supply of wood. In reality, such a reduction would have been slight at best, because lumber costs are only a small share of the costs of new housing.

Our relations with Carter cooled even more in 1980, which turned out to be his last year in office. Facing rising oil prices, inflation, and domestic restiveness, Carter had crafted a proposal for an Energy Mobilization Board, which would have been authorized to waive environmental controls. This was completely unacceptable to us. It was joined with a proposal to heavily subsidize development of synthetic fuels, particularly development of oil shale in the West. Oil shale development would consume vast amounts of scarce water and leave large waste piles of processed shale, posing pollution dangers. I wrote a major critique of oil shale development, expanding on its environmental problems, for a publication of the university of Utah Law School.[2] We bitterly resisted these measures in Congress and finally succeeded in killing them on the House floor with a strange alliance of votes from the left, which sought to protect the environment, and the right, which opposed the element of government subsidies for synthetic fuels.

While the fate of the Energy Mobilization Board was still in doubt, President Carter called me to solicit our support for his reelection bid in 1980. I held back, asking in turn for a pledge that he would veto any energy bill that contained waivers of environmental controls. He wouldn't go that far, but he did give me pledges that, were he to be reelected, we could interview candidates for various posts such as secretary of the interior and the assistant secretary of agriculture, the person who would be in charge of the Forest Service. This was an important breakthrough.

In 1979, when John McGuire resigned as chief of the Forest Service, the Sierra Club had been consulted by the Carter administration about who should be the next chief. The final choice was between Max Peterson and Doug Leisz, who had been the regional forester in San Francisco. Because I had strong policy differences with Leisz, I supported Peterson, who got the appointment and who I felt at least would give us a fair hearing.

In Carter's last year, the Sierra Club was in the thick of a battle for the so-called Superfund bill (more formally known as the Comprehensive Environmental Response, Compensation, and Liability Act, or CERCLA). This legislation was designed to clean up sites where hazardous wastes had been dumped in the past. It was a counterpart to the Resource

Conservation and Recovery Act (RCRA), which had been enacted in 1976 to control the disposal of newly generated hazardous wastes. Under the proposed Superfund law, those who contaminated properties in the past would be expected to bear the costs of cleaning them up, with a tax imposed on the petroleum industry, which was especially at fault, to clean up properties for which owners could not be found.

Doug Scott, in his new role as our director of federal affairs, led our forces in a brilliant campaign to enact this measure. Despite Carter's basic support of the legislation, we had to fight hard to get Congress to insist on "strict liability" and "joint and several liability" for dumpers. These provisions meant that negligence need not be proven and that all those who owned contaminated property were fully responsible. In the past, negligence law had done little to prevent gross contamination and in fact provided something of a shield to protect polluters. It was also fairer to hold those who had benefited from owning the property liable for its condition than to impose the costs of cleanup on the taxpayers at large. These stringent legal provisions sent a strong message to those who would generate these wastes that they were jeopardizing their property values because all of those to whom they might sell their property would find themselves liable.

Weighing all factors, the Sierra Club's board decided at last to let me go to a ceremony in the Rose Garden as an individual to endorse Carter for reelection. I was joined by many other CEOs of environmental groups. But it was fruitless; Carter would be a one-term president. In the final days of his administration, both the Forest Service and the Bureau of Outdoor Recreation gave the Sierra Club awards for its work. These were probably designed to enlist our aid in meeting the challenges to come.

The Sierra Club in the Late 1970s

The Carter years may have advanced our goals with respect to public policy, but they did not help the Sierra Club grow in size. Our constituency relaxed and became more complacent, and membership interest slowed, as it did among many environmental groups. During the four years of Carter's presidency, the Club's membership hovered around 180,000. We were in the doldrums again, just as we had been, at a lower level of membership, in the years 1971 through 1974. Our efforts in the Carter years to promote membership growth brought in new members, but they just replaced those who dropped out. Our constituents apparently did not feel the need for watchdog groups like the Club as acutely then as they would later.

By the mid-1970s, attitudes in the Club toward promoting growth in membership had changed. When Denny Shaffer became chairman of the Membership Committee in 1976, the Club enthusiastically embraced membership growth as a goal for the first time and began experimenting with various techniques to attract new members. With these changes under way, I was emboldened to suggest to the board that they set a specific goal for growth in membership, such as 250,000 members by 1980. The board approved that proposal, and by 1978 the Club began to use the firm of Craver, Mathews, Smith & Company in Arlington, Virginia, to advise it on membership development and fund-raising. Though the 250,000 membership goal was not met until 1982, the organization did grow appreciably (by more than 30 percent per year in those years), and we learned new techniques of recruitment.

Setting a membership goal was probably the Club's first introduction to strategic planning, though it had been doing another type of planning in connection with its conservation program. In the 1960s the board had adopted a couple of campaigns as its priorities, but only in the 1970s did it begin to set priorities among a longer list of possibilities. In choosing among potential campaigns. I suggested that the board weigh the intrinsic worth of a campaign, including factors such as the amount of environmental improvement that would be gained; its usefulness to the Club, including factors such as serving as a stimulus for raising funds and gaining members; its appropriateness as an undertaking by the Club, including its cost in terms of money and staffing; and the prospects for success, including factors such as the ripeness of the issue and the amount of opposition. As a checklist of things to consider, it was imperfect but useful.

We also began to distinguish measures of success. We saw that our legislative program sometimes had total wins and sometimes only partial wins, especially in the field of energy. We sometimes lost completely—again mainly in the field of energy, where we simply faced opponents with too much money—and sometimes the issue was put off for action in a following Congress. As a result, we also began to make distinctions in our planning between finishing up old campaigns, starting new ones, and merely building up public interest for future campaigns.

I insisted that the board set aside a pot of money, known as the Major Campaign Fund, that could be used flexibly for these campaigns. Then, depending on opportunities and the political mood, we could put our effort into the campaigns most likely to succeed. Because of tight budgets, the amount in this fund (originally about $150,000) gradually became worth less and less as inflation diminished its value through successive years.

For a while, we experimented with making the priority-setting process sophisticated—and thus overly complicated. In one effort, nearly seventy specific issues were listed as priorities under a complex set of headings. Obviously this was merely a way of finding a place for everyone's interests, rather than a way of setting real priorities. Usually the Club's board of directors ended up embracing whatever I recommended, although they usually modified it slightly. I got them involved in setting broad priorities too, for five- and ten-year periods.

As the 1970s wore on, it became apparent that the planning for major campaigns could no longer be done just by the board and staff. Activists in the Club in chapters and groups around the country had to be involved too. We began by surveying their interests. As they became more involved, we found that we had to simplify our priority-setting process. By 1978, we decided merely to pick "mega-campaigns" (such as the Alaska campaign) and some lesser campaigns. Nonetheless, the allure of planning was in the air. I was urged to set the stage for the 1980s in conservation. I prepared papers that tried to anticipate which issues would mature, which would unfold to a lesser degree, and which would not move at all.

As the Club involved thousands of its activists in priority-setting every two years, it found itself managing a complicated political process. Among its constituency were passionate advocates for almost every issue. Thus priority-setting was in danger of turning into a process that disaffected most of our activists, for most of the nearly one hundred proposed issues could not be picked; only a few could be true priorities.

So gradually the process became a sham. Broad headings came to be embraced as the ostensible priorities, because almost everyone could imagine that their pet issues would find a home somewhere in the list of meaningless generalities. In reality, the staff and the top officers decided what would get most of the funding and attention. Fortunately for me, as the Club grew, I became less involved in this process. As Doug Scott took over as Director of Federal Affairs in the late 1970s, the process came to have more of these characteristics. Ostensibly more people were involved in a popular process, but it was becoming more illusory.

Public Relations

In the late 1970s, I and others sensed that the political mood at large was growing less favorable to our cause. For about a decade, we had been easily able to find opportunities in our work before Congress. But the easy reforms were behind us. Increasingly, we were working on questions that might have widespread ramifications throughout society, such as Superfund. Reporters began to ask whether we had considered the side effects of our reforms. Moreover, our successes were pushing us into dealing with trade-offs. As we succeeded in stopping nuclear power, for example, we had to confront the many downsides of relying more on coal. And the media began to treat us as part of the establishment. In the skeptical post-Watergate period, they were inclined to think that even public-interest groups had feet of clay. The *Los Angeles Times* printed an article criticizing our foundation for holding stock in oil companies and others that were not "pure."

As the times became more conservative, new initiatives that would rely on the power of the federal government drew greater resistance. This was particularly true of proposals in the field of pollution control and energy, though we continued to do quite well with proposals to set aside new parks and wilderness areas. Our opponents in the latter case were largely local and had fewer resources to oppose us. In the case of pollution control and energy, however, we faced powerful and wide-ranging interests. To succeed here, we needed a better press.

To cope with these mounting problems, I proposed that the Sierra Club develop a long-range public relations strategy. I suggested that we needed to "consciously reach out, with some humility, to different sectors in society to explain our intentions and hopes and to listen carefully to their own." I saw four target audiences: our core believers, opinion leaders, the general public, and even our opponents, since I wanted them to have to factor us into their strategies. I urged that staff be hired and a program set up. This was not to happen until about six years later, however.

The Club had worked hard to secure media coverage. Whenever it had a good news hook, it would hold a press conference. The media typically turned out in good numbers whenever the Club filed a lawsuit and less readily when we announced a new campaign to promote or oppose a given

measure. Apparently the media thought they would be giving free publicity to one point of view if they covered such announcements. Often these
decisions of ours had more impact than our lawsuits, however.

I had good relations with a number of reporters. In addition to various journalists in the San Francisco area, I was called regularly by
Gladwin Hill of the *New York Times*, who covered environmental issues
out of an office in Los Angeles. Sometimes I visited him there, and many
of my conversations with him later blossomed into major stories. Later,
when I was stationed in Washington, D.C., I came to have a similar relationship with Philip Shabecoff, who covered environmental issues for
the *New York Times* from offices in the East.

Beginning in the late 1970s, many newspaper editorial boards were
eager to talk with us, so I started traveling around to meet with them,
visiting papers such as the *Milwaukee Sentinel* and the *Tulsa World*.
Because they would often raise questions regarding local issues, I would
usually bring along a local Sierra Club leader. A favorable editorial usually followed.

The boards of newspapers in the Midwest were most interested in
meetings of this sort. Those on the two coasts were much less interested,
with the exception of the *Los Angeles Times*. The *Times* editors were
always eager to meet with us and readily accepted the guest editorials I
wrote for them. Oddly enough, the editorial board of the *San Francisco
Chronicle*, our hometown newspaper, exhibited little interest in meeting
with us, even though I was personally acquainted with its owner as well
as its chief editorial writer.

I was often asked to write articles for various publications as well. I
wrote articles for the *Saturday Review*, *The New Republic*, *Harper's*, *Life*
magazine,[3] and scores of professional periodicals.[4] Over time I also
wrote more than a dozen pieces for various law reviews.[5] Guest editorials with my byline (usually written by me, but sometimes drafted by
our staff) were run in the *New York Times*, the *Christian Science Monitor*,
the *Wall Street Journal*, *USA Today*, the *Los Angeles Times*,[6] and other
papers. Some of my speeches were also printed in *Vital Speeches of the
Day*.[7] Once my words were even the quote of the day in the *New York
Times* and in an issue of *The New Yorker*.

After a while I convinced myself that I was fairly well known. A magazine that covered California politics named me one of the two dozen
most powerful people in the state. But I couldn't rest on those laurels.
Once when I was attending a reception at a conservation event in Palo

Alto, for instance, an elderly lady came up to tell me how much she admired me. I basked in her continuing praise until she finally told me that she had voted for me every time. With a shock, I suddenly realized that she was not talking about me at all but about Congressman Paul ("Pete") McCloskey, a Republican generally sympathetic to our cause who then represented that district. It was too late to confess that she had the wrong man. So I just responded by urging her to "keep it up."

This incident was not the only time the two of us were confused. My wife was often a member of U.S. government delegations to meetings of the International Whaling Commission. One year the meetings took place in Australia, and Congressman Pete McCloskey was in the delegation. My wife told me that it was assumed that she was the congressman's wife. She was treated with great deference and enjoyed it, but she drew the line when they tried to put her in the same hotel room with him!

Throughout my time as executive director, we struggled to find roles for Club members who were really celebrities. Actor Paul Newman agreed to star in a special television production that was prepared for us. When singer Linda Ronstadt was keeping company with Governor Jerry Brown, she volunteered to help us, although we never did work anything out. Actor Eddie Albert helped us by appearing at Club conferences, and actor Ted Danson spoke at one of our press conferences.

A succession of other personalities trooped into my offices on Bush Street in San Francisco at one time or another. Edmund de Rothschild of Britain, of the aristocratic banking family, once came to see me, supposedly to solicit support for a power project in British Columbia. But he spent most of his time telling me about his experience working with Winston Churchill many years earlier on the Churchill Falls power project in Labrador. Having spread out his very sizable maps underneath our feet, he spent his time crawling around on my office floor as he told his story. He was completely unpretentious.

For a while I felt that I should meet with anyone. As a matter of good public relations, I met with even those writers who were critical of us. On the Storm King Mountain campaign, one writer by the name of William Tucker had covered the issue of the proposed pumped storage project, which would have held water on the side of the mountain to be released to generate power when needed. It had been proposed by a New York City utility and would have defaced the scenery of that special place along the Hudson River. Environmental interests, including the Sierra Club, had stopped it through lawsuits.

Tucker had developed the preposterous theory that environmental groups were generally a front for wealthy people with estates and property to protect, along the Hudson and elsewhere. When he finished interviewing me, I found that he had left his notebook (with notes for many articles in it) in my office. Even though I had the chance to spare us further grief by disposing of it, I called to tell him that I had it. He was both alarmed and relieved.

I even met with Ron Arnold—on two occasions. Now a prime mover in the wise use movement, which opposes environmental objectives on public lands, in 1977 he was claiming to be an intermediary between environmentalists and the timber industry and to be writing articles in that vein. (He also claimed to have once been an activist in our Seattle group.) But the article he published about his second interview with me was laced with his invective, and I wrote to complain that he was anything but neutral.

I traveled a great deal to spread the word about the Sierra Club's programs and to give people a more accurate picture of what we stood for than they might get secondhand. At the behest of student groups, I spoke on many college campuses. I also spoke to many business groups, who wanted to meet their potential opposition. Many of these audiences were programmed to hear only what they expected, however. I would often say that we were not against all oil drilling, or mining, or logging. Usually the first question after my address would be "Why are you against all oil drilling [or mining, or logging]?" I began to wonder whether communication was really possible.

Once I was at the head table at a conference in Portland, Oregon, next to its governor at the time, Tom McCall. As he and I were chatting, I remember him cautioning me "not to be too hard on the timber industry." While McCall had a reputation for being an environmentalist, apparently he was not willing to go up against what was then the principal industry of his state. I didn't give him much satisfaction.

By the late 1970s, though, I had switched from speaking largely to outside groups to speaking mainly at meetings of Club chapters, often at banquets, to improve their sense of connection to the national office. I also traveled often to participate in a succession of policy dialogues and assorted other functions, which gave me a chance to see problems on the ground firsthand. I saw huge shovels tearing away the topsoil to reach coal. I saw mine fires that burned without end. I saw toxic waste stored in immense tailing ponds that would eventually leak. I saw berms of abandoned mines failing. I saw smoke from smelters polluting the skies for miles, offshore oil wells that had blown out, and birds smeared with oil from tanker crashes.

Naturally, I traveled often to Washington, D.C., for meetings to discuss strategy, to testify before congressional committees, and to lobby. The days were past when I was a lead witness at hearings, but I testified dozens of times as part of panels of witnesses from environmental organizations. While we would file our full statement for the record, we could usually speak for only a few minutes. Some of my colleagues felt they should speak extemporaneously for greater emotional impact, but I believed in preparing these comments carefully as well. It was surprising how many witnesses were unclear in their oral statement as to where they stood on the matter before a committee. Were they for it or against it, or did they deliberately take a qualified stand? Sometimes I acted in concert with other environmental witnesses and used my time for rebuttal, which of necessity had to be impromptu.

I took the same approach in lobbying. Most lobbying was handled by regular Club staff who specialized in the issues involved, but I was brought in to see key members of Congress who were undecided or wavering in their support. Although I would begin each meeting with some comments designed to break the ice, I tried to use the limited time for the visit carefully. Most members of Congress are skilled in putting visitors at ease and deflecting difficult decisions; I had to make sure that our discussion was not derailed by a member's jocular interjection. While members had to be indulged (we were trying to win them over, after all), at the same time we had to get our message across within the normal ebb and flow of the conversation.

On occasion, various entities paid my way to travel to events they were sponsoring. Once, *Town & Country* magazine decided to do a story on the Sierra Club, and wanted me and the presidents of the Club and the Sierra Club Foundation to be photographed at the edge of the Grand Canyon. The image would be featured as a two-page spread in the middle of the issue. They flew us to the South Rim, where we spent a strange late afternoon with a photographer who could not be satisfied. He wanted us to pose closer and closer to the rim, until I was about six inches from the precipice. And then he decided that the light was not right and had us wait until it was mellow. Then he wanted to wait until there was a rosy light as the sun set. By then it was almost too dark to photograph. It was beginning to get cold, and as he went on to take dozens of shots I began to get nervous about losing my balance. I was on the verge of getting vertigo and needed some food. I was a few inches from oblivion. But I gritted it out and kept my balance. Oddly enough, the photograph that was finally used in the spread was pitch black on one whole page. On the other page, we stood uneasily, with pained looks. I knew why.

But there were compensations too. Once I was approached by staff for a major public relations firm who wanted to fly me to New York City for a special event at Radio City Music Hall. A major firm was debuting an IMAX nature film, and their representatives had an unswerving notion that I had to be there. But it was not a convenient time for me to travel to New York. As I kept saying no, they kept increasing their offer. They said they would pay for my wife too. I said no. They offered to put us up at the Plaza Hotel. I still said no. They offered to provide a limousine and driver for three days, and I said no again. Finally, they offered to pay for our meals at restaurants of our choice for that period as well. Since no issues of principle were at stake, merely my convenience, I relented at last and accepted their offer and took some leave. I was introduced and took a bow at Radio City Music Hall (along with Russell Train, now with the World Wildlife Fund), and we thoroughly enjoyed ourselves.

Only a few times did I go on official Sierra Club trips; whenever I did, I would be plied with so many questions it felt like a busman's holiday. On vacations, I wanted to get away from work. Instead, every summer Maxine and I would take a trip of a week or so into the Sierra, or into other wilderness areas such as the Trinity Alps. Over time we got quite familiar with many areas on the John Muir Trail. Usually we would use pack horses to take us up from the steep east side to some area in the high country. After day trips spent hiking and acclimating ourselves, we would hike out to the roadhead. Whenever we could, we would repair to Hot Creek near Mammoth Lakes to soak ourselves in its soothing waters. Natural hot springs of just the right temperature bubbled up there in the bed of a cold, clear creek. One needed to move only a few feet to find water to cool off. Unfortunately, an earthquake ultimately ruined the spot; now scalding water pours out there.

Traditions regarding leadership on Club trips, like so much else, began to change during the 1970s. Originally the leader of the trip had total authority to make decisions on starting times, routing, safety, and pace. The leader was responsible for the welfare of the party. The changing mores of the 1960s, however, began to undermine this tradition of authority. I saw this firsthand on a trip up Crested Butte in Colorado with the Club's board of directors. We undertook the trip after a young man from the local Club volunteered to guide us up the mountain during a break in our meetings. While we had no trouble following him up, he virtually abandoned us on the way down. He literally ran down the mountain, leaving most of us behind and perplexed as to which was the right direction to head in. We ended up scattered over the mountain, straggling back to camp all throughout the afternoon. Another board member and I stuck together, fortunately, and at the bottom of the mountain we struck a road and thumbed a ride from a passing driver to get back into town.

Things could be aggravating in the city, too. One night at a Club banquet in San Francisco, I had to make a particularly difficult decision. As we made our way into the hall, demonstrators for a group led by Lyndon LaRouche were handing out leaflets protesting the Club's support for the "right to choose." As the crowd gathered and the proceedings got under way, the fire department called to tell me that a bomb threat had been called in. The department immediately sent investigators out to look for the bomb, but they found nothing. That did not mean there was no bomb, they cautioned me, and then put the decision on my shoulders: Did I want to call off the banquet and evacuate the hall, or proceed? The program was in midstream. The hundreds of people there knew nothing of what was going on, although some had noticed men looking into potted plants. Not having yet experienced direct violence against the Club, I thought it was an empty threat. I decided to go ahead, and luckily nothing untoward did happen.

A few years later I might have made a different decision, as the Club had begun to get more threats. Though the number of people who were bitterly opposed to us was small, some of them were gravely disaffected. A motorcycle group threw a brick through the window of one of our offices. A rag that was labeled radioactive was mailed to us; the innocent-looking package was opened by a Club employee who was pregnant. Fortunately, the police found that it was harmless. In rural areas, stories circulated of car windows with Sierra Club stickers being smashed. I had none on my car.

One day the FBI came to tell me the most amazing story. We were then conducting a second round of efforts to save more redwood forests on California's north coast. Members of the Manson family, who were already serving life sentences in Folsom Prison for murder, had taken an interest in this effort. They thought the Sierra Club and the Save-the-Redwoods League were doing too little, although the Club was actually then leading the fight. They had been writing threatening letters to the League, and the FBI thought their threats would soon reach us too. The FBI felt that the Manson family might have friends outside prison who were working with them and that we might be in danger.

At that moment, I decided to get an unlisted home telephone number. I did not want my address to be found easily or to get harassing calls. Moreover, I was tired of getting calls at 4 a.m. from radio reporters in New York who wanted an instant statement from me on the air about an oil tanker sinking in the South Indian Ocean. After such calls, I could never get back to sleep. Those making the calls never seemed to recognize that it was three hours earlier on the West Coast. I realized that I was simply too accessible. Now it was not only a matter of public relations, but a matter of my safety and that of my family.

Club Affairs

Dealing with such problems was not the norm, but I was spending about half of my time not on conservation but administering the Club. By the late 1970s, I had been entrusted with doing all the hiring. Fewer of the board members were interested in micromanaging the Club anymore; they were content to make policy. Even fewer had the time or desire to keep up-to-date on all of our operations. Many of the newer board members focused on specific subjects, and some became dedicated advocates for their favorite programs. Given all that was going on, I found that I needed to be in the office more. During the presidency of Richard Cellarius in the late 1970s, I decided as a consequence to limit my time on the road to about fifty working days each year.

I tried to unlearn the habits of subtlety that I had developed in college and to simplify my communications. Interestingly, the more I offered to share power and to collaborate, the more the Club's officers trusted me to use my best judgment. Conversely, senior staff who insisted on keeping their power strictly to themselves were more likely to be distrusted and hamstrung as a result.

The organization was becoming more complex and professional. Longtime staff were in a position to learn the intricacies of the Club, giving them a power of sorts, which was in turn resented by some of the newer volunteer leaders. Some staff began to develop alliances with powerful volunteers. I found that I had to spend more time managing the whole arrangement.

I spent most of my time in the office meeting with staff to review and plan operations. We always had a list of projects to improve operations. Problems of wider interest were addressed in frequent meetings with the heads of departments. These alternated with even larger meetings with them and midlevel managers. Our field representatives and lobbyists generally gathered at least annually to discuss plans. And the rank and file had their own loose organization, which was called the Stewards.

When criticism would come our way, my typical manner of replying was to provide an in-depth response, with lots of data and an explanation of the situation. If remedial action were needed, I tried to put the solution into effect without delay. This approach usually put an end to any effort to blow the situation into a big problem.

In the late 1970s we were testifying at about a hundred congressional hearings annually. We were preparing and mailing dozens of issue appeals each year. We had also developed a series of specialized newsletters on conservation topics, and we responded to tens of thousands of letters annually. On the average, we were involved in a hundred or more lawsuits at any one time.

Not only were our lobbying and litigation programs active, but our other operations were growing. We were publishing a dozen or more new books each year. We were turning out films by splicing together amateur footage. Our magazine (long the *Sierra Club Bulletin*, now renamed simply *SIERRA*) had doubled in size, its circulation was more than a quarter of a million, and it was sold in scores of outlets across the country. A serious effort was also under way to sell advertising in it, though we would not accept ads for products at odds with our conservation program.

We were selling 1.5 million calendars annually and now had the best-selling continuing line of commercially sold calendars in the country. I remembered advisors in book publishing in the 1960s warning us that the calendar was likely to be a short-lived business. It was not. We were receiving as many as 75,000 submissions of photographs for those calendars per year. As many as six hundred phone calls a day would come into our offices. Our accounting and membership staffs were handling about 700,000 transactions each year. Fortunately, dozens of volunteers would come into our offices each day to help with the mountain of work.

During these years, I read the copy for all issues of our magazine, which was published six times a year. I found commenting on the copy to be a good way to communicate in concrete terms with our editor, Fran Gendlin, about what I wanted. Because the lead time for articles was lengthening, they were becoming less topical and more generic. For a while I wrote editorials for *SIERRA* as well as introductions for our calendars and some books.

As the 1970s wore on, the Club welcomed an increasing number of Club presidents and other officers from the South. Though all quite different, they brought a broadly similar new attitude to the work and dealings with staff. They styled themselves as champions of the volunteers and were less inclined to defer to staff. Indeed, they were eager to challenge staff members and tended to treat us as "just the help." Their style of management was direct and hierarchical, and they had no reticence about using the authority of their offices. They could be brusque and difficult to work with.

They also brought various fresh talents to the Club. They started valuable new programs and helped solve intractable problems. Some had financial skills, some were experts in environmental law, and they all brought energy to our work. But they pushed me in a direction that was completely at odds with the pressures I was feeling from the staff.

In other parts of the nation, the use of naked authority had been discredited among the younger generations. This was particularly true of the younger staff of the Sierra Club, including those in the Conservation Department. They wanted a collaborative style of management, in which decisions were made by the group. They wanted to be part of a "management team."

I, on the other hand, had been practicing "management by objective." I worked with the managers to develop objectives that they would try to achieve; then I would follow up and assess their progress. I did not think many of the other department heads wanted to intrude into one another's business as part of a team. Nor did I think that they wanted to take orders from those who worked for them. Since ultimately the board of directors held me accountable for performance, I did not think it was right to acquiesce in decisions that did not make sense to me.

Over time, I tried to straddle the dilemma. I moved toward a more collegial style of management, in which I frequently consulted various groups of staff. But I thought that my judgment counted for something. Where there was no unanimity, I made the decision. The "Southern boys" on the board seemed to have no understanding that I was in the middle of a clash of cultures. At various times, their own headstrong ways precipitated outcries from staff and injured morale. When I was treading carefully, they were ready to barge in. Any hesitation on my part was regarded as ineptness. Finesse was not their long suit.

In the late 1970s, I faced never-ending pressures to add staff. Some board members wanted us to join with the Wilderness Society to hire "wilderness coordinators" to promote establishment of new wilderness areas. Board members such as Ted Snyder backed this proposal strongly; in 1976 the board went along, and four such coordinators were hired. No one knew where the money was going to come from, however. Board members were willing to "cut other things," though they never said which things.

The Club had already had to close down new programs after finding that it did not have enough money to continue them. Plans to expand the field staff, who handled all issues—not just wilderness-related ones—had come to a halt. The last field representative had been hired for the northern Great Plains in 1974, but the southern Great Plains wanted one too. Some on the board also wanted to put the New York office on a firmer footing. Even maintaining the staff at the same size (and it did not grow much in these years) took more dollars because of inflation. Other costs, such as insurance, were also going up, and chapters all wanted more money as well. But membership was static, and so were the revenues it generated. Donations were falling as complacency set in.

With the complacency engendered by the Carter administration, the process of preparing the budget for 1977 was difficult, with the board struggling to balance the budget by debating each element and beset by the contrary impulses of wanting to be fiscally conservative on one hand and trying to accommodate various clienteles on the other. For a while board members would cut things, and later they would fall into a mood of restoring things. They turned to me to figure out how to close the final gap of $70,000, and my recommendations were taken.

Their struggle foreshadowed the even greater problems we would face in preparing the 1978 budget. The practice then was for the board to adopt budget-preparation guidelines in the spring, with staff asked to collate information on expected revenues and expenses. The board's Budget Committee would undertake the first effort to wrestle the budget into shape. Usually they got only part of the job done. I made only limited reviews of the numbers; I was not then expected to "balance" the budget. At its meeting in the fall, the board would make the real decisions on what the surplus would be and what should be traded off to balance the budget.

In this case, when it met on September 11, 1978, the board received a budget that was still half a million dollars out of balance. Revenues were static at about $7 million, and inflation was driving costs up further. Club treasurer Denny Shaffer reported that cash flow was at a critical stage.

The board was in a very pessimistic mood. Shaffer and Snyder, then Club president, derided many revenue estimates as excessively optimistic—"blue sky," they called them. It was open season on almost every program. The board took straw votes, cut a little, and then cut some more. When board members ran out of ideas, they held a brainstorming session to come up with additional cuts. Various board members put together packages of projected cuts. Motions flew back and forth. Some failed, and some couldn't even get a second. Those who opposed the motions made substitute motions. In that contentious atmosphere, heavy reliance was placed on parliamentary procedure. The straw votes were even turned into binding votes.

Former president Wayburn called it "the most conservative budget meeting I have ever witnessed." Not every revenue estimate needed to be rock solid. While many of the staff in the various programs affected were present, the board acted as if they were not. Staff morale was wounded by the implication that what they were doing was not very valuable.

After a while the board itself became exhausted by the destructiveness of the exercise in which it was engaged. It began to turn on those who kept proposing further cuts. Finally a budget was adopted by the barest of margins—five in favor, four opposed, and two abstaining entirely. Three were absent. Board member Leslie Reid objected to a budget that cut so deeply being adopted by only a third of the entire board, and many recriminations about the whole process were voiced.

Snyder knew that the process had not gone well. Staff interpreted the freewheeling budget-cutting as a vote of no confidence in their work, and Snyder had to work hard afterward to repair the damage done to their morale. Furthermore, a major mistake had been made. When the operating year was over, the Club had compiled the biggest surplus in its history—nearly $400,000. More had been cut than needed to have been. It was clear that the board had been stampeded by its fiscally conservative Southern leaders.

Clearly a better process for budgeting was needed. Facing widespread resentment, the Southern boys bailed out. They made the executive director—me—responsible for bringing in a budget that met the board's guidelines. Thereafter, it would be the executive director, not the board, who would review each budget item and probe what it meant. It would be me who would confer in advance with program directors to find out what was at stake.

In the years that followed, I would work for nearly two months every year to get the budget into shape. I insisted on seeing how each revenue estimate was put together and on testing the math that was used. Again and again I found errors and hedging, and was able to identify ways to save money and close the budget gap. Week by week, the gap would close further. This was not my favorite work, but I think I did it well. Budgets were now adopted without great travail. And in all but one of the subsequent years, we generated surpluses when the year was finished. (The one exception involved only a slight deficit.) The board finally began to get over its distrust of staff.

As the decade ended, I also rearranged staff responsibilities in the Conservation Department, shifting Brock Evans to an outreach job in Washington, D.C., with John McComb in charge of organizing that office. As mentioned earlier, I moved Doug Scott from Seattle to San Francisco to become director of federal affairs. He would organize all of the Club's campaigns and seemed particularly well suited for this job. While his official title was not conservation director, that was his responsibility. Since I was now handling the budget, I needed to have someone else doing that work. And I was finally and formally recognized as the CEO of the Sierra Club. As the 1970s ended, the position of the executive director was securely established at last. It had taken ten years.

While the Carter years did not foster the Club's bottom line, they did force us to better manage our operations. On balance, they were good for the environment too, though there were still doubters.

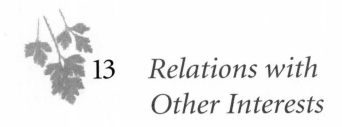

13   *Relations with*
       Other Interests

The rise of environmentalism in the 1970s engendered anxiety among many labor unions, various minority organizations, and business interests—all concerned with how we might interfere with their interests. All of them were anxious about the rise of environmentalism. I didn't think there were fatal antagonisms between what we and these other groups stood for, but at this time people from many walks of life were still in the habit of going about their business with little concern for the environment. It was true that they would have to change their ways if we were all to have a healthy planet.

Environmentalists were not all of one mind about how much change was necessary, of course. If the natural world was to be preserved for future generations, some believed, fundamental changes had to be made, particularly in the capitalist structure. They thought capitalists would never agree to give enough attention to nonmarket considerations such as conservation.

I was among the faction of reformers who believed that the flaw lay not in the ownership of capital but in the goals that society sought. We wanted to change the relationship of the built environment (and its management) to nature and to improve the design of the built environment. In our view, the Soviet Union's state-owned enterprises dealt even more harshly with the environment than did privately owned ones in this country. The problem, regardless of who owned things, was with what people sought to do and how. No one really knew how to change people's minds about the need for conservation, but we hoped by trial and error to find out.

Labor

I was inherently sympathetic to labor from an early age, an attitude I learned from my parents. I had organized and won a strike of newspaper delivery boys at the age of twelve. I had earned a college scholarship from the Oregon AFL-CIO by winning an essay contest on the history of labor. I had been a union member. And when I ran for the state legislature, I had been endorsed by the local unit of the AFL-CIO. Politically, I was a friend of labor.

Yet soon after I became the Sierra Club's executive director in 1969, I found myself at odds with the AFL-CIO in California. In much of the West, labor unions, especially in the construction trades, came to feel that environmentalists were fomenting a policy of no growth. They saw us suing to stop freeways, subdivisions, and new power plants. In their publications they derided environmentalists who, they claimed, wanted to turn cities into villages and stop any highway or dam construction that would displace a flower or tree. Together with the businesses involved, unions set up environmental trade councils to counter our efforts and raised a formidable war chest. Democrat Pat Brown, the former governor of California, even lent his name to one such effort.

We had a different perspective, of course. We thought we were trying to stop only ill-considered projects. And by pushing for enforcement of new environmental laws, we thought we were merely trying to even the scales, not to stop all growth. But there had been so little compliance with the new environmental laws, at least initially, that we actually had succeeded in stopping quite a few projects with court-ordered injunctions. We looked powerful, and labor unions were worried about our entry onto the scene.

Our efforts came to a head at a meeting of our board of directors in San Francisco in 1973, when the California AFL-CIO asked us to set up a task force to discuss improving our relations with the group. Its chief, John Henning, who attended our meeting, thought he had secured an agreement from our board to do this. On the other hand, our board thought it had agreed merely to set up a committee of its own to nurture better relations.

The board meeting had been stormy and difficult, with neither side understanding the institutional culture of the other. Because of the misunderstanding, Henning later took umbrage when the Club didn't start a dialogue with his group. Eventually the Club asked Les Reid, an active member of the machinists' union and one of its activists from Los Angeles, to form a committee to work with California labor. In the future, we would work more through intermediaries—people in the Bay Area such as Dwight Steele, a labor lawyer, and Dave Jenkins of the longshoremen's union—who better understood how each did business.

What the Club did do soon thereafter was to support the Oil, Chemical, and Atomic Workers Union when it struck a Shell Oil refinery in the Bay Area community of Martinez, John Muir's hometown. The strike was unusual because it was more over workplace and environmental issues than wages. The union was concerned about its members' exposure to chemical pollutants and wanted data on rates of illness among those who worked there.

Our support for the strike unfortunately spawned a backlash: some of our members were so alienated by our stand that they resigned. Shell denounced us for taking sides in a labor-management dispute and warned us against destroying our credibility (I didn't know we had any with them). We did not back down in face of this reaction, however.

As an upshot of this action, I was invited to Toronto in August 1973 to give a keynote speech to the annual convention of this union.[1] "The environmental movement can only succeed if it can find ways to advance its cause that are consistent with the other legitimate goals of our people, and job security is paramount among these," I proclaimed. "Environmental protection cannot come at the cost of social justice, and conversely, progress toward social justice will become ephemeral if it is earned at the price of a healthful environment." I went on to observe that "we have suffered the same things from the same people." I urged all of us to put myth-making aside and to work together. The union liked the speech so much that they reprinted it and distributed it widely.

In this speech, I also reviewed the Sierra Club's record of supporting labor in pursuit of our program. We had supported the enactment of the Occupational Safety and Health Act (OSHA) in 1970 and had subsequently called for its enforcement. To combat environmental blackmail, we had supported legislation to compel disclosure of background facts when industrial plants threatened to close because of cleanup requirements.[2] We had supported efforts to indemnify workers who might be displaced by such requirements, though most of the plants that closed were just obsolete. We had also supported efforts to tighten regulation of the use of pesticides in farm fields; this would better protect farmworkers as well as wildlife. And we had been one of the charter members of the Urban Environmental Conference, which Senator Philip Hart, Democrat of Michigan, had initiated to bring environmentalists together with labor and urban interests.

In addition, a few years after this speech, at Les Reid's behest, we endorsed the Humphrey-Hawkins Full Employment Act, committing the federal government to use various means to assure full employment, even though it had only a slight relationship to the environment.

As an outgrowth of this speaking experience, I began to perceive that environmentalists would have a better chance of relating well with industrial unions, which came from the former CIO, than with the craft unions, which came from the AFL. The industrial unions had begun to be concerned about workplace issues involving threats to health from the use of toxic chemicals. The craft unions faced fewer issues of this sort and had become preoccupied with allegations that we stood for "no growth," which led them to believe, incorrectly, that our success would put them out of work.

By that time I had also developed good relations with the United Auto Workers (UAW). Under Walter Reuther, that union had taken many farsighted stands. During the initial battle for the Redwood National Park, the union had supported us, and I had frequently been on the phone with its leaders about what they might do to help. The UAW also began to take an interest in problems of water pollution, initially in Michigan, and I attended a conference on these problems at their Black Lake conference center. Unfortunately, the UAW leaders who succeeded Reuther were less interested in these larger environmental issues. In fact, in later years the UAW even resisted efforts to improve fuel economy standards for cars and to tighten the Clean Air Act. It was worried about the jobs of its members in the future—even though foreign car producers were then gaining market share by being more fuel efficient.

Our ties with labor in the nation's capital began when Lloyd Tupling ran our Washington, D.C., office in the late sixties. From his days with the senators Neuberger, he was a friend of George Taylor of the AFL-CIO, one of the union's lobbyists. Our D.C. lobbyists also later became friends with Jack Sheehan, the lobbyist for the steelworkers' union, and they worked together on pollution issues. Even though the steel industry was threatened by cheap foreign steel from dirty plants abroad, the steelworkers' union worked steadfastly to clean up the industry in the United States.

In the late 1970s the Industrial Union Department of the AFL-CIO, which coordinated the work of its unions in plants of basic industries, was looking for political allies. It conceived the idea of forming a partnership with us to promote interest in issues of workplace health and safety, with a focus on toxic chemicals. We agreed, and the OSHA-Environmental Conference was formed. I was asked to co-chair it along with the chairman of the Industrial Union Department, Howard Samuel. The new partnership was widely publicized in union publications, and the conference had periodic sessions for activists around the country. A network was established, with counterpart groups created to promote cooperation at the state level, and it bore some fruit in states such as Wisconsin. The network was staffed by Sheldon Samuels at the AFL-CIO, who was also a member of the Sierra Club.

Through Samuels, I also became a member of a select group that operated at the international level to promote concern about occupational health, particularly cancer risks. This group, the Collegium Ramazzini, named after the founder of the field of occupational medicine and headquartered in Italy, operates principally as a forum for verifying research findings and exchanging information. I spoke at some of the group's conferences in Bologna, Italy, and I was one of the Collegium Ramazzini's few members who was not a scientist (I was regarded as a specialist in public policy).[3]

After about a decade, the effort at cooperation embodied in the OSHA-Environmental Conference withered away. The AFL-CIO was disappointed that we did not find a way to involve more environmentalists in this work. While our lobbyists had been active in getting two different Superfund measures enacted by Congress, as well as the Toxic Substances Control Act, many of our activists at the local level were already committed to other issues. Moreover, they were volunteers who were free to work on what interested them most, which was more often something like our campaign to protect lands and waters in Alaska.

Many of the issues involving chemicals and occupational medicine were too technical for our members, who often were not scientists, to feel comfortable with them. On a philosophical basis, most of our followers would agree that factory workers were merely the first to be exposed to toxics and that these same threats would then reach those who lived in nearby communities, but our activists could not be abruptly redirected to these new issues. Interest in newly introduced issues typically develops slowly and builds only gradually, we learned. People tend to be most interested in the issues that have been promoted the longest and that have the most meaning for them personally. Indirectly, class may also have been a factor, since most of our members did not cross paths regularly with union members and thereby become acquainted with them and their concerns.

Those of us in the Sierra Club were also somewhat disenchanted with our relationship with the AFL-CIO. We found that our investment did not translate into much concern on its part over issues that were fundamentally important to us and for which we had strong feeling. Again and again, its ruling council would take stands opposed to ours on such issues as drilling in the Arctic National Wildlife Refuge. The Industrial Union Department apparently had only limited weight in the inner councils of the AFL-CIO. When a given union would opt to support industry on an issue, the AFL-CIO seemed only too happy to go along, regardless of the implications the decision might have had for cooperation with us and other environmentalists. Short-range "back-scratching" seemed more important to them than building long-range strategic alliances. That was the stark reality.

Moreover, the Sierra Club and the AFL-CIO unions' work together was focused on a single area of overlapping interest: toxics in the workplace. To the members of each group, such overlapping issues too often appeared peripheral, making it impossible for them to compete effectively for time and attention with the core issues that mattered most to each group.

Over time other issues would emerge on which we could cooperate, such as the North American Free Trade Agreement (NAFTA), but the fundamental problems remained.

Minorities

Demographically the Sierra Club's membership has always been largely upper middle class and very well educated. Most of its members are in the professions, education, or middle management. As with most other American institutions with this kind of membership profile, the Club's members are largely white.

When the environmental movement first emerged in a major fashion at the beginning of the 1970s, some leaders of the black community were uneasy. When I spoke on panels, I sometimes heard black leaders disparage environmental concerns as issues solely for the comfortable and imply that they were of secondary importance. They were clearly worried that we were gaining the support of white liberals and thereby might divert their attention from civil rights as a primary focus. Meanwhile, in a public relations counterattack in 1971, industry-led coalitions were themselves trying to attract black leaders. They wanted to paint us into a political corner, leaving us isolated, and this was one of their tactics. They had enough success in the next few years to give us cause for concern.

In the mid-1970s Sydney Howe, who ran the Urban Environmental Conference, suggested that we sit down to discuss the problem with Bayard Rustin, who ran the A. Philip Randolph Institute in New York City. Rustin had recently written an op-ed piece in the *New York Times* that sounded some of these themes, suggesting that environmentalists were diverting attention from primary concerns of his constituency. Our discussion was polite, although he did not soften his view, nor did we. But our meeting did demonstrate that we were both willing to listen.

Under the leadership of Bill Futrell as president of the Club (1977–78), we decided to give more emphasis to the urban environment. This became the focus of our office in New York City under Neil Goldstein, which dealt with issues of human habitat, such as safe housing, air and water quality, traffic, and planning. We sent a delegation to the annual NAACP convention, and we prepared a recruitment pamphlet aimed explicitly at attracting black members. While our work did not pay off immediately, before long Willie Hyman emerged in California as a black leader in the Club. He first chaired our new Urban Environment task force (1977) and soon thereafter became the vice chairman of our regional conservation committee in northern California. But overall, black leaders remained scarce in the Sierra Club.

In 1978, the Sierra Club joined with the Urban League to sponsor a conference in Detroit on urban environmental problems—the City Care Conference. The kind of blight that had befallen the inner city there became our focus. I also served for a short time on the board of the Joint Center for Urban Environmental Studies, a group working to interest minorities in environmental issues.

None of these efforts put an end to the doubts in the black community, but gradually environmental issues achieved greater legitimacy and were seen as less of a threat. In fact, in due course it became clear that the strongest support in Congress for environmental programs came from the Congressional Black Caucus. Indeed, with the emergence of the environmental justice movement in the 1990s, black people increasingly expressed concern about the environment in which they were living. They wanted their fair share of governmental attention for the environmental problems afflicting them. Our Louisiana chapter has forged particularly strong links with environmental justice groups there, and the Club ultimately hired a number of black organizers.

Latinos were not immune to these crosscurrents either. One day we woke up to find that the oil industry had scored a success in its lobbying efforts: a Latino group in Los Angeles had endorsed more oil drilling offshore along the southern California coast. In an effort to understand what was going on, I went to see Raul Yzaguirre of La Raza, a national group devoted to the welfare of Latinos in the United States. Talk among environmentalists in Los Angeles about the need to control population growth and immigration, it turned out, had offended many Latinos there. To get our attention, they had jumped into an issue that we cared about and lent support to our adversaries.

Yzaguirre and I agreed that it would be a good idea if both of us worked to keep our organizations out of each other's hair. I would try to keep the Sierra Club out of the immigration issue, and he would try to keep his members out of the oil issue. For a while, this seemed to work. In the future, though, these issues would return to plague our respective groups.

In 1974, we got into trouble with the Native American community. In working for the expansion of Grand Canyon National Park in Arizona, our board backed the position suggested by our chapter there and supported the inclusion of lands around a waterfall in the canyon that had belonged to the Havasupai tribe. We then persuaded Congress to implement our position.

In return, we were deluged by a torrent of angry comments in publications sympathetic to the tribe and by an influx of critical letters. The Club tried to mollify the tribe by calling for the government to acquire, and then give to the tribe, a large block of privately owned grazing land on the plateau above the canyon. The tribe already had special rights to graze their cattle in a small portion of the park. The Havasupai had not wanted to lose their lands in the canyon, however, and they did not think they had received enough compensation from the Indian Claims Commission, which adjudicates unresolved claims over compensation for land taken from tribes. But there was no way we could intervene in the work of that very independent government commission.

Our relations with Native American groups were complex and varied tremendously. For the most part, we found common cause with the traditional factions in tribal councils and often got drawn into opposing schemes proposed by the "modern" factions, who usually embraced heavy development such as coal mining and logging. (This was before the advent of the Native American-run casinos.) Control would shift among these factions from time to time, and the balance of power varied from reservation to reservation. In many ways, Native Americans' views toward the environment were as varied as those of the rest of the country. But whenever we opposed the projects being pushed by one of the "modern" factions, we would find ourselves branded as anti–Native American.

We were not, of course; we were simply at odds with those who were pushing what we saw as ill-advised development. Over time, we tried to point out that we had supported a long list of measures desired by the Native American community. We had backed enactment of the Alaska Native Claims Settlement Act in 1971, for example. We had gone along with the transfer of Blue Lake in New Mexico, which Native Americans held sacred, even though it was located in a Forest Service wilderness. We had supported the call by Native Americans for more water for Pyramid Lake in Nevada. We had lent our support to Native Americans who opposed coal development on the Cheyenne Reservation. We had called for protection of Doctor Rock, also revered as a sacred site, in the Six Rivers National Forest in northern California and had sued to oppose construction of the Gasquet-Orleans Road near there. But still the Havasupai case had stigmatized us.

For a brief while we tried to gain traction on this dilemma by setting up a special Native American Issues Committee. But it was virtually impossible to find people willing to serve on it who not only had expertise on such issues but understood how the Club worked. Later we took the approach of setting up a committee on archaeological sites, which tried to secure protection for areas once occupied by indigenous people.

We got a further grounding in these relationships through our deep involvement with events in Alaska. Some of the new corporate bodies established in Alaska under the Native Claims Settlement Act were strongly pro-development. These were often so-called urban corporations established under that act for natives in towns and cities. They were mainly interested in promoting viable enterprises in logging, mining, and other fields, and sometimes we opposed their projects on environmental grounds.

There were also rural native corporations, however, which often had a traditional mind-set and were not interested in promoting logging and mining. We could more easily form alliances with them. We developed a particularly close relationship, through Dr. Wayburn, with the Angoon Village leadership on Admiralty Island in southeast Alaska. They wanted to keep the forests pristine and the salmon runs healthy.

From my wife's work in the save-the-whales movement, though, I learned that the Club could have differences even with some of the traditionally minded native people. We disagreed over whether the bowhead whale was endangered and should be protected. Some natives on the North Slope in Alaska wanted to take whales from that stock, even though it seemed for a while that it might be on the verge of extinction. They felt that continuing such a take was necessary to maintain their culture.

While the Sierra Club was aware of the natives' feelings on such issues, it was not ready to surrender its judgment. It might either support or oppose the natives' position, depending on the specifics and the environmental effects. The Club could not avoid taking positions on these matters; they were just too bound up in the landscape about which members cared deeply.

The Poor

Advocacy groups for the poor were also concerned about the environmental movement. They worried that the costs of cleaning up the environment would simply be passed on to consumers, many of whom could ill afford them; "poor people will be essentially given a regressive tax," as one critic put it. The Club needed to meet these concerns head-on, and one of our efforts to do so was through an address I gave at Reed College in Portland, Oregon, in 1974. I scoured the literature for good rebuttals to the assertion that environmental concerns were at odds with the interests of the poor and buttressed my case with citations. The speech was well received, and I went on to make similar arguments on subsequent occasions.[4]

In my speeches, I argued that installing required pollution-control devices on new plants would have only a slight impact on the price of goods, econometric studies suggested. Only about one-half of 1 percent of the rate of inflation at the time (and there was double-digit inflation then) was attributable to these requirements.

Moreover, the growth in gross national product (GNP) was being retarded only one-tenth of 1 percent by the required cleanup. And this was at a time when the greatest investments were being made in putting devices such as scrubbers on new plants in response to new statutory requirements, after years of indifference to environmental concerns. Less than 2.5 percent of the cumulative investment in new plants was related to controlling pollution.

At this time, EPA kept track of jobs that were lost through closure of factories that were too old and dirty to be cleaned up. It found that fewer than 40,000 cumulatively lost jobs could be attributed to that cause. On the other side of the ledger, some studies estimated that more than a million new jobs were being created by environmental programs. More-conservative studies suggested that two to three new jobs were created by environmental programs for every one lost. Moreover, most of the jobs lost at old sites were replaced by jobs at new plants built elsewhere in the country. I challenged our critics to show any increase in unemployment in places such as Alaska and California as a result of blockage of controversial plants by environmentalists. Finer-grained studies might have shown shifting patterns of community growth and decline, but economic change produced such shifts all the time; environmental requirements were not changing that pattern.

I also pointed out that the savings from most pollution-control programs were expected to be twice as great as their costs. Americans would enjoy better health, less damage from phenomena such as acid rain, and more productive waters, lands, and forests. "The market costs of pollution are very real, and somebody pays them," I pointed out. It is cheaper, as well as better for society, to prevent injury than to pay for correcting it.

"Inner-city residents are the prime victims of environmental abuse and the prime beneficiaries of environmental programs," I reminded my listeners. "Their air is five times worse than in the suburbs. The lowest-income neighborhoods usually chart out to have the lowest air quality. . . . Air pollution curtails vigor, reduces resistance to disease, and shortens life spans." Inner-city children suffer more from lead poisoning, and inner-city residents in general suffer more from noise pollution. Poor farmworkers suffer from exposure to pesticides, and industrial workers suffer from occupational diseases, many of which have environmental origins.

Environmentalists were pushing energy-efficiency programs that were leading to products such as cars, air conditioners, and refrigerators that cost less to run since they used less energy. Over their life cycle, these products would cost consumers less. We also supported special, lower utility rates (often called "lifeline rates") for the poor, who consumed the least.

In suing to stop freeways from being routed through poor neighborhoods (routes often chosen because they were expected to entail the least resistance), we were trying to keep urban neighborhoods from being destroyed and poor residents from being pushed into even worse housing. In lobbying to allocate part of the federal Highway Trust Fund monies to mass transit, we were trying, among other things, to make it more economical for the poor to get to work. In pushing to revitalize existing urban cores, we were mindful of how much more environmentally benign multifamily housing is. Compared with single-family housing in the suburbs, it consumes less land, is generally less polluting, and uses only a third as much water and energy.

I concluded these speeches by saying that for many reasons, the poor would be better off, not worse off, as a result of environmental programs. I urged those whose passion was improving the plight of the poor not to regard environmentalists with suspicion. "Because the agenda of reform is long," I asserted, "there is room in American politics for a number of reform movements that have their own validity and can progress concurrently." Environmentalists and advocates for the poor were part of two such reform movements that could coexist.

As the years passed, we heard fewer assertions of such incompatibility. Our friends in Congress were relieved: they wanted to embrace environmentalism but still champion the poor. Securing adequate funding for programs for the poor, however, continues to be difficult, and we have not seen the end of efforts to set one group against another.

Business Interests and Policy Panels

I got to know business leaders best on projects that brought them together with environmentalists to discuss pending problems. These were "policy dialogues" put together by various foundations and other institutions.

I participated in these projects for a variety of reasons. In addition to believing that it was good public relations to be able to say that we talked with all of those affected by our initiatives, I wanted us to be seen as a major player that was at the table when future national policy was being discussed. In this manner, we would be increasingly seen as indispensable.

Moreover, not only did these projects facilitate mutual education, but participation in them also allowed me to assess various business leaders and learn about their thinking and intentions. I also thought it was wise for them to have an accurate basis on which to appraise us. They would then be less likely to give free rein to any inclinations to demonize us, and they might make better decisions as a result.

The ground rules for these projects were not always clear. Most pretended that you were participating as an individual, not as a surrogate for your employer. But project organizers always wanted to list your affiliation in their reports, and when it suited their interests, they wanted you to "deliver" the support of your organization.

I seem to have participated in a never-ending stream of such projects. After my involvement in the Ford Foundation's Energy Policy Project, discussed in chapter 9, I served on two successive panels of the National Petroleum Council (NPC), which was technically then a body that advised the secretary of the interior. In reality, it was a body that told the secretary what the oil industry wanted. Because Senator Lee Metcalf, Democrat of Montana, had complained that there should be somebody on the council representing the public, I was appointed as the token environmentalist by the Ford administration.

In the mid-1970s, the NPC developed reports that called for the establishment of the Strategic Petroleum Reserve and for environmental safeguards in pursuing efforts to recover more oil from old fields (called enhanced oil recovery), such as by the use of chemicals. I was outnumbered 20 to 1 on these panels but did find a way to participate effectively: whenever I would threaten to write a minority report, the oil company representatives would compromise. I believe today's strategic oil reserve is larger because I insisted on it. Having a large reserve was a way to reduce the risk of supply interruptions from importing so much oil and to curtail the impetus to drill everywhere in this country.

Following that involvement, I served on the National Coal Policy Project, which was funded by the federal government and foundations.[5] In the late 1970s, as discussed in chapter 9, coal appeared to be the most likely bridging fuel, supplying the bulk of the nation's energy until sufficient amounts of solar and other preferable alternative energy sources became available. Thus, it was important to find ways to buffer the negative effects of using this fuel. Congress had just passed legislation regulating strip mining for coal, but there was much still to learn about where and how coal could be produced with the least impact.

This was a well-funded project with a unique format: there were an equal number of environmentalists and coal-industry people in the groups, and expert staff were assigned to both sides, or "caucuses," as they were called. Various study panels had co-chairmen, with staff working for each of them. I was the co-chairman of the task force on mining techniques. We developed a process for unearthing the facts of contested issues and often found that each side was "right" under different circumstances. In this manner, we eventually found dozens of issues on which we could agree.

For instance, we found that two very different situations existed in the Illinois Coal Basin. North of the line of glaciation in southern Illinois, soils are deep and surface mining reduces fertility. But south of that line were instances where such mining did not have this effect. Instead it broke through a clay pan that impeded the rooting depth of crops such as corn. We thus were able to come to agreement about where surface mining should occur so as to meet the new law's requirement for maintaining "pre-mining levels of [soil] fertility."

Unfortunately, one key environmental group refused to participate in the project and attacked our report. Before our board, I had to defend the report (which I think was inaccurately portrayed) and my own board-sanctioned role in the project. I had been recruited to join it by Larry Moss when he was the Club president, and Moss was also the environmental co-chair of the entire project.

That project in turn led to my service on two successive panels appointed by the National Research Council (NRC), the sister organization of the National Academy of Sciences. One, the Committee on Surface Mining and Reclamation (COSMAR), was charged with recommending policy to Congress on buffering the environmental effects of mining for minerals other than coal, which Congress had just addressed through the Surface Mine Reclamation Act. I served as chair of the "environmental" group in that project.

To my consternation, I found that the NRC operated under the assumption that by pulling together a diverse group, it would have all the expertise it needed around the table and no research would need to be done to write a study report. When it came to assessing the environmental effects of various types of "non-coal" mining, I knew I didn't have the necessary knowledge in my head. I insisted that the literature on the subject had to be researched. In response, the NRC reluctantly arranged for the Forest Service's Intermountain Research Station in Ogden, Utah, to do such a study. It was excellent and provided much of the substance in the overall report.

In contrast, the efforts of the NRC's panel on geothermal power were cursory. Under the chairmanship of former Alaska governor Wally Hickel, this panel was willing to complete its work in one weekend. It had been asked by Congress for advice on how much funding was needed to study various problems with geothermal power production. I found that other panel members, mainly academics, were willing to pull figures out of the air—running into many millions of dollars. I am afraid that, when asked for my opinion, I did the same, not wanting the environmental problems that most concerned us to be neglected. My requests were in the same range given by the others, so these numbers were not questioned, and in due course Congress provided that amount of money.

Shortly after the National Forest Management Act was passed in 1976, I was visited by a representative of the timber industry, Jay Gruenfeld, who then worked for Weyerhaeuser timber company. We both expressed a measure of satisfaction with the final shape of the new statute, but lamented that the process of working it out had been so contentious. We were curious about whether having a regular channel of communication might save a lot of strife in the future. As an upshot of this discussion, we experimented for a few years with something we called the Western Forest Environmental Discussion Group. With Gruenfeld and me as co-chairs, the group met a number of times each year in the late 1970s, usually in Portland, Oregon. Represented on the committee were leaders of the major timber companies operating in the West as well as the major environmental groups.

We found a few areas of agreement. We both wanted the Forest Service to change its specifications for access roads. Environmentalists wanted smaller roads to be built that would do less damage to the environment (i.e., smaller cuts and fills, producing less erosion) and be easier to "put to bed" (i.e., take out). Industry preferred such roads because then it could avoid the trouble of having to build roads to more exacting and costly specifications. We got no response from the Forest Service. We got an even colder shoulder when we asked the Forest

Service's research arm to look at the impacts, over time, of fertilizing forests. In effect, they told us to get lost. In time, the Forest Service even derided us as the "odd couple" committee. We finally concluded that we were not getting anywhere and disbanded.

Toward the end of his term, Jimmy Carter appointed me to a commission he established, the President's Commission for a National Agenda for the Eighties. While its recommendations covered many subjects and ran to many pages, I worked hard to steer the commission away from anything troublesome for the environment. Though it called for deregulation of federal entities that had been regulating purely economic activity, such as setting railroad rates, it did not call for weakening of any environmental regulations.

I felt at the time that my service on these panels was justified simply in terms of good public relations. But in looking back, I can see that the conventional wisdom that reports from such collaborative groups just sit on the shelf is not entirely correct. The report from the Ford Foundation's Energy Policy Project provided the initial framework for the energy policies of the Carter administration. The Strategic Petroleum Reserve was set up, as the National Petroleum Council suggested. Geothermal energy research was funded, as the NRC panel requested. Deregulation of agencies handling commercial operations occurred, as Carter's commission recommended. Larry Moss, the environmental co-chair of the Coal Policy Project, claimed that its report had an impact. The COSMAR report was neglected, but it stimulated my interest in reform of the hard-rock mining laws and formation of the Mineral Policy Center, of which I eventually became chairman of the board. Thus I now feel that service on such panels can also be an effective way of shaping public policy.

Acquitting myself well on such panels was never easy, however. On most of them, environmentalists were badly outnumbered. The bulk of panel members were drawn from the business community, academia, and government. In a few cases, I was virtually alone. Eventually I learned never to accept an appointment to a panel where I was the sole environmentalist.

Most panels sought consensus usually by going beyond preconceptions to find versions of reality that few expected to find, by steering around our differences, or by retreating to bland generalities that all could accept. We were never asked to surrender our principles or our interests. While I often threatened to dissent, in the end I never had to do so (though in one instance, which I related in chapter 9, I had to write a response to a dissent by an oil company president).

Sometimes our various parent groups were shocked that any area of agreement had been found. This was true for both industry representatives and environmentalists. We live in such an adversarial culture that I came to wonder how much of the conflict in our society really reflects opposed interests and how much is simply programmed into us. But I also came to realize that the consensus process is a very personal one and that it touches only those who participate. It builds a modicum of trust among those who sit for hours around the table searching for things of a positive nature, but its impact is very hard to transfer to others, or to society in general.

And I learned that it is a delusion to suppose that government policy makers would really welcome a "coming together" of interests that are normally opposed. Instead, they seem profoundly threatened by this prospect and often foster friction among such interests. They want to be seen as the only ones who have the skill to find the "middle path."

Whether working with unions, minorities, advocates of the poor, or business interests, I tried to show that the Club was not fundamentally at odds with their interests or what they cared about most. I think that many I dealt with came to realize this. It would be some years, though, before we would begin to have better relations generally.

Author at age four, on a pony, Palo
Alto, California, 1938

Author at age thirteen, with fish, Oregon
Coast, 1947

With parents and brother Dave at home in Eugene, 1952

Rappelling off Mt. Thielsen, Serving in the artillery, Ft. Sill, Oklahoma, 1957
Oregon Cascades, 1956

With Ted Kennedy at the University of Oregon, 1961

Hiking up Cascade Pass with step-
daughter Rosemary, North Cascades,
1966 *Photograph by Maxine McCloskey*

In the redwoods, 1969

Author and Dave Brower confer with staff at a break in a Sierra Club board meeting
in San Francisco, 1967 © *Photograph by Joe Munroe*

A Sierra Club board meeting, 1968 (author is behind the standing microphone at the end of the table) *Photograph by John Flannery, courtesy of The Sierra Club*

Press conference announcing the first Sierra Club lawsuit to stop Disney's development of Mineral King, 1969 *Photograph by Susan Landor*

Being interviewed shortly
after becoming the Club's
new executive director, 1969

Exchanging words with President Carter in the White House, 1978

With the petitions to oust James Watt, Sierra Club Library, 1981

Photograph by Mush Emmons

Being shown how to pan for gold, southeast Alaska, 1983

With a giant oak in Maryland, 1987
Photograph by Maxine McCloskey

Enjoying tropical forests, the
Amazon, 1990 *Photograph by Maxine
McCloskey*

Conferring with Vice President Gore when he meets with the Sierra Club's board, Washington, D.C., 1996

Inspecting a dragonfly park with Maxine in Japan, 1996

At Ed Wayburn's 90th birthday, Bolinas, California, 1997

14 *The Worst of Times, the Best of Times*

When Ronald Reagan was elected president in 1980, we did not know what to expect. We knew, of course, that he would make some effort to back away from the environmental policies of his predecessor, Jimmy Carter, but we did not know how much.

When Reagan was governor of California, he had appointed a former Sierra Club board member and lumberman, Ike Livermore, to head his Resources Agency and to make environmental policy, and he had made William Penn Mott the director of his state parks agency. Both men espoused moderate policies and had some understanding of what the Sierra Club was all about. Once I was even granted an audience with Governor Reagan in his office in Sacramento; he offered me some of his jelly beans.

In the days following the presidential election, their political positioning seemed to start out in the same vein. Ike Livermore, as well as some other moderates, served on Reagan's transition team in Washington. We decided not to jump on the bandwagon to denounce Reagan before we found out what he was going to do. When he appointed James Watt as his secretary of the interior, though, I began to be deeply concerned. Watt had headed the Mountain States Legal Foundation in Denver, which had brought scores of anti-environmental lawsuits since its founding in the mid-1970s. I had first known him as the head of the Bureau of Outdoor Recreation during the Nixon administration, when he was not a "fire breather," but the head of our legal office in Denver warned me that Watt had become very combative since then.

In December 1980, Watt invited a delegation of environmental group representatives, including me, to meet with him in Denver at the Brown Palace Hotel to get further acquainted. He was personable but noncommittal, though he and I did get into an argument about which of us had been operating in the mainstream of American opinion. Both of us claimed that the other was the extreme one. Future developments would show who was correct.

The Watt Years

While the Sierra Club testified against confirming Watt as secretary of the interior, the Senate—as usual—wanted to give a new president the appointees he sought. We found, to our dismay, that the "Hickelization" technique did not work anymore. Watt emerged from the confirmation hearings not having moved a bit from his prior stances. More appointees of the same ilk followed.

I decided that I ought to try to do more to size up Watt. He agreed to see me and brought Don Hodel along for lunch in the Interior Department cafeteria. Hodel, who was then his assistant (he eventually became secretary himself), had gone to both Harvard and the University of Oregon Law School with me. At Harvard he had been president of the Young Republicans, while I had been president of the Young Democrats. We always seemed to be on opposite sides, and this time was no exception. As I tried to get specifics from Watt and Hodel about what they planned to do, they blurted out that they were so clever that they planned to "fix" things in the Interior Department so that their adversaries would never be able to reverse them.

It soon became clear what they meant. Reagan chose not to reprise the moderate approach he had taken in California. The context and times had changed, and he became the most conservative, and anti-environmental, president in memory. Almost all of his initial appointees tried to roll back the environmental gains of the 1970s. These were gains that had been made under not only Carter but Nixon as well—under both Republicans and Democrats.

Reagan's appointees decided not to enforce the laws that controlled pollution and strip mining, for instance. They tried to emasculate the Clean Air Act; acid rain was characterized as a "non-problem." Watt tried to sell off 35 million acres of public lands. He tried to sell oil and gas leases in wilderness areas (such as the Bob Marshall in Montana), end purchase of lands for the national park system, and commercialize wildlife refuges through permitting excessive oil drilling and grazing. He also tried to open millions of acres of national park land in Alaska to hunting. Everything we cared about was under siege.

Watt was trying to do more than roll back the gains we had made, though. He was, I told our board, "challenging the basic ideas of what national parks are for, what wilderness means, and how national wildlife refuges should be managed." His approach was insidious; he was trying to fundamentally change the premises underlying the nation's system of protected areas.

By the spring of 1981, most leaders of the environmental movement realized that we had to pull together to counter this onslaught. Bob Allen of the Kendall Foundation in Boston suggested that the staff directors of the ten largest groups should meet regularly to coordinate strategy. We all welcomed the suggestion, deciding to meet quarterly and rotate the job of chairing and organizing the meetings. Under the auspices of this Group of Ten (its informal name), our staffs produced a series of reports documenting how bad the administration's policies were. The first one was styled as an "Indictment" of the Reagan administration. The second, "Hitting Hard," recounted the impact of Reagan's policies on various communities. We also organized a series of conferences around the nation to rally public opinion, and we coordinated our lobbying and media outreach efforts.

Over time, I supported efforts to expand the Group of Ten, but the National Wildlife Federation and other organizations opposed this, arguing that the group would become unwieldy if it got larger. They wanted it to remain exclusive. Only many years later was it finally expanded, with its name changed to the Green Group.

The Sierra Club unleashed a concerted effort to reveal the extreme nature of the Reagan administration. In a speech in San Diego to the American Right of Way Association, an organization of people who acquire rights-of-way for utility lines, I went into the specifics of the administration's plans. The Interior Department had been leasing 1 to 2 million acres offshore for oil drilling each year. The Ford administration had tried to increase that tenfold, and the oil industry wanted it increased to 50 million acres per year. "What does James Watt speak of? Two hundred million acres per year—a figure that is absolutely, physically impossible."

With 28 billion tons of federal coal already leased and still undeveloped, and 700 million tons mined annually, Watt was also trying to drastically step up leasing of coal on federal lands: he wanted to lease another 7.2 billion tons in the years to follow.

In that speech, I also addressed the administration's timber sales target for the national forests. At that time, the level of cut had been about 12 billion board feet each year. The upper limit of what the Forest Service saw as possible (if heavy investments had been made in so-called stewardship programs) was 17 billion board feet. "Some of the wildest people in the timber industry had talked of 22 billion board feet as an outer-limit figure that they would lobby for as their heart's desire. What does John Crowell [the Reagan administration overseer of the Forest Service] ask for? Thirty-five billion board feet!" I exclaimed.

Watt opposed expanding nature reserves, including ones already authorized by law. Reagan's Council of Economic Advisors was hatching a plot to sell to private corporations as much as 100 million acres of the public domain, I asserted. These lands, which millions of Americans use for hunting and fishing, "would then be behind private fences saying 'no trespassing.'"

"James Watt has proposed leasing for oil and gas development within the established, statutory wilderness areas of the United States—in hundreds of cases in the Rocky Mountains—in the so-called 'overthrust belt.' He doesn't see what's wrong with having roads and fields of oil derricks pumping away in areas which are supposed to be nature sanctuaries, which are characterized by law as areas where the marks of man are absent, areas where nature prevails and man is a visitor." I pointed out that Watt had also asked for a twenty-year extension of the loophole in the Wilderness Act of 1964 that allowed the mineral industry to continue staking mining claims in federal wilderness areas.

In our rhetorical counterattack, I also drew attention in subsequent speeches to the huge cuts that Reagan's people had proposed in the budget for an already overburdened EPA and how much was already being given away to industry. The level of subsidies and handouts was astounding. I estimated that more than $10 billion worth of existing subsidies were then being given away each year to various industries. Nearly $7 billion was given to the oil industry through the oil depletion allowance, while $2 billion was lost annually through the absence of a royalty for mining on federal lands. That industry also benefited from a depletion allowance that netted $460 million each year. Through sales of federal coal leases on a flooded market, $40 million had just been lost. Capital gains treatment for timber producers gave them the equivalent of $300 million each year. Grazing interests enjoyed the equivalent of $100 million annually through underpricing of federal forage, and they got another $23 million in price supports. Over time, the nuclear industry would get $35 billion as well.

Watt and his cohorts wanted to add to these amounts by flooding a saturated market for natural resources with even greater levels of sales and dispensations. By dumping so many new oil leases on the market, Sierra Club staff later estimated, the gigantic sum of $77 billion would be lost; another $20 billion would be lost in pushing development of oil shale. Even more would be lost in trying to push disposal of public lands. In a speech setting all of this out at the State University of New York at Buffalo, I commented: "Never in history has anyone attempted such outrageous raids on the environment, the public domain, and the Treasury at the same time. The cost is truly staggering, and one can only wonder why the country puts up with it."[1]

While the problem lay in the basic orientation of the Reagan administration as a whole, the Sierra Club decided to train its fire on James Watt. He had embraced the outrage of the so-called Sagebrush Rebels, who wanted massive amounts of the public domain turned over to the Western states, and was riding it as far as he could. We decided to launch a drive to gather signatures on petitions to get him fired. This drive, which Carl Pope on our staff thought up, would serve as a vehicle for organizing and garnering publicity. It would also give us names and addresses of interested people who could be asked to join the Sierra Club and be added to our lists of activists. Bill Turnage of the Wilderness Society later claimed that we "stole the idea" for the tactic from him, but I don't recall his ever mentioning it to me. We did not ask the Wilderness Society to join us in this drive, but looked to them to contribute in other ways. Friends of the Earth did help us.

The petition drive was an incredible success. Our activists stood in front of supermarkets and at subway stations to gather signatures, and in the process explained why we were concerned and handed out pamphlets. Ultimately, we gathered more than l.3 million signatures around the nation on these petitions; we then delivered them to the speaker of the House of Representatives following a rally on the Capitol steps.

Throughout 1981 and 1982, teams from the Sierra Club and other environmental groups also visited the editorial offices of newspapers and other media to carry our message. We held press conferences and thought up other pretexts for generating publicity.

Cartoonists responded with especial alacrity. Tall, bald, and bespectacled, Watt was easy to caricature, and they had a wonderful time pillorying him. We could hardly keep up with the gush of critical cartoons that appeared on editorial pages around the nation. My favorite was one that showed one grizzly bear explaining to another, as he used a toothpick nonchalantly, "Yes, the very same James Watt, the despoiler of nature, so finally I just ate him."

In response to our campaign against Watt, membership applications flooded in, as did contributions. During Watt's years (1980–1985), our membership grew by more than 30 percent each year, from about 180,000 members to nearly 350,000. Fortunately, the Club was now organized enough to take advantage of this opportunity. We began to roll out membership solicitation mailings by the millions. Early on, Watt himself recognized that he was a boon to our efforts to develop our membership. One day, to my surprise, I opened an envelope containing one of our solicitations—on which this note was scrawled in big blue handwriting: "I assume I will be your best fund raiser. Interesting! [signed] Jim Watt."

I usually drafted the outline for our quarterly direct mail appeals. The outline, as well as supporting material, was then turned over to the professional writers at Craver, Mathews, Smith, and Company. They were experts who knew how to hit just the right note, and their mailings proved to be the most successful we had ever done.

The Reagan administration fought back. We received a flood of letters complaining that we were insensitive to the needs of business. Because these letters were so similar and arrived within a short period, I am sure that they were stimulated by the Reagan administration, and few of the writers were actually Club members.

Watt scoffed at our criticism, suggesting that it was just trumped up as part of a routine membership drive. He went on to charge that the environmental movement was evolving into Nazism. To that I replied in the press: "Only James Watt could fail to see the difference between Hermann Goering and John Muir." Californian Ed Meese, then a presidential counselor, belittled the Club as made up of just "people who already own their cabins at Lake Tahoe." When the leaders of the three largest environmental groups—Audubon, the Wildlife Federation, and the Sierra Club—asked to speak to Reagan himself, we were turned over to Meese instead. In that January 1982 meeting he dismissed our various concerns as "misperceptions." We warned him that relations between the administration and our community were becoming polarized and that they were forcing us to move into the electoral arena.

Later that year a Utah group devoted to motorized recreation, Outdoors Unlimited, filed a complaint with the Postal Service accusing us of "fraudulent misrepresentation" and charging that we had distorted Watt's record in our fund-raising mailings. I firmly believe that they were put up to doing this. The Postal Service took their charge seriously, however. Even though we were certain that our mailing fell within an area of protected free speech, we too had to treat this complaint seriously and hire lawyers to mount a full-scale response. We had once lost our mailing permit; we would be seriously injured if we lost it again. Fortunately, we had the facts on our side, and our lawyers prepared a solid defense detailing the factual basis for each of our charges. It was a good thing that we hadn't shot from the hip, as some had wanted us to do.

Our opponents kept at it, though. Two years later, in 1984, the National Conservative Political Action Committee filed a complaint with the Federal Election Commission alleging that we had violated the law because we had mentioned the "green vote" in one of our member-recruitment mailings. Under the law, activities in support of candidates for public office had to be paid for with separately raised funds. Again we had to summon our lawyers to rise to our defense. And again they prevailed: the commission voted to dismiss this complaint as having no merit.

These complaints prompted us to wonder whether we had also been subject to politically motivated investigation by the FBI. Under the Freedom of Information Act, one of our lawyers, Peter Koff in Boston, obtained copies of an FBI file on the Sierra Club, but there was not much in it. Former FBI director J. Edgar Hoover said in response to a query that the agency had never investigated the Sierra Club, though it did have a file containing a few letters from cranks accusing us of being communists. Oddly enough, the file also contained an interview with Nate Clark, who had been president of the Sierra Club in 1960. Agents had asked him whether we barred communists from joining. Clark said no; we asked only about people's views on conservation. (At that time, one had to have a sponsor to join the Club.)

One of the wonderful dividends of our campaign against Watt was that the breach with Ansel Adams was healed. After he left the Sierra Club's board in 1969, he had been adopted as an icon by Bill Turnage of the Wilderness Society. After the Club and the Society started working together in the campaign against Watt, Adams began writing me chatty notes on a regular basis. Finally, the Club decided to resurrect our old enlargements of his photographs, which were left over from a traveling exhibit entitled *This Is the American Earth*. Adams agreed to supervise repair of the damage they had suffered in being shipped about. When they were ready, he came into our offices to sign them. Staff crowded around to shake his hand and celebrate.

As our campaign progressed, public opinion moved strongly in our direction. As Watt became intensely controversial, polls showed that by a 3–1 margin people said they wanted more, not less, environmental protection. More people supported us now than had during the complacent years of Jimmy Carter. A significant number of people even claimed that next time they would cast their vote primarily on the basis of a candidate's environmental positions. Polls also indicated that political independents were turning against the administration.

As a consequence, Congress was emboldened to intervene in various ways. It blocked leasing for oil drilling off the shores of California, Florida, and Massachusetts and killed Watt's coal leasing program. It also killed the Clinch River breeder reactor, the Synthetic Fuels Corporation (Carter's idea for oil shale development), and the MX system for basing missiles in the Nevada desert. It increased appropriations and passed more prescriptive legislation for pollution control. In response to lawsuits brought by us and other groups, the courts also blocked Watt in various ways, decreeing repeatedly that he had exceeded his authority. By the summer of his first year Watt was on the defensive, and the *Washington Post* even published an article recounting how he was backtracking on his record.

After two more years of skirmishing, the administration had enough of him as well as Anne Gorsuch, Reagan's embattled EPA administrator. In the face of congressional investigations, Gorsuch, who had been cited for contempt by the House, resigned in the spring of 1983. By the fall of that year, Watt was out too. While an ethnic slur he made was the immediate cause of his downfall, the truth was that he had become politically too costly for the administration.

William Clark, chief of staff during Reagan's governorship, replaced Watt at Interior. As soon as his appointment was announced, I arranged to see him at his ranch near San Luis Obispo in California. He was polite and heard us out but had little to say. While his basic thrust was not all that different than Watt's had been, he scaled back the leasing goals and toned down the rhetoric. He turned out to be only a caretaker for Don Hodel, however, who succeeded him before long.

The Reagan administration also brought William Ruckelshaus back to EPA, where he had been an effective first administrator. After a while William Penn Mott was made director of the National Park Service. I had known Mott in California when he headed the state parks agency under Reagan as well as various park agencies in Oakland. He had been active in conservation societies and had actually joined protests against Watt. Mott invited me to his swearing-in ceremony at Yellowstone Park, and I went. After that, I visited him periodically in Washington, and he gave us useful information. As one of the few environmentally sympathetic people in the Reagan administration, he was a curiosity. He was frequently overruled and came to realize that he was being used as a mere figurehead, but he stuck it out.

The greatest long-term environmental damage done during these times was more leasing of oil and coal lands. No vast "scale-up" in leasing, though, ever occurred. It was blocked. In time, the consequences of enforcement failures were overcome, and the demoralized agencies grew effective again. None of the basic environmental laws had been repealed.

Some good was done even during this period. Reagan signed a farm bill that we helped to pass, the 1985 "sodbuster" bill, which withdrew financial aid from farmers who tried to till erosion-prone lands. Reagan also went along with Congress's decisions to designate additional national forest land as wilderness; all together, Reagan signed wilderness bills protecting packages of land in fourteen states. We ran most of the campaigns for these packages. In 1984 alone, 8.5 million acres were added to the wilderness system. In fact, more acreage was protected as wilderness in Reagan's administration than in most others.

Reagan went along because these measures included a form of "soft release," which gave the timber industry more hope of eventually getting at the lands not designated as wilderness; these were lands that had been identified in prior studies as being roadless and that had been sidelined. Reagan also probably realized that public opinion would be even more inflamed if he vetoed these bills.

Even though Reagan dismissed nearly all of the staff at the Council on Environmental Quality (CEQ) when he came into office, he hired a small replacement staff, and I always had access to them. Alan Hill, from California, served as chairman. Though he felt embattled and unappreciated, Hill was always happy to see me. I helped nourish ties there that allowed us to find out what was happening and to provide help when it came time for CEQ to weigh in to get environmentally friendly legislation signed.

The experience we had with the Reagan administration convinced us that we had to jump into electoral politics. We realized that a really hostile administration, as well as an unfriendly Congress, could set us back appreciably. We first entered the field at the federal level in the congressional elections in 1982, where we enjoyed a modicum of success and would continue to do so. In 1984 we decided to go the rest of the way: for the first time, through its political action committee, the Sierra Club decided to endorse a candidate for president, Walter Mondale. While Mondale had not been the perfect official in the past, he was vastly superior to the incumbent.

Because of the case we had made against the policies of Reagan's administration, our decision drew little backlash from members. Only a trickle of letters came in, from a few who longed for the "old" club. But our endorsement proved to mean little in the general election, in which Reagan was reelected. For most voters, environmentalism was still not a first-tier issue that might determine their vote.

The period of confrontation with the Reagan administration did produce positive results beyond simply boosting the membership and finances of environmental organizations. It rejuvenated the environmental movement, which had assumed a lower profile during the Carter years. As already mentioned, the sense of embattlement brought the leaders of the ten largest environmental groups into close working relationships. The movement improved its public relations capabilities, and its visibility in the media jumped to levels reminiscent of the early 1970s. In weathering a withering counterattack from the Reagan administration, the movement demonstrated that it had staying power and was capable of mounting a spirited defense when its programs were attacked.

In the Sierra Club, a whole new generation of grassroots leaders were recruited. Those who joined at that time, the so-called Watt babies, came to run the Sierra Club in the next decade. And most of the new members recruited at that time did not drop out as soon as Watt was gone, but stayed with the Club.

The Watt years also added to the credibility of environmental leaders. As those attacking environmental programs were driven from office, the standing of environmentalists rose. In many polls of that time asking people who they trusted the most, environmental leaders stood toward the top in comparison to leaders in government, business, labor, and other fields. In its home base of San Francisco, the Sierra Club was actually at the top of the list as the most credible group in the city.

The Club After Watt

The end of the Watt era brought an end to the Club's explosive growth. If we had gained recruits, we had lost the villain against whom we had campaigned. While there were others in the Reagan administration whose policies were objectionable, there was no one as colorful as Watt. Media coverage dropped by 40 percent or more, so our members read less about problems with the Reagan administration. People wanted to believe that we had vanquished the villains and that they could relax.

Within a few months of Watt's departure, the responses to our direct mail recruiting new members dropped by more than half. Donations solicited from mailings to our members also dropped sharply. I realized that a financial crisis was looming, and thus in January 1984 I imposed a freeze on paid travel and other discretionary spending. I consulted the board; they were not ready to insist on this move, but neither did they object to it.

My decision was not popular among Club activists. Many among the rank and file thought that I should have anticipated this turn of events and planned for it. I did not know how I could have anticipated Watt's sudden outburst, which prompted his departure.

When the fiscal year was over, however, I produced the surplus that the board had originally asked for—$164,000. The result was just blind luck, some of my critics muttered. But that surplus would not have been possible without my prompt belt-tightening action. The final audited numbers were even better, showing a surplus of $358,000. We were in the best financial condition ever and enjoyed a net worth nearing $3 million.

As we honed our direct mail program to solicit both members and donations, I concluded that our sources of funds needed to be diversified. I asked our administrator, Len Levitt, to look for new sources of revenue. After winnowing out many possibilities, he brought two solid ideas to me. One was an affinity credit card, which I mention in chapter 10. The credit card company would pay us a royalty, varying according to amounts purchased, for letting them solicit customers from among our members and would then issue them credit cards with our logo. While the practice is widespread now, we were among the first to try it.

After testing various approaches, we found a successful way to structure the arrangement. We were soon netting about $300,000 each year, with almost no trouble or further investment. Our members were happy to use our affinity credit card when they shopped. This was the kind of revenue source I wanted.

The other source of new revenues proved to be complicated as well. We sought to earn revenue by selling products through a catalog related to nature or use of the outdoors. Quite a few board members were dubious. Some pointed out that we had little experience in merchandising, while others thought our members would react negatively to something so clearly commercial in tone. By the margin of a single vote, the board allowed us to launch the venture. After the business was set up, we encountered good news and bad. The good news was that our members accepted the catalog without any trouble, and we quickly learned how to sell the merchandise. Starting about 1983, the business grew quickly, and revenues started soaring.

The problem was that our managers had trouble controlling costs. As fulfillment centers started charging more and more, we moved from one to another, searching for more reasonable charges. From year to year, the growing business would generate either handsome profits or sizable losses. With growing capital costs and risk, the operation began to affect our bottom line unpredictably. After a few years it was shut down, no one having any confidence that the long-term record would be positive.

Our search for new sources of revenue also brought our fund-raisers into contact with telemarketers whose specialty was calling members at dinnertime to solicit donations. We began to use them and had very good success. Some members enjoyed talking to a "real live person" who represented the Sierra Club. They were eager to learn about the latest issues and donate to us. Others deeply resented intrusive calls into their homes. I got a steady flow of complaints from people who felt that way, and we quickly removed their names from the call lists. This program was too lucrative to drop, but board members were never enthusiastic.

After I hired Audrey Berkovitz (née Rust) as our director of development in the early 1980s, our approach to raising funds and acquiring members became much more professional than it had been in the past. She brought us state-of-the-art development techniques and built new fund-raising systems. We no longer depended on the talents of one person, such as Denny Wilcher, her predecessor, who had raised money for us by himself throughout the 1970s before leaving in the early 1980s to found the Alaska Conservation Foundation. From time to time, Wilcher had brought me along to meet donors to tell them of the latest developments in conservation. But under Berkovitz the emphasis shifted away from cultivating large donors toward direct mail designed to cultivate a greater number of smaller donors, an approach that brought in more money.

Our approach to personnel questions also became more professional in the early 1980s. Staff positions were graded and salaries set in terms of these grades. We looked at the salaries paid by other nonprofits in communities where we operated. We advertised publicly to fill vacancies and observed the equal opportunity laws. From time to time, we used headhunters to help fill specialized positions.

As we became more professional, we had fewer personnel problems. For instance, in hiring I learned how important it was to check references and to listen carefully to what was not said. But from time to time I did have to let people go, as with a person who misrepresented his credentials and an unsatisfactory acting editor of the magazine who sought retribution by putting a ridiculous cover on our magazine as his last act. It was a photo of a cat sitting beside a sewer pipe. Strangely enough, no one ever wrote me to complain; perhaps they thought there was some deep message there. Our personnel director used a law firm that was very pro-management. Having been sympathetic to labor over the years, however, I didn't like to be told how to give management "the whip hand." I tried to avoid acting in the harsh way they wanted me to. I never provoked the staff into organizing a union to protect themselves, as eventually happened under one of my successors.

In 1984 I had to come to grips with complaints I was receiving about Carl Pope, who was then managing our political program on a half-time basis. He spent the other half of his time running the California League of Conservation Voters. Pope, who became the Club's executive director in the 1990s, had enmeshed himself in a controversy over state water problems. Some of the Club's volunteers took a position different than his and wanted to know whether Pope was speaking for the Club. On that issue, Pope claimed to be wearing his League hat instead, but I felt it was too confusing. I told him he had to make a choice: either work full-time for the Club or quit. Fortunately, he chose to work full-time for the Club.

By the 1980s I had been in my job long enough that I began to be a well-known figure. I would get letters from people who wanted to know whether I was related to them, or who claimed to have met me years before. Friends of my father wrote. Wives sought solace over the death of their husbands. Others wrote about friends who had died. I even received a letter from a couple who wanted to put the Sierra Club logo on the headstone of their grave when they passed on. In a way, I was ministering to a flock. Quite naturally, I also got endless pleas to pay more attention to issues that we had not made a priority. And of course, all the letters to the Club raising complicated questions landed on my desk.

As we came to struggle more with Republican administrations, people increasingly came to view us as closet Democrats. One of our surveys in the mid-1970s had suggested that about one-third of our members were actually Republicans, however. When I began, the leaders of the Club, including Ed Wayburn and Dave Brower, were registered Republicans, albeit progressive ones. But times were changing. I was under growing pressures to have the Club identify itself with all of the policies of the Democratic Party. Some of our members expected us to have positions on issues of every type—even those that had little to do with the environment. They expected us to behave just as if we were a political party—and a very liberal one at that.

I resisted such pressures. Even though I came from the progressive wing of the Democratic Party, I thought the Sierra Club could be more effective as a group that addressed only environmental questions. I also did not want to alienate our Republican members. A growing number of our activists wanted the Club to develop a fixed ideology, however, as fewer of our members seemed to be committed to flexible pragmatism. Even as the Democratic Party became less of a cohesive force and continued its ambivalence about environmental issues, an increasing number of members wanted the Club to act as though it was the home of true believers with a liberal bent.

These pressures eventually led to the formation of the Green Party, which has adopted the task of trying to make the liberal wing of the Democratic Party more consequential. The Club staff, which is still strongly committed to pragmatism, now finds itself challenged by new activists for whom ideological purity is more important. The Club agonizes over congressional elections in which splits between Greens and Democrats end up electing very conservative Republicans.

Throughout the 1980s, the Club also struggled internally with the concept of organizational planning. We developed annual objectives for each department, wrote goals for five- and ten-year periods, and tried to develop strategic plans. These involved statements of purpose, beliefs, goals for society and for our organization, and other matters. Some of our officers were enthusiastic about this process, but others were skeptical. Over time, I became skeptical too. There was some value in trying to set a few targets and fix things that were broken, but I found that weighty planning documents were soon ignored. They were simply too long for most staff to keep in mind. And the process was time consuming and seldom fruitful.

Although the Club had moved from Mills Tower in 1975 to larger quarters a few blocks up the street at 530 Bush Street, by 1985 we needed more space again and our lease was up once more. Phil Hocker headed up the search process, which eventually put us in a renovated building in the Civic Center area of San Francisco, which we bought through a limited partnership. To raise money for it, I brought a long-time friend from my Oregon days, Carleton Whitehead, onto to our staff. He had been the development director at Reed College in Portland, Oregon, and had retired and moved to the Bay Area. Not only was he very successful in raising money for this purpose, but while working for the Club he also built a thriving program to cultivate bequests.

As the Club's resources grew, in the 1980s I was able to hire more people with specialized duties. About 150 staff were now working in the main office. Many of the operations, which had been run on a shoestring in the 1970s, a decade later were now properly staffed and handled in a routine manner. Club office work was becoming institutionalized.

Moreover, the difficulties I faced in having too many people reporting to me were over. Following a reorganization, only five managers reported directly to me, while once twenty-nine had. I felt that at last I had a solid senior staff. It was composed of Doug Scott, director of federal affairs; Audrey Berkovitz, director of development; Fran Gendlin, director of public affairs; John Beckman, director of the books department; and Len Levitt, administrator. John McComb had succeeded Brock Evans in running the Washington, D.C., office and had brought it into the computer age.

As the Club grew, we began to acquire more field offices. By the early 1980s we had ten, and I asked Doug Scott to develop a system for managing them. In response, he came up with the idea of having them work only on our campaigns involving the federal government and having them report directly to him, thus removing them from the control of the regional conservation committees (RCCs). They were to become organizers in their regions for the national office programs, which would come to embody the priorities adopted by the national Club. They would be the means of reaching the key members of Congress in their region. While I was not completely comfortable with his plan, suspecting that such a degree of centralization might be resented, I had delegated this job to him and decided to live with his decision. Moreover, the status quo was not satisfactory, and his plan did have an internal logic to it.

Many administrative jobs performed in the past by volunteers were gradually turned over to paid staff as the Club grew. (Volunteers continued to have strong roles in conservation and outings, though.) The operations had become either too complex or too large for volunteers to handle. The transition was not always easy to manage; the tradition of volunteerism in the Club was very strong, and some grumbled every time this happened. Moreover, the aura of distrust of staff, left over from the Brower era, remained for a long time.

Because the Sierra Club has continued to grow in the ensuing years, a myth has developed that the Club must have been easier to manage a few decades ago. It was not. As soon as the Club had hundreds of thousands of members, hundreds of local units, and tens of millions of dollars in its budget as it did by the early 1980s, it became a complex organization. If you add the Club's very involved board and large number of committees, you have complexity writ large. Management expert Peter Drucker claims that nonprofits are even harder to manage than profit-making entities, not only because a large number of units may have to be coordinated, but because many of their players are volunteers who cannot be given orders and because their work has to be judged in subtle, qualitative terms, not just in financial terms.

Initially, I may have been too subtle in the way I sent signals to staff. Over time I learned to be more direct, so that I would not be misunderstood. My staff, in turn, learned to read me. At meetings of the board, I would usually sit at a table directly in front of them. Apparently, staff told me, whenever I was uncomfortable with a party making a presentation, or with a proposition being entertained, I would get up and walk to the side of the room, ostensibly to stretch. In reality, it was a way of disassociating myself from whomever was speaking.

I not only had to manage the interplay between staff and volunteers but was sometimes called on to investigate conflicts that broke out in our chapters. After about a decade of relative calm, feuds developed in some of them in the early 1980s: in our Redwood Chapter in Santa Rosa, California; in our chapter around San Francisco Bay; and in our chapter in New York state. At first glance, the problems seemed to involve conflicting personalities.

Late in 1982, I was sent to investigate the New York conflict. I found that it involved not only rival personalities but differing ideas between those who came from New York City and those who came from upstate. Struggles typical of various states' politics were beginning to surface in the Sierra Club's structure too, it seemed. Not only were there conflicts between our groups in the metropolitan areas and those in less populated areas, but folks from each of those areas disagreed over which stands seemed radical.

While I was spending more time on the management of the Sierra Club than before, I still did find time to collaborate with the executive directors of other major environmental groups in fashioning plans for better days. The first, in 1984, was a project called "An Environmental Agenda for the Future," for which I chaired the working group on public lands. It was designed to produce a compendium of policies to recommend to the president in 1985, should he be sympathetic.[2] The right-wing Heritage Foundation had had great luck with its similar report for incoming President Reagan in 1981, but our hopes of working with a President Mondale were dashed.

In 1988 we prepared an update of the agenda, which we called "Blueprint for the Environment."[3] I also worked on a project to give an environmental slant to labor unions' call for an industrial policy.[4] The time was not right for any of these studies, unfortunately, but the exercises did create greater cohesion among environmental groups and caused us to think more deeply about what we stood for.

In 1982, I traveled to London for a celebration of the tenth anniversary of the United Nations Environment Programme. I joined with such figures as Edmund Hillary, Peter Scott, Thor Heyerdahl, Jacques Cousteau, and Richard Leakey, Jr., in commenting on the state of the world. I spoke in support of Leakey's proposal to restrict trade from endangered tropical forests, and later I tried fruitlessly to implement it in the United States.

At home, I helped launch a new long-term campaign to get Congress to protect millions of acres in dozens of designated areas in the Mojave Desert of southern California; some were intended to be parts of the

national park system and some to be wilderness under the BLM's management. The launch was held at the offices of *Sunset* magazine in Menlo
Park, California, whose owners at the time were supporters. This campaign, initiated by our leaders in southern California, took more than
a decade to accomplish. When it finally came to the Seante floor in the
mid-1990s, it was won by one vote: Senator Carol Moseley-Braun of
Illinois, who arrived at the last minute, having been delayed at home
by a balky electric garage door.

I also participated in a thorough review of the status of federal law
governing wilderness, including recent court decisions, which I presented in remarks to the American Law Institute–American Bar
Association in 1983.[5]

Throughout the Reagan years, the Sierra Club was berated by conservatives for being insensitive to the needs of business. In response, I
prepared a major speech on business and environmentalism, presenting
it in Fort Worth, Texas; in Birmingham, Alabama; and in a number of
other places.[6] It was a forceful rebuttal to these arguments:

> We are not opposed to active business enterprises, nor to those who seek a
> return on invested capital. We are seeking responsible behavior by those in
> business, behavior which does not degrade the environment that others must
> share nor impoverish the future. We are seeking constructive growth, which
> improves general conditions at reasonable rates. We are opposed to mind-
> less growth, which demands a narrow advantage regardless of the social costs.
> We are against that brand of progress that means only a few gain and most
> lose. . . . We have not stood in the way of most conventional progress. Most
> of the subdivisions have been built without objection from us, and the same
> can be said for the freeways, and the dams, and the power plants and the log-
> ging plans. . . . Usually it is only when natural values become scarce and devel-
> opment becomes extremely widespread that resistance begins to break out.
> But the resistance is to the imbalance in the equation. . . . We are for mass
> transit, for solar power, for recycling, for reclaiming waste water, for water
> and energy conservation, for reforestation and true sustained yield, for inte-
> grated pest management, for reclamation of derelict lands, for clean air and
> water, for more open space and parks, and for better public health programs.

Businessmen who heard this speech seemed intrigued, if not convinced. Most of them had never heard our viewpoint. The Reagan
administration wanted them to believe that we wanted to close business

down and that we were chronic "aginners." But it was they who were "aginners" vis-à-vis the environment.

In the summer of 1983, at a Sierra Club convention in Vail, Colorado, I paid tribute to the environmental movement, which had been able to bring so much of the Reagan administration's anti-environmental endeavors to a standstill:

> It is a movement that has emerged from a collection of lonely voices to now embody the common desire of the vast majority of the American people. Those in the early 1970s who dismissed it as a fad were wrong—it has continued and spread. Those who gravely warned of a backlash against it were wrong too—it never happened [as a popular phenomenon]. And those in power who are [now] deriding it as extreme are finding that it is they who are regarded as extreme and out of step with public opinion.

We are usually outspent five and ten to one by commercial interests; we face the country's top law firms, first-line public relations firms, and massive advertising campaigns. Their panoply of PACs have contributed lavishly to many key members of Congress. The staffs and budgets of the environmental organizations are minuscule in comparison to those massed against us in industry. And yet we have had the conviction that we could prevail.

We have persisted with cases where our advisors thought we had run out of stratagems and have prevailed in the end. We have brought parks into existence that are larger than anybody said was possible, and we have rescued places that had long before been sold and lost. Experience has taught us the value of hope:

- the trees are not lost until they are logged;
- wild rivers are alive until engulfed or lost by a dam's rising waters;
- birds, fish, ferns, and salamanders still have a chance as long as their habitat has not been paved over.

In the spring of 1983, I was invited to give the commencement address at my alma mater, the University of Oregon Law School, which in the years following my graduation had developed an outstanding program in environmental law.

I told the new graduates about how environmental law had emerged: "We had a sense, almost a vision, that environmental law had to come, and that they could hold us back only so long. There had to be a remedy in court when the laws were not being enforced or were being improperly applied or interpreted. . . . I remember early cases where our lawyers put our chances of prevailing at less than 10 percent, but I urged us to go forward, and many of these cases were won. In fact, some of these became landmark cases, forging new doctrines of law." We faced demands to post bonds along with countersuits and harassment, I reminded the graduates. We overcame all of these obstacles.

"We have rebounded from adversity; we did not accept the counsel of those who claim that the tide has turned," I concluded. "We believed in what we stood for and, again, stood up against those who were whipping up a contrary tide." And, I added, referring to the Reagan years, "we are turning things around again." When Reagan finally left office in January 1989, things improved even more.

But I was to face new personal challenges in the years ahead.

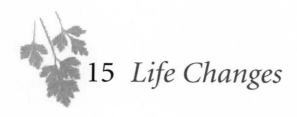

15 *Life Changes*

All things considered, in the mid-1980s I thought the Sierra Club was doing well. We had vanquished Watt. We had steered the organization through budget difficulties and were planning for the future. Personally, I had developed a national reputation and was in wide demand as a speaker and as a participant in projects. I was looking forward to celebrating my fifteenth year as the Club's executive director.

But I should not have been complacent. I knew there was resentment over my having put the brakes on spending in 1984, but I took that as just momentary grumbling. It turned out to be more. A collection of people within the organization had begun to wonder whether I had been around too long. They had never known any other executive director and began to ask whether they might do better. Because the organization had grown so much, they felt a professional manager might be preferable to a policy person like me.

A new generation of leaders, such as Denny Shaffer, viewed me with some skepticism. A voluble businessman from North Carolina, Shaffer had served both as treasurer and as president of the Club. He was one of the "Southern boys" who were rough on staff, and he viewed me as someone against whom to test his mettle. His tendency was to challenge whoever was in power. Often seeing problems before anyone else did, he was quick to criticize. He and his supporters were restive, their discontent also fed by a few younger Conservation Department managers who wanted me to share my job with them. In essence, they felt the

Club should be run by an oligarchy built around them, and they were on the phone with Shaffer frequently.

My first impulse was to resist these pressures, which built up during the spring and summer of 1984. My critics on the board had no specific complaints to lodge against me, other than my lack of formal training as a professional manager. But then I realized that in fact I had filled the role of executive director for a long time already and could not go on forever. On the average, people lasted only about five years in this kind of high-pressure position. I had lasted three times as long. And at age fifty-one, I was still young enough to have a second career.

Moreover, the management portion of the job was growing. I was spending more and more time balancing the budget, raising funds, and handling personnel problems. As a consequence, there was less and less time for conservation, which I enjoyed most. So in the spring and summer of 1984, I began a dialogue with the board about what the future would hold for me. Did I want to continue and for how long, they asked. Was I open to anything else?

An idea took form that I might move into a senior policy position. I would continue to be at the top of the Club's salary scale, but I would no longer be burdened with day-to-day Club operations. I would try to identify new issues, help the Club think through difficult questions, advise in the planning process, and become something of an ambassador at large. I could also turn more of my energies to the Club's international program. This sounded appealing, though I also wondered whether, once shorn of power, I would feel edged aside.

Longtime Club leaders, such as Ed Wayburn and Dave Brower, who had rejoined the board, urged me to reject these proposals to change jobs and to stand fast as executive director. They did not have much empathy with the newer board members. Factions were forming with older and newer board members on opposite sides. My supporters were predominantly the older board members, of whom there would, of course, be fewer around as time went on.

Finally, Denny Shaffer put it to me: Did I want to move into the new job or not? It was up to me. I could continue in my present position if I wanted. Someone reminded me that in a new position I could continue to be influential through the value of the ideas I put forth. I decided it was time for a change.

We haggled over the title of my new position but finally decided that I would be known as the chairman of the Sierra Club. I would participate in hiring new executive directors and in counseling them. I would provide "conservation analysis, guidance, and leadership on policy and strategy to the Executive Director and the Board of Directors," and I would act "as a major Club spokesperson and lobbyist on key conservation issues in coordination with the Club President and Executive Director, aiding in interpreting Club policy and shaping the Club's image."

While I had decided to go along with a change of this nature, not everyone was happy with the way the board was behaving. Longtime Council leader George Shipway wanted to rebuild the board and change how it was chosen. This was an implicit, if obvious, criticism of the board at that time. I had always had a lot of support on the Council, which was composed of delegates from chapters. Shipway circulated a proposal to amend the bylaws specifying how the board would be selected. That prompted Shaffer to try to mend fences with me, hoping that I would not encourage this idea. Having made my decision about the chairmanship, however, I decided not to encourage Shipway's amendment.

I was to step down as executive director on July 1, 1985, but first we had to hire a replacement. The committee gave serious consideration to a candidate who had been a bank manager, thinking that the Club might benefit from his management experience. But he did not share some of the Club's views. I finally threw my weight toward Douglas Wheeler, a candidate with whom I had worked well in Washington, D.C. He had been an official with the Interior Department during the Nixon administration and would later found the American Farmland Trust. He seemed less of a risk than the banker, he had worked with the Club on Alaskan matters, and I knew him and thought I could work with him.

It was clear that the board wanted to try an executive director who was very different than what I had represented. Doug Wheeler was a Republican, though a moderate one. Since this was a time of Republican administrations at the federal level, some thought his party affiliation might be an advantage; he might have greater entrée. Doug Scott and other restive Conservation Department staff welcomed him with open arms. They wanted to believe that he would share the job with them in ways that I had not. The new executive director, though, responded with restraint.

Wheeler and I both wanted to avoid becoming rivals and antagonists. Our polite discussions led us to negotiate a kind of private nonaggression pact. He agreed not to criticize what had happened on my watch, while I agreed not to criticize him while I was chairman. I would avoid getting drawn into the arguments of factions that might take "shots" at him.

To help him get up to speed on the lore of the Sierra Club, I drafted a long memorandum on what I thought he needed to know about the "house rules" that had developed over time (but had never been pulled together in one place), and I gave him a number of background briefings.

On May 4, 1985, I gave my last regular report to the board as its chief executive officer. I had served in this role (under various titles) since 1969. I took the opportunity to celebrate what I saw as the major steps forward the Club had taken in that period: "In the time between then and now, the Sierra Club has come of age as a national institution. It has become recognized as the premier organization of grassroots environmental activists; as a model for effectiveness as a large advocacy organization; as one of the most sophisticated lobbies that works Capitol Hill; and as a pacesetter for the environmental movement."

The Sierra Club's membership had grown fivefold in this period, its net worth and budget had grown five times too, and the net worth of its family of institutions had grown twenty times. It had grown from a medium-sized organization into a large one, and its staff from 70 to 200.

Although we had not achieved all of our conservation or financial goals, we had achieved many and had built a powerful mechanism to work for those goals. Whereas we once had only three field offices, we now had had twelve. Our Washington, D.C., office had grown from two to twelve people. Twenty-seven of our staff were registered with Congress as lobbyists, and they were teamed up with an active and motivated cadre of grassroots volunteers.

Over that period, I reminded the board, we had chalked up an incredible record of success, much of it during the glory years of the 1970s:

> In this time, the Club has played a major role in enacting over one hundred important pieces of environmental legislation. We stopped the Timber Supply Act, the SST, and a bad Public Land Law Review Commission Report; we ushered in EPA and NEPA, which we defended again and again. We led the fight for TOSCA [the Toxic Substances Control Act], the Superfund, and tighter controls over offshore oil drilling. We were in the thick of three winning battles over energy legislation. We were in the forefront of the drive for the National Forest Management Act and FLPMA

[the Federal Land Policy Management Act]. We pioneered the PSD [prevention of significant deterioration of air quality] for clean air areas, and mobilized the defense of both the Clean Air Act and the Clean Water Act. We got the Mineral King area put into Sequoia National Park, and the Redwood and Grand Canyon National Parks expanded, and scores of other parks, preserves, and recreation areas protected, including the BWCA [Boundary Waters Canoe Area in Minnesota], Voyageurs, Hells Canyon, and the Escalante. We originated the idea of marine sanctuaries, and put an end to staking mining claims in various national parks, and quashed the threat of turning federal wildlife ranges over to the states. Over most of this time, we led the fight for wilderness—critiquing RARE I and RARE II [roadless area review and evaluation surveys], adding wilderness in the East to the system, and championing the addition of tens of millions of acres to the wilderness system. And, of course, we spent well over a decade in the biggest battle of all: spearheading the lobbying for Alaska National Interest Lands. And in the 1980s, we rallied the grassroots against Watt, stopped the disposal of public lands, and sued again and again to stop Watt and his cohorts. They didn't succeed in repealing or rolling back any of the corpus of environmental legislation.

I concluded by hoping that I had "set a tone for this Club that will endure: a belief in working cooperatively; a willingness to trust people with responsibility; a seriousness of purpose and a willingness to take on a tough agenda; and, most of all, a belief that we can make a difference and a determination to do so."

I stepped down after sixteen and a half years with ambivalent feelings, realizing that an extraordinary period in my life was over. When in July 1985 the handover occurred, I was touched by the many gifts and notes that began to arrive: a new briefcase from the board, an engraved Sierra Club cup from the Stewards, books and other keepsakes from various staff members. The Rules Committee of the California State Senate passed a resolution extending "their congratulations and compliments to . . . Michael McCloskey for . . . outstanding accomplishments as Executive Director of the Sierra Club and . . . sincere wishes for every success as Chairman of the Sierra Club." (Our lobbyist there undoubtedly had a hand in this!)

The *San Francisco Chronicle* carried a story about my change of jobs, including flattering appraisals, as well as some wry comments, by contemporaries who ran other organizations. Huey Johnson, the former state Resources Agency chief, felt that I had done an "excellent, canny job." Dave Brower, my predecessor, was lavish in his praise and observed that I "profited from seeing what happened" to him. Martin Stern, head of the Trust for Public Land, said I had "the gift of being underestimated by . . . [my] adversaries."

As I turned to my new job, I knew I had to demonstrate that the new position was worthwhile—that I was delivering value for the money invested in me. And I had to make a sharp delineation between what others were doing and what I would be doing. I now worked directly for the board. In effect, I had to reinvent myself. Once again, I was the first to hold a position and had broad latitude in determining how it would actually develop. I wanted to use my time to think strategically about where the field of environmentalism should move.

One of my first endeavors was to prepare a substantial memorandum for Doug Wheeler which explained the changes that our international program was undergoing. The new focus of that program was to encourage the environmental movement where it was emerging abroad and where great issues were at stake. It was also to focus on the U.S. government's international activity. Influencing how the U.S. government behaved abroad with regard to the environment was the responsibility of Americans, I wrote; no one outside the United States could do the job. "And with our grassroots power base here, no one in this country is as well equipped as us to tackle it." Bills were being introduced in Congress that provided handles for us to use to influence the overseas behavior of our government. We could lobby Congress to effect reforms in this regard, and I would come to do that.

In my new work, which involved a kind of ambassadorial role, I started receiving visitors from abroad. They came even to our offices in San Francisco frequently, seeking information and ideas about how they might organize environmental efforts in their own countries, and they provided me with information. I expanded our correspondence with environmental groups in other countries and sought their newsletters. For many, I became their person to contact in the United States.

After a year in the new job, I came to the conclusion that I should relocate to Washington, D.C., and the board agreed. Many visitors from abroad came to our office there, and I could lobby more readily if I were there on a regular basis. And I could more easily stay out of Wheeler's hair if I were not in the San Francisco office every day. Staff needed to relate to Wheeler now, not to me, and I wouldn't be drawn into the circles of those who wanted to criticize him.

In July 1986 my wife and I sold our East Bay home and moved to Washington, D.C. That spring, Maxine had been shown a very nice townhouse near American University. Its owner had not yet moved. All over the walls she saw quotations from the Bible posted in frames. Being curious, she looked for a photo of the owners. To her consternation, she discovered that the owner was none other than—James Watt! Had we bought this house rather than another, people might have said that the Sierra Club not only drove him out of office but out of his home as well.

While we did eventually find another nice townhouse farther away, when I arrived at the Club's Washington, D.C., office I found that no arrangements had been made to provide a space for me to occupy. Frankly, the director of that office, John McComb, probably would have been happier if I had stayed in San Francisco. The Club had already outgrown its offices on Pennsylvania Avenue Southeast, and he put me in what was little more than a glorified closet. I fixed it up as best I could, but it represented a distinct comedown. I could not but wonder if McComb was also worried about having someone underfoot whom he did not control.

While I would attend weekly office staff meetings, I decided not to put myself into a position where others would feel free to give me directions or treat me in a way that I found demeaning. Instead, over time I went around to senior staff, one by one, and offered to help on problems they were confronting. I could do research, and I offered to lobby senior officials when the time was right. I took away any opportunities to criticize by offering to help before even being asked. Gradually I developed good working relationships with most of the people there.

Policy Projects

In addition to my direct Washington, D.C., work, I continued with projects I had begun earlier. While still in San Francisco, I had plunged into writing a series of think pieces about issues with which the Club had to grapple. In one I tried to make sense of a persistent contradiction in surveys of public opinion: while most polls showed environmental goals were given high standing, those that probed to find which problems were most important (i.e., salient) to respondents found that environmental issues were seldom mentioned.[1] This confronted us with the paradox of low salience but high levels of support.

One possible answer lay in what has been called the "issue-attention cycle": after a problem gets a lot of publicity and the government addresses it to some degree, the media turn their attention elsewhere or become bored, and public interest in the subject declines. But in the mid-1980s the media had not gotten bored, nor had the public lost interest. There was greater demand than ever for strong environmental regulations. So that was not the explanation.

Others suggested that salience really measures the sense that there is a crisis. According to this view, once the government pays attention and intervenes, the issue becomes more of a management problem and no longer a crisis. Under this definition, few issues are likely to stay as crises with high salience for very long. This made sense to me, but I doubted that it was a complete answer.

Finally, I found a theory put forth by a sociologist, Riley Dunlap, who suggested that salience was merely part of a spectrum of questions that could be asked. The pollster could ask alternatively about beliefs, or commitments, or the sense that there was a crisis (salience). Dunlap suggested that commitment, which was the demand that solutions be implemented, was the most important. He also observed that questions about salience often drew low responses because respondents were asked to volunteer information, which they did not have, or were asked to address questions that were simply too complex. I found Dunlap's analysis to be most persuasive and continue to think so.

By the mid-1980s, the unity in the environmental movement that had lasted for about a decade, from 1973 to 1983, was breaking down. For various reasons, a new breed of radicals was emerging in the movement. They were taking stronger stands on issues, using demonstrations as their main tactic, and renouncing pragmatic tactics of political persuasion. Leaders in Greenpeace and Earth First! were also making sharp comments about the Sierra Club, although we were not disparaging them. Perhaps the extremism of Watt prompted others to stake out extreme positions in the opposite direction. I began to look at the literature regarding splits in the movement.

A plethora of explanations had been offered for the new cleavage lines.[2] Some saw the splits in terms of a "dominant social paradigm" putting human welfare first versus a "new ecological paradigm" that places nature first, or at least at the center of things. I thought the Sierra Club believed in the "new ecological paradigm." Others thought there was a split between old-fashioned "nature conservationists," who viewed nature largely in aesthetic terms, and the "new environmentalists," who were more concerned about consumption. I thought the Sierra Club now had a foot in both of these camps, though we clearly had been old-fashioned "nature conservationists" in earlier years.

Others saw these distinctions in terms of political differences between liberals in the nation at large and conservatives. Surveys showed that about two-thirds of those in the Sierra Club considered themselves to be liberals, whereas nearly one-third thought of themselves as conservatives. But conservatives and liberals supported environmentalism almost equally, so clearly this distinction was not very helpful in explaining the new split.

Still others made a distinction between "deep ecologists" and others. I had written reviews of books on deep ecology for *SIERRA*. Proponents believed in the equality of all species, among other things, and wished the human population were smaller. They tended to disparage members of groups like the Sierra Club as "shallow." This was a case of what academics call the appropriation of ideology, because the Club also believed in many of these things; our founder, John Muir, had even called for them. Because of its obscure nature, I did not think this distinction was that useful.

Finally, some academics saw a distinction between "norm-oriented environmentalists" and "value-oriented" ones. The latter want to change the relationship of individuals to society and the way it works, whereas the former merely want to curb irresponsible conduct through laws and regulations. This distinction, I suggested, turned on whether it is wise to work within the context of the basic social, political, and economic institutions to achieve stepwise progress or whether prime energies must be directed at replacing those institutions. I thought this was the most useful distinction of all in explaining the split that had emerged, but I thought it might better be styled as a distinction between reformers and radicals, and that was the characterization I would use in subsequent talks and articles.

In the paper I wrote on this distinction, I outlined the following characteristics of the reformers, which we clearly were as an organization. The reformers focused on public policy so as to change the rules of the game for all, and political action was the method they used to effect pragmatic, incremental change. They were willing to take what they could get now and come back for more later. Their mood was one of studied optimism. In contrast, the radicals focused on changing both the system and personal lifestyles; their methods involved direct action, preaching, and bearing witness. Their cast of mind was more rigidly ideological and pessimistic; they had an apocalyptic outlook and tended to see crises at every turn.

In fact, these characterizations regarding reformers verses radicals were standard distinctions in political thought and history, but they were now emerging with great strength in the environmental movement. Perhaps the normal political spectrum was merely filling out as the movement matured.

I also saw a distinction between those who were embracing civil disobedience and those who believed in observing the law. The Sierra Club was clearly in the latter camp and always had been. I was afraid that the tactics of those who were engaging in sabotage (such as burning Forest Service buildings) as an extreme form of civil disobedience could polarize the public very quickly and create a difficult political environment for us all. Many people would not draw a distinction between environmental groups committing sabotage and the Sierra Club. But regardless of whether their tactics were well advised, it was clear that we would be dealing with a radical branch of the movement from now on.

Another problem we needed to face was the crisis in implementation. The belief was widespread that diminishing returns were setting in from environmental protection strategies that relied on the courts and Congress alone. After spending a decade or more to get a piece of legislation passed, environmentalists then needed to find a way to secure its implementation. The relevant government bureaucracies moved cautiously, and when hostile people were in power, such as during the Reagan administration, our challenge was even greater.

Slippage away from legislative intent will inevitably take place during implementation unless there is continued monitoring and lobbying, I wrote at the time.[3] Administrators make of statutes what they want to, particularly when funding and staffing are in short supply. Many in agencies have common advanced training and are members of related professional societies. These ties, as well as agency traditions, give them a sense of where public policy should be heading. They resist those who try to lobby them in different directions. And almost inevitably, onetime reform-minded agencies such as EPA lose their zeal and sense of commitment and become harder and harder to move.

In trying to determine what we could do, I also pointed to the difference between political appointees and career civil service staff, and, among political appointees, the difference between those who were more loyal to their peer networks and those who were loyal to the president himself. "The White House itself [the Executive Office of the President, or EOP] now needs to be thought of as a special target separate and apart from departments and agencies," I argued. "Because of the weakness of [political] parties and the diminished responsiveness of political appointees to a president, the EOP now does more to cultivate constituencies and intervene in departmental issues. The EOP intervenes especially on intractable issues that threaten political harm. Realizing this, lobbyists need to position themselves as representatives of constituencies that are to be cultivated and to use this entrée to move their issues." This approach should not be overused, and it would afford very limited success with hostile administrations. With regard to agencies such as the National Park Service and EPA, I suggested we seek out "soulmates" and "comers" on their staffs, with whom we could collaborate over time to advance our shared interests.

In dealing with midlevel and lower-level bureaucrats, I suggested a different approach. Because they are more comfortable "dealing with issues on a technical basis, we should cast our arguments as much as possible in unthreatening terms that are consistent with the agency's other suppositions and supported by data. The more rational we look, the more they will fear looking irrational and unsupported in the record if they rebuff us. . . . Lobbyists who become expert in specialized fields can meet the bureaucracy on ground that it can relate to."

Bureaucrats were cynical about contrived mail, I pointed out. They tended to view public participation in general as an empty charade, which they were all too happy to manipulate themselves. But we couldn't afford to be bested in contests to generate citizen mail to their agencies, or they would use our apparent lack of support against us. I argued that we had to play the game, hollow though it may be.

I concluded with the suggestion that we develop long-term efforts to lobby both the Forest Service and EPA. I recommended that we develop a "strategy of maintaining diplomatic relations with high figures of each administration (EOP, the secretary of the interior, CEQ, and so on), or if this proves to be impossible, we should then develop a public relations strategy to apply pressure to them." In the future, I would find myself doing just that.

Because we had been shaken by the hostility of the Reagan administration, I thought we ought to diversify our approach more, mainly by putting fewer of our eggs in the federal basket and looking for opportunities to make progress in various states. Through the vagaries of politics, it was likely that we would find promising circumstances in some states—even when the federal government turned its back on us. Through a survey of our chapters, I found that we were already active in lobbying legislatures in twenty-six states.

I developed the case for more Sierra Club lobbying at the state level in a paper for the board of directors.[4] After all, state governments control land use on two-thirds of the surface area of the country. These bodies regulate not only urban development but agriculture, mining, and forestry too. They control the beds of navigable watercourses, many wetlands, and ocean beaches and seabeds out to three miles or more. They control surface waters, groundwater, and resident wildlife, and have primary responsibility for abating and preventing most kinds of pollution. They control public services and most facility siting.

State and local levels of government, furthermore, in the previous decades had been growing even faster than the federal government—four times as fast. Apart from the military and trust funds, they then accounted for 70 percent of the domestic spending by government. And I learned that state legislatures could more easily be lobbied than before: those serving in them were better educated, salaried, and more professional; more of them had staff; and they tended to meet more often and for longer periods. And because there were fewer one-party states and more competition between the parties, state political parties had to deal directly with interest groups.

The emergence of greater professionalism in state government, I argued, allowed public-interest groups to press their case on the merits and be less at a disadvantage because they could not afford to wine and dine legislators. With the breakdown of the hegemony of old commercial interests in this arena, I felt we had new opportunities in the field. States continued to be incubators of innovation and reform. Intervention at the state level was also important because many issues such as land use could be addressed thoroughly and directly only at the state level. "If we care about results, we must bring forces to bear where they are achieved," I wrote.

I also pointed out that "many state legislators and bureaucrats, comparatively speaking, feel under-lobbied by constituents and environmentalists and would welcome our interventions; many feel they see too much of the other side and not enough of us." I recommended that the

Sierra Club weigh in with lobbying even more heavily in this arena. When Sue Merrow became president of the Club in 1990, she secured implementation of many of my recommendations. The board allocated more funds from its budget on a matching basis, for instance, to help more chapters hire lobbyists.

Reaching Out More Broadly

While I had endeavored to maintain relations with labor and business while I was executive director, I now tried to establish working relations with an even broader array of interests. I visited some of the officers of the Consumer Federation of America, for instance, to learn about their current efforts. I found that they agreed with us on many energy conservation issues, but they were concerned about trying to limit use of resources through higher prices.

When Larry Moss had been Club president in the mid-1970s, he had embraced and advocated the economists' notion of marginal cost pricing, which keyed prices of goods to the most expensive new increments obtained. For instance, he believed that the price of oil should be set at the cost of the most costly amount of oil produced from offshore wells, even though much of the overall supply might cost less. This approach stood in contrast to the more common notion of averaging the costs of production. Supposedly, its proponents argued, marginal cost pricing would retard demand. I had never been enthusiastic about this notion, though. I supposed I had absorbed the biases of the regions of the country where power was provided through public utility whose managers believed in keeping prices low (that is, reflecting costs plus a fair profit).

The folks at the Consumer Federation were willing to reject industry's blandishments with regard to drilling in wilderness areas and offshore areas if we stayed away from advocating increased prices as means of limiting consumption. I agreed, and I imagined that labor unions would agree too.

I saw Raul Yzaguirre, the head of La Raza, again. To my consternation, I learned that the organization had been further annoyed by a California congressman's charge that members had been duped by the oil industry on the issue of offshore oil drilling. I reminded him of our earlier agreement to stay out of each other's hair, noting that we had not gotten involved in supporting the Simpson-Mazzoli bill, which limited immigration and which Hispanics had viewed as a racist measure. From our conversation, I judged that La Raza was likely to stay out of the off-shore oil issue in the future, which I believe they did.

I also began to speak and write about the use of lawsuits against companies as a tool to protect the environment. In a speech to the Collegium Ramazzini and labor unions, I dealt with the idea of relying on tort suits instead of regulation, but ultimately rejected the idea.[5] This notion had been put forth by some right-wing think tanks opposed to regulation. "But surely the victims would want prevention over compensation," I said. "Damage suits themselves don't provide prevention, just compensation after the fact. . . . The claim is made that the regulatory process is slow and ponderous, but so is litigation."

But then I joined the advisory board of the Toxic Law Project of the University of Houston Law School. As I was exposed to more information, I began to see more potential for using such suits to supplement, though not replace, the regulatory system. "Regulatory standards are set to deal with average situations," I wrote. But "tort law can deal with egregious situations . . . demanding a higher level of care than is embodied in regulations. . . . It is potentially a kind of supplementary regulation demanding a higher level of performance." I saw, moreover, that some of the standards of care in statutory and tort law were influencing each other.

In the mid-1980s, I also began to explore deeper relations with the liberal wing of the religious community, being aware of the affinity between conservatives and fundamentalists. That liberal church community seemed to have a growing interest in environmentalism, especially in notions of sustainability—recognizing that the carrying capacity of the planet was limited. Many in this community were already active in energy issues and in combating acid rain. Now they were getting involved in preventing hazardous wastes from being disposed of in communities where the poor live, particularly poor blacks in the South. Their work laid the foundation for the concept of environmental justice.

One of their principal concerns, I wrote in a 1986 memorandum, was "the reconciliation of questions of economic justice with questions of environmental sustainability. They want to look at each of these questions through the lens of the other. They claim that 'the church may be the only institution capable of healing the often bitter distrust and disdain felt by activists on either issue for those working on the other.'" The dominant trend in that wing of the religious community, it seemed at the time, was "directed at absorbing environmentalism into their framework."

I thus thought that we might develop an alliance that would counter the involvement of fundamentalists with the political right, which was already evident. Accordingly, I joined the Eco-Justice Working Group of the National Council of Churches and began to attend its meetings on a regular basis. The group included not only Protestants but Catholic and Jewish representatives, and met in the United Methodist Building on Capitol Hill.

In the fall of 1985 I went to a Presbyterian conference in New York state on the sacred nature of creation, trying to learn all I could about these religious groups' interest in environmental issues. I found that a whole series of books and articles were being written by church leaders on the theological basis of environmentalism. I subsequently visited a number of these writers and thinkers. Many of them were trying to combat the thesis that the Bible gave sanction to those who were exploiting the earth. No explicit alliance ever developed, but the emergence of the environmental justice movement marked an important rapprochement between blacks and environmentalism, which continues today.

A Surprise at the Club

While I was preoccupied with these issues, all was not well in the Sierra Club home office in San Francisco. When I had taken my new position at the Sierra Club, I thought that I would still stay in touch with the executive directors of the Club. The board encouraged my successors as executive director to consult me on various matters. But little of that happened in practice. I came to recognize that confident managers would likely not want to admit that they had to rely on the "old guy." Understandably, they wanted to run their own show.

And I didn't want to get in their way. I did my best to avoid getting embroiled in internal Sierra Club operations, so successfully that I did not pick up on what was happening in the San Francisco office that first year. Because of the implicit "nonaggression pact" between Wheeler and me, I had discouraged confidants from phoning me to complain.

One day in the fall of 1986, Larry Downing, then Club president and a close friend of Denny Shaffer, telephoned me. The staff was chafing under Wheeler, and he thought Wheeler might not last long. If Wheeler resigned, would I consider coming back to San Francisco to mend the rift that had developed, serving as executive director again until a new one could be hired? Knowing that I was happy to have moved on to other work, Downing said the situation in the home office had become desperate. They needed me. Would I come back for at least a short while?

I had very mixed feelings. On the one hand, I was shocked that Wheeler would have barely lasted a year. I had just moved across the country and had projects already under way that merited my attention. I was glad to be out of it all, and now they were asking me to jump back in. But on the other hand, it was gratifying that they had turned again to me. They now must recognize that they could not plug just anyone with managerial skills into the job. But would I be welcomed back by those on the staff who had been restive under me?

I made a round of calls to find out more about what was going on. Apparently, the very staff who had been restive under me had rebelled against Wheeler. Doug Scott was their leader, but many more were involved. In fact, most of the staff were at odds with Wheeler. A few days later, I learned that he had resigned.

I couldn't resist the call of duty. I worked out an arrangement wherein I would fly on Mondays to San Francisco from Washington, D.C., and return on Friday afternoons to be with Maxine, which I did for six months.

When I arrived back in the home office, I was welcomed with joyous enthusiasm. At a staff assembly, I was given a standing ovation. I had delivered them from a terrible fate, they felt. Wheeler's Republican bias was a bad fit with the liberal ways of the Sierra Club, and his particular management style was also unwelcome. Apparently, he consulted hardly anyone before acting. Some said he walked confidently into open elevator shafts. He did not know where the pitfalls lurked and was too proud to ask. In a very short time, he had simply made too many enemies.

Wheeler had made a number of missteps. He wanted to seek corporate donations in a major fashion. He tried to change the Club's logo, not something to be trifled with at that time. He tried to lead the Club down the path of setting up a land trust, which the Club had already decided not to do. He tried to convert the Club to zero-based budgeting, but had to call in a consultant when that didn't work. After trying to turn over the budgeting to a staff team, he found the budget mired in controversy at the board level, then balked when the board tried to approve a budget that, he felt, had too small a surplus. And he focused mainly on policy questions of greatest interest to Republicans, such as the President's Commission on Americans Outdoors and the federal budget.

I invited the ringleaders of the rebellion to lunch. I asked senior figures like Doug Scott and Carl Pope whether I could get anything accomplished. I worried that their appetite for rebellion might now make the job untenable. Would I be anything more than an impotent caretaker? To my surprise, they begged me to come back and pledged their cooperation. They seemed worried that they had gone too far. Perhaps they were eager to be rescued from their own actions.

The board had also become polarized over Wheeler. Michele Perrault, who had been president when Wheeler was hired, stood by him; some on the board supported her. But Denny Shaffer, who had pushed me upstairs, had lined up against Wheeler now, the rebellious staff having convinced him to embrace their viewpoint. With Shaffer having his supporters too, bad blood had developed between the contending board factions, and the friction between Perrault and Shaffer had gotten caustic and personal. I was amazed at how quickly things could fall apart.

I needed to rescue them from these roles too, I realized. It was time for them to move on. And both of them then made friendly overtures to me.

In my second stint as executive director, I faced two challenges: to put operations back on an even keel and to lead the way in hiring a new executive director who would be a better fit than Wheeler had been. Accomplishing these tasks involved meeting with a lot of people who were seething with frustration. I sat down and talked with all of the department heads and some of their deputies. I took many of them to lunch. And I met with the head of the Stewards, the employees organization. We held a number of more general staff meetings, and I spent time with members of the board as well.

I moved into Wheeler's office, which was a larger office than I would ever have chosen or thought appropriate. In his desk I found correspondence from the dissidents, who had sought initially to ingratiate themselves. It was an interesting position in which to find myself. Many of those who had been so restive had now adopted me.

But rebellion was still in the air elsewhere. I got calls from one of the Club's groups asking me to fire a field representative. They thought he was undermining their positions and taking soft stances on a key issue. I made inquiries and concluded that he probably was, but I also concluded that this group was unrealistic in its expectations and overly combative. During my short time back, I was not about to fire someone of the field representative's rank. That would have roiled the waters again in the home office.

As always at this time (Fall 1986–Spring 1987), the Club was in the thick of some climactic public policy battles. It helped pass Proposition 65, a California initiative requiring businesses to post notices when they sold products that were contaminated by toxic materials. It succeeded in persuading Congress to enact a major overhaul of the Superfund law (the Superfund Amendments and Reauthorization Act, or SARA), and Reagan signed it too. Permanent cleanups were to be the order of the day, communities were given the "right to know" about toxics in their midst, and EPA was put on a schedule to clean up old sites contaminated with toxic chemicals and given a vast increase in funding for this purpose.

The amendments to the Clean Water Act, on which the Club worked hard, had to wait to be passed in the next Congress—over Reagan's veto. But before long, the Safe Drinking Water Act would clear Congress by margins that would make it veto-proof. Bills adding more wilderness to the system in Tennessee and Georgia were passed. A new Great Basin National Park was established at last in Nevada, and protection was extended to the Columbia Gorge in Oregon and Washington. In 1986, nineteen bills on which the Club worked were approved by Congress. And in the spring of 1987, the Club successfully pushed for new legislation to improve the energy efficiency of appliances.

Gradually the San Francisco office began to simmer down. For me things quickly fell into familiar routines. I was making decisions, preparing budgets, seeing donors, and developing strategies as once before. I was also drawn into the early stages of planning for a drive to raise major amounts of capital in connection with our centennial a few years hence. This was an initiative of the Sierra Club Foundation, which wanted to raise $100 million for this purpose (a goal they eventually achieved). It was the beginning of a period of "thinking big" about money, which continues to this day.

I had positive news to report to the board as I settled back into the job. Our affinity credit card program was bringing in new funds, catalog sales were up substantially over the prior year, and we had also started to produce videocassettes for television programming. We reinstated our children's books program in cooperation with a commercial publisher who underwrote it. We had increased our mailings to solicit new members, and our membership now exceeded 400,000, with 339 local groups. Cash flow was positive, and we had no bank loans outstanding.

The board gave me a Special Commendation for my work in restoring good relations. I felt that I had been vindicated and that any doubts among observers over the meaning of my change of jobs had been dispelled.

At meetings of the Group of Ten again I found myself the "dean" of the executive directors, and elsewhere I found that I was still in demand as a speaker. In the spring of 1987, I gave a keynote speech to the American Society for Environmental History, which met at Duke University. In it, I offered an interpretation of the historical phases of the environmental movement that was different from the notions of the "third wave" offered by those who were more business-oriented, such as Fred Krupp of the Environmental Defense Fund. Krupp and others were arguing that the time for confrontation with business was over; instead, they thought, it was time to negotiate and collaborate. I argued instead that the next phase should be seen as the time when the public actually received the environmental protection that it wanted and had so often been promised, rather than as a time when we should try to placate our opponents. In the future, I would sound more alarms about collaboration.

I also warned of new splits in the movement: "There is some evidence that the environmental movement now is in the process of realigning itself into three camps representing . . . differing views of what approach is most likely to get results. One camp represents disillusionment with government and resorts to direct action, including on occasion sabotage. Another represents a continued commitment to using the political process, with whatever confrontation it implies because of differing interests, while the third represents a faith in dialogue and a backing away from confrontation." I lamented the end of "the era of good feeling and cohesiveness in the movement." Our part of the movement, with its commitment to the political process, would now have to carry on without the help of people in the other two factions, and sometimes despite them—with them either criticizing us or opposing us.

Through the spring, I worked with a new search committee of the board to find someone to replace me. I involved staff in the search process, they helped me to check references, and I conferred with them on their evaluations. We all had a lot riding on this choice, and no one wanted to make a mistake a second time.

The board still wanted to search outside the ranks of our own staff. They wanted to avoid the dangers of becoming ingrown, and they wanted fresh insights. But this time, they especially wanted to avoid ideological incompatibility. They wanted to find someone who understood our environmental work and politics, but who had managed a staff.

This time the board chose someone who was already a Club member, Michael Fischer. He was a Californian, was an outdoorsman, and knew the Sierra Club, and I knew him. He had been the head of the California Coastal Commission, which the Club helped to create.

Finally, the day came to hand over the job again. Fischer, who was outgoing and relaxed, seemed confident also. At a staff assembly, I introduced him and gave him my best wishes. I thought that the staff would feel somewhat invested in this executive director's success. The board members seemed happy that the issue was behind them, but the tensions between some of the personalities on the board abated only gradually.

I was the only person who had ever served as the Sierra Club's executive director on two separate occasions. All together, I served in this position for a total of seventeen years. It was now really long enough. Oddly enough, Dave Brower and I ended up serving in this position for the same length of time, but he served only once. In my case, I was glad that the process of commuting across the country every week was finally over.

Once back at my job in Washington, D.C., I found that I was in an even better position than before. I sensed that everyone in the Club now viewed me in a new way. I was not just a hanger-on, with a sense of rejection hanging over me. I was now considered a mainstay of the Club's operation, a person who kept things together. And I had a new and trusting relationship with the board as well. At each meeting, the board was eager to hear from me, and I was no longer asked to confine myself to two oral reports a year.

During my six months as the interim executive director, the Club had also decided to buy a building in Washington, D.C., for our offices (we had been renting, and our lease was up). My wife donated her time to the search while I was out on the West Coast, and it was she who found the Club's new home. Located across the Hill on the Senate side, on Massachusetts Avenue Northeast, it was a recently built suite of offices designed to look like townhouses.

In that building, I chose as my office a small room on the top floor that would give me lots of exercise to reach. It also gave me a view of the Capitol Dome and its cupola, which was lit up at night when Congress was in session. I could also look out on the cherry trees in a small park. I had found my new home for the next dozen years.

16 *Wilderness Work Again*

By the 1980s, worldwide forests were being felled at a record rate, with wildlands and wildlife habitat shrinking in the face of development. The situation was becoming desperate with the International Union for the Conservation of Nature and Natural Resources (IUCN) shifting its focus from nature protection to sustainable development, and I felt that someone needed to champion nature protection without apology. I wanted to give support to those battling tall odds in trying to save wildlands. I launched a newsletter, *Earthcare Appeals*, to share news of their battles, and I built a mailing list comprising hundreds of such groups around the world.

But in championing this cause, I immediately faced the question of defining how much we were trying to save. At the level of individual cases, I was prepared to back indigenous groups in whatever choices they made about areas they thought were worth saving. But ultimately, I felt a more comprehensive answer was needed.

Through its new program in Washington, D.C., established in 1985, the Sierra Club's international office now had the ear of agencies in the development funding community, and we needed to be able to tell them which areas we believed should be off-limits to development. Having successfully encouraged passage of legislation that kept the U.S. Agency for International Development from making loans for development in protected areas (an approach I had conceived), we now, for example, wanted to persuade the World Bank to stop promoting development in key areas in the tropics.

Mapping Wilderness

To formulate such broad recommendations, we first needed a comprehensive picture of the world's wildlands. Various efforts around the world to map wildlands had failed in the past because experts insisted on using methods that were too costly and sophisticated. No one had the money to gather the data to apply them. In these cases, the perfect had been the enemy of the good. I wondered whether it would not be better to get the process started by using cruder but more affordable techniques. While all the details might not be right, the orders of magnitude of the estimates should be. The general picture that emerged might point the way toward follow-on studies that could refine the particulars.

Shortly after arriving in Washington, D.C., Peter Thacher of the World Resources Institute (WRI), a supporter of this approach who, while serving as an executive at the United Nations Environmental Programme, had learned much about what did not work, encouraged me to pursue my ideas and found money in WRI's budget to give me a $5,000 grant to get started. He also arranged for me to use the digitizing equipment in the environmental department of the World Bank. I hired a young woman just out of college, Heather Spalding, to do the work and added to that money from my own sources.

I cast about for the best approach. I found that the LANDSAT and SPOT satellite images were too detailed. It would take forever to examine them for the entire earth; and in the tropics, clouds sometimes obscured views of the land. I decided to use the approach the Forest Service had used in its RARE I and II surveys to find de facto wilderness and that I had employed years before in my own wilderness studies: use maps to look for areas devoid of any settlements, roads, or marks of humans. Essentially, we were looking for "empty quarters."

I soon discovered that only one type of map covered the entire planet: the Jet Navigation Charts (at a scale of 1:2 million) developed by the U.S. Defense Mapping Agency. Related to them were the Operational Navigation Charts (at a scale of 1:1 million), developed for the military but then used by commercial pilots who needed visual aids for navigation.

These charts were ideal for our purpose. As areas become more and more remote, these maps indicate increasing levels of detail with respect to artifacts in such places constructed by human beings, and the approach used to create the maps was consistent throughout the world.

Because pilots use human constructs to orient themselves, these charts show not only roads, rail lines, settlements, and airports but also power lines, pipelines, canals, mines, wells, buildings, and even shrines. The wilder an area, the more they are likely to show such constructs.

We decided to concentrate on blocks of undeveloped land of at least one million acres (400,000 hectares) in size. Bob Marshall had once suggested this as the minimum size for wilderness. Areas at least this large were likely to have the greatest chance of harboring biodiversity that might survive for a time.

On each Jet Navigation Chart, we identified the areas that showed no signs of human development, included an appropriate setback from all development (to allow for undisclosed development), and then digitized these sections of the charts. When questions arose, we consulted the more detailed Operational Navigation Charts and Library of Congress maps. Once we identified the areas, we asked environmental groups in a variety of countries to spot-check our findings in areas they knew and made adjustments to reflect their feedback.

In September, after intense months of teamwork preparing the materials, I found myself giving the keynote address on our results at the Fourth World Wilderness Congress in Denver. The findings of the first World Wilderness Inventory, done on a reconnaissance scale, were revealing: one-third of the land surface of the earth appeared to be generally wild and undeveloped still, but only half of that was in biologically active regions. All told, more than 48 million square kilometers of wilderness appeared to be left, but more than 41 percent of it was in the high Arctic or Antarctic. Of the remainder, 20 percent was in warm deserts, 20 percent in temperate regions, 11 percent in the tropics, and the balance in mixed mountain systems and cold winter deserts.

The audience for my talk was large and enthusiastic. The information presented had never been available before, and the *New York Times* gave a full account of it. In due course, I arranged with *Ambio*, the publication of the Royal Swedish Academy of Sciences, to publish our full report, jointly authored by Heather Spalding and me.[1] Subsequently, at the request of the Royal Geographic Society of the United Kingdom, I wrote a shorter version of the report that was published the following year.[2]

After we showed what NGOs could do in gathering such information on remaining wildlands, the United Nations Environmental Programme asked to incorporate our data into its system. Our visual images of the world's wilderness began to show up in other publications as well. A few years later I was glad to see the World Resources Institute begin to tackle more refined studies. I felt that I had not only done some pioneering but had stimulated others to get involved too.

I soon began to perceive that these wilderness maps could be used for other purposes. From data of the World Bank, for example, I found the locations of all the nearly one hundred new dams that were proposed in Brazil. It appeared that about a third of them would fall within areas of wilderness, little of which was officially reserved—another reason to be concerned about the environmental impacts of these proposals. And in the early 1990s, I overlaid our maps on maps of the tropical rain forests created for a Smithsonian Institution exhibit, finding that two-thirds of the forests around the world had been badly fragmented. In Africa only 20 percent of the equatorial rain forests were within large blocks of wilderness; the rest had been fragmented. At that time the situation was much better in South and Central America, where 41 percent of the rain forests fell within wilderness and the Amazon was in slightly better shape. Once again I published these results in *Ambio*.[3]

I thought about making further use of the Smithsonian's data to try to calculate the rates of loss for such forests, but I quickly discovered that this set of data was too crude for that purpose. I could not push my generalized techniques beyond their appropriate uses in gaining a general picture. But it did prompt me to wonder what could be done to stem the tide of loss. I noted that countries in Central America, East Asia, and Africa were decimating their tropical forests much faster than other countries.

By the spring of 1990 I had gathered a great deal of information about imports of tropical wood (volume, species, and so on). I also put together information on which countries had most depleted their forests, which species were most endangered, and what these countries had done to set aside protected areas. I thought a boycott could be organized to put pressure on the countries that clearly had the worst conservation records. With the data I had, we could apply pressure in a selective fashion. We even got Al Gore, then a senator from Tennessee, to introduce a bill that would have required labels to be placed on imported wood showing the country of origin. This would allow activists to make informed choices in the marketplace.

What I had not counted on was dissension among our constituency. Other conservation groups did not like the idea of boycotting countries per se. They thought that efforts in the market should be aimed at individual producers, not entire countries. They ignored the fact that it was governments that had allowed unrestrained logging to go on and that had decided not to set aside many protected areas. And they ignored the fact that certain species were endangered and could not stand more pressure.

These groups were also concerned about appearing to be hostile to given countries. That stance might have been poor diplomacy, and some of the groups had overseas operations that thereby might have been put in a difficult position. Moreover, I discovered that I had done too good a job of acculturating Sierra Club activists to the notion that our business was influencing public policy. Now they just wanted to do public policy and were not ready to engage in boycotts. Thus I turned my attention to persuading the governing elements of the Club that boycotts were a legitimate tool for activists in the international arena, where few tools were available.

I was disappointed by the lack of interest in boycotts, but Bill Mankin then emerged from the Sierra Club's International Committee to organize a different, specially funded project to save tropical forests. He was a determined young Georgian who had once been a driver for Newt Gingrich (when some thought he might be a conservationist). In due course, Mankin played a pivotal role in organizing the Forest Stewardship Council (FSC), which adopted the approach of certifying producers who were doing a better job—for instance, by protecting vulnerable areas and limiting their logging. By implication, those who were not certified were not to be patronized. While certification was a laborious and complicated undertaking, in the end it may have been a better approach than mine. The FSC's efforts are now beginning to make substantial progress in the retail lumber market, causing more producers to seek certification.

Mankin and I went on to work together, joined by other environmental groups, to encourage the United Nations Conference on Environment and Development (UNCED) in 1992 to develop a strong statement on forests. We lobbied the staff at the embassy of Brazil, which was hosting the conference, and traveled to Geneva for advance negotiations. We probably pushed UNCED to develop a stronger statement on this topic than it otherwise might have, but this experience made clear to us how contentious and difficult the work on this subject was.

Once the Club embraced the broader perspective of environmentalism in the 1970s, I no longer focused much on wilderness issues for the next fifteen years. I left this to Doug Scott and others, while I concentrated more on issues of energy, mining, planning, pollution, and international policy. After I prepared the first World Wilderness Inventory, however, I began to be invited once again to address wilderness issues, but now in my role as Sierra Club chairman and often in front of forums that had a professional caste, such as the Forest Service's Southeast Experiment Station in Athens, Georgia, which was then charged with doing scholarly work on wilderness. These invitations gave me a chance to expand some of my thinking on these issues.

In one of these talks in early 1988, titled "Understanding the Demand for More Wilderness,"[4] I reviewed the progress in the literature since 1966, when I had done my major article on the Wilderness Act and the values behind it. In addition to the eleven reasons for valuing wilderness that I had identified then, I found six more values that had been identified in the intervening years.

Saving more wilderness, I also argued, was not about determining how much citizens wanted to pay to have wilderness. In trying to impute monetary value to these lands, economists assume that the public has to pay to buy back the opportunity to have these areas. I suggested the reverse was the case: "The public owns wilderness on public lands, and private commodity interests are trying to buy rights, or seize them, to take away wilderness values—to take the natural resources in them for private gain."

I cited public opinion surveys that showed strong public support (82 percent) for the idea that "government has a responsibility to protect large areas of land for wilderness." And, more specifically, another survey showed that the public, by a 2–1 margin, supported the proposition that trees in the national forests should be preserved "in their natural state" rather than be logged. Only 7 percent felt there was too much wilderness. Amazingly enough, that survey was done for a timber industry group. Furthermore, according to another study, the counties in the American West with wilderness were enjoying greater growth than others in that region because having wilderness areas nearby was viewed as an amenity.

Congress had by then increased the size of the national wilderness system tenfold since it was started. Moreover, apparently Congress often thought that the administering agencies were too timid in their recommendations: it had increasingly been enlarging areas beyond the size that these agencies had suggested. In a decade, Congress had gone from increasing their size by an average of 25 percent to increasing their size by an average of 41 percent. The system could easily reach 150 million acres. Some even suggested it should reach 300 million acres.

Wilderness Values

Helping people to better understand why wilderness was valuable would help justify preserving more land in this system, in my view. Accordingly, I revisited my 1966 article on the Wilderness Act and the values behind it and reorganized my scheme for listing wilderness values, from the most abstract to the most concrete. In a 1986 conference address at the University of Minnesota to celebrate the act's twenty-fifth anniversary, I discussed wilderness as an expression of the notion that nature has rights.[5] Wilderness can be viewed as providing "regions of ecological freedom." Wilderness is one of the places on the planet that we allocate to other forms of life; it is the balance in the equation between humans and nature. These areas thereby become refugia for all of the species that survive there and can reemerge again. It is the place where evolution can still work to produce its wonders—a place which provides the rich, raw material that it needs. By allowing enough wilderness to survive, we recognize that we are not wise enough to presume to plan how the whole planet should work.

There were many utilitarian reasons to value wilderness areas as well, I argued, building on my 1966 article. I discussed not just their role as a source of genetic material and a homeland for indigenous peoples, but also their importance as watersheds and providers of geophysical services. They provide a measure of insurance against ecological disaster too. All in all, I listed twenty-five different values in this talk.

I thought I probably dealt with this topic in too abstract a way, but I soon found that there were those in the Forest Service's Southeast Experiment Station who wanted to hear more. Over the next year, I worked with Pat Reed of Colorado State University, who was associated with this station, in developing a taxonomy of wilderness values.

In the spring of the following year, 1990, at another conference sponsored by the Southeast Experiment Station, I set forth a revised scheme based on our combined analysis, elaborating on what I saw as more than fifty values, uses, and benefits of wilderness.[6] Not all of these values, benefits, and uses were found exclusively in wilderness (that is, roadless, undeveloped land such as that in the U.S. wilderness system).

Many were merely associated with wilderness but could also be found in parks and wildlife refuges and on undeveloped land. Nonetheless, they helped people justify saving wilderness, and increasingly they would be found more in wilderness areas. The Forest Service seemed to be satisfied with this rendition and put the material in one of its official publications.

In 1992 I attended the Fourth World Parks Congress in Venezuela, where I was scheduled to deliver some papers. Sponsored by the IUCN's Commission on National Parks and Protected Areas, the commission had long recommended that countries put at least 10 percent of their land under management that accorded it strong protection. Environmentalists were urging that a larger percentage be set aside. I succeeded in persuading the IUCN to call on nations to apply these percentages to their large biomes, such as tropical forests, not just to their total land mass, thereby avoiding the danger of limiting wilderness to swamps and deserts.

I realized that I might face questions about how well the United States had performed in this regard. Had we been able to protect more than 10 percent here? While some of the figures were readily available, I had never seen anyone put together the complete picture. With the aid of interns, we did so.[7]

I was reassured to a degree by what I found. If one looked at just federal holdings, only 9.2 percent was protected. But if one also looked at other holdings—those in the hands of state, local, and tribal governments, as well as private land conservancies and trusts—another 1.8 percent could be added, meaning that 11 percent was protected. I was gratified to find that even the IUCN's staff for North America was soon using these figures in their reports, citing me as their source.

At the World Parks Congress in Venezuela, I again was confronted by claims that the notion of wilderness was something only Americans were interested in. Some Latin Americans seemed to believe this, as did some Britons. Having attended World Wilderness Congresses, I knew this was not true. In fact, there was considerable interest abroad, and from Vance Martin, who ran the series of World Wilderness Conferences, I obtained specific information about a number of other countries that had established government programs to protect their wilderness.

In 1993 Martin and I collaborated on a piece in this vein, with me providing the legal analysis, for the *Journal of Forestry*.[8] We found that wilderness was officially maintained by ten other governments. They were mainly English-speaking countries, such as Australia, Canada, South Africa, and New Zealand; but they included Sweden and Finland too. Five of them had statutory systems; the others maintained their systems by administrative fiat.

These wilderness systems in other nations followed the basic law of the United States in many particulars. In some respects, Canadian wilderness law was more strict than U.S. law, while the rule for wilderness in African countries was less strict. The Scandinavian countries had made political compromises not unlike those we had made. Argentina also maintained roadless zones in its national parks, and Russia had substantial roadless areas in its nature preserves; however, I left them off our list because their approaches were not modeled on the American law.

For quite some time, I had been bothered by the fact that too many people in the IUCN seem to think that protected areas were justified only through preserving biodiversity. Having spent so much time identifying all the reasons for protecting wilderness (many of which applied to other types of protected areas as well), I was eager to address this oversimplification. In 1995 I did so in a speech to the North American branch of the IUCN's parks commission, at Lake Louise in Canada's Banff National Park.[9]

I accused some vocal conservation biologists, such as Edward Grumbine, of what historians call "present-ism." These biologists wanted to see the justification for protected areas through the lens of the single interest that consumed them—biodiversity protection—rather than see these areas as the product of many historical forces. Protected areas exist for a great variety of reasons, and their boundaries were drawn with different ideas in mind. A large and diverse constituency had supported the establishment of these areas, and I feared—and still fear—that the constituency for their continuation would shrink if only one value were to be used to manage them. Designated wilderness areas often do not serve the purposes of conservation biologists very well because they were not set aside with such notions in mind. I rejected their criticisms of these areas as anachronistic, however, or as simply token gestures that encouraged abuse of land elsewhere.

I also characterized as overblown historian Alfred Runte's assertion that protected areas such as the national parks consist mainly of "worthless lands,"[10] which some conservation biologists cited in depreciating the value of what had been set aside. While it was true that Congress had trimmed the boundaries of some of the original national parks to avoid valuable timber stands and bodies of ore, this was by no means true of the entire system. I pointed to Sequoia and Olympic national parks, which included valuable timber stands, while Kings Canyon and Yosemite contained valuable sites for dams. And the Redwood National Park contains timber that cost the federal government $1.3 billion to purchase. In terms of forgone commodities alone, these and other wilderness areas were far from worthless lands. "It will be all too easy for the public to conclude that protected-areas systems should be dismembered if this is the message they get from leaders in the biological community," I said, citing bills pending in Congress at the time that called for culling from the national park system areas thought to be of lesser value.

But there was something more disturbing in thinking of biodiversity as the only justification for protected areas: in fact, we want these areas protected even if the biota on them should change. At the very time that these conservation biologists wanted to build a system of protected areas around the traditional habitat for given species, the latest science was calling into question expectations that given species will permanently reside in given areas. The related equilibrium theory was giving way to more dynamic paradigms. "Because chance [disturbance] factors and small climactic variation can cause very substantial changes in vegetation," I explained, "the biota and associated ecosystem process for any given landscape will vary substantially over any significant time period. Instead of knowing more about what to do, it almost seems as if we know less about what to do and how best to plan for the future."

After reflecting on indications that some conservation biologists wanted to control the vegetation that grows in protected areas (principally through controlled burning), manipulate it in other ways, and grant local managers carte blanche to do what they felt best in the name of advancing biodiversity, I called for an end to so much presumption and hubris. I felt that such well-intended but amateurish meddlers in the political process of wilderness designation might well do more harm than good. They might undermine much of what we had spent so many years accomplishing.

In this speech, I sought to be deliberately provocative to get attention. Those who had been assuming that all those who wanted protected areas were working for the same ends began to think more deeply about the matter. These included the former head of the IUCN's parks commission, Hal Eidsvik of Canada. Afterward he wrote to say: "We need to apply biodiversity concepts where they can enhance our traditional objectives, not to try to break down the very foundation of the conservation world. . . . I agree with you that it is a dangerous time to be casting doubt on the validity of over 100 years of concerted conservation action."

My speech was published in a 1996 issue of *Wild Earth*,[11] which was then produced by the Wildlands Project to champion conservation biology. I then engaged in an exchange, in the *International Journal of Wilderness*, with conservation biologist Reed Noss. When he lamented the difficulty of enlisting recreational users of wilderness in his effort, I replied: "A crusade for biodiversity (i.e., richness of species and genetic variation) ought to be focused on the lands where it is found, which is not in the high-elevation wilderness in the American West. Rather, it should be focused on semi-natural lower-elevation lands. . . . Noss's desire to appropriate federal wilderness areas into his intellectual framework is like trying to draft 4-Fs into the army. They are the wrong conscripts. They have little to offer, and little is gained by turning their management on its head." Manipulating wilderness areas, as through burning and poisoning, would do little to advance the cause of biodiversity, both because the ranges for the few keystone species, such as grizzlies, found there are larger and because the biodiversity is largely elsewhere. "Let's work together," I concluded, "to design a new formula and manage vegetation to protect biodiversity where it is found and leave traditional Western wilderness alone." Nothing came of the invitation, however.

Park Service Wilderness

The question of how protected areas should be managed came up in other ways as well. In the mid-1990s, I was asked by Wes Henry, then director of the wilderness program at the National Park Service, to speak to its headquarters staff about the importance of wilderness in the mission of the Park Service. Many there apparently did not understand why the Park Service was a part of the National Wilderness Preservation System. As I prepared notes for my talk, I was surprised to find that little had been written on the topic, and I had to draw heavily on my own knowledge.

After my talk, Henry suggested that I collaborate with Frank Buono of their staff to prepare a technical paper on the subject, which they could distribute to field staff. I agreed and presented an expanded version of this paper at an agency conference on wilderness in Santa Fe that fall.[12] I also realized that I had the makings of a law review article that could fill a void in the literature, and I published the resulting full-fledged paper, "What the Wilderness Act Accomplished in Protection of Roadless Areas within the National Park System," in a 1995 issue of the *Journal of Environmental Law and Litigation*.[13]

People in the Park Service had always wondered why they needed the Wilderness Act. Couldn't they maintain as much wilderness as they wanted under their 1916 organic act, which governed administration generally? Since the Park Service was supposed to protect nature in national parks, could they not decide to protect more or less of it as they chose?

My reply was "Yes, but." They could, but they did not. The Park Service did not always want to maintain a lot of wilderness, while conservationists wanted more to be maintained than the agency did. We had worked to get the Park Service put under the Wilderness Act to restrict its administrative discretion in building roads and lodges.

After the Wilderness Act became law in 1964, the Park Service was in denial for a while. It embraced the "purity" doctrine to minimize how much land could qualify for wilderness status. This involved the faulty notion that areas had to be untouched in the past to qualify for inclusion in the system. The Park Service ignored the wording of the statute that spoke of an area's appearances (not its history) and its condition on the whole (not that of every part). Moreover, it was slow to complete the required studies of its holdings.

Gradually the Park Service put this unfortunate history behind it. But it took a lawsuit and pressure from Congress to persuade it to abandon another unfortunate practice. In response to a recommendation of the Outdoor Recreation Resources Review Commission report, the Park Service had adopted a misguided system for classifying all federal recreation lands and had been using that system to determine how each of its areas should be managed. But this practice caused the Park Service to fail to look for direction to the statute setting up each of its areas in the first place. As a result, many national seashores tended to be managed as if their primary purpose were mass recreation. That was far from the case; many of their statutes directed that their natural attributes be preserved.

I had long complained to Interior Department officials about this. They were inadvertently convincing us of the need to put even more of their lands in the wilderness system. At my behest, Assistant Secretary

Nat Reed issued orders to the Park Service in 1972 to change its regulations regarding this practice. A few years later, as part of the second Redwood National Park bill, Congress put in systemwide language to make this even clearer.

Future court cases would also shed light on Congress's intentions. One went even further, casting doubt on the notion that the Park Service must operate under dual mandates (to pursue "use" as well as "conservation"). It said the Park Service's organic act speaks of "but a single purpose, namely, conservation."[14]

In 1994, as the thirty-fifth anniversary of the Wilderness Act was drawing near, students at the University of Denver law school decided to publish a symposium issue of their law review on how well the act was faring. Because my 1966 piece on the act was remembered (and was often used in teaching), they invited me to contribute a piece.[15]

What most struck me in 1994 was how little the act was honored then among professionals of various sorts. At a time when the wilderness system had grown to record size and drew unprecedented approval from the general public, the idea of wilderness seemed to have also attracted a record number of critics, including many besides the normal commercial opponents.

Various writers and academics were debunking the very notion of wilderness. Perhaps we had oversold the concept and they were reacting to that. In many respects, they were railing against straw men they themselves had erected. For instance, they felt they had to point out that no areas are pristine. Greenhouse gases affect all areas; sulfates and pesticides drift into wilderness areas. Fire suppression has built up fuels in backcountry forests. Some areas had been burned at one time by native populations.

Apparently these critics did not realize that we had never asserted that the remaining wilderness is pristine—only that it is less disturbed than other places. In fact, we had been explicitly arguing that areas did *not* have to be pristine to be eligible to enter the system, only that the imprint of humans should now be *substantially* unnoticeable. These areas need only *generally* appear to have been affected *primarily* by the forces of nature. This is what the Wilderness Act says.

But others, such as historian William Cronon, accused wilderness lovers of turning wilderness into a fetish. They thought we were avoiding the real world and devaluing the rest of the environment. A few might be guilty of that, but the environmental movement as a whole certainly was not. It had been engaged in an endless series of struggles to combat pollution, curb sprawl, and protect open space. We had not been writing off other places.

I found that some conservation biologists had an ambivalent feeling about the wilderness system, as suggested earlier. On one hand, they tended to see the units in the present wilderness system as too small, in the wrong places, and too far apart. They did not want to acknowledge that the system was built not to protect biological diversity, but rather to protect rugged, wild country. Moreover, it had not been easy to get that much protected. By deprecating the value of these lands, I warned, they were playing into the hands of those who would dismember the wilderness system.

Simultaneously, though, these conservation biologists wanted to co-opt this system into a new system of mega-reserves for a few species, which they wanted to build. Oddly enough, though, even these larger reserves would not be in the places where most of the biodiversity is found. The more diverse lands, such as valleys and coasts, have largely been preempted for other purposes. Only small niches of natural places can be found in the more species-rich lowlands. This is like looking for your lost keys where the light is shining rather than where you dropped them.

If some of these conservation biologists were put in charge, I suggested, they would depart from the approach of letting wilderness alone (the "hands-off" approach). They were willing to use herbicides and pesticides to eradicate unwanted species and to employ fire as a tool to manipulate the biota in wilderness. Along the boundaries of wilderness areas, they were prepared to place barriers and salt blocks to control the flow of wild animals. Some of them wanted to relax restrictions on motorized equipment, such as snowmobiles; others would allow wood to be removed for fuel.

Some agency managers were prepared to go in this direction too. They were ready to manipulate the biota to achieve the desired "composition, structure, and function" in designated wilderness areas. They felt they must choose between the status quo, pre-settlement conditions, or some other desired condition.

They would use fire as their tool of choice in shaping the wilderness. Forest stands would last only as long as they chose. After they had burned continuously over a long time, the entire stand would be an artifact of their choices. It would not be natural in any sense of the word. I believed instead that wildfires, which have little chance of escaping onto other lands, should be allowed to burn themselves out in wilderness, rather than being suppressed.

Yet they argue that they must do these things and make these choices because they are obliged to preserve "natural conditions." While that wording can be found in the Wilderness Act, they cite it out of context. In context, it is clear that wilderness is to be untrammeled by humans.

What they should really be maintaining, I argued, are natural processes—processes that minimize human interference. Management should just consist of protecting designated wilderness from human influences. Those who would argue that humans are part of nature and that our interventions are part of nature will be able to excuse anything in such terms. By definition, wilderness is that part of nature which has few human interventions.

I also found that some conservation biologists would even go so far as to let each manager decide his or her own prescriptions. Despite the sad history of local managers being all too susceptible to pressures from vested interests in their locality, these biologists would do away with uniform legal standards to protect wilderness. The wilderness system would gradually degrade as managers would go in different directions.

I concluded by observing that a wilderness debate was taking place almost in ignorance of the actual provisions of the Wilderness Act. Too many people had lost sight of the fact that the Wilderness Act is actually a legal device for zoning. It sets forth what may and may not be done in these areas. It did not set out to address all of the problems afflicting humanity.

These debates continue today. Some of the critics may be arguing about the almost mythic status that wilderness has achieved in the popular mind, but other critics are very specific in directing their comments to units within the official wilderness system.

Wild Rivers at Global Level

After making a hit with my World Wilderness Inventory, I found that I could not easily drop that line of work. Vance Martin wanted to showcase new inventories of qualities of the wild at his future World Wilderness Congresses, and in the early 1990s he urged me to tackle some new topic along this line. I immediately thought of the subject of wild rivers. Having looked at the land, why did I not now look at the rivers that drained the land? How many of the world's rivers were still pure, wild, and free flowing?

Martin's fifth such congress was meeting in Norway in 1993 and would focus on the Arctic as a region, so he suggested that I determine how many of the rivers in this region were wild and give a presentation at the meeting. I now called my overall mapping endeavors the Natural Value Mapping Project. I hoped to raise grants from foundations for it, but this never worked out, so I used a succession of very dedicated interns instead.

In this study, we did not demand that a river be wild in its entirety, as some foreign experts have. Instead, we used standards similar to those employed in the United States. We would accept segments of rivers upstream from dams and impoundments, but we wanted the rivers to be free of bankside development and contamination. For purposes of convenience, we chose fifty kilometers as our minimum length for stretches of wild river. This was similar to the twenty-mile minimum length once used by the U.S. Bureau of Outdoor Recreation in its inventories for the U.S. system of wild and scenic rivers, established in 1968.

Once again we used the Jet Navigation Charts as the base maps for our work. They showed the principal impoundments. In addition to other local maps, we consulted the *International Register of Dams*. We eliminated reaches of rivers with closely paralleling roads, which suggested too much development. In the inferences we made, we were stretching more than we had with the wilderness surveys, but I felt that the overall percentages we calculated would still be representative. This had to be viewed as only a first approximation, however. In doing our calculations, we totaled all the lengths of portions of rivers that were still wild and determined what fraction they were of the total lengths of rivers in a country and region. And, at least in our study of the wild rivers of the north, we did check with the local experts in Scandinavia, who confirmed our findings about their region.

In September 1993, I traveled to Tromso in northern Norway to present our findings at a plenary session at the Fifth World Wilderness Congress. Examining rivers in Canada, Alaska, Scandinavia, and the Russian Federation (north of 50 degrees latitude), I found that 45 percent of the river mileage in this region was still wild. But whereas Canada and Alaska (considered together) had 75 percent of their river mileage still in wild condition, only 34 percent of the mileage in the Russian Federation still had wild qualities, and even fewer—11 percent—in Scandinavia did. The actual total length of all wild rivers in Canada/Alaska and the Russian Federation, though, was similar (more than 200,000 kilometers), as were the numbers of wild rivers.

Potentially the Russian Federation could have had the largest number of wild rivers. Not only are the world's large land masses in the north, the Russian Federation is half again as large as Canada and Alaska combined. However, the Soviet Union had pursued a binge of dam building, as well as industrialization and settlement, in its northern regions. Many of its rivers, which flow into the Arctic Ocean, are heavily polluted, yet the Russian Federation gives little attention to preventing pollution or abating it. My presentation was published as part of a book on the meeting.[16]

In 1998 I completed my survey of the world's wild rivers and presented my findings to the Sixth World Wilderness Congress meeting in Bangalore, India, to a boisterous audience. If all of the rivers of the world were laid end to end, I estimated, only about 20 percent of that length would be wild. I found about 6,000 river segments that could be thought of as wild, totaling more than 700,000 kilometers.

I now combined the figures I had developed earlier for the northern regions with figures for the balance of the world. In a relative sense, more wild river mileage was left in North America—nearly 38 percent, mainly in Canada and Alaska (the lower 48 states had only about 5 percent). South America had the next greatest amount—26 percent, mostly in the Amazon basin—followed by Eurasia, with 17 percent of the river mileage still in a wild state, mainly in eastern Siberia. Surprisingly, Africa had the lowest percentage left in wild condition—7 percent (though the percentage was much higher in Mozambique and other countries).

In absolute terms, Russia had by far the greatest total length of wild rivers—more than 260,000 kilometers. Canada, Brazil, and the United States (Alaska mainly) were next in line. The countries with the greatest density of wild rivers (kilometers of wild river per square kilometer) tended to be in South America (in places such as Peru and Suriname). Looking at the average length of wild rivers, most of the longest tended to be in South America also. Two-thirds of the total number of wild rivers were in Eurasia and North America.

The summary of my longer study was well received by the leaders of the wilderness congress.[17] The audience may have thought such reports were routine; they probably did not appreciate that this one was the first of its kind, wrapping up nearly a decade of work. To complete it, I had directed the work of perhaps a half dozen interns, who had intently inspected maps and measured river lengths. In appreciation, the conference organizers conferred on me a Lifetime Achievement Award. They called me a "Wild Man."

I had never expected to get into this work, but I felt that it needed to be done. Instead of dealing with wild country as an abstraction, we were identifying where it still existed and how much of it there was. We could speak of it in real terms. Some interested in this work, particularly in Australia, thought of me as the instigator of this movement to map wild-lands. Institutions such as the World Resources Institute, the World Wildlife Fund, and others are now bringing out a succession of reports and maps dealing with trends in wild country around the world.

It is ironic that at a time when wilderness studies are drawing more detailed and professional attention than ever on a worldwide basis, others continue to debate the concept at the most basic level. They would benefit by studying the historical record of how conservationists worked their way through this debate a half century earlier.

17 Working in the Capital

My time in Washington, D.C., 1986–99, reflected the frustrations of dealing with a government that was no longer promoting environmental reform, as well as with a harsher regulatory climate for advocacy groups, a search for new strategies, and a need for NGOs to assume heavier burdens. The heavier burdens ultimately affected me in a personal way. But it all began differently.

Soon after I began my new job as chairman in the summer of 1986, I received a phone call from the secretary of the interior. At that time, during the Reagan administration's second term, it was Don Hodel, whom I knew from my college days and with whom I generally disagreed.

This time he took me by surprise. He said he now believed it was time to take down Hetch Hetchy Dam within Yosemite National Park. It had been a long time since any interior secretary had stood for doing that. He said he had just called Dianne Feinstein, then the mayor of San Francisco, and she had not been pleased. He planned to direct the Bureau of Reclamation to do studies on what would be involved with the dam's removal, and he wanted my support.

Ever since John Muir's time, the Sierra Club had favored the removal of Hetch Hetchy Dam, as it had opposed the construction of the dam in the first place. Building it seemed a tragic mistake; it had been put there simply because the site was cheap and convenient, though it ran contrary to the notion that national parks were supposed to be inviolable. How could I turn down Hodel?

Yet this was out of character for him. He ordinarily stood against what we stood for. He told me he was on his way to Alaska, where he was expected to push for oil development in the Arctic National Wildlife Refuge. Perhaps this was a way to take the sting out of that thrust. Some thought he was trying to drive a wedge between San Francisco Democrats and the Sierra Club. In any event, I realized that he would enjoy seeing us at odds.

I encouraged Hodel to proceed and met with him a number of times thereafter. He had valuable studies done that showed that San Francisco could get the same water, which was used for municipal drinking purposes, from the river downstream at another reservoir built later, one that adjoined the aqueduct already bringing water to San Francisco. While the city would lose the revenues it got from selling the power produced by the Hetch Hetchy project, the city was never supposed to get those monies anyway. By law, the energy was supposed to be used for a municipal power system, which was never established.

Hodel had artists depict what the restored valley could look like in time, and he used those visualizations to produce a video, which he presented to us. I wrote an op-ed piece that fall for the *Los Angeles Times*[1] in which I pointed out that this dam, and a related dam at Lake Eleanor—also within the park—"represent a monumental embarrassment to the nation that originated both the idea of national parks and the standards for their protection. More and more countries are establishing national park systems modeled on ours, and are being urged to adhere to the standards that we worked out—that nature is to be fully protected in national parks and there will be no factories, powerhouses, or commercial exploitation within them. . . . It is time to look seriously at how we can rectify this calamitous mistake and restore Hetch Hetchy to Yosemite."[2]

While Congress failed to give Hodel further funding to investigate the idea, his call to me on the issue did mark the beginning of an effort by Republican administrations to reestablish communications with us. And Hodel's initiative, which garnered lots of publicity in California, caused the Sierra Club to take the issue up again. The Club set up a task force on the issue, which eventually blossomed into a new group calling itself Restore Hetch Hetchy, on whose advisory board I serve. Some of us feel that the dam should still be taken out and the area restored, at least by 2013. By then, San Francisco will have had the valley for a hundred years—long enough by just about any standard. From then on, the people of the nation ought to get their "second Yosemite" back and have their national park restored.

The First Bush Administration

In the fall of 1988, George Bush, the elder, was elected. In his campaign, he declared that he was going to be the "environmental president." Though he had been Ronald Reagan's vice president, he suggested that he would make a real shift from the policies of his predecessor.

When he assumed office in January 1989, Bush did make some encouraging appointments. He put an environmentalist, Bill Reilly, in charge of EPA. An effective person, Michael Deland, was chosen to head the Council on Environmental Quality. A Hill veteran who was sympathetic to environmental goals, Bob Grady, was given the post at the Office of Management and Budget (OMB) that oversaw policy on natural resources and the environment. Other spots affecting environmental policy were given to people who were at least not hostile. This was a promising change from the Reagan years.

I was our point person in maintaining contact with the administration. I spent a lot of time at CEQ and worked well with Deland and his staff. On a number of occasions, I was invited to the White House for events. The administration seemed to be eager to court us—at least at the outset. I even enjoyed lunch at the White House mess. Various officials at the Interior Department invited me for briefings and to confer. I saw the secretary at that time, Manuel Lujan, on a number of occasions and ate lunch with his solicitor in his private dining room. I met at various times with almost all of the officials in Interior who handled matters of interest to the Sierra Club.

I also visited with officials of other agencies: EPA, OMB, the Office of the Trade Representative, and the State Department. In these generally cordial meetings, I gave them our view of what they were doing (and ought to be doing) and picked up useful intelligence.

This was the most complete access to the executive branch nationally that I ever enjoyed. For a while, the administration treated us as if we were part of their constituency. Once one of the president's sons, Neil Bush, came to see me at our offices. He sounded us out about an idea he had for a television channel carrying environmental programming, perhaps as a way to cultivate us further. In due course, I found myself appointed to a presidential panel on awards for environmental service.[3]

Not all of these meetings turned out well. The chief of the Forest Service at that time, Dale Robertson, and his deputy once took me to lunch. We covered lots of issues. When he suggested that we might do this again, I mentioned that his agency had trained us to discount the value of face-to-face meetings. He wanted to know what I meant.

I told him I had learned the hard way that time spent in cultivating personal relations with Forest Service officials did not pay off. I could not recall any appeal I had made to them that had yielded positive results. Not one official had ever come back to say that they had thought more about what I had suggested, that I had a good point, and that they would be modifying their approach. Instead, we learned to view these encounters as wasted time and to take our points to Congress and the courts instead, where we usually got a fair hearing and a response. Needless to say, Robertson and I never had lunch again.

As time passed, I realized that the supportive people in the first Bush administration were being checkmated by others who had opposite views. Bob Grady, for example, was put under Richard Darman, who headed OMB. Darman thought environmental programs cost too much, and he ridiculed environmentalists as "strange people who were trying to make the world safe for green vegetables." The influence of Michael Deland at CEQ was more than blunted by John Sununu, Sr., a fierce anti-environmentalist, who happened to be chief of staff. And Bill Reilly's clout at EPA was stymied by Vice President Dan Quayle's Competitiveness Council, which came to control the regulatory process. It became increasingly obvious that the environmentalists in the administration were there as showpieces. The real power lay elsewhere.

Andrew Card was among the hard-liners who stood against us. Once I was part of a delegation that went to the White House to make a presentation on global warming. Instead of just listening and thanking us, he was rude and argumentative. I remembered this well after he became chief of staff during the second Bush administration. By happenstance he was at a restaurant in downtown Washington one night, where he barged into a dinner being held by the Sierra Club Foundation and lectured us on treating that administration with courtesy and avoiding rudeness. He was the last person who should have been lecturing us about courtesy.

While there were a few creditable policies at the outset of the first Bush administration, such as initiating action in Congress on the Clean Air Act of 1990, after a while things turned sour. The administration of the senior Bush opposed taking action on global warming, tried to cut the number of protected wetlands by half, tried to weaken the Clean Air Act, pushed hydrocarbon production (including in the Arctic National Wildlife Refuge), balked at signing the treaty on biodiversity (after having weakened it), stymied efforts to extend the reach of the Endangered Species Act, and let Quayle completely hobble the EPA's process for developing new regulations.

While the Sierra Club came to denounce the backward policies of this administration, initially we had been hopeful. The Club was ready for a change after the Reagan years, and I enjoyed the promising beginning. Oddly enough, it was the best treatment I have ever received from any administration in my entire career. Perhaps it was because the administration was counting on riding on appearances rather than substance.

As our relations with the administration cooled, I found myself working more closely with the key Democrats in the Senate. For instance, during the battle over the Clean Air Act's renewal in 1990, the chairman of the Environment Committee, Senator George Mitchell, Democrat of Maine, who later became majority leader, invited me to join him to campaign for the act in Philadelphia. We spent an afternoon on Rittenhouse Square buttonholing passersby asking for their support. I acted as the person who snagged people and fed them to the senator for a few words.

I also found myself being courted by the Canadian government because of its concern about the acid rain falling on its eastern provinces, which was caused by emissions drifting across the border from old, dirty power plants in the United States. It wanted us to do everything possible to secure enactment of amendments to the Clean Air Act in 1990 to curb this pollution. I met a number of times with officials from their embassy to discuss progress.

As chairman of the Sierra Club, I was supposed to help identify new issues that deserved attention. In this vein, I had laid the groundwork for the Club's increasing its effort at the level of state government. Now I tried to get the Club to take on another issue of great importance that was receiving little attention at the time.

In 1989, officials at EPA invited me to a series of expert presentations on the issue of global warming at a conference near Washington, D.C. Previously I had not been convinced by claims that global warming was occurring. I had heard from an environmental group in Berkeley that cited evidence which they thought suggested that a new Ice Age was beginning. On the other hand, Rafe Pomerance, whom I had known from his days as CEO at Friends of the Earth, was convinced that human activities were instead causing a new warming trend, and he was on a mission to persuade everyone that this was so. At that time, I thought these voices counterbalanced each other. I was not really sure whom to believe or what was true.

But after listening to the scientists at the conference, I was persuaded that carbon dioxide levels were rising, that greenhouse gases were accumulating, and that it was probable that average temperatures were rising as a consequence. At a meeting shortly thereafter at Wildacres, a retreat center in North Carolina, I persuaded the Sierra Club's board of directors that this was an important issue that they should address. In due course, grants from foundations permitted us to hire staff to deal with this issue and build a program that continues to this day.

Regulatory Concerns of Nonprofits

As the opportunities to influence the administration on environmental issues shrank, I began to pay more attention to other matters, such as regulatory issues affecting the finances of nonprofits. Attacks on the tax status of nonprofits were a favorite tactic of the political right, and they were increasing.

When I had served as the executive director of the Sierra Club, I had learned how the finances of nonprofits were affected by the regulatory climate in which they operated. In this respect, we had something in common with for-profit enterprises. I had been there when the Sierra Club lost its tax deductibility, and I had lived through the days when the Postal Service withdrew our eligibility for preferred rates. I was aware that right-wing groups had tried to get the Club into trouble with the IRS, and I had seen election commissions question our filings. And I was still there when the IRS claimed we owed taxes because of our affinity credit card arrangement.

Since we had a high profile and took tough stands, regulatory agencies assumed we were an easy mark—that we could be intimidated. We had to teach them that this was not so, I decided. We had to fight back with top legal talent and stick with our cases as long as it took.

The political right had a long-nursed notion that progressive groups thrived on government "handouts." Under Bush and Quayle, the right strove to modify various provisions in the tax and regulatory laws that allowed not-for-profit groups to be vigorous advocates. Under the heading of a campaign to "defund the left," which was originated by the Heritage Foundation, some groups tried to stifle us. One leader of a conservative group boasted that "we will hunt these groups down one by one and extinguish their funding sources."

These adversaries were also trying to delegitimize lobbying by nonprofit groups of all stripes so as to leave the field to commercial operators, who would be the only ones able to pay experts to find their way through the maze of new restrictions placed on advocacy. Many nonprofits would be crushed by the record-keeping burden for lobbying, our opponents hoped, and would become even more "gun shy" about engaging in it. Thus they hoped to thin the ranks of the vigorous advocates for independent positions.

Unfortunately, few environmental lobbyists understood these regulatory issues or had any interest in them, since they often seemed esoteric and simply a distraction. I not only knew these issues affected our bottom line, but had become interested in them and had learned to follow their twists and turns.[4] I saw our action in this sphere as part of the larger goal of defending the rights of the advocacy community, which was critical to making democracy work effectively.

I was eager to find allies in this struggle. When I arrived in Washington, D.C., I identified Independent Sector, an organization that styled itself as the voice for tax-exempt groups with public purposes, as the base from which I could best do this. The Sierra Club had joined Independent Sector a few years before, and I quickly joined its tax committee, a working group of its larger policy committee on government affairs. Before long, I was invited to join this committee too. I plunged into this work and enjoyed many of these associations.

In one of our first efforts, we worked furiously to stop a bill in Congress that threatened the Sierra Club's bottom line. Sponsored by Representative Jake Pickle of Texas, the bill sought to increase the degree to which any income nonprofits derived from "unrelated" businesses would be taxed (that is, subject to the unrelated business income tax, or UBIT). We feared we might owe a great deal more in taxes were this bill to pass, as it would limit the business expenses we could charge against the income we received from our outings, our catalog, our affinity credit card, and advertisements carried in our magazine.

At one stage in the struggle over the bill, our critics also tried to impose taxes on our books program, including our calendars. Under that proposal we might have owed a half million dollars or more, on top of the UBIT taxes we were already paying on income from renting our mailing lists and selling advertising in our magazine.

The Pickle bill had been introduced at the behest of retailers, who felt nonprofits were competing with them. They wanted to define any income we gained by competing with them in "their marketplace" as taxable. They meant to do away with the test of "relatedness," which waived taxes on products related to a nonprofit group's chartered purpose, and make taxable anything they considered to be "inherently commercial."

The Sierra Club had endorsed Pickle, a Democrat, in the prior election. I strove to meet with him, but he refused to see me. I finally got a full meeting with his key staff person, but to no apparent effect. I ended up working more with the ranking minority member of Pickle's subcommittee—a Republican, Richard Schulze of Pennsylvania.

As a result of the lobbying by the coalition we forged, the scope of the bill was narrowed, and finally the bill was bottled up entirely in subcommittee. Pickle chaired this body, but he could not get his subcommittee to report out his own bill. He wouldn't survive the next election either.

Independent Sector's tax committee spent years persuading the IRS to issue decent regulations to implement the Conable Act, named for onetime congressman Barber Conable. This provision allowed tax-deductible groups to do a limited amount of lobbying, and if they exceeded the limit, they would only be fined rather than suffer the loss of their exemption. This measure grew out of concerns in the tax-deductible community following the IRS crackdown on the Sierra Club in 1966. It had taken a decade for the community, led by the National Audubon Society, to get this measure enacted, but even another decade later, implementing regulations still had not been issued in final form.

Finally in 1990, through the law firm of Caplin & Drysdale, Independent Sector got the IRS to settle on a definition of lobbying that had a number of the elements we sought: it applied, for the most part, just to legislation; it applied just to measures that were specifically identified; and the organization had to have taken a stand on the measure and had to have issued a call to action. In the end, it took thirteen years for the IRS to issue these regulations, which ran to almost forty pages.

There was hardly a regulatory issue affecting the Sierra Club that I did not work on in these years. In retaliation for our opposition to such judicial nominees as Robert Bork (who Reagan sought in 1987 to put on the Supreme Court), for example, the General Counsel of the IRS proposed taxing the money that advocacy groups spent lobbying against such nominees. This proposal had to be (and was) defeated. The House tax committee also successfully promoted a change in the law to require groups such as ours to print a notice on all our solicitation literature stating that donations to us were not tax deductible.

Administration forces also sought to discourage nonprofit lobbying in every way they could: by trying to change the law so groups that focused mainly on public policy or were supported mainly by foundations could no longer qualify for tax exemptions, for example; by imposing burdensome reporting requirements on lobbying groups; and by prohibiting advocacy groups from conducting fund-raising efforts among staff of federal agencies. We had to fight off a proposal to impose a 30 percent excise tax on nonprofits' lobbying expenditures. Senators even tried to deny us access to the nonprofit postal permit if any of the funds we raised via the mail might be used for lobbying.

I was involved as an expert witness in litigation that dragged on for more than fifteen years about our affinity credit card arrangement with a bank. The matter had grown so controversial that Congress even tried, during the UBIT fight, to take the issue away from the courts. Ultimately the Sierra Club prevailed, however, which had broad repercussions for other groups as well. The tax court ultimately held that the monies that nonprofits receive from such ventures are properly regarded as royalties and are not taxable. Many other groups with these arrangements were jubilant at the ruling.

I was active too in the broad coalition that bottled up a bill by Representative Ernest Istook, Republican of Oklahoma, in the mid-1990s.[5] Among other things, it would have prevented tax-exempt groups that receive government grants from lobbying Congress—even with their own money (that is, from sources other than the grant). Unfortunately, the only part of the bill that was enacted was the part that applied to advocacy groups—501(c)(4) groups—that could no longer get government grants at all anymore. But government grants were never an important part of the club's finances.

Through these many struggles, I found that advocacy groups tended to be treated as pariahs. Independent Sector was oriented more to traditional charities—501(c)(3) groups—than to groups set up for advocacy per se. These latter groups were thought to have forfeited most of their rights as nonprofits. Because they were granted the right to do unlimited lobbying and advocacy, they were denied deductibility for their donors. But I found that Congress was also discouraging them by treating them differently than (c)(3)s in other ways: by not letting them set up tax-deferred retirement income plans for their staffs, by treating income from renting mailing lists differently, and by denying them eligibility for government grants.

I came to understand that few other (c)(4)s had business arrangements which were as complicated as those of the Sierra Club. Staff in the tax-writing committees and the Treasury Department seemed to believe that we had gotten too big and powerful and needed to be "cut down to size." That was my challenge.

At the outset, I found that Independent Sector was loath to work on too many issues. Those of us who wanted to draw a firm line on many issues were often outvoted, so we eventually formed a rival group, the Advocacy Forum, and I was chosen to chair it. We met in a union office and invited Independent Sector staff to sit in our sessions. Faced with competition, Independent Sector became more willing to deal forthrightly with issues of concern to us, and I soon was invited to join its board of directors. As Independent Sector became more responsive, we let the Advocacy Forum die.

While I did lobby various bodies on regulatory issues, I worked hardest to get umbrella organizations such as Independent Sector, whose coalition included a long list of organizations, to address them. This was the main way I saw of mobilizing a constituency to bring pressure. I felt I was helping to make more organizations aware of how their future was influenced by tax and regulatory policies. In this work, I was often in alliance with a group called OMB Watch, run by Gary Bass. In due course, I joined the board of that organization, which works on tax and regulatory issues as well as on pollution control policy and other matters.

As the coalitions sponsored by Independent Sector and OMB Watch involved more and more groups, we were recognized as a powerful bloc of organizations and began to enjoy a measure of success. These groups were no longer cowering before regulators, waiting for the axe to fall. Independent Sector lobbyists began to see that they could be effective, and the cooperating groups began to feel an esprit de corps. In the battle over the Pickle bill, for example, we went from trying to slow down an onslaught to, in effect, killing a bill in committee. One of the Republican members told us after our victory that members did not feel "suicidal" about that bill—that is, willing to back it even in the face of such opposition. They simply had no taste for tangling with large, mainstream organizations over esoteric tax doctrines.

We now felt that we could hold our own on such issues. And I had found another cause: the rights of nonprofit advocates.

Engaging Business Directly

As we faced frustration in looking to the government and the courts for redress of environmental abuses in the 1980s, I began to think about alternatives. Surveys were showing rising rates of public opinion favorable to environmentalists. Some of this was attributable to broad resentment over the failures of the Bush and Reagan administrations to embrace environmental policies, but some grew out of media coverage of the run-up to another Earth Day, scheduled for 1990—the twentieth anniversary of the first one.

Nearly 90 percent of the public said they were willing to buy "green" products or pay more for them. More than three-fourths of the public now claimed they were willing to exert power as consumers to boycott irresponsible firms. I thought that green consumerism might be developing into a second front for us. When the Sierra Club held a convention for its leaders (called an International Assembly) in Ann Arbor, Michigan, in July 1989, I used the occasion to call for a move in that direction.

I developed the themes of green consumerism at greater length in remarks that fall to an audience at Bentley College in Massachusetts.[6] "Spending or investing money is another way to vote," I said, "to put power in the hands of those in the economy who behave responsibly vis à vis the environment."

Other groups were beginning to enjoy successes in persuading business to respond. NRDC had gotten the pesticide Alar withdrawn from use as a result of an exposé in the media—even though EPA was not ready to act. The Environmental Defense Fund had persuaded McDonald's to stop using Styrofoam packages. The Rainforest Action Network had gotten Burger King to stop using beef from a country relying on pastures that had been created at the expense of tropical rain forests.

My work with the campaigns of our international program made me realize that progress in this mode might be possible domestically. The Sierra Club had persuaded an agency of the Austrian government to withdraw financing for an objectionable dam on the Danube River by threatening to join a boycott of skiing there. The threat itself proved to be enough; we didn't actually have to mount a boycott. The mere threat of bad publicity by the Sierra Club also induced Citicorp not to loan money to help finance a dam in the Brazilian rain forest. A Club letter-writing campaign persuaded a major American oil company to drop its plans to drill for oil in a national park in Ecuador. And major canners had been persuaded to back out of selling tuna fish that was not "dolphin safe."

Occasionally a real campaign had to be waged, but some firms were ready to be "tipped" in our direction by just a little pressure. In these cases, environmental groups went around government and dealt directly with businesses. Various companies now wanted me to address their middle managers and their boards of directors. Something interesting was under way. Even CEOs often claimed to be ready to act.

Major U.S. retailers were promising to bring out green lines, and all sorts of new green products were appearing in the marketplace at home and abroad. I traveled to Canada especially to see what the reputed leader, Loblaw's supermarkets, was offering. I saw shelves stocked with products with bright green labels, each proclaiming a special feature: "no chlorine," "no dioxin," "dolphin safe," and so on. Huge green banners proclaimed "You can make a difference" and "Buy green, buy clean." Loblaw's enjoyed a boost in sales by taking this tack.

Various new institutions, such as Green Seal, were established to capitalize on these trends. I conferred with Green Seal's founders and sat on its founding board. Since the U.S. government did not have an official eco-label (as Germany does), we decided to form a new nonprofit to help consumers easily choose environmentally responsible products. When they saw Green Seal's bright green check on a product's package, they would know it was acceptable. In time, its seal was carried on hundreds of products, such as lightbulbs and tissue.

In another development in this area, the Council on Economic Priorities (CEP), a public service research organization based in New York, found it had a best seller on its hands with its book *Shopping for a Better World*, which evaluated products and firms in terms of their social responsibility. The Sierra Club agreed to reprint it, since its rating system included environmental factors.

CEP set up committees to identify the most and least socially responsible companies. Its annual selections were given wide publicity; the awards themselves were presented at a major dinner in New York

City. Separate committees handled citations for the most and least responsible. I served on both over time, beginning with the awards for good conduct. After a while, I switched to the other committee. Its work had grown more interesting, as it began to be treated differently by the companies it was charged with investigating.

At the outset, the companies being studied refused to provide information when asked. They just hoped CEP would go away. But CEP persisted, using public information to make its evaluations instead. Staff evaluated firms by category (such as oil and chemical companies), gathered data on industry averages (such as emissions), and then showed which firms in each category performed above and below the average. When CEP cited the companies at the bottom of their list, it would indicate what they needed to do to improve.

Since the media were taking CEP's findings seriously, the companies involved began to take them seriously too. They stopped stonewalling our committee and started talking. Before long, we were flooded with information. Boxloads of data would arrive in my office. When the paper flow finally became overwhelming, I had to resign from this committee, though I stayed on CEP's advisory board. We had found a new way to change behavior.

In the early 1990s, firms that specialized in socially responsible investing found that the issue their customers cared about the most was the environment. These firms wanted to develop a process to become more credible on environmental issues—a process that would bring them more reliable information. A number of us were invited to a meeting to figure out how to do this.

The upshot was the formation of the Coalition for Environmentally Responsible Economies (CERES). I joined its board of directors and served on it for the next decade. I was asked more than once to be its co-chair, but each time I turned it down. I didn't want to become too prominently associated with the business community.

CERES issued a code of conduct to which it asked companies to subscribe. Subscribing companies would also have to agree to file annual reports disclosing how well they had lived up to those principles.

While Green Seal focused on model products, CERES did not entirely attract ideal companies. At first it drew small New England companies with niche operations, which were indeed model firms. But in time it began to attract major manufacturers. In a few years, CERES had fifty or more firms in its ranks, and it has continued to grow steadily.

CERES always had an implicit partnership with the Interfaith Center on Corporate Responsibility, an offshoot of the National Council of Churches. Each spring the Interfaith Center would prepare a list of companies it would target with petitions on behalf of its members' shares, which ran into the billions of dollars. They would often ask that companies subscribe to the CERES principles and to other environmental propositions. Some targeted companies would eventually try to settle the question by joining CERES. In this way, CERES often took in flawed companies as members—companies that were improving but were hardly ideal.

CERES included some major institutional investors, such as the New York City Pension Fund. The Fund had too much money to limit its investments to model companies, but wanted investment guidelines that would improve performance generally. Their tolerance for flawed companies created tensions within CERES. I was part of the group that was bothered by the growing number of flawed companies associated with CERES. But I wanted to hold on to the institutional investors that we had.

I began to stress that we had to have a way to remove firms from CERES that were not showing good faith by living up to the code of conduct to which they had subscribed. I worked on teams that wrote up amendments to CERES's bylaws that set forth the circumstances under which signatory firms could be removed.

I was also disappointed that CERES was not doing more to analyze the annual reports that were filed with it. At the outset, the founders discussed the possibility of evaluating and grading annual reports, but realized that few companies would join if they thought they would be graded. I felt CERES should do more to get these reports into the hands of activists who could use them, however, and that it should do more to encourage good patterns of conduct among its members and identify trends. I summed up my views in a well-received farewell speech to the annual convention of CERES at the Roosevelt Hotel in New York City in 1999.[7]

When I joined these various institutions to "green up" the business community, I perceived that we were beginning a set of related undertakings. We would get firms to pledge to abide by a sound code of conduct and disclose data about their actual performance (CERES). Then we would cite the firms that were doing the best and the worst jobs (CEP) and put the worst performers on notice to improve. And finally, we would aid consumers in the marketplace by giving them guides to find the best products (Green Seal and CEP). In all instances, we were starting organizations that were independent and credible. Together they would constitute a system to affect reform, regardless of the swings of the political pendulum that influenced government.

But I soon discovered that we were overreaching. None of these new organizations was well funded, and foundations were reluctant to make grants to them. Perhaps our work was too close to the source of their own capital. Green Seal never had the money to adequately advertise and promote its seal, and consequently, demand for the seal remained low. CEP never had enough money for research, and CERES and Green Seal took several years to assemble a critical mass of staff and experience.

But most importantly, too few among the body of environmental activists took these efforts seriously. They were culturally attuned to the idea of fighting with industry and looking solely for governmental solutions. They could not get used to the idea that progress might be made in a different fashion. They were stuck in a culture of political conflict. People who otherwise should have been sympathetic would hold back because they thought we were wasting our time or—even worse—"selling out."

Moreover, widespread disillusionment was setting in over the way green merchandising was being handled. Consumers looked for new, clean products. Instead, they mainly got advertising gimmickry. The green virtues of existing products were simply heralded, or packaging was reduced. In some cases, the producer simply promised to do more recycling or to make donations to environmental groups.

The emphasis among those interested in green marketing began to shift toward identifying firms making bogus claims. Government authorities, such as the Federal Trade Commission, began to intervene to identify firms that were making false claims of greenness. Instead of capitalizing on the huge potential market for green products, industry had chosen to view it simply as an advertising opportunity. The moment passed and became characterized by "green scammers."

My experience with CEP, though, had convinced me that at least some companies would respond to efforts to green up business. I also saw companies negotiate with the Interfaith Center to get their names removed from its annual lists. I saw a major oil company work with CERES to pass their five-year review, and I saw General Motors negotiate with a supplier to clean up its act after CERES had pressed them.

But many in our ranks could relate only to sticks, not carrots, in relation to the business community. They could only conceive of fighting with firms, never praising them. I had learned over the years that both were necessary. When a firm improved or did what you asked, you had to give them credit. The logic of the system suggested that you had to be able to do one if you did the other.

Fortunately, help began to come from a different quarter. Generational change among industrial managers now began to bring greater acceptance of environmental responsibility. As firms were required to report their release of toxics and other emissions, they gradually began to measure various aspects of their environmental footprint. Some CEOs were appalled to learn that their firms were high on the list of egregious emitters. They didn't like the bad publicity, and they began to press their managers to lower the emissions.

As more and more firms got used to issuing annual environmental reports (and CERES probably prompted this growing practice), firms measured more and more parts of their footprint. They began to compete in designing well-drawn reports. There is now an institutional impetus to want to deliver better environmental news each year in these reports.

Moreover, large firms are hiring more and more staff to attend to this cleanup. They are professionals with their own standards and pride, and are pressing to make their firms more environmentally responsible. They may not be in the driver's seat in business, but they are becoming an institutionalized force in their own right. In a way, they are adding weight in place of the interest lacking in the environmental movement itself. It is also they who are pointing out that pollution prevention pays and developing solid arguments to win over the hard cases in their firms. By reducing nonproduct output such as pollution, they note, more input can go toward producing products that can be sold. Less waste can mean more profit. Lower environmental liabilities can translate into higher stock prices.

Progress was slow, however, on the effort to get the Sierra Club substantially involved in greening business. I had been all too successful in convincing the Club that it should keep its eye on politics and government, it seemed. I had made headway in convincing the board of directors that it should embrace the idea of trying to influence corporate action via direct engagement, but getting them to do something substantial was an entirely different matter. They had the Club join CERES at my behest, but no real resources were diverted then to this second front (although this has now changed). Only slowly, too, did they come to understand the theory of graduated use of a threat to boycott.

I realized that I was dealing with the challenge of changing institutional culture—on both sides. It would take time, perhaps many decades. Gradually new institutions were becoming rooted; it would remain to be seen whether their efforts would bloom in an important way.

Natural Resources Council of America

The Sierra Club had been a member of the Natural Resources Council of America (NRCA) since it began shortly after World War II. NRCA is an umbrella group that aims to bring together a broad array of organizations concerned with various types of conservation. For the most part, its groups are concerned with public lands. Dave Brower had been active in it and served as its president in the late 1950s. Brock Evans, who headed our Washington office in the mid-1970s, had also served as its president for a time.

I had been active in NRCA when I was the Club's conservation director in the late 1960s. The group was then dominated by the more conservative hunting and fishing groups. I worked with Russell Train, who at that time represented the Conservation Foundation, to develop an understanding that its officers should be drawn as much from the groups that do not consume resources as from the groups that do, such as the hunting and fishing organizations. I also worked to raise the dues so that the group could hire staff.

When I went to Washington, D.C., as the Sierra Club's chairman, I decided to become active again in NRCA. I hadn't had the time to be an active participant in the 1970s and 1980s, but my situation had changed now. NRCA had always been a useful place to meet people in other parts of the older conservation movement. The contacts made there could be useful on issues where it helped to show a broad front, and representatives from more conservative groups were helpful allies when meeting with more conservative legislators. While NRCA itself did not take stands, those who met there could quickly form alliances. In considering how the Sierra Club should develop in the coming decades, I thought it would also be useful to learn more about the interests of the various groups and their plans for the future.

In turn, I promoted NRCA as a place for the newer and smaller environmental groups, which could not gain admission to the Group of Ten, to find a home on the national scene. Most of them wanted to feel part of something greater than themselves and to be in regular touch with peers. Groups fighting billboards, building trails on old rail rights-of-way, and setting up land trusts were now joining NRCA. I began to see NRCA as an umbrella group that might serve the institutional needs of our broader movement. It could provide a place to talk about regulatory problems affecting us and our various relations with funders, and could be a place to address training needs and promote concern for our history.

I was elected president of NRCA for the 1992–93 terms, and for a while I also served on its awards committee. NRCA proved to be the only place where the staff of our groups could earn awards from their peers. It also bestowed awards on those in government and politics who befriended us, presenting its awards at an annual banquet at the National Press Club, where I often spoke at press conferences. During most of the year, NRCA had monthly luncheons there, at which we heard speakers. We invited figures in government and business to attend also, making these a good place to meet people outside the movement.

Gradually NRCA's membership began to reflect more of an environmental slant. I even had to assure the director of the Society of American Foresters, whose members were often at odds with environmental groups, that he had a place there and could aspire to move up in the organization.

For about twenty years, I also served on the board of the League of Conservation Voters, which, as the electoral arm of the environmental movement, endorses candidates. I had gotten involved in the League before the Sierra Club developed its own electoral program. For many years, I had been frustrated because, in my opinion, the League did not give enough weight in its legislative scorecard (which rated legislators on their voting records) to votes on wilderness, parks, and other issues of nature protection. For years the scorecard slighted issues of particular interest to the Sierra Club in favor of issues of interest to the Environmental Policy Center and Friends of the Earth; for instance, dam projects these groups were opposing and various other non-mainstream issues.

Many years later I heard a similar complaint from Senator John McCain, Republican of Arizona. I was part of a delegation that sought him out in the mid-1990s to see whether he could encourage more Republicans to support environmental positions. He dodged our plea, but revealed that he felt the League's scorecards were unfair to Republicans because they gave too much weight to social issues such as international family planning, which he did not consider a conservation issue. In different ways, we may have been responding to similar feelings. While I would not have eliminated the issues with a social edge that he would have, the balance would have been different if traditional conservation issues had more of a place in the League's scorecard.

The Sierra Club went ahead to develop its own system for tracking votes as well as the stands legislators took on issues of interest to us. I saw the League through a transition in management and then got off its board in the late 1980s as we developed our own program.

NGOs in Governmental Roles

In what I was saying and writing in the late 1980s and early 1990s, I was looking for new approaches that would permit the environmental movement to move forward. While I was resisting efforts to hamstring NGOs through tax and related measures, my interest in a second front with the business community was growing, as I had become frustrated with the federal government. I was also quite mindful of the failures of federal agencies to deliver, especially as the presidency of the elder Bush moved along.

On the twentieth anniversary of Earth Day in 1990, I was asked to address a group meeting at Walden Pond in Massachusetts. "Gradually the nonprofit environmental community has been inventing instruments of public purpose outside the framework of the federal government," I pointed out. "Environmental NGOs have taken over the role of a defaulting federal government."

I cited a number of examples in which the roles had been reversed. I had first thought of this reversal during the Club's early environmental litigation (in federal courts), when we were characterized as serving as a "private attorney general." In effect, we were deputized to serve as the attorney general because the actual attorney general was defending wayward public officials; he was really acting in a private capacity. As litigants, when we prevailed we were sometimes awarded attorneys' fees because we were serving public purposes. I cited other examples: the Conservation Foundation was then doing studies on the state of the environment, which CEQ had failed to do, while the National Parks

Association, another NGO, was doing surveys on the state of the parks. The Trust for Public Land was acquiring land and holding it for the government. The Sierra Club was bringing actions to enforce the Clean Water Act. At one time, the Club had more enforcement actions pending in the courts than did the Justice Department. Meanwhile, it was NRDC rather than EPA that was doing the studies whose results led to pesticides such as Alar being dropped from use.

"The NGOs are acting more like government, and the government is acting more like private parties," I suggested, calling this practice vis à vis NGOs "delegated government." "The delegation is by inference or by a kind of adverse possession that is sanctioned by time. A government too apathetic to exert itself acquiesces in the exercise of public functions by others, particularly as public opinion comes to approve of the results."

In a subsequent article in the *Renewable Resources Journal*,[8] I elaborated on these themes. "Increasingly the line between the government and the governed is getting blurred in practice." Nonprofits were doing as much to shape many regulatory outcomes as was government, though obviously business may do even more to promote its own ends. "[Nonprofits] have lobbied through most of the pollution control laws; most of the laws to conserve public lands bear their imprint. Their court cases have forced issuance of a large body of regulations." They do more to screen out bad projects than do supposed regulators. They almost resemble a "shadow government," I claimed. They are, in effect, quasi-regulators.

I began to see ways too that American NGOs might play a role on the worldwide stage. When I spoke to an international environmental law conference at the Hague in the Netherlands the next year,[9] I drew on ideas set forth at that time in the *Harvard Environmental Law Journal*. I suggested that U.S. courts might have extra-territorial reach for American laws. This had happened in the Bhopal case, in which the New York federal district court kept jurisdiction (because a U.S. company was involved, with most of its assets here), while remanding the case for initial trial in India. I found many cases in which U.S. courts asserted jurisdiction over U.S. nationals for their behavior abroad (for instance, in cases of taxes, military service, labor laws, and patents). This was now beginning to happen in the environmental field as well, as in dealing with injuries from pesticides. After reviewing recent decisions along this line, I concluded that this assertion of "extra-territoriality is designed to get justice for victims worldwide of U.S.-based perpetrators. Foreign victims can track their attackers back to their lairs and get satisfaction from those with deep pockets."

Centennial

When the Sierra Club celebrated its centennial in 1992, I was asked to speak at Club commemorative events.

At the banquet held that night in a San Francisco hotel to cap the celebration, I tried to look ahead. In trying to imagine what kind of world people might live in when the Sierra Club celebrated its next centennial in 2092, I explored three alternative scenarios. In the pessimistic scenario, 90 percent of species had been lost, and human numbers had quintupled. Two-thirds of the globe was choked by heavy pollution. The glaciers were melting, the seas were rising, and desertification was spreading across the American Midwest.

But I reminded my audience that things do not have to get worse. The bison had been brought back from the edge of extinction. Gray whale stocks had recovered. Levels of ambient lead were declining, and nuclear fallout had abated. By 1992 new cars were emitting 98 percent less pollution than those built before the first Earth Day. The wilderness system had grown tenfold. Political will could make a difference.

I then told them what a mildly optimistic scenario might look like. Among other things, the level of human population might stabilize (albeit at still too high a level). The levels of industrial pollution would stabilize too, and the percentages of land put in protected areas would grow. More farmers would turn to sustainable agriculture. Rains would return to some drought-stricken areas.

But then I asked whether there was any hope that we might do better still? Oddly enough, I thought there was. There was a chance that multinational corporations might even provide the impetus because they wanted rational, stable, and predictable operating conditions. They were seeking these through trade agreements such as the General Agreement on Tariffs and Trade. But so far they were not granting parity to environmental concerns and democratic values, pursuing instead a one-sided approach that would only bring more instability and uncertainty.

If these contending forces of business leaders and environmentalists could arrive at a detente, the result would be a better world. This would be a world where the human population stabilizes at sustainable levels; "where literacy and education rise to meet the needs for technological competence . . . and public health improves to protect employers' interests in that workforce." Energy would be provided by photovoltaics, fuel cells, and hydrogen. Tropical countries would value their rain forests more for biotechnology and carbon storage than for logging. Employers would decide that they do not want to foul their own nests.

"The world would gradually learn that life is better in every way when it practices good earth care," I said. "Corporations would come to understand that the price of getting global trading rules for their economic operations carries with it the obligation to provide for parallel rules to require environmental cleanup."

With this vision, I may have filled my listeners with hope. And they knew that many around the world shared their hope, as good wishes for our centennial had flooded in from environmental groups in many countries. In due course, my remarks were reprinted in the *Congressional Record*.[10] Today, I still think this scenario is possible.

Even while I was trying to move beyond looking to government in the conventional way, I did respond repeatedly to invitations to testify before Congress, on such diverse topics as rejuvenating CEQ, giving cabinet status to EPA, and extending NEPA's reach overseas to cover American foreign aid projects. I was constantly on the run giving speeches to such varied groups as the International Bar Association in New York City, the Society of American Foresters, and the American Library Association; and at conferences on such topics as trade (delivered in Mexico), EPA's future, and global warming. The pace did not slow down.

Before I knew it, five years had passed since Michael Fischer had become the Club's executive director in 1987. He had begun to consult me a bit more, but the Club officers were beginning to grow restive with him. He did not have the same problems as his predecessor, but he did not seem to be bonding with Club folks. After he laid off employees to meet a budget crunch, the remaining staff organized a union. They were not happy. I found myself drawn into performing a kind of shuttle diplomacy to interpret Fischer to the board and vice versa.

Soon it became obvious that a parting of the ways was in the offing. I wanted to minimize bad feelings and tried to make the transition as smooth as possible. Soon Fischer announced he was leaving. I remained on good terms with him. He performed as well as anyone from outside the staff probably could have.

I was even more involved in this transition than the previous one. I participated in round after round of interviews. Many very credible outside candidates applied, some of whom I later recommended for jobs inside government. But our inside candidate looked just as good and seemed less of a risk. We had gone outside two times in a row, and we had not found a long-term answer. This time we went for the inside candidate, Carl Pope. He had been serving as associate executive director and had practically been an understudy for the job. He turned out to be the right answer, and his competence is now widely acknowledged. As I observed at the time, I think it is a healthy sign that one can still work one's way up through the staff ranks and aspire to this position.

Things may have been finally set right with the Club, but something was not right with me. One morning in 1993 I woke up at an international conference to find that all my energy had drained away. It felt as if someone had turned down the rheostat on my energy level; I could barely get out of bed. This was all the more curious because I had been fine the day before and had just given a number of papers. My wife and I had also just traveled to see Angel Falls in the southern part of Venezuela.

After a day or two, my wife got me to the airport and home, where I repaired to my bed. The doctors could not find anything wrong. Since I had been in the tropics, the natural supposition was that I had a tropical virus. But when I went to a top expert on tropical medicine, he could not find anything wrong either. No other specialist among the twelve or so I consulted could find the source of my problem. I had some symptoms of chronic fatigue syndrome, but not enough of them to be conclusive. But I was buoyed after I joined a network for those with this malady. Talking to them helped.

For six months, I was prostrate and confined to bed. I took to plotting the ups and (mostly) downs in my energy level. My brain was still working normally as I lay there. After a while I wanted to use it, so I read a lot and wrote a few papers, including one on the record of the first Bush administration in subverting science.

Finally I realized that I would have to find my own way out of this dead end. I discovered that the medicine prescribed for my high blood pressure had a side effect that caused fatigue. So I switched to another.

I learned that lying prone caused fatigue (this had been learned during the space program). So I began to force myself to get around a little. In a book on herbal remedies, I noticed that various herbs relieved fatigue. When I inquired to my doctor, he sent me to a special pharmacy near the National Institutes of Health, which he thought might help. The key person there told me to take five herbs. In two weeks I would feel a bit better, he said, and in two months I would be all right. Then I should stop taking these substances one by one, to see which was most helpful. It turned out to be potassium.

It worked exactly the way he said it would. In late summer while still on sick leave, I returned to Oregon and began to walk a little. Each day I went a bit farther into the deep, soothing forests. Gradually I began to feel like myself again. Finally, in the fall I returned to work, restored to health.

No one may ever determine exactly what happened to me. A few years before, I had had a short bout of the same malady. But I may have been suffering from a form of profound exhaustion. I had been working in a high-stress environment, testifying, speaking, and writing, as if I were a machine. I was happy and doing challenging work. But there is a limit to how much anyone can do. I may have finally gotten to the bottom of my bottomless pit of energy.

18 *Trade Matters*

Just as I had not been convinced at first about global warming, it also took me a while to see that trade matters were a bona fide environmental issue. But eventually, I changed my mind about trade too and in 1990 persuaded the board of the Sierra Club to take up this important issue. In the ensuing years I became caught up in it in a major way, and the Club is still involved.

In the late 1980s I was approached by Lori Wallach of Public Citizen, one of Ralph Nader's organizations, about the subject. Public Citizen was concerned about the social impact of various free trade agreements, both those then in force and proposed. At that time, no environmental group had taken on the issue of the proposed North American Free Trade Agreement (NAFTA) between the United States, Canada, and Mexico and the effects it might have on the environment. As a traditional Democrat, I initially tended to see the proposal simply in terms of lowering tariffs and easing restrictions on trade. It was not clear to me what stake environmentalists had in this issue.

Because I had few preconceptions, I was appointed during the Bush administration to a trade and environment working group on the General Agreement on Tariffs and Trade (GATT), to advise EPA on this issue. I found myself surrounded by specialists, most of whom were completely committed to the NAFTA proposal, while I wanted to research the arguments on both sides and weigh them.

So I worked alone to gather a lot of international literature on environmental arguments about trade agreements. Using scissors and paste,

I arranged the arguments by categories and then by logical progression in order to try to make sense of what was a confusing issue. By the time I was done, I was convinced that we did have reason to be concerned. The EPA staff liked my "cut and paste" document so much that they published it. It gave them the basis for trying to slow down the first Bush administration's march toward a NAFTA agreement.

In testimony I subsequently delivered to the Senate Foreign Relations Committee, I outlined the concerns that had emerged from my study.[1] "Environmentalists have begun to notice that environmental protection standards and programs are beginning to be challenged as non-tariff trade barriers," I said. And proposals "we are beginning to advance . . . are being rejected because it is asserted that they violate free-trade rules." I mentioned that we were looking at legislation to regulate trade in imported wood from countries that were decimating their tropical forests. Since the United States already regulated trade in endangered species of plants and animals, it was but a logical step to regulate trade in products stemming from endangered habitats. I was also worried about efforts to phase out subsidies to producers in order to comply with proposed NAFTA regulations. Conservationists had just been involved in efforts to deny agricultural subsidies to farmers who refused to stop tilling fragile lands and draining wetlands (the "sodbuster" and "swampbuster" laws). We were talking about making these subsidies conditional on additional conservation practices—that is, engaging in "cross compliance." Ending all subsidies would end these programs too.

I worried too that a growing number of our already established environmental protection programs might be vulnerable to challenge as "non-tariff trade barriers" under NAFTA because they barred imports obtained in violation of U.S. environmental standards. Such interpretations would provide the basis for punitive action against us. Mexico, for example, was already challenging our standards to protect dolphins from being snared in tuna-fishing activity. "Will Mexico challenge our standards to minimize pesticide residues on vegetables as a 'disguised trade barrier'?" I asked. Under a NAFTA agreement, I wondered, "will trucks from Mexico have to meet our air pollution standards for tailpipes," or would this requirement be waived for them?[2]

I summed up my concerns in this way:

> The negotiators [of a new trade agreement] could agree to a harmonization process [for the environmental laws of both countries] which could weaken

our domestic environmental standards; they could expose our environmental programs to challenge as being non-tariff trade barriers; they could disallow federal support programs for public benefits produced by farmers and others; and they could eliminate justifiable restrictions on foreign ownership [as with respect to concessionaires in national parks].

We were concerned about potential increases in the level of gross environmental injury on the continent. With this agreement, I foresaw that Mexico might serve as a magnet in attracting industry that would no longer have to comply with the higher cleanup standards of the United States. After all, pollution was already crossing the Mexican border from the *maquiladora* factories producing for the U.S. market.

Independent authorities had already said this border region of Mexico had become an ecological disaster area. Border rivers were choked with raw sewage; 50 percent of all border inhabitants lacked access to sewage systems. Groundwater in these communities was badly contaminated with heavy metals, aquifers were being depleted, and the people living there had poor health. Four-fifths of the manufacturing plants on the Mexican side of the border were not then meeting Mexican laws governing handling of hazardous wastes, and Mexico's environmental agency was starved for funding.

Nor were our fears about "harmonization" hypothetical. In the aftermath of a similar pact that had recently been concluded with Canada, I pointed out, that country had been forced to weaken its own environmental laws regulating pesticides and other products when they were stronger than those of the United States. In turn, Canada was suing the United States to weaken our laws that called for phasing out asbestos.

NAFTA was not a treaty per se. Therefore, it did not need to be ratified by the Senate. It was an executive agreement. But Congress would need to pass legislation to implement it, and the administration was worried that Congress would try to revise the agreement retroactively. Because Mexico shared this concern, the Bush administration sought so-called fast-track legislation. It would call for congressional approval or rejection by simple majorities, allowing no amendments; interested parties would have little time to study the final document. Congress would be committed if it agreed to this process. Thus the political struggle over NAFTA really focused on the effort to pass fast-track legislation.

I persuaded the Sierra Club to oppose such legislation. This matter was too complex and of too much public interest to be handled in this shorthand way. Many trade agreements had been negotiated without fast-track legislation. We made it clear that our opposition could be withdrawn if our concerns were met. We hoped that we could tip the issue our way by bringing environmentalists into the equation.

I was part of a delegation that met in April 1991 with Carla Hills, the U.S. trade representative at the time. We explained our concerns to her; she listened politely. We asked that U.S. environmental laws not be impaired, through either harmonization or challenges; that an environmental protocol be negotiated that would be an integral part of the agreement; and that there be an implementation hammer: if environmental conditions along the border deteriorated, a new tariff would be imposed on imports—to build an earmarked fund to address the impacts.

By this time, a number of other environmental groups had become interested. On this issue, we felt the closest kinship with the Humane Society of the United States, which was concerned with the impact of NAFTA on laws and treaties to protect endangered species.[3] We also found ourselves viewing technical questions in a similar manner to the Natural Resources Defense Council (NRDC), but we began to differ over questions of tactics. And we began to differ more substantially with the National Wildlife Federation over how to cure the problems, an issue on which they entered into separate negotiations with the Office of the Trade Representative.

I did most of our lobbying on NAFTA. When I began, I approached Senator Dennis DeConcini for help. He was a Democrat from a border state, Arizona, where we had active members. I was welcomed by John Audley, an aide of his who seemed to share many of my concerns and was eager to pursue them. In a memo that I wrote to him and his boss, I explained our position and urged some fresh ideas. Citizens in both countries, for example, could be empowered to file legal actions to enforce environmental laws in the courts of the country in which a firm is domiciled; environmental improvement districts could be set up to span the border, with a special fund established to assist in this cleanup.

In due course, Audley found that DeConcini's office was not as good a fit for him as he thought the Sierra Club might be, and we hired him to lobby for us as the battle continued. He was an ideal choice. He both knew the Hill and the issue and was a Club member.

I also found it rewarding to be working closely with the labor movement. The AFL-CIO opposed NAFTA because of fear that it would accelerate the process of deindustrializing America. In the corporate search for cheap labor, America would lose even more good-paying jobs through NAFTA. Traditional labor laws, such as those barring import of goods produced with child labor, were also at risk. Labor was eager to find allies in this anti-NAFTA effort and began to add environmental concerns to its litany of problems posed by the proposed trade agreement. Labor gradually brought a large block of Democrats to its side, and we brought some more.

Oddly enough, there was a bloc of nationalistic Republicans who were also opposed to NAFTA, lending a strange political dynamic to the campaign. They saw a threat (which I think is real) to U.S. sovereignty in these agreements. Our laws are being compromised to suit foreign powers, with the public hardly aware that this is happening. Too many think trade agreements of this sort are just about lowering tariffs, but they also involve an effort to integrate many of the laws of the affected countries. Already we had seen the U.S. trade office quietly pressuring various federal agencies to bring proposals to Congress to revise or weaken U.S. laws in order to comply with trade agreements.

Thus we were playing "both ends against the middle," mobilizing a bloc of liberal/labor Democrats together with a bloc of conservative Republicans to oppose NAFTA. We even had joint meetings on the Hill.

The Bush administration began to be worried about the furor that we were stirring up over NAFTA and promised to try to protect federal environmental laws and regulations from being weakened. Eventually, it added a "no diminution" clause to the agreement, to suggest that it would not require any reduction in the stringency of environmental laws. This was progress, but we were also concerned about what would actually happen. Mexico had weak laws on pollution and did little to enforce those it did have. We sought binational guarantees to enforce "the strictest environmental standards [of either country] and a joint commitment of resources." The Bush administration merely promised to study environmental problems along the border and to undertake parallel discussions to resolve concerns.

In our letters to members of Congress that spring, we also took up another problem of concern that would grow in importance in subsequent years. A provision in these agreements provided grounds for challenging environmental regulations: they had to be justified "scientifically." The business community wanted the evidence to be nearly incontrovertible. This is what they meant when they called for "sound science."

That demand attacked the very nature of the practice of public health, which rarely dealt in such black-and-white certainties. Public health warnings often depended on correlations, not proof, and biological research was plagued by apparent contradictions. Officials had to make decisions based on the balance of evidence and set prudent margins of safety. "Sound science" was a catchphrase for those who opposed what EPA did. This provision in trade agreements thus amounted to an egregious "end run" around U.S. pollution laws and gave business a new weapon to use to attack U.S. environmental laws. Few in the trade field understood any of this, unfortunately.

We had trouble getting through to many in Congress who were wavering. They perceived NAFTA as a business issue and, to a lesser extent, a labor issue—so when we expressed our environmental concerns, they thought we were intruding into an issue that belonged to others. If NAFTA's disguised, collateral attacks on the environment had been frontal ones, they might have paid more attention.

We came close. We never had a chance in the Senate, but had we been able to shift just fourteen more votes in the House, NAFTA would have failed. We had been gaining support among the public, but time ran out on our efforts to educate more people. The Bush administration pushed for an early vote before it lost any more support, and the NAFTA measure passed.

To respond to all of our criticisms of NAFTA, in the fall of 1991 the Bush administration quickly cobbled together a document that purported to review environmental problems along the border. For us, it simply whetted our appetite for a real environmental impact statement.

John Audley and I reviewed the Bush document in detail. The NAFTA crowd clearly wanted to intrude into the pollution control process of each nation. They planned to establish "disciplines on the standard-setting process in each country." The document offered no real answer to the concerns over industrial flight to Mexico; it merely hoped that Mexico would discourage such flight by raising its standards over time (ignoring the fact that Mexico had been cutting its funding for pollution control). The authors claimed that new factories in Mexico no longer would hug the border to be close to U.S. markets but would be placed in the interior instead; they could offer no convincing reasons to explain why this would happen, however, since the factories were exporting to the American market. The authors also could only hope that economic growth would provide the wealth to cope with new environmental distress. They never faced the reality that this growth would also generate more pollution.

Mexico also realized that the U.S. public needed to be reassured. Their officials made a number of raids on the worst-polluting factories in Mexico and shut them down—only to allow them to reopen later. At the same time, the Mexican president cautioned that "environmental concerns cannot stand in the way of economic progress."

NAFTA was in so much trouble that the Bush administration decided to put off signing or implementing it until after the 1992 presidential election. The agreement became an issue in the presidential campaign itself, as independent candidate Ross Perot complained about the "giant sucking sound" of jobs being siphoned off south of the border. I was asked to do various radio call-in shows and was even invited onto the Larry King radio show to elaborate on the issue. Most of the phone calls I got on the show were friendly; it seemed that the public was beginning to understand what was at stake.

During the campaign, Democratic presidential candidate Bill Clinton addressed the problems of NAFTA in detail in an October 1992 speech in Baltimore. He called for procedural safeguards in NAFTA that would protect the environment and pledged to devote substantial resources to the job of cleaning up the border. He promised to include enforcement powers, including citizen lawsuit provisions, and more democratic processes. While his pledges did not go as far as we wanted, they did please us. We worked hard for his election, and we were hopeful when he won.

But the Bush administration changed its mind about putting off further work on NAFTA when it saw that it would not return to office. As a lame-duck administration, it signed the agreement it had negotiated, leaving implementation of legislation to its successors.

The Clinton administration promised not to send legislation to Congress to implement NAFTA until it had decided what to do about the problems it had pledged to address. As incoming vice president, former senator Al Gore had been given the job of coordinating environmental policy for President Clinton. I wrote him a memo that spelled out exactly what was wrong about NAFTA and needed to be changed.[4]

Because our objections now were rooted in the details of the legal language of the agreement, they were often not easy to follow. But I summed them up in these terms: "It should not be too much to call for a trade agreement that leaves the United States free to pursue strong environmental laws and treaties; that removes incentives for industrial flight; that delivers a better environment along the border rather than a worse one; and that assures open, democratic processes in decision making."

I spelled out the various problems in the text. Wherever U.S. wildlife laws failed to confine themselves to the characteristics of a product, they would be at odds with NAFTA's requirements. An example involved U.S. laws to protect sea turtles by banning poorly designed nets, which could snare them when fishers tried to catch shrimp; most of the other parties to NAFTA were using such nets. Other laws protecting vulnerable species would also be affected, and the United States would find it difficult to enter into future international agreements designed to protect such species.

Similarly, our country's efforts to protect our food against pesticide residues were open to attack for not being based on "risk assessment and science." Many of our domestic regulations were based instead on notions of risk avoidance or shifting the burden of risk away from consumers.

In NAFTA, only three of the hundreds of environmental conventions to which the United States is a party were finally acknowledged and not adversely affected. Through NAFTA, an executive agreement was being used—in a kind of end run—to supplant existing legislation in the United States, just as we had feared. There were other tricky pieces of language designed to give opponents in the business community tools with which to attack U.S. environmental laws: the least onerous measures had to be used, means had to be used that minimized effects on the agreement, and the environmental laws of all three countries had to be uniform—regardless of circumstances.

Other provisions also pushed the idea that the environmental laws of the three countries would have to become "equivalent." A committee on standards would be set up to advance that agenda. The United States would be discouraged from adopting laws that were stricter than international norms, except in cases where such norms were completely ineffective. Businesses would be able to bring lawsuits in which they might claim, for instance, that they lost a business opportunity because environmental standards in this country were too high. Disputes would be resolved by panels that met in closed sessions, thus preventing environmentalists from intervening or following the proceedings. I thought a protocol might be negotiated to fix many of these problems, and I later furnished Gore with specific language to do that.

But of course, not all of the problems lay in the language of the text. Because the very existence of the agreement would create incentives for U.S. firms to move their factories to Mexico, for example, that fact alone would trigger pressures to weaken U.S. environmental laws to forestall job flight. And we needed safeguards to prevent a bad situation from getting worse along the border. Funding was needed for cleanup; profits from new factories, I argued, should be plowed back into cleanup through a tax. More than pious promises and "talk shops" were needed to provide enforcement, and I suggested a way this could be done.

I am sure that Al Gore heard a similar message from Ralph Nader and his Public Citizen staff. The coalition of forces opposing NAFTA had now attracted a number of lawyers to our side who specialized in these matters.[5] Had Gore had his experts work with them, the problems with NAFTA could have been resolved. But Gore didn't want to come to grips with these questions. They were left to Mickey Kantor, who had become the U.S. trade representative. He begged for time to address them, but he was soon captured by the trade establishment and other "true believers" in such agreements. He was worried that Congress was turning against NAFTA.

I appeared with Nader on many platforms and knew how strongly he felt about NAFTA. Had he been treated better and taken seriously, I believe Al Gore would have become president. Nader was infuriated by Gore's unwillingness to stick by what Clinton had promised. I am sure that these feelings were a key reason why he decided to run against Gore in the 2000 race, siphoning off crucial votes, and also why he kept running thereafter.

No one in the administration was willing to get serious with us. Sandy Gaines, whom I had known when he ran the Toxic Law Project at the University of Houston Law School, had joined the trade office to look after environmental interests, but he did not fight those to whom he was responsible. Even if he had wanted to, he was too low in the hierarchy to carry the day.

We were hardly treated like a core constituency of the Democratic Party. The Clinton administration acted as if it had to deliver this agreement for the business community to assure prosperity (which was doubtful). In the end, we were given a series of only cosmetic fixes, since the administration did not want to reopen discussions about the agreement itself.

The principal fix was a so-called environmental side agreement, which established the North American Commission for Environmental

Cooperation. It would study environmental problems in North America and would receive complaints about faltering performance. But it would not be able to compel change, unlike the protocol we wanted.

Jay Hair, then the CEO of the National Wildlife Federation, later told me that he had broken ranks with other environmental groups to get the commission established. He was proud of it and regarded it as his achievement. Because we had pursued conflicting tactics, Hair and I had a testy exchange, and feelings between us were strained for a number of years. Eventually, he wrote me a note apologizing for his harsh words.

NAFTA's opponents found a way to strike back. In the summer of 1993, Public Citizen, joined by the Sierra Club and others, filed a lawsuit to challenge the process by which the Bush administration had brought NAFTA to Congress. No legislative environmental impact statement (EIS) had been prepared, as NEPA required. A federal judge then issued an injunction against proceeding with any efforts to implement NAFTA until one had been prepared. This caused great consternation, and we were perceived as trying to kill NAFTA entirely.

I remember speaking at a press conference immediately afterward, facing the largest swarm of microphones I had ever confronted. Later, friends abroad told me they had heard my voice in places as far away as India and Ireland. I had rashly prophesied that "trade agreements can never again be negotiated without conscious consideration of the environment."

The *Wall Street Journal*, which was in the camp that considered NAFTA a threat to U.S. sovereignty, ran an op-ed piece by me, in which I said:

> The Clinton administration is beginning to act in a proprietary way about the NAFTA that it has inherited. It is finding reasons not to tackle most of these problems. It is hard-lining the question of doing an environmental impact statement, which could give it breathing room to get a firm grip on the best way to resolve these problems. It has fecklessly put itself on a schedule for wrapping up negotiations, which throws away bargaining leverage. It is acting as if its future is tied to getting this agreement through with only minimal change.[6]

In a few months, however, an appeals court overturned the ruling by the lower federal court judge, finding that he had tried to interfere impermissibly with the president's foreign policy powers. We could then only persevere with related questions as they came up in Congress.

In the fall of 1993, the critics of NAFTA faced a vote on implementing legislation. Because the Clinton administration had now staked its prestige on getting the legislation through unchanged, together with the side agreements it had negotiated, it put this package under the fast-track process used by the Bush administration, allowing only an up or down vote.

The environmental community was split on whether to oppose the package. While we all agreed that it had negative aspects, some saw positive ones as well, and various organizations weighed them differently. In the Sierra Club's eyes, the shortcomings still outweighed the gains. Others, however, wanted to salvage the gains; they felt that the package would set valuable precedents that they did not want to see defeated.

This split had begun the previous spring after our joint meeting with Mickey Kantor, the new U.S. trade representative. We could not agree on a follow-up letter to him. The Sierra Club thought that the letter NRDC had drafted asked for too little. Now we were facing what we were going to get, not what we might ask for. Kantor's office managed to convince six mainstream groups, including the National Audubon Society and the National Wildlife Federation, that the gains were more important. Our relations with the National Wildlife Federation became distinctly frosty.

We had some three hundred groups around the country in our faction, however. Friends of the Earth and Greenpeace joined the Sierra Club in opposing the NAFTA package, as did the Humane Society of the United States and, of course, Public Citizen and Nader's trade network. All together, the groups opposing NAFTA had more than twice as many members as those supporting it.

People on the Hill still found it hard to believe that NAFTA would in any way jeopardize U.S. laws governing trade in wildlife. I prepared a technical memo citing the exact portions of the agreement that posed problems, for which I drew heavily on the work of Steve Charnovitz, a legal scholar who was an expert on trade. Few, however, wanted to get into these details.

The Clinton administration wanted to rush a vote shortly after it released the results of its efforts to negotiate side agreements. It had not even finished negotiating a program to clean up the border, and it was asking for only one-third of the funding that we felt was needed for that work. In a statement to the press, I said the Clinton trade negotiators had neglected most of the agenda for curing NAFTA's environmental deficiencies. And any pledge not to weaken environmental standards could hardly be enforced. "The process [of enforcement] is so tortuous that it is unlikely ever to be applied," I said. "Two-thirds of the parties have to start it, evidence can be withheld, and sanctions can be dodged whenever [one of the countries] wants to claim it had different priorities."

Moreover, the Clinton negotiators did nothing to cure the unfairness of excluding environmental groups entirely from the dispute resolution process set up under NAFTA. They attempted to offset that by later putting us on various panels clustering around the environmental side agreement, which was a powerless "playpen" they created for us. The dispute resolution process depended entirely on the goodwill of the parties and could not override the NAFTA agreement itself. Subsequently, people from the environmental groups that had supported the Clinton folks were put on the more prestigious panels set up under the environmental side agreement, while I found myself appointed to another EPA advisory committee on trade. Though I enjoyed my time on it, it put me on the sidelines.

On October 28, shortly before the vote on legislation to implement NAFTA, the environmental opponents staged a press event in a House of Representatives meeting room. We brought in people from all three affected countries to speak in opposition. Sixty groups in Mexico were now opposing it, and eighty in Canada. When it came to my turn, I explained that "we are not at odds with each other as peoples. We are at odds with political leaders who are forcing flawed policies upon us through NAFTA. . . . We are at odds with those who want to sweep away social concerns in the single-minded pursuit of trade dogmas. We are not willing to have all social, environmental, and cultural values subordinated to economics. We are not willing to accept window-dressing formulas that ignore our substantive concerns."

In the end, we lost in the House on the legislation to implement NAFTA by a vote of 234–200. This vote was not all that different from the vote on fast-track. The Clinton administration considered this a pivotal vote and had pulled out all the stops, encouraging members of Congress to support the agreement by promising rewards on other matters. It was something of a Pyrrhic victory for the administration, however. In the years that followed, most House Democrats would vote against further fast-track arrangements, and in future years Congress as a whole began to turn down fast-tracking requests.

From GATT to WTO

As the NAFTA battle matured, I began to realize that many of our problems with the agreement could be traced back to the General Agreement on Tariffs and Trade (GATT), which had been adopted in 1946. Much of the language in NAFTA that we found most objectionable was taken from GATT. An agreement among nations to reduce tariffs and unfair trade practices, GATT was heralded at the time as a progressive step to assure greater prosperity. Most of the thinking in it about unfair trade practices came from economists and the international business community, though Democrats and their administrations backed it solidly. But few who liked its aims ever looked at its details.

Negotiations had occurred to update GATT and restyle it as the World Trade Agreement/Organization (WTO), and Congress needed to concur. I thought this would be the next big battle over trade. For this struggle John Audley, who had returned to graduate school, was replaced on our staff by Dan Seligman.

In a move that paralleled the NAFTA struggle, Senator Max Baucus, Democrat of Montana, who was influential on trade matters, had called in 1991 for an Environmental Code of Conduct for GATT and had urged a new round of negotiations to "green it up." GATT had responded to this pressure by reviving its Environment Working Group, with an intent to block any such effort.

The G-77 bloc, representing the poorer countries, now dominated GATT. It thought the environmentalists were trying to restrict the G-77's exploitation of their own natural resources and were trying to impose obligations on them that they could not afford. In fact, we were trying to avoid being forced to reduce our own environmental standards. As globalization spread, this different way of viewing the issue came to a head.

The effort to turn GATT into WTO came out of the Uruguay Round of trade negotiations, which concluded in 1993. In addition to reducing tariffs, this round addressed many new issues, including a few of our environmental concerns. In response to efforts made by the Clinton administration's trade negotiators, the GATT secretariat at least agreed to provide summaries to the public of the decisions made by its dispute resolution panels (my wife, once in Geneva on whale business, was once denied even that). The question of whether member countries would be required to bring their various laws into alignment, even if alignment might mean they would be less effective, was also obscured. (We called this downward harmonization.)

Language was also added to slightly relax the yardsticks by which the legislation of member countries would be judged, thus giving U.S. environmental laws a greater chance of surviving. While regulations still had to be supported by "sufficient scientific evidence," an exception was added to dispense with that requirement if no evidence was available. Risk assessment no longer had to cover economic factors, as conservatives had wanted, but just deal with physical probabilities of injury. The necessity test—whether a given measure, such as an environmental law, was the only way to provide the public benefit—was now extended to include protection of plant and animal life as well as human health.

In April 1994, Mickey Kantor met with a number of environmental groups to put a good face on these gains. But despite them, WTO now struck us as worse than NAFTA. It did not contain the concessions obtained in NAFTA. Instead, the revisions we had obtained showed that the problems we were complaining about were real, not fanciful.

The parties to the agreement also refused to begin any new round of "green" negotiation, despite the many underlying problems that remained.[7] WTO today remains at odds with all the provisions of our domestic wildlife and environmental laws that deal with how wildlife-related products are made. WTO allows only regulation based on the characteristics of an end product, whereas many American laws go beyond that: many of our laws governing trade in wildlife look at whether the species is endangered. Many of our environmental laws consider other factors, such as fuel economy standards, costs over a product's life cycle (which are often lower with green products), recycling and amount of packaging, whether products are made with problematic chemicals such as CFCs and chlorine, and whether animals are humanely slaughtered.

Moreover, WTO is at odds with the many environmental conventions that try to restrict trade for environmental reasons, such as the Montreal Protocol, which restricts trade in substances that degrade the ozone layer. WTO does not include the exceptions for the three specific environmental conventions contained in NAFTA.

WTO still imposes tests (termed disciplines) for judging U.S. laws dealing with items that enter the flow of trade. Though the latest round liberalized these disciplines slightly, they still do not allow the United States to base its environmental regulations simply on the amount of risk it will accept, nor to reflect political feasibility. The tests hobble the search for the most effective environmental remedies. WTO also makes assumptions about the field of environmental regulation that are at odds with the practice of public health (e.g., by demanding unambiguous evidence).

And WTO still asks nations to harmonize their laws with one another. It pushes the United States into an undertaking that can only go poorly for it. In such a large pool of nations, just as with the Environmental Working Group of GATT, a less enlightened approach is likely to prevail, perhaps even the lowest common denominator. WTO pushes the developed countries into a political arena where they are outnumbered. The difficulties the United States encountered in trying to harmonize its laws with Mexico will be multiplied many times over in such a forum. We should recognize that countries have different outlooks at various stages of economic development. The developed countries will be outvoted in this arena by the nations that are not yet ready to seek high environmental standards. While downward harmonization is not inevitable, it is likely.

Moreover, the United States and other developed countries face an erosion of their sovereignty. While it is argued that, technically, countries violating WTO will only face penalties from dispute resolution panels (that is, greater levies on goods they import), in reality they will be pressured to conform to WTO. Our executive branch will work to change U.S. laws so that they are consistent with WTO. Our nation will not want to be in violation of WTO on many counts. It is also required to take "reasonable measures" to ensure that state governments bring their laws into conformance.

"All of this adds up to the United States being a party to an arrangement that will put pressure on us to weaken our environmental laws for the sake of reduced tariffs," I wrote at the time. "This is not a debate about free trade. It is about the struggle to get a fair-minded trade agreement that respects the rightful sphere of environmental regulation and does not willfully intrude upon its proper domain."

Quite fortunately, this time the environmental movement did not split. A broad array of environmental groups were unified in opposing WTO. We certainly did not want to repeat the painful split over NAFTA. Organized labor was on our side, and the business community was far from unified. On the surface, WTO then looked like a more winnable issue, and many of us were hopeful.

The Clinton administration wanted to pass the legislation to implement WTO quickly, before the public became even more aroused. But because of the opposition already evident, Congress delayed acting until after the fall 1994 congressional elections. By then, it turned out, people were already exhausted by the issue. Members of Congress and their staffs wished the issue would go away, and the opponents were burned out. I was bitterly disappointed that the Sierra Club too was no longer equipped to put many resources into this battle.

Thus a lame-duck Democratic Congress came back after the elections and passed the implementing legislation by handy margins. It was never a contest in the Senate, and our support in the House had melted away; many felt the problems had been resolved by Clinton's trade negotiators.

Moreover, Congress thought it could stonewall pressures to weaken U.S. laws. For instance, by heavy margins it voted to block EPA from weakening a regulation on reformulated gasoline that then was under challenge by WTO. It also denied the administration new trade negotiating authority. Members thought they could have it both ways.

Not only did we lose on this issue, but the Democrats lost too in the fall elections, so they would not run succeeding Congresses. But we would lose by less in future legislative battles. In a fast-track contest over the Free Trade for the Americas agreement in 2001, for instance, we lost by only one vote in a Republican-controlled House of Representatives.

Many so-called free-trade Democrats began coming our way. Columnist David Broder explained this new support: "Trade agreements now go far beyond tariff reductions and involve tradeoffs on intellectual property rights, environmental standards, basic labor laws and other issues of such importance to [members'] constituents that they are reluctant to delegate sweeping authority to any administration to negotiate them away."

These battles awakened a larger constituency to the fact that those promoting trade agreements had overreached themselves. In trying to reduce tariffs, they had sacrificed too much that the world also cared about—not only environmental protection but the concerns of labor, and the distinctiveness of countries and cultures as reflected in trade. Thereafter, protests began to break out around the world whenever trade negotiators met to draw up new pacts. Protesters broke up negotiations in Seattle and in Cancún, Mexico. Efforts to negotiate a multilateral agreement on investment (MAI) collapsed because the opposition was so intense. Trade negotiators began to look for obscure places to meet that protesters wouldn't be able to get to.

When trade ministers from 140 countries met in Qatar in 2001, they were forced to concede that they needed to take environmental concerns into account as globalization proceeded, and they pledged to negotiate a relationship between WTO rules and various international environmental treaties (called multilateral environmental agreements, or MEAs). It is a start.

Were any of the NAFTA concerns we raised borne out in the years that followed? In the decade since the battle began over these trade agreements, pollution along the U.S.-Mexican border has not diminished; it has grown worse. Environmentally related disease rates at the border are two to three times the average rates in the United States. Industry has not moved into Mexico's interior, as the first Bush administration assured us it would. Twice as many people now work at the border, in nearly three times more factories. Cleanup efforts have lagged far behind the rising levels of pollution. More than a half million U.S. jobs have been officially certified as NAFTA casualties, and an estimated 3 million more have been lost as a result of WTO. Those who have found replacement employment usually get much less pay in service jobs. The U.S. trade surplus with Mexico has turned into a huge deficit. And Mexico itself is no longer gaining an advantage. Factories that once flocked there have now fled to countries in Asia, where wage rates are even lower. More than a million Mexican farmworkers have lost their livelihood as imports from U.S. agribusiness have displaced their crops in Mexican markets.

Just as we predicted, corporate polluters have brought claims under these trade agreements to force weakening of cleanup laws. If the cleanup laws remain in force, then polluters will demand to be compensated under a claim that their property has been "taken," or expropriated, by government through its environmental regulations—arguing that the value of their property has been diminished. For example, a Canadian company, Methanex, which supplies methanol for an injurious gasoline additive called MTBE, won $1 billion from the U.S. government after California phased out MTBE, which had shown up in water supplies there. The Mexican government lost a case brought by Metalclad after the government tried to close a toxic waste dump. When Canada tried to require less alluring packaging for cigarettes, former U.S. trade experts, now representing cigarette companies, threatened legal action and forced it to back down. And more cases of this type keep being brought.

These cases are all settled by specialized trade courts under NAFTA's chapter 11, which promises recourse from regulations that arguably diminish the value of an investor's assets. One trade expert has estimated that 80 percent of American environmental regulations are vulnerable to such challenges under WTO. EPA was forced to back down over its efforts to tighten regulations to improve air quality with regard to gasoline additives after their manufacturers challenged the agency's actions. A WTO trade panel ruled against the European Union's efforts to ban the use of artificial hormones to grow beef.

It is now clear to me that the events in which I participated were just the beginning of a long-term struggle over these ill-advised pacts. More and more, unfortunately, will learn their costs as the story unfolds year by year.

19 *Continuing International Work*

One of the reasons I moved my operations to Washington, D.C., was to make it easier to participate in and help shape the Sierra Club's international program. The Club's board of directors wanted me to lend my experience to that program, which in the mid-1980s was launched in a new direction and moved to Washington. Those who had run the old program in New York suspected that I wanted to set myself up as the new director of that program, but I did not. I did want it to succeed in its new form, though, and wanted to help.

Larry Williams was made the director of that program. A skillful lobbyist, he had been working for the club to procure more funding for the federal clean water program. During the Carter administration he had worked for CEQ, and prior to that he had founded and run the Oregon Environmental Council. After all these years, it was a surprise to be working with him again: we had known each other in Oregon in the early 1960s and had involved ourselves in some of the same groups. We enjoyed each other's company and often lunched together. While he was a few years younger than me, we were of the same generation and came out of the same milieu in Oregon. We tended to react to office politics, and people, in the same way, and we tended to have similar outlooks on behavior and politics.

We also valued each other's talents. He was innovative, and because of his sunny personality, he was good at outreach. Through the grants he gained from foundations, he soon had a number of people working for him. I, however, had traveled abroad more widely and had a notion of how things worked internationally. I had studied international law in college and understood the theory behind many of the international institutions that we dealt with. So he tended to look to me for theory and grand strategy. I often dealt with things at the conceptual level, while he grappled with them at the practical level. He handled our campaign to reform the World Bank and funding institutions of a similar nature, for instance, while often consulting me about situations he faced. We made a good team.

Aside from my advising Larry, I also tackled projects of my own: publishing a newsletter about global threats to nature, together with organizing a worldwide network of like-minded groups; helping environmental groups in various countries cope with environmental problems caused by U.S. firms or our government; maintaining established relations with environmental groups in the Soviet Union; and immersing myself in fresh projects in the Arctic.

An issue that arose frequently in international work was that of the relationship between economic development and conservation. A series of talks I had heard at the Fourth World Wilderness Congress prompted me to try to clarify my own thinking on the subject, which I shared with the Club's board of directors. After hearing bankers and U.S. Treasury Department officials argue that "development is a necessary precondition of conservation—you can't have conservation progress in the Third World without more development," I heard others warn us to "beware of bankers bearing gifts." Canada's environment minister spoke of "altruistic disasters" in development abroad that his country had funded. I recommended that we be wary of the idea of development as it was being practiced by so many international development agencies. Pasting new labels on an old product won't wash, I cautioned: "No one can state categorically that development and environmental protection per se are compatible or incompatible. Their compatibility can be judged only in specific contexts.

"But the one thing we know," I continued, "is that those who are in charge of producing development have yet to demonstrate that they can practice it sustainably." Despite claims to the contrary, much of development was not designed to alleviate the misery of the poor, and we should not be intimidated into signing on to support every program whose sponsor claimed it would cure poverty. "Sustainability is still more a slogan . . . than a proven body of theory and practice ready to be applied," I said. I had heard Gro Harlem Brundtland, chair of the United Nations World

Commission on Environment and Development, tell our Congress about her commission's report on sustainable development, and I was not persuaded. Later I set forth my view of its shortcomings in an article arguing that meeting the needs of the present without compromising the needs of the future was too anthropocentric and assumed too many things, such as never-ending foresight about future needs.[1] In dealing with projects on the global level, in my view we were likely to make fewer mistakes by helping local environmentalists protect natural values than we would by taking the word of someone with a vested interest in development.

Environmentalism Abroad

By the 1980s environmentalism had become a worldwide movement.[2] "We are seeing the flowering of a great social movement on a global scale," I declared in a 1988 speech to a conference of law students held in my hometown of Eugene, Oregon. I continued:

> This movement's emergence both reflects public opinion, and in turn helps mobilize it and deepen its concerns. This movement provides the key to moving governments and to developing their political will to act.
>
> As a social movement, environmentalism is a driving wedge for greater democratization of life. Our movement stands for empowering citizens to share control over the conditions that shape their environment. It provides a channel of access for citizens . . . to participate in the procedures of government—to play a part (often for the first time) in shaping public policy. It is forcing governments to open themselves up.

I gave examples of this from around the globe, including Chile, Czechoslovakia, and the Soviet Union.

I reminded my audience that the naysayers at the 1972 U.N. Stockholm conference and other places had asserted that this would never happen: "They said that environmentalism is a product of Northern cultures . . . that there is no interest in nature and the environment in the South." They said that only rich countries would show this interest, and it could really function only in democracies. And they claimed that it would take a very long time before this movement would spread around the world. But that is not what happened.

"A vast environmental movement now exists in developing countries like Brazil and India," I went on. There were then more than three hundred environmental groups in Brazil, while it took two directories to list all the groups in India. I read a list of environmental organizations in African countries and in South America too. Groups were flourishing even though there was no tradition of volunteerism in many of their countries, they lacked the tax and postal subsidies that U.S. nonprofits enjoy, they had no way to recruit members through direct mail, and they had little money and few staff. Traditional political parties could not make much sense of them. Often they faced authoritarian regimes, even oppressive ones, and some activists even languished in jail. Despite such adversity, many still flourished. What they needed was not just resources but encouragement, recognition, and acknowledgment that their work was legitimate. "By our visits, by our testimony, and by our letters," I concluded, "we can help cure their problem as 'prophets without honor' in their own countries."

I decided that I would focus on helping such groups—when they asked for our help. I thought we could be useful when American firms were involved whose overseas branches were injuring the environment in some way, such as by polluting too much or proposing a project in an inappropriate place. We could also be useful when a U.S. government agency was the offender. Then there would be a logical reason for such groups to ask for our help. And I decided to focus on cases where nature was endangered.

Over the next few years, I built up a network of about two hundred groups around the world that wanted to cooperate. The Sierra Club had coined the term "Earthcare" in connection with a global conference it had put on in New York City in the prior decade. I decided to put it back in use by calling this consortium the Earthcare Network.

To focus the network, I developed a newsletter that I sent to the groups several times a year. Called *Earthcare Appeals*, it carried stories about threats to national parks, nature reserves, and wild country across the globe. The cooperating groups sent me the stories. The newsletter called for letters from around the world to be sent to the officials who were responsible. Our interns helped me write the stories and put out the newsletter. It seemed to fill a niche and generated growing interest.

Issues Abroad

As an outgrowth of these efforts, I got involved with a series of issues abroad. In the late 1980s, at the outset of this phase of my work, I tried to assist the Wild Bird Society of Japan, which was concerned about the Japanese government's efforts to build a jet-landing strip for the U.S. Navy on Miyaka-jima, a southern island of Japan. This island was in a national park and harbored the greatest variety of bird life in Japan. I filed protests with the U.S. Navy, arguing that it should not be a party to an undertaking that compromised the integrity of a national park and potentially violated treaty obligations to protect migratory species and endangered species.

But we kept receiving the same frustrating response. Under post-war agreements, our Defense Department asserted that it was empowered only to ask for the facilities it needed; it did not pick the sites in question. The Japanese government, in turn, argued that it had little leeway; it had to build the facilities the U.S. government wanted. Each side was locked into denial and blame of each other, and the environment itself fell into a kind of no-man's-land. No change was made in the plans.

This question of who was responsible arose most forcefully in another case in which I became deeply involved. This concerned the future of forests on the Ikego Hills, around the town of Zushi near Yokohama. This area harbored the largest amount of healthy natural habitat in the Tokyo metropolitan area and provided some of the best bird habitat on Honshu. It was a former ammunition dump that had been closed to the public for more than fifty years. The area had grown back nicely, with the ammunition stored in tunnels. Signs on the fences around the site claimed that it was the property of the U.S. Navy.

Conservation-minded local residents wanted it preserved, but the Japanese government chose it as the site for midrise apartments to house U.S. sailors attached to a nearby base. When these residents could not get their local government to support their protests against this development, they organized a campaign to recall the mayor and succeeded. When the city council balked as well, they campaigned door-to-door and succeeded in recalling enough members of the council to gain control of it. They then launched a long campaign to persuade the national government to relent.

I helped on the U.S. side by writing letters and trying to persuade the U.S. government to turn this site down. The Navy refused to budge, and the State Department stoutly defended the Navy. I tried to get a congressman from Hawaii, who was on the Armed Services Committee, to help. He was friendly, but nothing came of it. We looked into lawsuits; one was filed futilely in Japan.

I helped the mayor of Zushi prepare a full-page advertisement that ran in the *New York Times*. At various times, I guided a succession of mayors of Zushi around Washington D.C., when they came to lobby. At one point, in the fall of 1990, the group brought me to Japan to see the site and to speak to a local audience on the significance of the issues. I compared Zushi, Miyaka-jima, and one other case to various battles that we had fought in the United States, and proclaimed that it was a scandal of world proportions that they had not been resolved, that no recourse was available. My words were carried on television and in the Sunday newspapers in Tokyo.

I went to this trouble because I thought this contest was important. It was an exceptional case of a grassroots uprising, of housewives and others who would not take no for an answer. They went to the polls seven times and won. They collected more than a million signatures on petitions. They used all the means of procedural recourse that a democracy affords to try to change things. This was the most heavily publicized environmental issue in Japan, and it entailed the kind of grassroots environmentalism that we wanted to encourage. In a country that lacked much of a national environmental movement, I thought the protesters needed every bit of encouragement they could get.

We did make some headway. The issue became so controversial in the United States that control of the issue was taken away from the Defense Department and put into the hands of the White House and the State Department. But in the end, we lost.

It turned out that the matter was caught up in a larger issue. It had become a pawn in a tug-of-war between the United States and Japan over "burden sharing" on defense matters. It was felt that Japan had gained a trade advantage by spending too little on defense, and the U.S. government wanted to be tough on this issue to force Japan to assume more of the costs of its own defense. Behind the scenes, this issue had been chosen as the one to force Japan to "do something." It was tragic that such valuable habitat came to be held hostage in such a game.

Half way around the world, I helped a local group deal with an American business in the Ecuadorian Amazon—Conoco, an oil company then owned by DuPont. As that region was being opened to oil drilling in the early 1990s, a group there by the name of CORDAVI asked the Sierra Club for help in fending off Conoco's proposal to drill for oil on land that had been a part of Yasuni National Park. On the eve of granting the lease for drilling, without notice the national government revised the park boundaries to eliminate the area it proposed to lease. It could then claim it was not drilling in a national park. CORDAVI challenged the legality of this action. We agreed to approach Conoco to urge them not to drill in this area.

Other groups were involved too, both in Ecuador and in the United States, and they did not all have the same ideas. But in CORDAVI, made up mainly of environmental lawyers, we had a reputable partner in Ecuador and felt that the sanctity of national parks was at stake. The New Delhi principles of the parks commission of the IUCN (named for a meeting held there, which had promulgated rules against the exploitation of natural resources in national parks) would have decried oil development of this sort on parkland. We saw a role for ourselves in promoting due process for nature reserves and in encouraging other countries to abide by these principles.

After attending a meeting to learn the company's side of the story, we launched a letter-writing campaign to persuade DuPont to back out of this project. Their CEO, Ed Woolard, had made a speech promising that his company not only would practice sustainability but would give the public what it expected with regard to high standards of environmental protection. He had garnered a lot of publicity with this promise, and I pressed him to live up to it in this case.

Woolard came to my office to see whether we could work something out. I explained that we were not interested in mitigation. The Sierra Club was committed to the principle that extractive development must be kept out of national parks. Such places were sacrosanct. This was not a question of how much money they would spend or the care they would exercise; it was a matter of principle.

Woolard kept probing for how he could make a deal. He offered to put Club representatives on a committee to oversee a mitigation effort. Then he trumped that by offering to make me the committee's chairman. Finally, he actually offered to give me the power to close down the project if I found that Conoco was not living up to its promises. But I said no. It was the idea of drilling there that was wrong. We did not want to be regulators of something that should not take place at all.

That did it. DuPont pulled out, but unfortunately it sold its rights to a smaller company, which did go ahead. History will be the judge of whether we did the right thing. NRDC, which was also involved, took a different line, trying to negotiate a monetary settlement for the region's indigenous people. In return, it was attacked by CORDAVI for presuming to make such an arrangement. The entire struggle eventually ended up as the subject of a *New Yorker* article and a case study of the Harvard Business School.[3]

A few years later, odd circumstances turned my attention once again to this region of the Amazon in South America. Our fund-raising office was thinking of embarking on a cooperative arrangement with an adventure-travel firm known as Society Expeditions. Our members would be encouraged to go on the firms' trips and then would be asked to donate to the Sierra Club. To try out this idea, I was asked to give lectures on conservation issues embroiling the area and to serve as temporary staff on one of the cruises on the upper Amazon River.

While enroute in Lima, Peru, we discovered that the Shining Path (Sendero Luminoso) guerrillas had bombed the power station, throwing our hotel into darkness. The next morning the police bomb squad searched our bus before we headed for the airport, where we would fly to Iquitos to board our ship. That was disquieting enough. But then the staff leader pulled me aside to tell me that the regular airline crew (from Fawcett Airlines) had gone on strike, so air force pilots were replacing them. He asked me to help prevent panic among the passengers. I didn't fully grasp what was going on, but I said that I would try.

Once we were in flight, I started to plot our course on the detailed maps I had brought. To my dismay, I saw that we were not heading straight for Iquitos at all. We were going a bit farther to the south. Then I learned why he was worried. We were headed into the heart of the Huayaga Valley, where soldiers unloaded military cargo at an airport that was rimmed with sandbags and machine guns. This was the last government outpost that the rebels had not seized. Because of where I was sitting, I saw everything—but most passengers did not. We were in a war zone. Fortunately, we got out of there before conflict enveloped us.

I had little taste for further adventure after that tense experience, but my wife, Maxine, was undaunted. I was content to enjoy the giant lily pads in the rain forest (*Victoria amazonica*) and the blue-green macaws, but she volunteered to swim in the waters of the Rio Negro near its junction with the Amazon, where piranhas lurked. Supposedly the piranhas wouldn't enter the sterile waters of the Rio Negro, but I was happier eating them for dinner than risking having them eat me for lunch.

In 1999 we attended a conference in Tromso, in the far north of Norway, after a visit to Helsinki, Finland. We found that Tromso could be reached by bus via a highway from Helsinki that reaches north across much of Lapland. We saw the spindly pine forests (*Pinus silvestris*) shrink in size and disappear as we traveled so far north, ultimately all by ourselves. We later learned with dismay that on the longest wild river in Finland above the Arctic Circle, relatives of Maxine ran a lumber mill that cut these forests. While in northern Norway, we also toured a dam that had been built in the face of protests: conservationists had tried to save another wild river but had failed. On earlier trips, we had seen the sites of other battles over dams—in New Zealand's Fiordland National Park (unsuccessful) and in Tasmania (successful).

Soviet Union

Arrangements made some years earlier continued to involve me with the environmental movement in the Soviet Union and that, in turn, led me to focus on environmental problems in the Arctic region.

The Sierra Club facilitated a visit to this country by a delegation from the All-Russia Society for the Conservation of Nature in 1988. This was in return for the visit we had made to the Soviet Union in the 1970s, though it was much delayed. Their delegation was composed mainly of bureaucrats whom we took to see sights such as Yosemite Valley, which did not impress them—though giant sequoias did.

Despite the lackluster tenor of this experience, both sides agreed to continue the series of exchanges, so in 1990 we returned to the Soviet Union. The All-Russia Society was now feeling less secure, as glasnost was introducing competition on the environmental front. Members now felt challenged by the new Socio-Ecological Union, a group for which I felt a greater affinity.

During our time in Moscow, we made a round of visits to agencies with environmental responsibilities. At the forestry ministry, officials told us of their troubles in controlling logging concessions in the Far East. Not only were Korean companies taking the timber they had bought, but they were hauling away the topsoil as well in railway cars and ships. The situation was getting out of hand, but the agency no longer had the means to assert control. Everywhere we heard environmental agency officials tell of their fears and uncertainties about the future. Glasnost afforded a brief moment when these agencies started to flourish, but they have not done well since, nor had they in earlier times. In earlier times they had more power but little interest in protecting the environment. In later times, they have had more interest but little money or power.

After a few days, we traveled by train a few hundred miles south of Moscow to Voronez, where the forest belt gives way to steppes with black soil. Soil sciences began in universities there.

The area was also the center of Soviet research on nuclear power. The Soviets wanted us to visit their complex of five nuclear plants, which were supposed to be their newest and safest. Perhaps they planned to publicize our visit to give much-needed reassurance to their public in the aftermath of Chernobyl. Despite our misgivings, we went ahead, but with our own Geiger counter to verify its safety.

This trip convinced me that these exchanges were an anachronism. We were dealing with an organization whose time had passed. With the end of the old regime and the Cold War, there was no longer much reason for us to continue the exchanges. We may have contributed a little to reduce tensions, but probably not much, and that was not our purpose. We always talked optimistically with the All-Russia Society about expanding cooperation, but we had neither the funding to do it nor the base of interest. Moreover, we were very different kinds of organizations. While technically we owed the Soviets another visit here, the amount we had spent for their single visit to the United States about matched the amount they had spent to bring us there on two occasions. So at my behest, we discontinued the program.

This trip was not my last visit to Russia, but it was my last under these auspices. In the future, the Sierra Club championed dissidents there who were pushing the environmental cause, but we stopped dealing with this organization representing the establishment. While Russia needed environmental help in all sorts of ways, we were not in a position to provide it, nor could it be done effectively through the All-Russia Society.

Seeds

In the early 1990s, the Sierra Club hired Steve Mills to take over some of the overseas programs I had begun. This was in keeping with the idea that I should get programs under way and then move on. I was also becoming quite busy with other matters. But Mills was not keen to maintain *Earthcare Appeals*, the newsletter I had started, and he was having trouble getting enough facts from foreign sources about threats to parks and reserves. He was more attracted to the plight of those who were protesting and being persecuted. He chose to champion the cause of the indigenous peoples who were losing their forests, rather than the cause of the forests as such. Alas, I watched him shut down my newsletter.

He wanted to go in a different direction. He wanted to establish a connection between human rights and the environment. Bowing to the inevitable, I helped him by writing a paper elaborating on this theme, suggesting that we "focus our involvement on those civil and political rights that must exist as preconditions for environmental activism to be able to prosper." Activists "cannot rally public opinion in their countries if there is no freedom of speech nor of assembly," I wrote. "Public opinion will not matter if people cannot vote. Their protests will be muffled if they are jailed or put under house arrest." In time, Mills got a grant for a cooperative project with Amnesty International and began a kind of green Amnesty. His program became quite successful and took him all over the world. The seeds each of us planted grew in quite different directions.

I was disappointed that another seed did not turn out so well. I had long involved myself in an organization known as the American Committee for International Conservation and eventually became its vice chairman. While historically it had focused on the work of the IUCN and the relations among its U.S. affiliates, it also provided a forum in Washington, D.C., to discuss international environmental matters, and it brought agency and NGO personnel into regular contact with us.

In the early 1990s the committee elected George Rabb of the Chicago Zoological Park to serve as its chairman. He hardly ever called meetings and let the group wither away. Perhaps he felt it was no longer needed because IUCN had now opened its own office in Washington, D.C., to forge closer relations with its U.S. members. In any event, I was sorry. If he no longer wanted to keep it going, I wished he had simply asked me to take it over. No other group filled its niche.

But if I had my disappointments in the international field, I found in time that some people did appreciate my contributions. The WILD Foundation, which ran the world wilderness congresses, gave me its Lifetime Achievement Award. Somewhat later, the IUCN's World Commission on Protected Areas (formerly the Parks Commission) gave me its Fred Packard Award.

The Arctic Environment

In the last few years of my career, I worked on some of the problems affecting the Arctic, particularly chemical contamination. In connection with our Russian work, I took an interest in controversies over schemes, fortunately eventually blocked, to reverse the current of rivers that flowed from Siberia into the Arctic. Many of these rivers were grossly polluted and were contaminating the ecosystems of the Arctic region. I also came across an American researcher who had once worked for the Environmental Defense Fund, who believed that this contamination often attached itself to icebergs at the mouths of rivers, which worked their way across the Arctic Ocean—depositing these chemicals in places, such as the Fram Straits near Greenland, far from their sources. In addition, the Russians planned to vastly expand their oil production in Siberia (Russia is now among the world's leading oil producers) and were considering transporting the oil to market via the Arctic Ocean. I was alarmed at the prospect of spillage, adding to already existing levels of contamination. Most people thought of the Arctic Ocean as pristine, but that is far from the truth.

In 1989, the nine nations around the Arctic undertook a project to evaluate these problems, called the Arctic Environmental Protection Strategy (AEPS). Various teams were formed to study different aspects of the problem, with scientists detailed from agencies and universities. Because the United States includes Alaska, our country was involved. The State Department and the National Oceanic and Atmospheric Administration (NOAA) paid close attention to this project, but strangely enough, EPA showed little interest. U.S. involvement was coordinated through the State Department's office of Oceans, Environment and Science, which held regular briefings for interested parties.

I started going to these meetings and over the ensuing few years filed a series of comments on draft documents. I also began to attend briefings sponsored by the only organization that focused just on this matter, the Circumpolar Conservation Union (CCU). Despite its impressive name, this was primarily a project organized by one person, Evelyn Hurwich, to bring conservationists and indigenous peoples in the Arctic together for a dialogue (which was slow to happen). She had a background in both law and anthropology. But she did not really have much of a background in conservation, though she came from a family in California with strong conservation interests.

My role was primarily to prod the State Department into asking that more be done to protect the Arctic environment. Its basic tendency was to try to stay out of harm's way. It wanted to keep the environmental focus paramount and to avoid having the AEPS ripen into a new institution that would compromise our sovereignty. Canada wanted to change the focus of the project to one that promoted sustainable development in the Arctic (without really defining that term). Canada also sought to set up a new institution called the Arctic Council, which Evelyn favored. In contrast, I agreed with the State Department and sought to keep the focus on solving environmental problems. I was concerned that the Arctic Council would become focused on self-determination for the region, regardless of its environmental condition.

The state of Alaska wanted to monitor the AEPS process, but did not want to alarm its residents over pollution reaching their shores. The Alaskan delegation in Congress prevented the release of data in the federal government's possession on the health effects to date of contamination in Alaska, mostly from abroad. Basically, Alaska's government seemed to prefer a head-in-the-sand approach.

Some of the Scandinavian countries had a similarly conflicted position. Norway invested heavily in researching these problems, but would not admit for the record that its waters and fish were anything but clean. Iceland felt the same. Greenland (through Denmark) and Canada were mainly interested in placating their native populations, who still consumed a great deal of bush food. They did not want to face the facts that harmful chemicals were moving up the food chain to become concentrated in the foods that natives ate. The issue was really the level of chemicals in the tissues of sea life, birds, and people and the dangers they posed. Canada allowed birds to be consumed in the bush that could not be served in restaurants in Montreal because of the chemicals in them. Natives in the northern bush saw our work as an attack on their type of food, rather than an attempt to protect their health.

Native populations also chafed under restrictions that the European Community had imposed on selling seal pelts there, and Norway, Iceland, and Greenland all resented the restrictions on whaling that the International Whaling Commission had imposed. For many years, they prevented the CCU from even obtaining observer status at AEPS meetings. With Evelyn and me prodding it, our State Department tried to liberalize AEPS rules to allow more observers. As the AEPS proceeded with its studies and reports, the evidence accumulated that the problems in the Arctic were severe. I wrote a number of papers summarizing the results.[4] The conditions I described continue to this day.

Volatile pollutants throughout the northern hemisphere (often from agricultural pesticides) work their way northward to find their final resting place in the Arctic Ocean and its biota. The volatilization process ends in the Arctic when the air becomes too cold for it to continue. High levels of persistent organic pollutants (POPs) such as PCBs and chlordane show up in the milk of human mothers—for example, in the Russian north, eastern Greenland, and northern Quebec. Reproduction is failing among polar bears and foxes on the Svalbard archipelago because of elevated levels of POPs. These animals prey on ringed seals, which in turn are contaminated.

Heavy metals are concentrated along the Russian coasts in the Arctic and in nearby seas. The levels of mercury in Canada's eastern Arctic are high enough to affect the health of breast-fed children, exceeding tolerable daily-intake levels. A plume of air with high levels of sulfates reaches across the Arctic Ocean in the winter from Russia and moves into North America. It acidifies lakes and reduces the numbers of fish they can support. In the springtime, children in eastern Greenland have to limit the time they spend outdoors because of elevated levels of UVB light. Exposure to these levels affects human health by causing immunosuppression, making people more vulnerable to disease. The protective ozone layer has already been reduced by 40 percent. And warming temperatures stemming from climate change are reducing areas of sea ice, affecting the global climate as well as the habitat for marine mammals. Climate change will also cause melting of the permafrost, which will release trapped methane and increase concentrations of greenhouse gases.

To my consternation, I found that I could not persuade others to take these problems seriously. When I made efforts to get these facts into the hands of leading media, they thought I was "crying wolf." They were tired of hearing how bad things were getting. The revelations were embedded in ponderous reports. They did not always find my concerns reflected in the summaries, which they examined; they would have had to dig more deeply to find the dire information within the texts. I finally resorted to making a presentation to a panel attached to President Clinton's Council on Sustainable Development. I was a co-chairman of this panel, so participants had to listen to me. But they too wanted to get beyond "gloom and doom."

When I began my involvement with problems in the Arctic, I thought I would find less contention than in the tropical forests. Because there were fewer people living in the region, I thought that agreement would come more easily. And in this region, we were not focusing on nature reserves, which might be viewed as taking land from someone; instead, we were trying to help stop the deposition of harmful chemicals and the disruption of natural systems. We were trying to help those who were being victimized.

But many of those who resided in the Arctic, especially natives, did not seem to want any outside help. They felt that people from the United States really did not have any business being involved. But at some point, they may change their minds. They may see that because the assaults on their region are coming largely from outside, they need people from the outside to help deal with them. They may at last come to see that it is not provincial questions that are at stake, but the integrity of world systems. I hope these realizations will not come too late.

My work abroad in the 1990s certainly deepened my conviction that environmentalism was spreading across the globe, but unevenly. It had yet to develop an indigenous base in the Arctic and had not developed a strong national presence in Japan, although its local base was strong. On the other hand, it was emerging strongly in the Soviet Union as the old regime there broke down and leadership among groups began to change. And the Sierra Club itself was changing its focus, beginning to champion the rights of those who were championing the rights of nature. Ideas were taking hold that could not be held back.

20 *The Bittersweet Years*

During the years of the Clinton administration, 1993 to 2000, we expected renewed progress, but our actual experiences varied immensely. Some ended in frustration. Some resulted in engagement with parts of the administration in unexpected ways. Some forced me to struggle to defend the pollution control laws of the 1970s. It was a bittersweet time of defensive battles, punctuated by a few momentous breakthroughs.

The Clinton Administration

When Bill Clinton was first elected president, the environmental community thought that it would fare well under his administration. The presence of Al Gore, who had courted the environmental movement as a U.S. senator, on the ticket had suggested to many that Clinton's term in office might be like the Carter administration all over again, and they immediately established contact with his transition team. They organized their own working group, representing the principal mainstream organizations, to draw up a list of their members whom they would propose for appointed positions in the new administration.

I was among the active members of this working group. In a quite unrealistic way, we politicked among ourselves to work out a place for each of us on this list, which was proudly presented to the administration. The group put me down for three positions that interested me: director of the National Park Service, chairman of the Council on

Environmental Quality, and assistant secretary of state for oceans, environment and science.

I have no evidence that the administration ever seriously considered this list. A former field representative of the Sierra Club in Los Angeles, Bob Hattoy, who had resigned to work for Clinton, was then on the White House personnel team. The Club had endorsed my candidacy, and he may have pushed my name. I was even mentioned in a column in the *Washington Post* as a candidate for the Park Service post. I solicited an interview with Interior Secretary Bruce Babbitt and got one, but his interest was not evident.

Babbitt made it clear to the White House that he wanted to control the appointments within Interior. He ended up appointing Roger Kennedy, a Republican, as Park Service chief. Kennedy was a lawyer from Minneapolis who had gotten interested in history. Some months later Kennedy was startled to recognize me at a meeting and seemed to regard me initially as some sort of threat to him, though later he became quite cordial.

For reasons that baffle me, recent Democratic administrations seem to think they have no reason to humor environmentalists by appointing the people we favor to positions that are important to us as an interest group. Instead, the administrations seem to think these are good positions to use to cultivate other constituencies. The Clinton administration was no exception. Besides Bob Hattoy, who eventually went to a minor post in Interior, only two other people from the Club's ranks were asked to join the administration, and they were in positions with little impact. I may simply have been too strongly associated with a major advocacy organization; my peers who received appointments either were not associated with such strong advocacy or were from organizations with a lower profile. Apparently I am indelibly a Sierra Club man.

I might have sought help from people who knew me, but I remembered what had happened when Jerry Brown became governor of California. Club officers had decided to suggest that I be appointed to head that state's giant Resources Agency and had asked the Club's vice president, Claire Dedrick, to lobby the governor on my behalf. But she seemed to have sold herself rather than me: in due course I found that she, rather than I, had been appointed to the position.

In the end, only about half as many environmentalists were appointed in the Clinton administration as had been in the Carter administration, and those that were did not leave much of a mark. In retrospect, I may have been better off staying with the Sierra Club. The prestige once attached to serving in public office has waned, and most appointees do not stay long enough to accomplish much. I may have accomplished more by staying for such a long time with an organization where I was able to build my expertise.

There was another source of consolation as well. When the Sierra Club celebrated its centennial in 1992, I suggested to the executive director that steps be taken, from time to time, to remember staff for their contributions to conservation, just as volunteers were recognized. Some time later, I was delighted to learn that such a program had been set up, and I was even more delighted to learn that the staff had chosen to name one of the awards after me. The Michael McCloskey Award is made annually for "a distinguished record of achievement in national or international conservation."

While the Clinton administration was better disposed toward the environment than the Bush administration that preceded it, it did even less to court environmentalists, including those of us in the Sierra Club. The Clinton folks were trying to court big business instead and wanted to project an impression of moderation. Thinking they had a number of appointees within their ranks who came from environmental organizations, they felt that they already understood us and did not need to go out of their way to consult us.

Vice President Gore, in fact, was trying to change his image. He now felt he needed to court Wall Street rather than the environmental community and suggested that the regulatory role of government needed to be softened. This was what his "reinventing government" initiative was really all about. He wanted to reduce regulatory costs, move toward performance-based approaches, and share decision making with companies and other stakeholders. He and his staff quarreled with the EPA administrator, Carol Browner, who was less excited about having her agency soften its approach.

Carl Pope, the Sierra Club's executive director at that time, made clear to the new administration that it should deal with him, not me. He wanted to handle high-level politics. That was appropriate. But I suspect that he was not cultivated by the Clinton administration the way I had been by the earlier Bush administration. The Clinton folks basically felt that we had nowhere else to go. Labor got the same "arm's length" treatment from them.

Along with thousands of others, I did get invitations to attend Clinton's inauguration and celebratory events. Maxine and I sat on the west lawn of the Capitol for the swearing-in and later enjoyed watching fireworks from the balcony of the diplomatic rooms of the State Department.

After that, little more occurred to suggest that the Clinton people wanted a close relationship. I was seldom invited to meet with cabinet officers. Perhaps our frictions over trade policy explained this, but I felt that they wanted to establish distance. Bureaucrats down the line, however, assumed that we were now "persona grata," and they were quite willing to meet to discuss specific projects I was pursuing. I often saw officials in the trade office, in EPA, and in the environmental section of the State Department.

In the past we had found CEQ to be a place where we could always get a hearing and gather intelligence, in both good times and bad. CEQ officials had generally seen their job as maintaining liaison with us. But the Clinton administration began by trying to abolish the agency. We had to lobby Congress to save it and to get it funded. Katie McGinty, who came to run it from Gore's office in the Senate, had little time for us. She acted mainly in a political role to advance Gore's interests and did not seem to identify deeply with environmentalism. We still had contacts in CEQ after she took over, but it was no longer such a warm and welcoming place.

Interior Secretary Babbitt spent his first years with the administration working out settlements to outstanding environmental disputes. Wherever we had challenged questionable programs, he characterized our actions as having caused "train wrecks." He generally worked out awkward compromises to resolve these disputes. In his final years, he pushed Clinton to set aside many national monuments on Interior Department lands that few had ever heard of. Only a few were on our list of proposed monuments.

After the Republicans gained control of Congress in 1995, Clinton changed his tactics and began to take a firmer line in dealing with our adversaries. He fought back over budget blockages and other things, and we applauded him. His new backbone served him well in the next election. As the Clinton folks began to mend their fences with the environmental community, we sought a meeting with Vice President Gore to talk about our feelings.

At a closed meeting with Gore in earlier 1996, we complained bitterly about the administration's failure in its first term to get the Forest

Service's direction under firm control. The person the administration had chosen as chief, Jack Ward Thomas, while the prime mover in protecting Northwest old growth, was more of an ingrown U.S. Forest Service person than the administration had assumed. When I met with him over the fate of the sequoias, he seemed indifferent. Gore told us that he was also frustrated and that he and Clinton were determined to do better—if they got a second term. When they did and appointed as chief Michael Dombeck, a biologist from the Bureau of Land Management, the policies and practices of the Forest Service finally improved. I think our meeting with Gore made a difference.

I was asked to meet with Clinton himself on only one occasion. It was a staged event designed to cultivate me, as well as a leader of Public Citizen, to get us to support EPA's Project XL, one of Gore's reinvention projects, which would allow industry more leeway in accomplishing pollution abatement goals. After Clinton read a prepared statement praising the program, he chatted with me about a visit he had just made to Franklin Delano Roosevelt's home at Hyde Park in New York. He knew that Roosevelt had been a tree lover, as I was, and he clearly had been briefed on topics that should interest me and establish a connection. I must say that he could be very charming, though I did not change my negative opinion about Project XL.

From an environmental point of view, Clinton did do a few things of historic importance. Most significantly, he pushed down the level of logging in the national forests by 75 percent. The allowable sale level (once called the allowable cut) went from more than 12 billion board feet to less than 3 billion board feet by the end of his time in office. In the Pacific Northwest, the level of logging declined even more—by 87 percent. It was his boldest stroke, and it resolved stalemates arising out of litigation brought by the Sierra Club Legal Defense Fund over the plight of the northern spotted owl.

In a related action in Clinton's final term, his appointees declared an end to road building on 58 million undeveloped acres of national forests. It remains to be seen whether this order will survive over time; the administration of George W. Bush has worked hard to undo it.

Clinton's action in setting aside two major national monuments was also noteworthy: the Grand Staircase–Escalante National Monument in Utah and the Giant Sequoia National Monument in California. Unlike many of the other monuments he set aside, these were widely known and did have constituencies. I was also glad to see protection come to Steens Mountain in eastern Oregon, which I knew from my early fieldwork. Under prodding from Clinton's people, who suggested that declaration of the area as a monument was likely unless Congress acted, members finally legislated to protect it with a combination of wilderness designations and various other restrictions on exploitation. A monument would have been fine, but this legislation got enacted, while actual declaration of a monument was less certain.

Whereas Jimmy Carter often met with environmental leaders, the Clinton administration wanted to avoid the impression that it was giving us special access. Clinton usually put environmental leaders on panels set up to discuss contentious topics with leaders of the business community. He would hold off committing himself while encouraging the two sides to come to a consensus. He did this, for instance, on the topic of improving automobile mileage to reduce greenhouse gas emissions, creating a panel informally known as the Car Talks. Nothing came of this effort, but it did permit him to dodge the issue for most of his time in office.

President's Council on Sustainable Development

Clinton's principal device for promoting such dialogue was the President's Council on Sustainable Development. This was a major project that lasted for eight years and consumed huge amounts of time and energy. It was composed of various cabinet officers, CEOs from large firms (including Ken Lay of Enron), a half dozen representatives of major environmental groups, and representatives of labor unions and minority communities.

The president of the Sierra Club in 1993, Michele Perrault, was appointed to the Council. Her appointment continued throughout the eight years of Clinton's administration, even though her term as Club president soon ended. She appointed me as her chief deputy, and when she could not be present, I took her place at the main meeting table in the plenary sessions. At various times, I drafted the statements that she offered for the record.

Much work for the Council was done between the quarterly meetings of those who were presidential appointees. There were three or four levels of staff working on various study projects. Because Michele was far away on the West Coast, I represented her interests in a number of these groups. As it turned out, that participation gave me considerable access to cabinet officers and their high-level staff. I trekked regularly to the White House conference rooms on Jackson Place Northwest.

These meetings were important occasions at which to pick up intelligence and lobby government officials on various matters. I also learned exactly what industry leaders wanted and how they argued their case. In responding to their arguments, I probed for weaknesses in their rationale while honing my own arguments.

Most of the participants on the Council had no real interest in finding out how sustainable development might best be defined or work; after all, there were more than 250 definitions of it in the literature. When I sat on an early panel that was asked to identify its underlying principles, for example, I found that only one other person, a staffer from EPA, was interested in probing the subject. The others' idea of the project seemed to be that we would endorse bland versions of what each wanted in order to produce a balanced, but meaningless, document. This was justified under the notion that sustainable development involved reconciling notions of environmental protection, economic development, and social justice. No one knew how to do that—though that would have solved many problems for politicians. When I tried to identify theories that might help do it, I got blank stares.

We quickly found that we could look for a sufficiently abstract version of a point so that no one could object. In this way, the business community found it could be viewed as "green" without actually committing itself to anything definite. For our part, environmentalists could feel hopeful that business was at least interested in the idea of sustainability. And the Clinton officials went through the paces to keep us busy and generate a final report. Everyone felt they were playing a role, as actors do, although few had any confidence that the effort was leading anywhere.

Through three phases in two presidential terms, this project ground relentlessly onward. Michele grew weary of flying back and forth from the West Coast, so toward the end I found myself sitting at the main table more and more. In the third phase (1997–98), I co-chaired a new project on environmental management along with an industry person. By now, I knew the process well and could help guide it.

Pollution Control Policy

During my time in Washington, I found myself increasingly asked to defend the underlying rationale for federal laws dealing with pollution.

Gradually I became a spokesman on this matter for the environmental community, along with Dave Hawkins of NRDC, who dealt mainly with air pollution. While in my early years I had focused on other issues and did not consider myself a pollution expert, I began to address this topic more and more simply because hardly anyone else was doing it. I remembered the rationale for these laws from the 1970s and was interested in policy, while many of the younger generation seemed to take the laws for granted or, in a simplistic manner, thought pollution could be ordered out of existence by edict. They did not seem to have an appetite for grappling with the complexities of the laws enacted to control it.

Thus when I became chairman of the Club, I began to write articles on pollution policy and speak at conferences. While I had first written an article in 1971 for the *Duquesne Law Review* about the promise of EPA when it was formed, I did not return to the topic until 1987. Then I wrote a provocative piece, "The Crisis of Failing Bureaucracies," for the *Natural Resources Journal.*[1] I argued that EPA seemed to be "immobilized and ineffective" after the trauma of living under the Reagan administration. Though EPA was underfunded and overworked, I suggested that its problems might be more deep-seated: it was being asked to do too much on issues where too little was known, and it did not seem to possess the can-do attitude of other bureaucracies such as the Corps of Engineers.

The following year, when I was asked to address a waste control association in the Midwest, I used the occasion to respond to the policies that were guiding EPA under the first Bush administration. As directed by its administrator, Lee Thomas, EPA was trying to minimize concerns over toxic chemicals in the environment and was advocating a go-slow, low-cost approach.

In my critique, I argued that people felt they were being immersed in a "chemical bath" without their permission. I asserted that most people think "it is not moral [for businesses] to take risks with other people's lives and health." Only a few of these chemicals had been tested for their safety by impartial experts. Deaths were occurring around the world because of chemicals that were degrading the ozone layer. Chemicals such as dioxin concentrate in biota and move up the food chain. Some of them were showing up in mothers' milk. I argued that regulators should err on the side of safety, especially because scientific estimates of safe exposure levels were constantly being lowered. Moreover, in light of the "polluter pays" principle, it was right that much of the costs of cleanup should be borne not by the public, but by those who created the problems.[2]

In an address at an international audience of independent experts on industrial medicine, the Collegium Ramazzini in Italy, I extended my critique of "the crisis of failing bureaucracies" by setting forth further reasons that might explain why EPA was bogged down. For one thing, the agency was not drawing the public support that it needed. Instead of welcoming public support, EPA was disempowering the public— holding it at bay—by resorting to too much jargon and by doing its work in secret. Few were able to intervene in its procedures. Its processes, furthermore, had so many steps that they played into the hands of those who opposed regulations. Each step in the process became another "failure point"—a place where a legal or political ambush could occur. I felt too that there was a great mismatch in resources between those who were defending EPA's regulations and those who were attacking them.

There also seemed to be a breakdown in "administrative regularity": the presumption, which lawyers make, that the laws will be loyally and efficiently executed. Society was giving too many jobs to agencies for which they were ill suited. "We should not send bureaucrats to do politicians' jobs," I suggested. "We need to match up politicians, not bureaucrats, with the crucial questions of political consequence." Agencies such as EPA were being asked to take on the task of balancing competing claims, when it is elected officials, not bureaucrats, who are the experts in balancing claims.

Finally, I argued, "we need to accept the fact that simplified approaches will seem to sacrifice some element of economic efficiency." Sometimes polluters will be obliged to follow uniform reduction approaches rather than having an approach tailored just for them. This will be the price for programs that can be readily administered and that are intelligible to the public. I felt I had broken through to new levels of analysis with my remarks, which were subsequently published in the *American Journal of Industrial Medicine*.[3]

On EPA's twentieth anniversary in 1990, I was asked to share with the readers of its journal my latest thoughts about the reasons for its difficulties.[4] This time I suggested that the agency was also suffering from a "brain drain" as senior people took early retirement to flee hostile administrations. It seemed to me that a kind of agency decay had also set in, wherein an agency loses its initial zeal and settles into doing business hesitantly and cautiously. I also thought that EPA was seeing itself less as a results-oriented agency and more as a process-oriented one—"concerned with moving paperwork along as an end in itself." It was seeking to defend itself from attack by searching for iron-clad science, which in turn produced endless delays, often in defiance of deadlines set by law.

EPA's managers probably wished they had not asked for my opinion. But before long, I would find myself taking their side.

Regulatory Rollback

At a conclave of the Sierra Club for its lobbyists at the state level in 1996, I described a campaign by conservatives to discredit the whole federal system of regulating pollution—a campaign that continues to this day.[5] These conservatives preached that the current system was broken and in need of a major overhaul. They associated our system with the "command and control" systems found under communism, and in its stead they sought a system that offered the prospect of "perfect justice" for the regulated community, with little said about how much the environment would be cleaned up.

This right-wing campaign was aimed at federal laws that strove to set uniform standards for all those who were in like situations. Under those laws, over time all citizens were supposed to get similar levels of protection and all industrial plants were supposed to get into compliance so that ambient standards could be met. Most new plants would have to install state-of-the-art controls—so-called technology controls (with variations), which were supposed to stay abreast of emerging technology and embody the best available technology to abate pollution. The emphasis was on minimizing pollution rather than on arguing about how much to tolerate.

Industry attacked this uniformity of standards, charging that it required excessive cleanup in some cases. Industry objected to technology controls and wanted a system under which plant managers could determine, on a case-by-case basis, which controls should be installed. It wanted only to have to meet reduction goals, not to be told to achieve them in a given way. It wanted the regulatory agencies to sit down with each plant manager to negotiate on such matters. In effect, it wanted a customized rather than a uniform process. As a general proposition, industry felt it should not have to act until the underlying science was beyond dispute. It wanted to argue about every case that was not proven. It did not want to accept the authority of EPA and its scientists.

There were numerous flaws in these arguments, I reminded my audience. The prevailing system provided (and still does provide) a level playing field where the same standards apply to all. Business knows what will be required of it. Businesses are not set against one another to see who can negotiate the best deal. Agency permit writers are not put under pressure to grant special dispensations. There is no endless search for the "perfect way." The prevailing regulatory system acknowledges that self-interest and special pleading are involved and tries to shield the system from these pressures.

A uniform system, I admitted, does administer a kind of "rough justice." In some cases it may require more than a philosopher-king might demand, but in other cases it may not ask enough. In net terms, the cases probably balance each other. A uniform system uses an approach similar to that used for traffic lights. Though too much traffic may be stopped at times and too little at other times, on the whole the system works to control traffic.

In the case of traffic control as well as of pollution control, effectiveness is more important than the quest for ideal efficiency. Our standardized system of pollution abatement requirements avoids endless arguments about whether more or fewer reductions should be required. But it did not try to displace plants and facilities built before the law was passed; instead, it focused on new ones, which could more easily adapt. Eventually, it was thought, the old plants would be gone.*

Industry seemed to want cost-benefit calculations to be done on every question. Such calculations are used to shed light on major rule-making decisions by EPA, but it is not practical to attempt them on lesser questions because they are costly and time consuming to prepare. Moreover, they tend to overstate costs and underestimate benefits. Despite being inherently skewed in industry's favor, most studies after the fact have shown that EPA's regulations are justified—benefits exceed costs by large margins. Because they are such an imperfect tool, though, it is wise not to base decisions entirely on cost-benefit analyses.

The argument over "sound science" stems from industry's rejection of the "precautionary principle," on which the U.S. system is based. This principle stipulates that society should err on the side of protect-

---

*In the case of power plants built before 1970, it has taken longer to retire them than anyone anticipated. Because they can be operated cheaply as an exception to Clean Air Act requirements, industry has tried to keep them operating as long as possible.

ing public health in cases in which scientists still lack conclusive evidence. "We want to take prudent action to avert problems," I explained, "when there is a reasonable suspicion that a chemical poses a threat." EPA is appropriately attentive to the findings of science, while its critics, I alleged, "want to hide from them as long as possible."

In the midterm elections of 1994, the Republicans won control of Congress. They tried to advance a radical agenda in 1995–96, which their leader in the House, Newt Gingrich, called the Contract with America. One of their chief aims was to hamstring the environmental regulatory system, which they so disliked. They called their effort regulatory reform, while we labeled it regulatory rollback. Throughout most of that Congress, it was assumed that some sort of action would occur on this item in their agenda.

My role was to analyze the various bills introduced on this subject and to identify the issues for us. Occasionally I did some lobbying, but most often I armed our lobbyists with arguments that I hoped would prove powerful.[6] The bills in question were long, complicated, and numerous. They mainly dealt with requirements for risk assessment and cost-benefit analysis for EPA regulations. The chief bills were introduced by Republican senators Robert Dole of Kansas (S. 343) and William Roth of Delaware (S. 291), and Democratic senator Carl Levin of Michigan. There were comparable bills in the House, such as H.R. 1022. Dole's bill drew the most attention, since he was in a powerful position as the new majority leader. This bill was pushed by small business, with big business acceding to it. Not all major industries were firm in their support, though. Roth represented the position of the more moderate Eastern Republicans, while Levin's bill represented the position of Democrats who wanted to compromise.

The Clinton administration was ambivalent. Fundamentally, it did not like these bills, but it felt that it was politically unwise to position itself against "regulatory reform." It wanted to blunt the momentum behind the bills by pushing its own version of reform under the rubric of "reinventing government." Unfortunately, this latter program, even though it was more moderate, seemed to acquiesce in the notion that there was a need for change. Even the Clinton administration was talking about "place-based regulations" and criticizing "one size fits all" regulations, thus undermining the case for a uniform approach.

I pointed out that these bills would impose stringent new threshold requirements for regulations in the field of public health. Regulations would have to be cost-justified through cost-benefit analyses; they would have to achieve their goals through the least costly means, even if more benefits could be achieved through more costly means; and they could not be issued at all unless the benefits were quite large. Collectively, these requirements would have imposed a much higher threshold before new regulations could be issued. The public, accordingly, would have received far less protection from pollution.

The bills reflected confidence in risk assessment as the only firm guide and a belief that everything that regulators needed to bear in mind to protect the public's health could be readily quantified. Ignored were the many problems with such an approach—for instance, too little data are often available for the approach to be used with confidence, nor do data reflect cumulative exposures or exposures to multiple types of pollution.

The bills were one-sided, being concerned solely with mandating practices that would push the government toward reducing standards, not with giving the public more protection. The bills assumed that regulations should be confined to pollution problems that had already been identified. They curbed the application of the best professional practices in the field of public health. They armed industry with the basis for a whole new series of court challenges to EPA's regulations. Business could have even petitioned for review of all regulations then in force; EPA would then have had to reexamine all the regulations it had issued in the previous fifteen years, and, for a limited time, all deadlines for issuing regulations would have been suspended.

Throughout the spring of 1995, I generated a heavy flow of detailed analyses of these bills, pointing out their many flaws. Because I realized that my analyses were too complicated for our lobbyists to use as such, I experimented with different ways of framing larger issues. At one point, I summed them up as follows: this legislation undermines protection of public health; it would hurt our economy by introducing chaos into the regulatory picture; it would replace sound means of decision making with methods that are skewed toward the polluters; it would enshrine bad science (that is, it is based on a misunderstanding of the methods of public health); and industry, under the House bills particularly, would be given an unfair advantage in providing input.

In a speech at that time to a major chemical company that had committed itself to operating under high environmental standards, I argued that the company should not "stoke the fires of resentment among these populist forces," referring to the independent businesses allied with

Representative Tom DeLay. "They are going to destabilize a system in which you have invested huge sums [in cleanup equipment]," I warned.

The Sierra Club waged a furious grassroots campaign to bring pressure to bear on vulnerable members of Congress, mainly Republicans, to get them to back off. Other environmental groups joined in, and together they spent almost $3 million in a media campaign to turn the situation around. Republican Congressman Sherman Boehlert from upstate New York became our champion and succeeded in enlisting more than sixty Republican moderates in opposing these efforts to weaken EPA's laws.

Gradually the impetus behind these bills waned as Congress bogged down, as opposition grew, and because of the complexity of the approach. The issues carried over into the next Congress, but the campaign to enact the bills lost momentum. Finally, the Clinton administration produced a letter from OMB opposing them. Since there was now considerable doubt that the president would even sign these bills, many legislators wondered if it was wise to expose themselves by expressing support. They held back, and none ever became law. About this time, in a sandwich shop near our office, I overheard a lobbyist from the Heritage Foundation complain, "We can defeat other interests, but we don't ever seem to be able to beat the environmentalists." I was proud, in this instance, to have helped make that true.

As an antagonist in these battles, I was generally viewed with distrust by those in the chemical industry. More of this industry's plants are sited along the lower Mississippi River near Baton Rouge, Louisiana, than anywhere else. When Edwin Edwards reassumed the governor's seat in that state in the early 1990s, strangely enough he chose a Sierra Club state-level lobbyist, Martha Madden, to head his Department of Environmental Quality.

For reasons I did not understand then, Madden put on a reception in the governor's mansion to honor me. At the opulent mansion, built by Huey Long, I found myself in a receiving line accepting the good wishes of a long procession of chemical company executives. In light of my recent speeches, this all seemed very unreal. But since Madden's agency regulated the companies, I supposed they felt they had to play along. I later learned that the governor found her to be more pliable than her predecessor. She may have been using my presence to burnish her reputation; in any event, I am sure the effect was short-lived.

Over the course of the campaign opposing regulatory rollback, I
steadily improved my grasp of the opposition's arguments and weaknesses.
I developed a working draft of the industry's ten preferred approaches to
regulation and my responses to them.[7] I looked at risk assessment, cost-
benefit analysis, least-cost standards, performance-based standards, the
"bubble" concept, trading emissions reductions, taxing pollution as a
means of control, flexibility as a goal, the notion of self-regulation, and
finally collaboration as an alternative approach. I found limitations and
drawbacks to all of these approaches, particularly if they were to be put in
widespread use.

Many of these notions, designed to justify relaxing regulations, were
picked up by the more moderate business community and its friends,
such as William Ruckelshaus, an influential business figure who had
been EPA administrator at various times under Republican administrations. Before long, numerous reports either funded by business or influenced by Ruckelshaus were pushing these doctrines. I called them
reports from the "Ruckelshaus network."

The type of regulation that industry resented the most was technology controls—that is, obligations to install the best available pollution-
abatement technology in new plants—because it wanted to meet a permanently fixed standard in the cheapest way possible. The Clinton
administration, which felt it had to respond to industry's protests, did so
by advancing an alternative that it claimed would be not only cheaper
but cleaner: new industrial plants could escape technology controls altogether if they agreed to use an approach that would yield "superior environmental performance," a new term coined by the administration.

In the first phase of the President's Council on Sustainable Development,
EPA administrator Carol Browner convinced the Council to endorse the
superior environmental performance concept, with little elaboration on how
it might work. Under technology controls, not only was the best available
technology supposed to be applied, but it was supposed to be improved over
time as technology got better. This new standard, however, would be frozen;
it would never become more stringent. Thus a pollution device installed in
1995 might persist over the life of a plant, and an upgrade would never be
required. The administration's argument that equally good results would
ensue was plausible, but no one could be sure. Notwithstanding, environmentalists on the Council acquiesced in this waiver.

I was asked to join a working group that the Aspen Institute had
organized to examine the Clinton/Browner proposal in greater detail.

The group was composed of people from business, government, environmental groups, and other interests. Observers from key congressional committees were there as well, lending the impression that Congress might pick up the group's findings. Over a two-year period in the mid-1990s, I was heavily engaged in this work.

Many of the key questions about this notion had not really been thought through. How much had to be promised for performance to be regarded as "superior"? Who would make this decision? What was the benchmark for measuring the results? Who would monitor them? What would the penalty be for failing to deliver? Could this alternative approach be tested first, before changes were made across the board? Our group grappled with all of these questions.

The group had a knowledgeable facilitator, Don Snow. He tried to find positions that all of us could live with, after each of us had ample opportunity to explain our views. Gradually, through dialogue, we developed answers to most of these questions.[8]

We felt that only firms that were environmental leaders should be allowed to participate in this scheme, meaning that the rest would operate under the current laws. Superior performance should mean performance that was better than that now required by law. We felt performance needed to go beyond existing law because of uncertainty about whether existing standards were high enough. We did not accept the notion that "equivalency" would be enough—that is, that the new approach chosen could simply be equivalent to what was required under current law. Further, EPA should defer to a robust stakeholder group (as might exist, for example, in the case of a planned new manufacturing plant) to determine whether what the firm proposed was good enough. This group would frame an agreement with the firm, and it would join in monitoring the arrangement.

In this work, I played a leading role in developing our thoughts about how superior environmental performance would be measured from benchmarks. We developed a scheme that would have required new plants to go beyond what was now required by law and set forth requirements for other circumstances. Continuous improvement was also called for. While the choice to operate under these new rules would have been optional, those who did choose this option and then violated the rules would find themselves back under existing law. We thought that this was an acceptable version of the Clinton/Browner proprosal.

Unfortunately, although EPA was represented during our discussions, it chose not to follow our recommendations. When it came time to apply its suggestions about "superior environmental performance," it proceeded in a much less disciplined fashion than we had suggested. Under the banner of experiments to "reinvent government," it authorized a series of test cases as part of a program I mentioned earlier, Project XL. EPA chose the companies that would be the test cases—presumably companies that it trusted—and looked to each to invent an inclusive stakeholder process to work out a proposal, agreeable to all, to deliver "superior performance" in an alternative fashion. EPA would then decide whether to approve each proposal. After a series of test cases, the agency issued regulations for the program.

Few of the environmental stakeholders were prepared for the ordeal they were to face in the test cases. Local enthusiasts were up against industry experts. Sometimes the sessions were too numerous; in one case, there were more than a hundred. Promises to operate by consensus were not always kept. Some of the stakeholders near the plant site were not independent of the firm. Sometimes only perfunctory notice of meetings was given in the media.

The process was designed to keep national environmental watchdogs away. Under the guise of working things out with the people immediately affected, the process was structured in a way that allowed local industry to write its own rules. There was no such thing in practice as a robust stakeholder process because most participants did not have parity with the firms involved in terms of resources, expertise, and time.

EPA officials could not explain how the criteria for "superior environmental performance" would be met. They were not able to explain how what they sanctioned was "superior" to what would have otherwise been required. They did not attempt to set benchmarks to measure results. Moreover, comparisons were difficult because they permitted trading across types of pollution.

I opposed EPA's approach not only because it did not embrace the safeguards in the Aspen Institute report, but also because it contained other deficiencies. Its results were less transparent; because they were based more on matters of judgment than law, criteria were harder to challenge in court; its approach encouraged special pleading; and it entailed heavy transaction costs. It was expensive for EPA to track and evaluate these deals. The approach undermined the whole idea of a level playing field for all. It revealed the drawbacks of trying to customize pollution laws.

I persuaded the Sierra Club to come out squarely against this experiment when EPA revised its regulations after the 1996 election and dispensed entirely with the notion that superior performance would be required. After the first round of test cases, EPA acquiesced to industry's demand that "equivalency" would suffice. The agency also dropped its demand that the alternative results be measurable. Approving them became a subjective exercise: the agency would simply decide whether the new performance looked all right. With this change, EPA no longer even clung to the pretense that this approach was "cleaner." It was "cheaper and dirtier"; that was what the plea for flexibility came down to.

EPA was pushed into this position by the Clinton administration, in my view. Gore thought he had to deliver regulatory relief to take the edge off the claim that he was "too green," and he wanted campaign contributions from the business community in the next election.

ISO

EPA considered various factors when deciding whether to admit a firm to the XL process. I learned that one of them was whether the firm was certified under ISO 14000. After I looked into what this was, I found myself invited to share my thoughts before an audience that EPA assembled in Philadelphia in the spring of 1996.[9]

ISO 14000 was set up by the International Organization for Standardization (ISO), which had begun by establishing worldwide specifications for mechanical products in order to prevent problems of incompatibility. It is run by representatives of transnational businesses, and in its proper domain, I am sure it serves its purpose.

But in recent years, ISO has seen its domain expanding with globalization of the economy. Because of trends in the European Union, it has moved into the field of environmental management. In its 14000 series of standards, it has attempted to provide standards that firms might use to manage their environmental systems. Firms seek to demonstrate that they are responsible by getting certified as being in compliance with ISO 14000.

Such standards could have a useful impact if progressive firms required that their suppliers around the world be certified as well. ISO is entirely process-oriented, however, and does not forbid any kind of behavior or require disclosure of adverse impacts. "ISO logic is that a firm is vindicated by touching the right bases and saying the right words," I concluded, "not by treating the environment right."

ISO 14000 allows firms to certify and audit themselves, which undermines their credibility. It is not a badge of excellence at all. It involves no accountability to the public for what a company actually does. I became really suspicious of it when I found that in trying to sell it to U.S. industry, its apologists were claiming that "it is designed to obviate the need for 'command and control' regulations." Moreover, I found it curious that these same enthusiasts did not want ISO 14000 to embrace any performance standards. They insisted that process requirements would suffice.

In the U.S. regulatory field, these same people are dead set against technology-based standards and want performance standards instead. In this context, I saw that these standards were merely a way station as business works its way toward process standards, which ignore what businesses actually do. I sat down with some of the K Street lawyer-lobbyists working on ISO 14000 and learned firsthand what they were trying to do. I was not reassured. Rather, I saw a long, slippery slope in front of us.

From looking at XL and others like it, I came to realize how many forces were in play to weaken our pollution programs under various guises. What was startling was their variety and ingenuity. I wished that EPA had been able to spend more of its ingenuity on actually making the environment cleaner.

Because of their different interests and perspectives, industry and environmentalists had come to see the issues in entirely different ways. Early in the deliberations of the Environmental Management Task Force (which focused on moving firms to operate in a mode that was "beyond compliance"), I set forth, in a memo to its staff director, what I saw as the fundamental differences in the way industry and environmentalists view the regulatory process:[10]

- Environmentalists look at the issues from the perspective of morality—what is right. They do not think business has a right to pollute; rather, people have a right to be free of injury from pollution. Business looks at the issues from the standpoint of economics and engineering.
- Environmentalists seek to minimize the exposure of people to pollutants, while business seeks to minimize the intervention of government in what it considers to be its business.

- Environmentalists evaluate success in terms of whether regulations are effective. Business evaluates success in terms of efficiency—that is, whether interventions are cost effective.
- Environmentalists seek a system that is standardized, while business seeks a system that is customized.
- Environmentalists want the precautionary principle to guide public policy, while business seeks quantitative proof.
- Environmentalists want mandatory targets for improvement, while business prefers voluntary commitments on its part.
- If business must be held to standards, then it wants to be held to performance standards, and it wants flexibility in determining how to meet those standards. Environmentalists want business to be required to do the best that is technically possible, and they want pressure to advance the state of the art in pollution control technologies.
- Business wants to be able to make required reductions where it is cheapest to do so. It wants broad latitude to search for such places. Environmentalists want to promote a sense of stewardship everywhere and in all operations. They do not want some people or places to have to continue suffering from pollution, and they want an end to old, bad operations.
- Business uses science and data to defend itself against regulations. Environmentalists use science and data to identify problems and risks.
- Business seeks to avoid liability for low doses of toxics, while environmentalists seek to eliminate exposure altogether.
- Business seeks to focus funding on addressing the biggest risks (measured in quantitative terms), while environmentalists seek to focus funding on the risks that are most unconscionable (viewed in qualitative terms). Environmentalists feel particularly strongly about risks that the public does not voluntarily assume.
- Business seeks choice on its part to determine the rates by which it should improve its operations in the area "beyond compliance," while environmentalists seek to move toward preventing pollution entirely. They want that goal to be accepted.

Fundamentally, I found these two camps to be proceeding from entirely different premises. Too many business apologists were trying to obfuscate these differences and confuse people. I did not believe that their notions should be the wave of the future. Instead, they were a way of derailing progress.

When our Environmental Management Task Force, attached to the President's Council, finally produced a tepid report, it did not attract much attention. But its work did serve as an instructive process for those of us involved. There are probably not many firms yet ready to make more pollution reductions than they have to. There is now more reason instead to worry about their slipping backward, I concluded.

Despite the time so many of us spent in empty dialogues, the 1990s did produce results. Not only were the efforts to weaken pollution control laws blocked and an effective defense mounted, but the amount of logging in the national forests was appreciably reduced, with remaining roadless areas given a measure of protection. Moreover, two substantial national monuments were set aside. With the benefit of hindsight, these achievements seem to be of increasing importance.

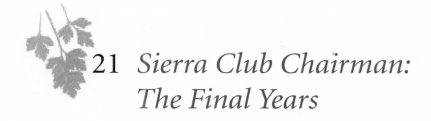

21 *Sierra Club Chairman: The Final Years*

As I approached my retirement—I would turn sixty-five in 1999—I found myself as busy as ever, involved with issues both in the world at large and within the Sierra Club itself. In the larger world I addressed the preservation of giant sequoias, reform of the mining laws, and attempts to displace governmental structures with collaborative strategies designed to suit businesses. Within the Club I mediated between emerging factions and advised the board of directors and key committees, but also found myself resisting new strategies, reorganization, and rejection of hard-earned lessons. Meanwhile, I was also called on to teach part-time at a university, to lecture, and to advise new organizations.

Giant Sequoias

I had known Martin Litton since the 1960s, when he had served on the Sierra Club's board of directors. A former travel editor for *Sunset* magazine, he had involved himself in many issues of interest to the Club. A tall bear of a man, he had a booming voice and an engaging manner. I had always gotten along well with him and recognized his value. He had a tendency to state things too strongly, however, and this did not sit well with everyone.

For decades, Martin had been concerned with issues affecting the southern end of the Sierra. Most of the giant sequoias are found there, and more than half of them were not protected in parks. They were located in the Sequoia National Forest, whose managers in the early

1980s began to permit logging around the edge of its groves, and on occasion even within them. This was occurring even though the Forest Service had assured us it would never happen.

While Club leaders in the area concentrated on trying to stop this logging and even negotiated an agreement to settle a lawsuit with the Forest Service on this matter, Martin wanted a more permanent solution. For more than a decade I worked with him to find it, and as I had on Mineral King where the situations were similar, I suggested that a legislative solution be sought.

Having legislation pending would produce a number of benefits, even though a bill might not pass for years. It would help define an alternative around which people could rally. It would reveal exactly what he and his supporters were seeking. It would legitimate them as the other side on the issue. And it would cause the Forest Service to become more cautious. Because Congress usually does not like to pass such legislation until it is ripe, I advised him to get a bill introduced soon to get the ripening process under way.

In the early stages of this effort in the 1980s, I helped with drafts, but soon Martin found a member of Congress from Los Angeles, Representative Mel Levin, to introduce his bill. Martin worked out the boundaries, and Levin got the legislative counsel to put the bills in final form. His bill put all of the giant sequoias in the southern Sierra under a new statutory management scheme to protect them against commercial logging; all told, it protected a large block of land totaling more than 300,000 acres, as well as some outlying parcels. The land would remain with the Forest Service, but the sequoias would be under statutory restrictions.

The ripening process went on for many years. In the early 1990s, Martin began to come back to Washington, D.C., regularly to lobby members of Congress. I suggested people he should see and things to stress. Year after year he built support. He always brought back striking photographs of the huge trees, standing alone in areas that had been logged. Trees standing alone in this way were especially subject to drying and being blown down, and these pictures were very persuasive arguments for the need to do something.

In the early 1990s, when Senator Bennett Johnson of Louisiana was chairing the Senate Interior Committee, Martin took Johnson's son, who was in California, to see the area. Awed by what he saw, the son persuaded his father to take up the issue. I worked with the senator's staff to insert riders in appropriation bills to stop the logging there. For a while, we had some success.

Then I hit on the idea of trying to get the first President Bush to designate the area as a World Heritage Site to burnish his image as he left office. I worked with CEQ staff, who liked the idea, and drew up a proposed executive order along those lines. After gaining some momentum, the idea faltered in face of opposition from the Agriculture Department, reflecting the Forest Service's antagonism. In the end, Bush merely issued an order that more or less reiterated what the Forest Service's settlement with the Sierra Club had said (imposing restrictions on logging but not ending it). But the idea had been planted that presidential action was an option.

We then shifted our focus back to Congress. The prime sponsor of the bill became Representative George Brown from southern California, Levin having left Congress by this time. Brown was a ranking member of the House Agriculture Committee, and he persuaded the chairman of the committee to schedule a hearing on his bill in the spring of 1994. I gave the lead testimony for the environmental side. It went well enough, except that Brown had neglected to tell the committee chairman that there would be opposition from the local lumber company, as well as the Forest Service. Given this opposition, the chairman apparently did not feel confident that he could move the bill out of his committee, and so the effort bogged down.

I could never find a way to get the Sierra Club folks in California to back this legislation in a big way. If they had done so, the bill might have moved in Congress. Instead, it was the victim of a factional fight within the Club in California.

Some of the Club's field staff in Sacramento and Los Angeles did not like working with Martin because they could not control him. They also concocted a theory that his was an old-fashioned approach and that it would be more appropriate to try to reform timber management generally in the Sierra rather than making more reservations, as he proposed. One of the Sierra Club staff people was married to a staff person for Senator Barbara Boxer, and they used their influence to erect roadblocks in that office. In other words, they spent their time sabotaging our efforts rather than saving sequoias. I tried to use my good offices to smooth things out and get activists to work together, but although I enjoyed some short-lived success, the deadlock did not abate.

Though the Sierra Club's board chose to give its highest awards to both Martin Litton and, later, his aide Carla Cloer, who did a lot of the organizing, oddly enough its staff in California always found excuses to be missing in action on this issue, and orders were never given to get them in line. The Sierra Club supported the legislation in theory, but did not do much in practice to promote it.

After many years of work, action came at last toward the end of President Clinton's second term. In his last year he set aside the Giant Sequoia National Monument, its boundaries taken, with limited changes, from the bills we had promoted. Ironically, in the end most of the behind-the-scenes work for the monument effort was done by NRDC, not by the Sierra Club. By then I was retiring. I felt satisfied, though, that this issue would not have risen high enough to get presidential attention had we not exerted ourselves in earlier years.

During the administration of George W. Bush, the Sierra Club at last began paying some attention to the sequoia issue. The Forest Service still has not stopped logging inappropriately. The area was left with the Forest Service, and not given to the Park Service, because Clinton was influenced by our bills. I had originally advised that the Park Service was the better answer. But Martin had embraced Forest Service management because he thought such a bill would be easier to pass. Now he regrets his decision.

As a confirmed tree lover, I was happy that I had not only helped create a national park for the coastal redwoods early in my career, but now also had contributed to the process of establishing a national monument for the Sierra redwoods as my career drew to a close.

Factions in the Club and the Movement

During the first fifteen years of the environmental movement (from 1970 to 1985), factional problems had been few. We were too busy getting things done. But in the mid-1980s, factional problems began to emerge in the Sierra Club and elsewhere.

Within the Club, a radical faction organized itself around our former executive director, David Brower. Through petition campaigns in the 1980s and 1990s, Brower had once again gotten himself elected to the Club's board of directors. Once there, he embraced a series of quixotic efforts to persuade the Club to endorse various actions, such as campaigning to have the immense Glen Canyon Dam torn down. On occasion, his supporters marched about the room with placards at board meetings. Brower himself was not abrasive, but his supporters seemed to want confrontations with those running the Club. By the 1990s they had morphed into a more determined radical faction that wanted to eliminate all logging in the national forests. Some of them also wanted to end all commercial activity on public lands, including grazing and mining. They began to attract a growing following in the Club.

Ed Wayburn and I began to be disturbed that the Club was losing its appeal to a younger generation by appearing to be too conservative on logging issues. This was happening particularly along the West Coast, where newer groups were taking a harder line, but it was cropping up elsewhere as well. In fact, the Club had been too cautious, reflecting Doug Scott's feeling that it was fruitless to push harder because the entrenched and powerful Senator Hatfield of Oregon would block such efforts in Congress. Yet the Oregon Natural Resources Council (ONRC), with whom Scott had been at odds, had succeeded in having Hatfield set aside many small wilderness areas and new wild rivers in that state. ONRC's zeal had not destroyed their working relationships, suggesting that Scott had carried pragmatism too far.

In the early 1990s, Wayburn and I persuaded the Club's board of directors to strengthen its policies on logging. Thereafter, many rounds of political skirmishing led to their being strengthened further. Meanwhile, Brower and Scott quarreled in the press on questions of policy and strategy, and before long Scott left the Club's staff.

Eventually, the radical faction began to work systematically to place petition candidates on the Club's board of directors. Functioning almost like a political party (they called themselves the John Muir Sierrans) and without organized opposition, they elected enough directors over time to potentially assume control of the board. However, their strategy was not without flaws. They usually ran candidates who were new to the Club—and even new to their faction. After these board members gained experience, most of them parted company with the leaders of the faction. Thus this faction never managed to get control of the board, though they came close.

At first I thought this was a battle between pragmatists and ideologues, and these people certainly did want to take a harder line on many issues. I later concluded, however, that it was a battle between established leaders and those who distrusted them.

Following my usual practice, I tried to get along with those in the various factions. I wanted to understand them and felt that some might turn out to be valuable contributors in time. They had the energy, skill, and outrage to become productive activists. But their young leaders did not yet have much experience in the realities of political combat.

I also realized that this new generation had not lived through the "glory years" of our movement. It had not had the opportunity to learn quickly on the political firing line, to learn what worked and what did not. Since deadlock has characterized the last quarter century of American politics, few anymore are learning the lessons of how to operate effectively. Everybody's notion of how to do it seems arguable, and few efforts lead to demonstrable results anymore. Success is no longer readily available as our teacher. I realized how lucky I had been to learn in better times.

The Club's board was also beset by a split on the issue of immigration. For some people, it was an article of faith that immigration into the United States ought to be strictly limited, otherwise our population would soar. Those preoccupied by population issues never had a secure niche in the Club or in the environmental movement, however; they operated partly within the movement and partly outside of it. And the Club's growing alliances with other progressive causes made it difficult for us to support limiting immigration. Mexican-American political forces regarded such efforts as racially inspired and discriminatory. Even the possibility that the Club might take such a stand had brought denunciations of the Club in the *Los Angeles Times* in the early 1990s. In historic terms, exclusionary efforts by nativists certainly have had such origins, and population control enthusiasts have, at times, kept company with reactionary forces.

Carl Pope and I both thought it prudent for the Sierra Club to sit out this issue. As a group, we were too split on it to be effective. The board concurred and chose to remain neutral. To population activists, this was tantamount to heresy. The Club had failed to stand up and be counted on an issue that had almost theological implications to them. Ever since, they have been running single-issue candidates for the Club's board of directors by petition, in an effort to take it over. Their efforts in 2004–5 fell far short when resistance stiffened, but few expect them to go away.

Working with a member of the board at its behest, I had once attempted to find a compromise on this issue. I had argued that the proper way to view the issue was on a planetary basis—the global population remains the same even when people crossed borders—and that population shifts from one place to another should be viewed in terms of their environmental impact on specific regions. (For instance, the

Soviet Union's "northern policy" of resettlement was probably a bad idea because it was not sustainable to try to resettle so many people in places that far north.) But no one wanted to compromise. The line had been drawn.

During the 1990s, the environmental movement nationally became even more factionalized. Its mainstream seemed to divide into those who were willing to become more accommodating and those who did not want to change tactics (I called them the "stand-patters"). The accommodators felt that they had to ask for less and be more cooperative during more conservative times, whereas the stand-patters wanted to keep the pressure on, feeling that doing so would hasten the return of better political times.

The Sierra Club was a stand-patter, while NRDC became an accommodator. Previously, our respective positions had been indistinguishable. Now NRDC and the Sierra Club differed over trade policy, forest policy, reform of the mining laws, and pesticide laws. (During the administration of George W. Bush, however, NRDC became more like its old self.) The Club also found itself differing often with the Environmental Defense Fund and the National Wildlife Federation. We now had to work at maintaining polite relations. On the other hand, the Club found that its positions were not as far from those of Greenpeace as they had once been, though that group had become more pragmatic too in the meantime. The Sierra Club's positioning reflected the internal pressures that it was feeling, as well as its desire to attract more young people. It was acutely conscious that it faced competition from new groups at the local level.

Issues within the Sierra Club

By the mid-nineties, I found myself increasingly questioning basic decisions that the managers of the Club were making. Some of this was natural. I was getting older, and times were changing. New leaders would approach questions differently than I had. I tried to restrain myself to avoid an open rift, but I could not entirely stifle my judgment.

I admired Carl's management of the Club's electoral program—its work in endorsing candidates for public office and marshaling support—and was pleased to see the Club gain even greater prominence under his leadership. He kept it in the headlines. But those who were managing the Conservation Department neglected the process of forming new Club policy on emerging issues. They claimed that the Club already had more than enough policy on its books. They feared that this process would cause the Club to spread its efforts too thinly.

I had an entirely different feeling about this process and saw it in a broader context. Developing new policy provided an ideal way to constructively engage volunteers on various national policy committees that had been set up. They typically liked such work, and in considering proposed policy the board gained a more active role. Moreover, such work kept the Club up to date on the latest issues and provided impetus for rethinking the Club's agenda for action. The whole process was a way to keep the Club from becoming moribund.

I decided to do my part to keep this process moving. I worked with the board over a four-year period to develop a perspective on social issues, which was finally embodied in an adopted policy statement.[1] This statement declared that the Club could become involved in social issues when they had a solid connection to environmental conditions. I worked up a proposed policy on trading credits for pollution reductions that generally viewed it in a negative light, not wanting to see pollution continue unabated at any place. I developed another on mitigation—policies requiring business to offset environmentally injurious action with positive steps—that reflected a similar mind-set. I brought a proposal to the board on campaign finance reform, which it adopted; took the lead in working with a task force to develop a worldwide forest policy; worked with the Club's international committee to develop an environmental code of conduct for transnational companies; and developed policies on various internal Club matters.

I am not sure the newer board members recognized that my efforts were something of an exception. Their policy process was otherwise drying up, in my opinion because of a drastic committee reorganization in the mid-nineties. Some felt that the Club had too many committees at the national level, and it did have almost a hundred, but many of them were making a contribution. Regardless, the number was cut in half.

When the reorganization took effect, almost all committee leaders over the age of fifty were let go. Instead of flattening the hierarchy, as promised, the reorganization steepened it. The work of the new groups was far less rewarding, and the Club had difficulty thereafter finding people who wanted to spend their time doing administration. The whole national volunteer operation began to atrophy. The new system was oriented toward central control and saying no.

It was ironic that the committee structure, which Ray Sherwin had initiated many years before to control me, was something I ended up feeling good about and defending. I had helped shape it and had worked with it for many years. I was sorry to see it throttled.

Toward the end of my time with the Club, I found myself asked to advise more and more of the remaining Club committees. I had done this for years with the International Committee. I was now also treated as an advisor to the Environmental Quality Team, which worked on pollution policy and was one of the new oversight groups that had been set up. I was asked to serve on the Conservation Governance Committee, the general oversight committee for the Club's entire conservation program as well.

Other trends in club management also began to bother me. Doubts had developed in my mind about our legislative approach about this time. Carl Pope, the Club's executive director, thought our traditional emphasis on lobbying Congress was passé. We were being checkmated in Congress because we had not built up enough support among the public. He said we needed to build more "demand" for change.

I recognized that we were no longer able to pass many bills. Congress was more polarized, with fewer moderates. Republicans were more anti-environmental than at earlier times, and they were now in control. There were fewer undecided, swing members who could be lobbied. Increasingly, we were in a defensive posture—defending the past gains we had made.

However, I also knew that Carl had not run many successful legislative campaigns, as I had. The fact was, we had rarely had an easy time in achieving our past victories in Congress either. While Democrats had been in control in those days, many were conservative and not all that receptive. Many of our campaigns seemed to be hopeless when we began. But we steadily built political support for our goals, by focusing on a specific measure that we promoted heavily over time. We made the issue understandable. And we picked achievable goals and concentrated on picking up Congressional votes in specific places. We learned to develop imaginative strategies to turn these situations around.

In recent years the Club has also sought to organize at the local level around issues that have some salience there. But these efforts do not seem to have had much enduring value for national campaigns. They have not taught people to focus on the overriding issues that are shaping the context for everything else. And our recent organizing efforts have taught people to focus on routines that could be managed and measured, such as counting the number of doors knocked on, not on achieving results through being resourceful or on finding a way to prevail. The emphasis is now on running our field operations in a systematic manner, rather than on winning.

I felt that we were not really looking for opportunities. In the House in the 1990s, we were able to cobble together a majority around the remaining moderate Republicans and most of the Democrats. This majority helped us to pass a moratorium on patenting mining claims and to defeat rollback of the pollution laws. Opportunities do exist during conservative times (for instance, to cut spending for bad projects), and sometimes odd coalitions can be formed, such as with both ends of the political spectrum. In some ways we were becoming prisoners of our processes, which dictated adherence to our priorities and "staying on message."

I wondered, though, whether I was living in the past. Before I retired, I had one last opportunity to test my confidence in the effectiveness of traditional techniques. The Park Service had declared the Club's outings program "commercial" because it charged fees for its trips and was excluding it from the national parks for this reason. The Club didn't seek a profit, no private parties benefited, and the fees charged just covered the costs of the program. Nevertheless, our efforts to change Park Service minds were unavailing. I even went to the office in charge of concessions, which was in Denver, to argue our case, but got nowhere.

Carl gave me a free hand to seek help from Congress to restore our ability to schedule outings in national parks. (They would still be subject to Park Service control over where and when the participants could visit, of course.) I found that those who ran commercial youth camps were having the same trouble. Through a Club board member who ran such a camp, I learned that these camps were represented by a trade association, the American Camping Association, which was also trying to get relief. I saw an opportunity for a cooperative effort among groups of a different character.

I met with their lobbyist and thrashed out a common plea for relief. We then teamed up to do the lobbying—he taking the Republicans and I the Democrats. We got ranking members of the House Resources

Committee to help us and won the support of other groups in this field as well. In the end, we got a corrective provision inserted in the National Parks Omnibus Management Act of 1998. This experience convinced me that these techniques still do work; they had not been bypassed by history.

In the final years of my career, a number of the presidents of the Sierra Club called on me for advice, as if I were their private consultant. I felt ambivalent about this. It would have been healthier for the organization if they had felt comfortable going to the executive director for advice and had worked to develop trusting relationships with him. And I knew that I sometimes approached questions differently than Carl. Even though I did not always agree with him, I didn't want to undermine him. On the other hand, the board was paying me and had a right to my advice. I felt I had learned a lot in serving for so long on the Club's payroll; Club leaders had the right to avail themselves of my knowledge. I found that the board needed someone to work with it.

But I began to have increasing doubts about what I was doing. I was no longer executive director and did not want to be anymore. These were problems and issues that should have been taken to Carl, not to me. I began to resist being drawn so much into his domain. Inexperienced board members, desperate for counsel, latched onto me because they could and because it was hard to get time from Carl. But I was no longer the right person. The board was better advised to work with the person who could make things happen and who would be responsible.

I felt that I could still help in appropriate ways, however. When Tony Ruckel was Club president (1992–93), he asked me to help the Finance Committee find new sources of revenue. I felt that we needed to better understand why Club revenue had fluctuated so much over time. I decided it would be helpful to do an analysis of revenue patterns over the past forty years for the Sierra Club and two other groups, and I persuaded NRDC and the National Audubon Society to cooperate. This was something I could do without getting in the way of the executive director.

There were two factors that most explained these fluctuations, I discovered. They were neither wars nor recessions, as many thought, but media coverage and a clear threat. Our revenues boomed during times when media coverage of environmental issues was intense, such as at Earth Days. Our membership grew rapidly then, and donations also increased. And fear of bad policy decisions by hostile presidential administrations also spurred growth. Conversely, our income went down when media coverage suddenly dropped, as after big pushes for Earth Days; and after sympathetic administrations came to power, when complacency set in. To stabilize our revenues, I suggested a number of new initiatives, including a green investment fund, which is now under way.

Other Roles

Since I had known and worked with a number of figures of importance in the conservation movement, I began to be asked by the Smithsonian Institution and universities to reflect on the work of such people as Howard Zahniser of the Wilderness Society[2] and Ansel Adams, as well as earlier figures such as Leopold and Muir. One university, the University of Michigan, asked whether I would like a closer relationship. I agreed to become an adjunct faculty member at its school of Natural Resources and the Environment, lecturing occasionally on the legislative process and lobbying in its public policy division. The faculty in that division seemed to fall into two camps. There were those in the so-called "advocacy program" who took the confrontational approach advocated by Saul Alinsky, a grassroots organizer and intellectual. The other camp believed in collaboration as a mode of operation. They wanted to minimize confrontation and maximize peaceful cooperation through dialogues that rely on consensus outside normal participatory processes of government. I fell in neither of these camps outside established channels of the political system.

The fact that I was alone in believing that things could be accomplished through that system told me how much the world was changing. I was a product of times that few now could even imagine. One graduate student complained that there was nothing left for her generation to do. She thought we had done it all. I tried to change her mind, but she viewed me as part of a world that no longer existed.

Mining Reform

During the 1990s, I devoted increasing attention to an issue in which I had been intermittently involved for many years: reform of federal laws regulating mining on the public domain.

When former Club treasurer Phil Hocker moved to Washington, D.C., in the late 1980s, he asked me for ideas about what he should tackle next. Hocker was a bright and energetic fellow, trained as an architect, who also could be very rigid. He had been active in Jackson Hole, Wyoming, in combating oil and gas leases in roadless areas. He now wanted to set up his own advocacy organization in Washington, D.C.

I suggested that he concentrate on trying to reform the antiquated General Mining Act of 1872. That was the most significant reform of our land laws still needing to be made, but reform legislation had always been blocked. I had testified hopefully on the subject in the early 1970s, but congressional interest had turned instead to simply reforming the laws affecting leasing offshore oil properties and coal lands.

The 1872 mining law allows miners to stake claims on the public domain for only a nominal sum and to get complete title if there is enough ore present to open a commercial mine. The act gives the government no authority to reject mines that would injure the environment. We needed an organization devoted to building up demand for change in the laws governing metalliferous ores, the so-called hard-rock minerals.

Hocker accepted my advice and set up an organization he called the Mineral Policy Center (MPC; now Earthworks). He enlisted me and former interior secretary Stewart Udall to serve on his first board of directors, along with Washington, D.C., lawyer Tom Troyer.

Udall chaired the board for many years, and I enjoyed renewing my acquaintance with him. He now looked to me as someone who was abreast of conditions in the capital, though he still had his own ways of finding out what was going on. I served for a time as the secretary-treasurer. Hocker agreed that as his treasurer I was easier on him than he had been on me when he was Club treasurer; he had fussed a lot over minor points. We both laughed as we realized this.

Hocker succeeded in getting grants from foundations and building a credible staff. Through its work, MPC turned out a series of valuable reports that built the case for reform. It also generated good media coverage and made some headway with Congress. For instance, it secured an annual moratorium on patenting mining claims, thereby preventing the land involved from passing entirely into private ownership.

Unfortunately, Hocker had difficulty getting along with his staff because he was a very demanding manager. By the latter part of the nineties, it became clear that changes would have to be made. Udall favored immediate change at the top, while I favored an orderly transition. I admired Hocker's achievement in setting up the organization and did not want to act in an abrupt way that would show a lack of respect for what he had accomplished. When Udall could not get enough backing on the board for his approach, he stepped down as chairman and resigned from the board. I then became chairman of MPC, a post I continued in for nearly four years.

I presided over a graceful succession as Hocker retired in due course. Before he left, he hired Steve D'Esposito, who had been an executive with Greenpeace, to succeed him. MPC continued to attract foundation funding, and its influence has continued to grow. Through its work, some of the bite has been taken out of the old 1872 mining law. MPC was very active during the Clinton years in helping to shape public policy, and it became a strong supporter of activists in the West who have been protesting mining projects. With MPC's help, an increasing number of proposed mines have been blocked.

I also encouraged the organization to become active in the international field. D'Esposito was ready to operate in this arena because of the global experience he had gained with Greenpeace, and MPC became the preeminent organization pushing for reform of mining practices at the international level. When companies that were planning mines abroad approached me, I steered them to MPC. Some asked what they needed to do to avoid bad international press, which would affect their ability to get financing in New York and Washington, D.C. MPC advised them on the best practices to use. Sometimes it told them that putting a mine in a given place was a bad idea.

I was disappointed that I could never persuade the Sierra Club to devote real resources to reform the domestic mining laws. But through MPC, I had at least done what I could to get this issue addressed. Though final action in Congress is as elusive as ever, little new mining activity is taking place in the United States—except for gold in Nevada. Low-grade ore bodies, high operating costs (partly because of environmental requirements), and widespread opposition at the local level are discouraging development of new mines. Because reform has been blocked by the mining industry, more public land has also been withdrawn from mining entirely. Economists have pointed out too that this industry is no longer very important to the economies of the Western states. By being so obdurate, the mining industry may be defeating itself. It might better serve its own ends if it cooperated with the reform effort.

Collaboration as a New Form of Governance

Through involvement for three decades in various policy dialogues, I had learned a lot about collaboration. I had seen how those in a minority can block action by the majority. I had seen how collaborative projects often end up being reduced to the lowest common denominator on which the parties can agree.

Politicians in the West were growing weary of having to deal with public land conflicts on issues such as forests, grazing, mining, and water. They were pushing the idea of collaboration as a way to reduce conflict. Under this notion, opposing factions would talk out their differences and find common ground. This would get the politicians off the hot seat.

Word was spreading of an experiment in the northern Sierra near Quincy, California, which encouraged the belief that this notion represented a "new and better way." The experiment was called the Quincy Library Group, after the location of its meetings. Stakeholders there were coming up with an alternative scheme for managing the Plumas National Forest—a plan that ostensibly gave something to each faction, though no national environmental groups were involved.

In the spring of 1995, I found myself urged to attend a conference on this subject at Blairsden, California, not far from Quincy. Many representatives of other environmental groups were shunning this conference, but I was intrigued. I wanted to learn more about the case that was being made for this approach. Some legitimate local environmental groups were participating, but most of the attendees were from the timber industry and local government. They liked the collaborative approach.

While I did offer some thoughts at this conference, I concentrated on listening and trying to learn. At the conclusion of the conference, the key organizer, Jonathan Kusel, was eager to know what I thought. Kusel was an extension agent for the University of California, concerned with the welfare of local communities. I told him I planned to write a report on the conference for the Sierra Club's board. He was eager to get a copy of it, and I promised to send him one.

When I got back to my office, I wrote up my thoughts as a memo to the Club's board and sent a copy to Kusel. Imagine my surprise on learning, soon thereafter, that my memo was being quoted unsympathetically in timber industry newsletters. Before long, *High Country*

News, the widely read weekly that covers the Rocky Mountain West, called me to ask whether it could publish the memo; its editors had heard about it and were interested. I gave them permission,[3] and soon academics and policy makers were discussing it. Before long, *Harper's* magazine wanted to reprint it.[4] I was asked to speak on the topic at various conferences, and I continued to write about it as well.[5]

In my *High Country News* piece, I reviewed the idea of collaboration and set forth the arguments for and against it. The basic notion is to turn over power to make policy on public resources to ad hoc groups of self-selected stakeholders in communities adjacent to tracts of land in the public domain (curiously enough, no one thinks this process should be applied to industry lands). These groups would make decisions only when a consensus exists. If there is none, no action could be taken.

The proponents of this approach argue that it will produce various benefits: the process will lead to more creative solutions because people will talk to each other and work out solutions based on their knowledge of local conditions. They will bargain to find win-win solutions. Having done that, they will buy into the conclusions and generate support for them. Working relations and trust will thus be improved in the local community. Agencies will become facilitators and implementers, politicians will no longer have such a burden placed on them, and people will in effect solve their own problems. At least, these are the claims.

Critics, however, doubt that this is how collaboration really works in practice. Collaboration allows local industry to escape from operating at the national level, where it is often at a disadvantage. Industry has a better chance of dominating these panels in localities where it operates, and it often can bring experience, training, skills, and financial resources that can't be matched locally. Public relations consultants are advising firms to embrace this approach, as it puts power into the hands of localities, where environmentalists are least organized. Moreover, there may be no way to monitor implementation of agreements, and all these processes consume large amounts of time, straining the capacity of local volunteers.

In my article, I asserted that these processes are designed to disempower our constituency in urban areas, which are far from the scenes where these collaborations take place:

> Instead of hammering out national rules to reflect majority rule in the nation, transferring power to a local venue implies decision-making by a very different majority in a much smaller population. But then it gets worse.

By adopting a consensus rule for the decision-making, small local minorities are given an effective veto over positive action . . . [thus] disempowering both local and national majorities. Those not represented by any organized interest in a community may be totally disempowered, and if the status quo is environmentally unacceptable, this process gives small minorities a death-grip over reform.

This collaborative process really empowers vested interests to act as spoilers. Small factions can prevent a consensus from developing and can remove pressing issues from the action agenda. Such processes can also take burning issues out of the spotlight of public debate and bury them in closed-door sessions. Fundamentally, this process takes public resources away from the people in the nation as a whole who own them. It acts as if they belong only to the people who live near them, as if only their interests are at stake.

Collaboration does not deserve to become the "new way" of doing business, I concluded. It is a cumbersome process plagued by disadvantages that outweigh its perceived advantages. Turning over the power of government to collaboratives is misguided and a departure from democratic ideals. Instead of public policy directions being set by those garnering the greatest support among the electorate, those directions would be set by collaboratives in which those with little support could thwart the will of the majority. This turns democracy on its head.

This approach, I argued later in a Tucson speech, "would go so far in protecting minority interests that it would overthrow majority rule. Majorities—even overwhelming ones—would be held hostage [under this process] to the views of tiny minorities."[6]

The central premise of the collaborative regime is that harmony is more important than all other interests. It presumes that the status quo is always preferable to discord. It reflects a lack of confidence in full-throated, open public debate as a way to develop the public's understanding and will. In fact, it delegitimizes public debate as the engine of democracy. My remarks were greeted with disdain by some and with almost delirious approval by others.

Collaborative and place-based programs* really represent an agenda for devolution, localism, and voluntarism (that is, the notion that things

---

*Place-based: the notion that national rules should be replaced by formulas crafted for each place affected.

of public value should be done only voluntarily). This is an agenda that calls for shedding federal powers, that wants small towns to be in charge, and that doesn't want government ever to govern. It is the agenda of rural America and the political right. This is not an agenda that progressive forces should have anything to do with. They should resist it with all their might.

Before long, the related idea of charter forests emerged. Under this concept, national forests would be turned over to councils representing state and local interests. At a conference at the University of Montana Law School, I denounced this idea.[7] I spoke too against the idea that the states should have sovereignty over federal lands. I warned that our national forest system was in danger of being dismantled. This is where such place-based notions were leading us. Why the Clinton administration had ever flirted with them was hard for me to understand. Now the ideas they sanctioned are appearing in debased form, such as charter forests. Officials of the Interior Department under President George W. Bush are toying with these ideas too.

Winding Up

I had decided to retire when I reached the age of sixty-five, which was in 1999. I would be eligible for my full pension then, and I wanted a change of pace. As I approached retirement, I began to reflect on larger themes in my speeches.

The environmental movement is not a passing fad, I emphasized in remarks to the Society of Environmental Journalists in Tucson in 1997. This movement has been active now in the United States for one and a half centuries, with differing phases and faces. Much of public policy for the environment bears its stamp and influence. Individual and corporate behavior does too. It has changed the rules governing large systems at the national level.

But, I warned, there are those who believe that the future lies in withdrawing from the real world of large assemblies of power into concerns with the community and the neighborhood. The forces that impose stress on the environment, however, are not moving in this direction. They are building ever larger aggregations of commercial power in the global economy, and if not opposed they will dictate the terms by which all of us will live. Withdrawing is a romantic strategy of abdication and victimization. Power must be met where it is found.

I concluded with a prediction: "It is likely that we will be led into larger and more difficult theaters of engagement, not into smaller and softer encounters."

At a fall meeting of the Council of Club Leaders the following year, I reviewed the critique of wilderness among academics and urged Club activists to join that debate. I pointed out that new theories that nature is inherently unstable, such as chaos theory, suggest that it is impossible in any event to "manage" wilderness to maintain stable conditions. It may be better just to leave it alone and let things change as they will.

That same year I gave an address in a similar vein to the Federation of Western Outdoor Clubs. I had begun with this group almost forty years before and had never lost touch with it. As I was retiring, one of its longest-serving leaders, 100-year-old Hazel Wolf of Seattle, phoned to urge me to take over its presidency. "Mike, do you recall that you recruited me to become active in the Federation almost thirty years ago?" she asked. I said I did. "I have done this long enough," she said. "It is your turn." I thanked her, but while it was hard to say no to someone so senior and beloved, I begged off for the moment, saying that I needed to get myself retired and relocated. But within a year of retiring, I found myself becoming president of the Federation, and I served for three years in that post.

At a meeting of the Club's board of directors in New Orleans in February 1999, I described the changes in the physical environment in the United States during my career. I asked: "Has all of our public policy work made any difference?" The picture was mixed, I thought. "Pollution is less severe; more land is protected; and conditions may be turning around on public lands. Moreover, some species may have been brought back. . . . However, more species are also in trouble; more land is under pavement; and most of the old growth has been logged. And pressures grow on the resource base. Little progress is in sight in reducing greenhouse gases," I said.

"But we do know that things would be a lot worse if we had not been on the job," I concluded. "We have shown that we can turn trends around. And in some cases, conditions have actually improved. We have every reason to keep at it. We have made a difference."

I made the rounds of the Sierra Club that year. In March I addressed the board of the Sierra Club Foundation and later the junior staff in the Washington, D.C., office of the Club, sharing lessons I had learned. The senior staff honored me at a retirement party in the office, and then the local chapter of the Sierra Club asked me to address its annual banquet. For the most part, I told them anecdotes, some of which are in this book.

I thought I was giving my farewell to the Club's board of directors with my last report in the spring of 1999. I told them it had been a fabulous experience to be the executive director of the Sierra Club at the time of the first Earth Day; during the time the environmental movement took off; and during the "glory days" of the environmental movement, when we wove the fabric of modern environmental thought and law. We accomplished things with dizzying speed. I am glad that I was young enough to keep up with it.

When I began in 1960, the Club had only 16,000 members; by 1999 it had almost 600,000 members and millions of supporters. In 1961, we had about two dozen staff members; in 1999 we had 385. When I took over as executive director, we had negative net worth and almost all the staff had left. When I finished my two stints as executive director in 1987, we had 220 staff and a budget of $25 million and had built a substantial net worth. The budget is much larger today, in 2005; the net worth has continued to grow as well as the membership.

The board made me an honorary officer of the Sierra Club and presented me with a framed plaque recounting my accomplishments, which they also listed in a resolution they adopted to honor me. One of the Club's former presidents, Richard Cellarius, gave me a framed print of a Northwest scene, and I was later invited to become a trustee of the Sierra Club Foundation.

Friends in the Natural Resources Council of America, which I had once chaired, wanted to say goodbye too. Hundreds turned out at their annual banquet at the National Press Club, where they gave me their Award of Honor and I made a farewell address. In the spring of 1999, still other friends in Washington (Bill Futreal and his wife and the Moormans) put on a retirement party for me at the Cosmos Club, which is housed in a stately old mansion on Embassy Row. It had been started by John Wesley Powell, the geologist, and was a traditional meeting place in Washington for those interested in natural resources. Once I had been urged to join it, and I had tried to in the late 1960s. I was blackballed by a forestry association executive who was on the membership committee and was turned down as a consequence—even though I was sponsored by the director of the Bureau of Land Management.

While I retired officially on May 1, 1999, the Sierra Club in San Francisco still had a surprise in store that fall. It honored me with a banquet and presented me with a bound volume of the second oral history I had given to interviewers from the Bancroft Library at the University of California. In my remarks I stressed the importance of visions and ideas, but then went on to say that

> if our visions matter, so also do the means for making them come true. Our dreams must make sense and constitute good public policy. Success lies in marrying the contributions of those with visions and those with the talents to get things done. To succeed, we must have both visionaries and pragmatists—in proper measure.
>
> Society will treat us as an important player if we engage ourselves in addressing its ills . . . and we must not shrink from addressing tough issues. Again and again, we have changed political reality over time. We have not accepted situations that looked hopeless; we turned them around, working patiently a step at a time. To do so, we must tailor our strategies to the situations we face. . . . To be effective, each situation must be analyzed in its own right and approached individually, with insight and creativity.

I am not sure my points were really grasped, but it was my last chance to say these things before Maxine and I returned to the state of our birth, Oregon. I thanked the board for giving me these opportunities. While on the platform, I savored the experiences I had had in the outdoors. I remembered the adventures my wife and I had hiking with "bear bells" in Glacier National Park, flying into volcanoes in the Aleutians, and riding the "billy pugh" to see the birds on the Farallon Islands— which involved being winched out of small boats in the heaving sea and hauled up a sheer rock face, while balancing on a rubber tire. These had been grand experiences.

The joys I felt outdoors were embodied in the names of so many of the places I had visited: Oh Be Joyful Creek in Colorado, Laughing Waters, and Happy Isles. Not only had I been able to enjoy these treasures of nature, but I had had the unforgettable opportunity to spend four decades working to protect such places and so many others—a lifetime in the thick of many of the most significant struggles to form America's environmental laws.

 *Endnotes*

My own memory provided most of the early material for this memoir. For the description of my work with the Sierra Club, I drew heavily upon the two volumes of my oral history that were prepared by the Bancroft Library of the University of California at Berkeley. I also consulted the library's Sierra Club Collection, which includes most of the papers from my years at the Club; the official files and newsletters at the Sierra Club Library in San Francisco; and my personal files, which contain many of my published articles as well as unpublished writings.

Many pieces that I prepared for specific occasions have not been published but are in the Bancroft Library as well as in my personal files. The articles from *Western Outdoor Quarterly*, published by the Federation of Western Outdoor Clubs, can be found in the University of Oregon's Knight Library.

I also consulted the oral histories of other Club members that were prepared by the Bancroft Library of the University of California at Berkeley. They can be found at the Bancroft Library as well as in the Sierra Club Library in San Francisco.

Finally, my wife and colleagues also helped me to remember various incidents.

Introduction

1. Political scientist Grant McConnell, cited in Robert Cameron Mitchell, *From Conservation to the Environmental Movement* (Resources for the Future, Washington, D.C., 1985), p. 2.
2. For instance, in the 1950s, economist Mancur Olson identified what he called the "free rider" dilemma: Because those who did not contribute to public interest organizations would benefit from their work as much as those who did and thus would get a "free ride," they had too little incentive to join such organizations. Accordingly, he thought, organizations defending the public interest would never prosper and become influential.

3. See Rose Gutfeld, "Eight of Ten Americans Are Environmentalists," *Wall Street Journal*, p. A1, August 3, 1991.

4. See Riley E. Dunlap, "The Environmental Movement at 30," *Polling Report* (vol. 16, no. 8, April 24, 2000).

5. Mitchell, *From Conservation to the Environmental Movement*.

6. Ibid., p. 9.

7. William K. Wyant, *Westward in Eden: The Public Lands and the Conservation Movement* (University of California Press, Berkeley, 1982), p. 379.

Chapter 1

1. My father, who knew Ammon Hennessey of the *Catholic Worker*, introduced me to the paper. In 1954 I wrote a few articles for the national edition, and in 1956 it published a chapter from my senior thesis at Harvard, which included a profile of the paper's political views over time. For a while the newspaper staff viewed me as one of their theorists, although I didn't agree with all of their positions.

Chapter 2

1. See Michael McCloskey, "The Meaning of the Multiple Use–Sustained Yield Act of 1960," *Oregon Law Review* (vol. 41, December 1961), pp. 49–77. I drew upon material that the Sierra Club had obtained the prior year in its legislative work on this measure.

Chapter 3

1. See Michael McCloskey, "Etiquette at a Public Hearing," *Western Outdoor Quarterly* (Winter 1966), pp. 6–8.

2. I elaborate on this theme in my introduction for Nancy Wood's *Clearcut: The Deforestation of America* (Sierra Club Books, New York, 1972).

3. I describe the campaign to protect Waldo Lake in Oregon in "The Waldo Lake Battle," *Western Outdoor Quarterly* (vol. 29, 1962), pp. 3–6.

4. I wrote about the high mountain policy for the national forests of the Northwest in the *Sierra Club Bulletin* (May 1962), p. 16.

5. I filed an earlier administrative appeal on the Waldo Lake issue while in law school, but it was handled through political channels. This later one was handled by the Forest Service's bureaucracy.

6. See Michael McCloskey, "The Oregon Dunes: The Sands That Time Will Not Save," *Sierra Club Bulletin* (April–May 1963), pp. 8–9.

7. I sounded the alarm over logging next to the boundaries of primitive areas in a publication of the Oregon Cascades Conservation Council: "Logging Along Boundaries of Wilderness," *Oregon Cascades* (January–February 1962), p. 5. Coverage of this issue can also be found in Kevin R. Marsh, *Drawing Lines in the Woods: Debating Wilderness Boundaries on National Forest Lands in the Cascade Mountains, 1950–1984* (University of Washington Press, Seattle, in press).

8. I describe my efforts to develop support for an expanded Mount Jefferson Wilderness in "Northwest Clubs Propose Mt. Jefferson Wilderness Boundaries," *Sierra Club Bulletin* (January 1962), p. 7.

9. I also helped Spokane-area conservationists address the issue of the future of Upper Priest Lake, in the northwesternmost part of Idaho's panhandle. They wanted to keep the area from being overdeveloped with summer homes, logging, and power boats. I helped them strategize and develop a proposal of their own that ultimately met with a measure of success.

10. Some of the history of the efforts to create an Alpine Lakes Wilderness in Washington state is set forth in Brock Evans's *The Alpine Lakes* (The Mountaineers, Seattle, 1971), pp. 109–119.

11. See Michael McCloskey, "The Wilderness Act of 1964: Its Background and Meaning," *Oregon Law Review* (vol. 45, 1966), pp. 288–321. This is probably my most widely cited article. I followed it up five years later with "Wilderness at the Crossroads," *Pacific Historical Review* (vol. 41, August 1972), pp. 346–361.

12. See Michael McCloskey, "Prospectus for a North Cascades National Park," North Cascades Conservation Council, Seattle, 1963. Copies are in the NCCC collection of the Allen Library at the University of Washington in Seattle. I followed up the prospectus with a series of articles in the *Sierra Club Bulletin* (September 1963, p. 18; October 1963, pp. 7–16; May 1964, p. 14; June 1965, p. 22; March 1966, pp. 17–18). I also wrote pieces on this topic for The Mountaineers; see, for instance, "Major Policy Changes May Presage North Cascades National Park Legislation," *The Mountaineer* (vol. 56, no. 1, January 1963), p. 1.

13. See William Ashworth, *Hells Canyon: The Deepest Gorge on Earth* (Hawthorne, New York, 1977), pp. 146.

14. In my years in the Northwest, I also answered many and varied calls for help. On behalf of an attempt to conserve the isolated Steens Mountains in southeastern Oregon, I served in 1963–64 on an advisory committee of the Bureau of Land Management. See Michael McCloskey, "The Steens Mountains— What Future?" *Western Outdoor Quarterly* (vol. 31, winter 1964), pp. 1–11. Many years later Congress conferred special protected status on that area. I also investigated mining operations in the Kalmiopsis Wild Area in the Siskiyou Mountains of southwestern Oregon. See Michael McCloskey, "A Complicated Job: Keeping the Kalmiopsis Intact," *Mazama* (vol. XLIV, 1962), pp. 13–16; and McCloskey, "Placer Mining Operations," *Western Outdoor Quarterly* (Fall 1962), p. 8. I persuaded the state Sanitary Authority to investigate the damage that mining was doing to the quality of the Chetco River, which drained the area. On that trip I also marveled at rare species found on the serpentine soils, such as the Brewer's spruce (*Picea breweriana* S. Wats.), with botanists from the University of Oregon (including Alexander Fabergé, a relative of the famous jewelsmith to the czars). I also completed work to organize a state committee

in Oregon to fight for "wild rivers," following an earlier effort to block a hydro-electric project on the upper McKenzie River. See Michael McCloskey, "Wild Waters—Do We Want Them?" *Western Outdoor Quarterly* (vol. 30, 1963), pp. 1–4. And much farther away in Colorado, I organized efforts to propose new wilderness boundaries for the Uncompahgre Primitive Area near Ouray.

Chapter 4

1. As an outgrowth of my efforts to help Dave Brower on the Grand Canyon issue and my role as a liaison with RAND staffers (who were helping the Club after hours), I was asked to write a technical paper for the National Water Commission in the late 1960s on the ecological and aesthetic impact of impoundments. I wrote further on this theme in "The Changing Context for Planning Water Projects," *Forensic Quarterly* (August 1970), p. 433.

2. I expressed some of the frustration I felt over the slow pace of congressional action on wilderness reclassifications in remarks to the Club's wilderness conference in Washington, D.C., on September 24, 1971, in an address entitled "Is the Wilderness Act Working?" It was subsequently published under the same title in *Trends* (January–March 1972), pp. 19–23.

Chapter 5

1. Not all foresters were willing to let even these redwoods in the state parks alone. For instance, Emmanuel Fritz, a forester whom the timber companies styled as "Mr. Redwood," kept harping on the need to thin the old trees in state parks. On a field trip in Bull Creek Flat, I heard him warning state park officials gravely about the danger of "leaner" trees, pointing to one giant that was leaning over a road, and complaining that he had been warning about it for more than twenty years. From the size of the buttress that the tree had grown to offset the span of the lean, it probably would be leaning there for centuries yet. But Fritz wanted to take it out now—and this was in parkland. It was no wonder that timber company officials revered him.

2. An account of the first battle for a Redwood National Park from the perspective of the Save-the-Redwoods League can be found in Susan R. Schrepfer, *The Fight for the Redwoods: A History of Environmental Reform 1917–1978* (University of Wisconsin Press, Madison, 1983).

3. See Michael McCloskey, "Why Worry About the Redwoods," *Saturday Review* (June 3, 1967), p. 18. I wrote frequently for the *Sierra Club Bulletin* on the initial campaign for a Redwood National Park (May 1965, October 1966, October 1967 annual, and June 1968). I also wrote for any publication that asked for a piece (see, for example, my article in *Per/Se*, Fall 1967).

4. I recounted the history of the redwoods campaign in "The Last Battle of the Redwoods," *American West* (September 1969), pp. 55–64.

Chapter 6

1. A number of the participants in these events, including Ansel Adams, Richard Leonard, Edgar Wayburn, Will Siri, and David Brower himself, discussed them in oral histories they prepared for the Bancroft Library. These histories are very revealing; even though most were prepared a decade or more later, many participants still had strong feelings about what had happened.

2. The controversy over David Brower's ouster from leadership of the Sierra Club is covered at length by Michael Cohen in his *History of the Sierra Club 1892–1970* (Sierra Club Books, San Francisco, 1988), pp. 395–434. A short account appears in Tom Turner, *Sierra Club: 100 Years of Protecting Nature* (Harry N. Abrams, New York, 1989), pp. 183–185. Curiously Brower declined to discuss his ouster from the Sierra Club's top position in his autobiography; see David R. Brower, *For Earth's Sake: The Life and Times of David Brower* (Peregrine Smith Books, Salt Lake City, 1990).

3. A scholarly account of the Club's struggle over the Diablo Canyon issue can be found in Susan R. Schrepfer, "The Nuclear Crucible: Diablo Canyon and the Transformation of the Sierra Club," *California History* (Summer 1992), pp. 212–237.

Chapter 7

1. These contests took place in closed sessions held in advance of the official, open meetings. These accounts are drawn from oral histories prepared by the Bancroft Library.

2. Our former advertising agency, Freeman, Mander and Gossage, had broken up after Gossage's death in 1969. Jerry Mander had helped form the Public Media Center, which Brower's Friends of the Earth was now using.

3. This case was originally taken to Robert Jasperson of the Conservation Law Society, who referred it to others. That group had an opportunity to get in on the ground floor of environmental litigation, but it chose not to do so and is now largely forgotten.

4. See 639 F.2d. 495.

5. See Oscar Gray, *Cases and Statements on Environmental Law* (BNA, Washington, D.C., 1970) for a review of early cases.

6. See *Ecotactics: The Sierra Club Handbook for Environmental Activists*, ed. John G. Mitchell (Pocket Books, New York, 1970), p. 11.

7. See my editorial in the June 1970 issue of the *Sierra Club Bulletin*, p. 2.

8. See H. Erskine, "The Polls, Pollution, and Its Costs," *Public Opinion Quarterly* (vol. 36), p. 120.

9. For his appraisal of the environmental accomplishments of the Nixon administration, see Russell E. Train, *The Environmental Record of the Nixon Administration* (Presidential Studies Quarterly, Winter 1996, No. 1), pp. 185–196. Also see his memoir, *Politics, Pollution, and Pandas* (Island Press, Washington, D.C., 2003).

10. Michael McCloskey, "Raiding the Forests," *The New Republic* (December 13, 1969), pp. 10–11.

11. See Michael McCloskey, "The Public Land Law Review Commission Report," *Sierra Club Bulletin* (October 1970), pp. 21–30. I wrote on this topic at greater length in a law review article, "The Environmental Implications of the Report of the Public Land Law Review Commission," *Land and Water Review* (University of Wyoming School of Law, vol. VI, 1970), pp. 351–368.

Chapter 8

1. I made my first detailed defense of the Club's new policy on nuclear power in a speech to the American Nuclear Society in Portland, Oregon, on August 26, 1974. In an unusual precaution, I peppered my prepared text with citations. I concluded with the observation that a "calamitous confrontation could occur in the coming decade if the [nuclear] industry chooses to blindly gamble on winning the race with the rising tide of doubt." In fact, the industry lost that race as licensing of new projects ground to a halt because of rising costs and growing opposition. The text of this address can be found in my files and in the files of the Bancroft Library.

    I addressed an American Nuclear Society convention in Boston several years earlier on June 15, 1971; here I did not confine myself to the problems of nuclear power but spoke more generally about the origins of the energy crisis of that time. See Michael McCloskey, "An Environmentalist Views the Energy Crisis," 19 pages. This speech is also in the Bancroft Library.

Chapter 9

1. These bills were handled by a succession of Club lobbyists: Dick Lahn, Jonathan Gibson, Rhea Cohen, and Greg Thomas, coordinated by Gene Coan at headquarters.

2. The NRDC lobbyists were Dick Ayres and Dave Hawkins.

3. See my editorial in the June 1970 issue of the *Sierra Club Bulletin*, p. 2.

4. Albert Hill, a volunteer activist over a considerable time, and I co-wrote a chapter on the struggle to save Mineral King, "Mineral King: Wilderness Versus Mass Recreation in the Sierra," in *The Patient Earth*, ed. John Harte and Robert Soclow (Holt, Rinehart and Winston, New York, 1971), p. 165.

5. Others who played significant roles at various stages of this campaign were John Harper, Club staffer John Amodio, and, as mentioned above, Albert Hill.

6. I revealed my changing thinking about the land use bill in a speech to the Georgia Conservancy on January 29, 1977. I had not yet reached a decision to jettison the measure, but I was close to it. The text of this speech can be found in my files and in the files of the Bancroft Library.

Chapter 10

1. This definition of what was then regarded as lobbying was set forth in the Supreme Court's ruling in *Harris v. United States* (1954), 74 S.Ct. 808. 347 U.S. 612, 98 L. ed. 989. For a number of years, the Sierra Club relied on that ruling.

Chapter 11

1. I set forth my own ideas about action in this arena in an article I wrote with Eugene Coan and Julia Hills, "Strategies for International Action: The Case for an Environmentally Oriented Foreign Policy," *Natural Resources Journal* (vol. 14, January 1974), published by the University of New Mexico Law School.

Chapter 12

1. The Group of Ten was then composed of the Natural Resources Defense Council, the Environmental Policy Institute, the National Wildlife Federation, the Environmental Defense Fund, the Izaak Walton League of America, the Sierra Club, the National Audubon Society, the National Parks Conservation Association, the Wilderness Society, and Friends of the Earth.

2. Michael McCloskey, "The Environmental Impacts of Synthetic Fuels," *Journal of Energy Law and Policy* (vol. 2, 1981), pp. 1–12.

3. My *Saturday Review* article is cited in chapter 5, endnote 3; my *New Republic* article is cited in chapter 7, endnote 10. My article in *Harper's* appeared in the November 1996 issue, pp. 34–35. I provided a statement on the meaning of life for *Life* (December 1988), p. 90.

4. My articles appeared in the following professional journals (other than law reviews): *Energy Review* (vol. 19, 1977); *Journal of Forest History* (vol. 25, 1981); *Ambio* (vol. 18, 1989, pp. 221–227; vol. 22, 1993, pp. 250–251); *Geographical* magazine (vol. LXII, 1990), pp. 14–18; *American Journal of Industrial Medicine* (vol. 17, 1990), pp. 755–760; *Environmental Conservation* (vol. 14, 1992), pp. 291–293; *Journal of Forestry* (vol. 91, 1993), p. 35; *Journal of Applied Communication Research* (vol. 24, 1996), pp. 273–291; *Renewable Resources Journal* (vol. 13, 1995), pp. 12–14; *George Wright Forum* (vol. 14, 1997), pp. 18–28; *Wisconsin Academy Review* (Fall 1998), pp. 32–33; and *Society and Natural Resources* (vol. 14, 2001), pp. 627–634.

5. In addition to the four law reviews that I have already cited, I published articles in *Pacific Law Journal* (vol. 2, 1971), pp. 575–602; *Duquesne Law Review* (vol. 11, 1973), pp. 478–494; *Kansas Law Review* (vol. 25, 1977), pp. 477– 543; *Environmental Law Reporter* (vol. 13, 1983, pp. 10278–10286; vol. 18, 1988, pp. 10413–10418); *Natural Resources Journal* (vol. 27, 1987), pp. 243–246; *Journal of Environmental Law and Litigation* (vol. 10, 1995), pp. 455–472; *Duke Environmental Law and Policy Forum* (vol. IX, 1999), pp. 153–159; *Ecology Law*

Quarterly (vol. 25, 1999), pp. 624–629; *Denver University Law Review* (vol. 76, 1999), pp. 369–381; and *Valparaiso University Law Review* (vol. 34, 2000), pp. 423–434. In addition, I addressed bar association symposia (for instance, in Denver in 1976) and published in *Legal Times* in Washington, D.C. (for example, in May 31, 1993).

6. My op-ed pieces appeared in the following newpapers, among others: *New York Times* (September 20, 1977); *Christian Science Monitor* (November 1, 1983, and April 11, 1995); *Wall Street Journal* (July 8, 1993); *USA Today* (July 12, 1984); and *Los Angeles Times* (February 18, 1983, and August 12, 1987).

7. My addresses were reprinted in *Vital Speeches of the Day* in 1971 (vol. 37, pp. 621–625) and 1999 (vol. 65, pp. 534–536).

Chapter 13

1. This address was printed as "Labor and Environmentalism: Two Movements That Should Work Together," in a booklet by the Oil, Chemical, and Atomic Workers Union (Denver, 1973). 14 pages.

2. I was invited to introduce a panel on the pollution troubles afflicting the steel industry in Ohio's Mahoning Valley on May 4, 1976, at Black Lake in Michigan. The text of my remarks, in which I raised many questions about industry's tactics in such cases, is in the Bancroft Library (see "Opening Remarks at UAW Conference").

3. See Michael McCloskey, "Re-Thinking How Public Interest Organizations Defend Public Health through Pollution Control in the United States," *American Journal of Industrial Medicine* (vol. 17, 1990), pp. 755–760.

4. See "Environmentalism and the Poor," address of Michael McCloskey at Reed College, Portland, Oregon (October 24, 1974). 17 pages. In my files and at the Bancroft Library.

5. See the report of the National Coal Policy Project, *Where We Agree* (Center for Strategic and International Studies [Georgetown University], Washington, D.C., 1978).

Chapter 14

1. See address of Michael McCloskey at the State University of New York at Buffalo (April 26, 1981). 8 pages. In my files.

2. See John Adams, Michael McCloskey, et al., *An Environmental Agenda for the Future* (Island Press, Washington, D.C., 1985).

3. See T. Alan Comp, ed., *Blueprint for the Environment: A Plan for Federal Action* (Howe Brothers, Salt Lake City, 1989).

4. See Industrial Union Department (AFL-CIO), *Deindustrialization and the Two Tier Society: Challenges for an Industrial Society* (AFL-CIO, Washington, D.C., 1984).

5. Michael McCloskey and Jeffrey Desautels, "A Primer on Wilderness Law and Policy," *Environmental Law Reporter* (vol. 13, 1983), pp. 10278–10286.

6. See "Business and the Environment: How They Can Live Together," address of Michael McCloskey to the Rotary Club, Fort Worth, Texas (March 10, 1978). In my files and at the Bancroft Library. A short, updated version of this address was published in *SIERRA*; see Michael McCloskey, "Environmental Protection Is Good Business," *SIERRA* (March/April 1981).

Chapter 15

1. See my memorandum to the board of directors of the Sierra Club, "Thoughts on the Paradox of Low Salience Rankings for Environmental Issues in Public Opinion Surveys" (February 13, 1986). In the files of the Bancroft Library.
2. See my memorandum to Sierra Club President Michele Perrault, "Emerging Thoughts about Developing Splits in the Environmental Movement" (January 14, 1986). In the files of the Bancroft Library.
3. See my paper, "Lobbying the Executive Branch: What Promise Does It Hold?" (March 15, 1986). 24 pages. In the files of the Bancroft Library.
4. See my paper, "Lobbying State Government: An Analysis of the Opportunities, Changing Outlook, and Arguments for Greater Involvement" (July 9, 1986). Also see my paper, "States as an Arena for Environmental Activism" (October 30, 1986). Both in the files of the Bancroft Library.
5. See my remarks to the Collegium Ramazzini at the conference "Living in a Chemical World," October 10, 1985, Bologna, Italy (response to remarks of Professor Johnson). In my files.

Chapter 16

1. J. Michael McCloskey and Heather Spalding, "A Reconnaissance-Level Inventory of the Amount of Wilderness Remaining in the World," *Ambio* (vol. 18, no. 4, 1989), pp. 221–227.
2. J. Michael McCloskey and Heather Spalding, "The World's Remaining Wilderness," *Geographical* (August 1990), pp. 14–18.
3. Michael McCloskey, "Note on the Fragmentation of Primary Rainforest," Ambio (vol. 22, no. 4, June 1993), pp. 250–251.
4. Michael McCloskey, "Understanding the Demand for More Wilderness," *Wilderness Benchmark 1988: Proceedings of the National Wilderness Colloquium* (Tampa, Florida, January 13–14, 1988), Forest Service, General Technical Report SE-51, pp. 38–43.
5. Michael McCloskey, "The Meaning of Wilderness," in *Managing One Wilderness System: The Next Quarter Century*, proceedings of the conference "Managing America's Enduring Wilderness Resource" (Minneapolis, Minnesota, September 11–14, 1989), pp. 22–25.
6. Michael McCloskey, "Evolving Perspectives on Wilderness Value: Putting Wilderness Values in Order," in *Preparing to Manage Wilderness in the 21st Century*, proceedings of the conference (Athens, Georgia, April 4–6, 1990),

Forest Service, Southeastern Experiment Station, General Technical Report SE-66, pp. 13–18.

7. Michael McCloskey, "Protected Areas in the United States: What Is the Record?" *Ramazzini Newsletter* (Bologna, Italy, no. 3, September–December 1992), pp. 20–31.

8. Michael McCloskey and Vance Martin, "International Laws Governing Wilderness," *Journal of Forestry* (vol. 91, no. 2, February 1993), p. 35.

9. "Conservation Biologists Challenge Traditional Nature Protection Organizations," address of Michael McCloskey to IUCN's Commission on National Parks and Protected Areas, Lake Louise, Canada, October 1995. 18 pages. In my files. A shortened version was published as "Conservation Biologists Challenge Traditional Nature Protection Organizations," *Wild Earth* (Fall 1996), pp. 62–65.

10. This thesis was propounded by Alfred Runte, *National Parks: The American Experience* (University of Nebraska Press, Lincoln, 1987), chapter 3.

11. McCloskey, "Conservation Biologists Challenge Traditional Nature Protection Organizations," *Wild Earth*.

12. See Michael McCloskey, "What the Wilderness Act Accomplished with Reference to the National Park System," in *Wilderness: The Spirit Lives*, proceedings of the Sixth National Wilderness Conference (Santa Fe, New Mexico, November 14–18, 1994), pp. 137–145.

13. See Michael McCloskey, "What the Wilderness Act Accomplished in Protection of Roadless Areas within the National Park System," *Journal of Environmental Law and Litigation* (University of Oregon, vol. 10, 1995), pp. 455–472.

14. See *National Rifle Association v. Potter*, 628 F. Supp. 903, 906 (D.D.C. 1980).

15. See Michael McCloskey, "Changing Views of What the Wilderness System Is All About," *Denver University Law Review* (vol. 76, no. 2, 1999), pp. 369–381.

16. See Michael McCloskey, "Wild Rivers of the North: A Reconnaissance-Level Inventory," *Arctic Wilderness: The 5th World Wilderness Congress* (North American Press, Golden, Colorado, 1995), pp. 130–138.

17. See Michael McCloskey, "Wild Rivers of the World—A Reconnaissance-Level Survey," in *Wilderness and Humanity: The Global Issue*, proceedings of the 6th World Wilderness Congress (Fulcrum Publishing, Golden, Colorado, 2000), pp. 20–25.

Chapter 17

1. See Michael McCloskey, "Hetch Hetchy Idea Deserves Hearing," *Los Angeles Times* (August 12, 1987), p. 5.

2. When Congress subsequently held hearings on the issue of nonconforming dams within the national park system, I reminded them in my testimony that Hetch Hetchy was the biggest nonconforming dam of them all.

3. I was a member of the Awards Selection Committee of the President's 1992

Environment and Conservation Challenge Awards program, The White House, Washington, D.C.

4. I recounted much of our experience with regulatory agencies in remarks to a Free Speech Coalition conference. See Michael McCloskey, "Serving as a Lightning Rod for Government Reprisal," in *Endangered Species: First Amendment Rights and Nonprofit Organizations*, proceedings of the Free Speech Coalition Second Annual Leadership Conference, Arlington, VA, October 6, 1994 (Free Speech Coalition, Washington, D.C., 1994), pp. 81–86.

5. See J. Robert Cox and Michael McCloskey, "Advocacy and the Istook Amendment: Efforts to Restrict the Civic Speech of Nonprofit Organizations in the 104th Congress," *Journal of Applied Communication Research* (vol. 24, 1996), pp. 273–291.

6. See Michael McCloskey, "Customers as Environmentalists," in *Business Ethics and the Environment*, J. Baird Callicot, ed. (Quorum Books, New York, 1990), pp. 139–144.

7. See Michael McCloskey, "Environmentally Responsible Business," *Vital Speeches of the Day* (vol. LXV, no. 17, June 15, 1999), pp. 534–536.

8. See Michael McCloskey, "Environmentalists as Quasi-Regulators," *Renewable Resources Journal* (vol. 13, no. 3, Autumn 1995), pp. 12–14. This article was derived from Michael McCloskey, "Reinventing Government under New Auspices: Finding a New Way to Make Environmental Progress," remarks to the Walden Earthcare Conference (April 19, 1990). 13 pages. In my files and at the Bancroft Library.

9. See M. McCloskey, "Extra-territorial Adjudication: A Means to an End," in *Biodiversity and International Law*, ed. Simone Bilderbeek (IOS Press, Amsterdam, 1992), pp. 151–153.

10. See Extension of Remarks by Honorable Wayne Owens, *Congressional Record* (May 12, 1992), pp. E1352–E1354.

Chapter 18

1. See "Testimony of Michael McCloskey, Chairman of the Sierra Club, to the Senate Committee on Foreign Relations, March 22, 1991, on the Mexican Free Trade Agreement Negotiations." 16 pages. In my files and at the Bancroft Library.

2. Early on, I tried to explain our concerns to an audience in Mexico—and to make it clear that we were not anti-Mexican. I chose this topic in remarks I made to a conclave concerned with wildlife in Guadalajara, Mexico: "Environmental Protection and Trade Agreements," remarks to the Third International Wildlife and Natural Resources Congress (Guadalajara, Mexico, May 21, 1991). 9 pages. In my files and at the Bancroft Library.

3. See Michael McCloskey, "NAFTA's Impact upon U.S. Wildlife Laws Affecting Trade: Questions and Answers," September 1993. 9 pages. In my files and at the Bancroft Library.

4. "Memorandum to Vice President–Elect Albert Gore from the Sierra Club, January 4, 1993, entitled: Changes Needed in NAFTA." 11 pages. In my files and at the Bancroft Library.

5. One of the most helpful of these lawyers was Steve Charnovitz. He subsequently worked for the International Trade Commission. See, especially, his articles: Steve Charnovitz, "Environmentalism Confronts GATT Rules— Recent Developments and New Opportunities," *Journal of World Trade* (vol. 27, April 1993), p. 37; and Charnovitz, "NAFTA: An Analysis of Its Environmental Provisions," *Environmental Law Reporter* (vol. 23, February 1993), p. 100067.

6. See Michael McCloskey, "Rescue NAFTA—Safeguard the Environment," *Wall Street Journal* (July 8, 1993), p. A13.

7. See Michael. McCloskey, "Questionable Provisions of GATT" (memorandum to file), October 13, 1994, 12 pages. Also see extensive notes I prepared for a panel on GATT in North Carolina on November 15, 1994. 10 pages. Both documents in my files and at the Bancroft Library.

Chapter 19

1. See Michael McCloskey, "The Emperor Has No Clothes: The Conundrum of Sustainable Development," *Duke Environmental Law and Policy Forum* (vol. ix, 1999), pp. 153–159.

2. See Michael McCloskey, "The Emerging Worldwide Environmental Movement," remarks to the Western Public Interest Law Conference (Eugene, Oregon, March 5, 1988). 12 pages. In my files and at the Bancroft Library.

3. See Susan Hall and Charles Williams, case study prepared for the Harvard Business School on the Conoco case in the Amazon, July 1, 1993, N9-394-001-007. Also see Joe Kane, "With Spears from All Sides," *The New Yorker* (September 27, 1993), pp. 54–79.

4. See Michael McCloskey, "Globalization of Pollution," a presentation to the Environmental Management Task Force of the President's Council on Sustainable Development (December 15, 1997). 6 pages. In my files and at the Bancroft Library.

Chapter 20

1. See Michael McCloskey, "The Crisis of Failing Bureaucracies" (guest editorial), *Natural Resources Journal* (University of New Mexico School of Law, vol. 27), pp. 243–246.

2. See Michael McCloskey, "Debating the Problems That Underlie Pollution Control Problems," *Environmental Law Reporter* (vol. xviii, no. 10, 1988), pp. 10413–10418.

3. See Michael McCloskey, "Re-Thinking How Public Interest Organizations Defend Public Health through Pollution Control in the United States," *American Journal of Industrial Medicine* (vol. 17, 1990), pp. 755–760.

4. See Michael McCloskey, "What Do You Expect of EPA: An Environmentalist," *EPA Journal* (September/October 1990), pp. 52–54.
5. See remarks of Michael McCloskey, "The Campaign to Discredit 'Command and Control' Regulation," a presentation at the State Colloquium of the Sierra Club (December 6, 1996). 16 pages. In my files.
6. Our lead lobbyist in the successful effort to block rollback of the pollution control laws was Kathryn Hohmann.
7. See Michael McCloskey, "Limitations of Proposals for Regulatory Change," third draft (June 16, 1995). 11 pages. In my files. I published articles on some of these concerns during the prior year, such as Michael McCloskey, "The Environmentalist Viewpoint on Risk Assessment and Cost/Benefit Calculations," *Risk Policy Report* (December 16, 1994), pp. 23–25.
8. See report of the Aspen Institute, *The Alternative Path: A Cleaner, Cheaper Way to Protect and Enhance the Environment* (Washington, D.C., 1996), especially chapter 4.
9. See Michael McCloskey, "ISO 14000: An Environmentalist's Perspective," remarks to a Roundtable Meeting of EPA Region III (Philadelphia, April 26, 1996). 15 pages. In my files.
10. See my memo to David Monsma, staff director of the Environmental Management Task Force of the President's Council on Sustainable Development: "Ideas on Contrasting Paradigms" (March 24, 1998). 2 pages. In my files.

Chapter 21

1. See my memorandum to the Sierra Club board of directors, "Proposed Policy on Club Involvement in Social Issues," February 21–22, 1998 (agenda item #B13), fifth draft. In my files.
2. See Michael McCloskey, "Remarks in Honor of Howard Zahniser," prepared for the Hall of Fame of Prince George's County, Maryland (April 25, 1999). 7 pages. In my files and at the Bancroft Library.
3. See Michael McCloskey, "The Skeptic: Collaboration Has Its Limits," *High Country News* (May 13, 1996), p. 7.
4. See Michael McCloskey, "The Limits of Collaboration," *Harper's* (November 1996), pp. 34–36.
5. See Michael McCloskey, "Local Communities and the Management of Public Forests," *Ecology Law Quarterly* (vol. 25, no. 4, 1999), pp. 624–629; See Michael McCloskey, "Problems with Using Collaboration to Shape Environmental Public Policy," *Valparaiso University Law Review* (vol. 34, no. 2, spring 2000), pp. 423–434; I participated actively in a project to provide environmental activists with guidance on when they should join in collaborative projects. See Franklin Dukes, *Collaboration: A Guide for Environmental Advocates* (Institute for Environmental Negotiation, University of Virginia, 2001).

6. See comments of Michael McCloskey on "Guidance for Environmental Advocates Considering Use of Collaborative Processes" panel, Alternative Dispute Resolution and Natural Resources conference (Tucson, Arizona, May 18, 2000). 7 pages. In my files.

7. See "Public Lands: Whose Interests Should Be Served, and How to Get Greater 'Buy-in' Among Stakeholders over How They Are Managed," address of J. Michael McCloskey at the University of Montana Law School (April 12, 2002). 21 pages. In my files.

Acknowledgments

This memoir got written because of the steady encouragement of my wife, Maxine. She knew that this story needed to be told. It also got written because my editor, Jonathan Cobb, encouraged me to believe that it was a story that others would want to read. I am grateful for his help in finding the best way to tell this story.

I did not keep a journal that I could consult to write this memoir. But I did keep files of what I had written over the years, and I was surprised by how much I could remember. In writing this account, I have found more patterns than I thought I would. In a way, this effort makes sense of my life. This may seem more like an autobiography, but it really isn't; I have left out most of the aspects of my life that did not relate to my career in environmental work.

Because my work was for the Sierra Club, I have told some of its story too, although this book is really the story of the big issues I faced, how I reacted, and how it felt to be playing the role I did. But those who are interested in the Sierra Club will find much here that can help inform a history of the Club in the years after 1970. That history has yet to be written.

I want to thank those at the Sierra Club who helped me conduct research in the organization's files. Gene Coan was particularly helpful in giving me easy access to the minutes of the Club's board meetings. Ellen Byrne and Caitlin Lewis in the Sierra Club Library guided me in using its resources, particularly the oral histories.

The staff at the Bancroft Library of the University of California, at Berkeley was also very helpful. That library houses the archives of the Sierra Club, including many of the files of my own work. Theresa Salazar and Susan Synder made my research efforts possible. I also want to thank Ann Lage of the library's oral history program, who helped me prepare my own two oral histories, which I also consulted for this book.

Finally, I used the files of the Multnomah County Library in Portland, Oregon, periodically to check various facts, and found their staff most helpful as well.

Michael McCloskey

Index